MW01503745

Freemasonary in the Revolutionary Atlantic World

This book is part of the Peter Lang Humanities list.
Every volume is peer reviewed and meets
the highest quality standards for content and production.

PETER LANG
New York • Berlin • Brussels • Lausanne • Oxford

Hans Schwartz

Freemasonary in the Revolutionary Atlantic World

PETER LANG
New York • Berlin • Brussels • Lausanne • Oxford

Library of Congress Cataloging-in-Publication Control Number: 2022009082

Bibliographic information published by **Die Deutsche Nationalbibliothek**.
Die Deutsche Nationalbibliothek lists this publication in the "Deutsche
Nationalbibliografie"; detailed bibliographic data are available
on the Internet at http://dnb.d-nb.de/.

ISBN 978-1-4331-8278-5 (hardcover)
ISBN 978-1-4331-8279-2 (ebook pdf)
ISBN 978-1-4331-8280-8 (epub)
DOI 10.3726/b17360

© 2022 Peter Lang Publishing, Inc., New York
80 Broad Street, 5th floor, New York, NY 10004
www.peterlang.com

Contents

Part I Introduction

    1 The Ancient and Honorable Society   3

    2 Global Growth, Politics and Persecution: The Grand Lodge and Universal Freemasonry   17

Part II Print Culture in Creating and Connection Franklin's "Masonic Democracy"

    3 "Lovers of the Liberal Arts and Sciences": Freemasonry and the Scientific Enlightenment   49

    4 From Noah to Newton: Creating the History of an Ancient Society   67

    5 Navigating the Masonic Globe: Print Culture, Masonic Communication and Connection in the Eighteenth-Century Atlantic and Beyond   89

Part III New World Networks: The Craft from Puritan New England to the Sugar Isles

6 St. John's Grand Lodge Boston: "Masonry in British America has Wholely Originated from Us." 127

7 The Grand Lodges' Correspondence: Communication and Connection in the British Masonic Atlantic 155

8 Making Headlines: The Craft in the Colonial Press 173

9 The Lodge of St. Andrew: "Headquarters of the Revolution" 193

10 Revolutionary Boston and Beyond: Freemasonry and the Sons of Liberty 211

11 Boston's African Lodge: Hub of the Black Masonic Universe 237

12 Freemasonry Across the Black Atlantic 257

13 Perfect Scots, Peevish Gauls, and American Republicans: The Far—Flung Masonic Networks of the French Caribbean 279

14 Commerce, Connections, and Conspiracy Theorists: Pennsylvania's Grand Lodge of Santo Domingo 307

Epilogue: "To Vie with the Best Established Republic" 331

Works Cited 341
Index 361

List of Illustrations

Figure 5.1. The *Engraved List* of 1736. Left: frontispiece and first page; Right: page 10, showing "Boston, in New England", the first lodge in the Americas, at number 126. Later editions included the meeting place, days of meeting and date of establishment. From the Collection of the Grand Lodge of Massachusetts.   91

Figure 5.2. On the left, the frontispiece and first page of Benjamin Cole's 1761 list, featuring The West India & American lodge "constituted time immemorial" at number 1. The page in the center features two lodges from the Carolinas at numbers 250 and 251. On the right is the list of Provincial Grand Masters from the final edition, 1778. It begins with "America North Henry Price Esq. of Boston" and features Antigua, Bahama Islands, Barbadoes, Bermuda Islands, Canada, Carolina South and Carolina North in the Americas, with two India entries. More American PGMs featured in the rest of the list. From the Collection of the Grand Lodge of Massachusetts   92

Figure 5.3.   The 1775 *Freemason's Calendar*. This was the first, unofficial edition. From left to right: frontispiece; first page of London, or "Town" lodges, listed by day of meeting; the list of foreign lodges; each number represents a lodge in a given location. In this edition the publisher made no attempt to include meeting days for foreign lodges; the first page of the list of provincial grand masters. The list begins with, *"America, North*. Henry Price, *Esq*; of Boston." Other American entries are identical to those in figure 5.2, right, above. From the Collection of the Grand Lodge of Massachusetts   93

Figure 5.4.   German sources for lodge listings. Top Row: Title pages of various German masonic publications dating from 1776 to 1801. This is not a conclusive listing. Bottom Row: selected pages from the 1796 *Taschenbuch fur Druder Freimaurer*. Left: the list of English provincial Grand Masters, beginning with *"America – Nord*, H. Price, *Esq*. en Boston". Center: this page begins with a complete listing of lodges in St. Christoph (St. Kitts), followed alphabetically by listings in India, England, and Germany. Right: Indian lodge listings for Bencoolen and Bengal. From the Collection of the Grand Lodge of Massachusetts   95

Figure 5.5.   The title page of Adam Boehme's *Alphabetisches verzeichnis aller bekanntenfreimaurer logen aus oeffentlichen urkunden dieser ehrwurdigen gesellschaft* and the pages listing the first six of eight sources he cited in compiling his list of 903 lodges around the world. From the Collection of the Grand Lodge of Massachusetts   96

Figure 5.6.   The frontispiece of the 1767 *Almanac des Franc Masons* and its listings for Asia, Africa, and the Americas. From the Collection of the Grand Lodge of Massachusetts   97

Figure 5.7.   Downes Dublin pamphlet of 1804 with lists of lodges under the English Ancients, the Grand Lodges of Ireland and Scotland and extensive lists for many American States. Right: a page from the lengthy list of Pennsylvania lodges features those under Pennsylvania's Provincial Grand Lodge of Santo Domingo in Saint Domingue. From the Collection of the Grand Lodge of Massachusetts   98

Figure 5.8.   Samuel Stearns 1793 *Freemason's Calendar and Continental Almanac*. Right: the first page of the almanac's history of masonry in America beginning with Boston's First Lodge. The almanac also included lists of lodges in the Americas under English authority and listings of lodges in many US states, as well as a reprinting of the English *Calendar's* "Remarkable Occurrences in Masonry". From the Collection of the Grand Lodge of Massachusetts   99

Figure 5.9.   Bernard Picart and Claude Du Bois' Les Free Massons, 1735; the first international reproduction of the English *Engraved List of Lodges*. Boston appears at number 126. From the Collection of the Grand Lodge of Massachusetts   101

Figure 5.10.   The second Glasgow edition of Wilson's anti-masonic pamphlet *Solomon in All His Glory*. A much less successful work than Pritchard's, this edition was nevertheless slated for a pressing of 40,000 (top of page). Pro-masonic pamphlets such as *Hiram, Jachin and Boaz,* and *Mahabone* had more sustained print runs. They spread masonic history, moral claims, ritual and administrative knowledge as well as listings of lodges around the world, serving to promote and connect masonry across the European diaspora. From the Collection of the Grand Lodge of Massachusetts   105

Figure 6.1.   Original ballot box of the Boston Marine society next to a standard masonic ballot box. Note the white balls and black cubes, used to elect or reject candidates. Courtesy Boston Marine Society   151

Figure 9.1.   Summons engraved by Paul Revere for St. Andrew's (1772), St. Peter's, Newburyport (1772), and Tyrian (Gloucester, 1773) lodges in Massachusetts. Courtesy American Antiquarian Society   198

Figure 9.2.   Receipt from Paul Revere to Tyrian Lodge bearing Revere's signature dated Boston February 13, 1770 for instruments delivered to the hand of Epes Sargent Jr., property of Tyrian Lodge, Gloucester, Massachusetts . Courtesy Tyrian Lodge   199

Figure 10.1. March 2, 1770 Minute Books of Gloucester, Massachusetts' Tyrian Lodge Signed by Sons of Liberty Joseph Warren, GM, William Burbeck, DGM, Joseph Webb, SGW, Moses Deshon, JGW, William Palfey, Grand Secretary, three of whom were also North Caucus Members, and Gloucester Selectman, Patriot leader and lodge charter member Epes Sargeant, Jr. Courtesy Tyrian Lodge   217

Figure 10.2. Lodge of St Andrew minutes for December 16, 1773. "Lodge closed (on account of the few brethren present) until tomorrow evening." Thomas Urann served as Master Pro Temp- he is listed among Drake's Tea Party Participants. No other flourishes like those on the bottom of the page occur anywhere in the minutes. From the Collection of the Grand Lodge of Massachusetts   228

Figure 10.3. John Johnson's 1773 Watercolor of the Green Dragon Tavern, bearing the legend "Where we meet to plan the consignment of a few shiploads of Tea." Clearly visible in the upper left hand corner in the Masonic square, compasses, and letter G. (Courtesy American Antiquarian Society).   229

Figure 14.1. 1790–91 Tableau of lodge No. 47. Of the members, only the two "frere Sevans", both tailors, were natives of Saint Domingue. Of the 45 members and five honorary members (including Dupleissis, listed as Notary in Philadelphia), there were: 16 merchants, 8 planters—all immigrants from France; two ships captains, one of whom was also listed as "merchant"; 2 lawyers, an employee and a guard of the royal magazine, a pharmacist, a royal contractor, 4 building contractors, a surgeon—dentist, a regimental officer, military official, bailiff, a notary, a seneschal and 4 regimental musicians. Courtesy Masonic Library and Museum of Pennsylvania   320

Figure E.1. Left—Allyn Cox's 1793 depiction of George Washington laying the cornerstone of the U.S. Capitol in a masonic ceremony. Note the masonic apron and gloves of Washington and his assistant. Right- a second contemporary mural. Public domain   332

Part I

Introduction

1

The Ancient and Honorable Society

"As the success of every political affair depends in a great measure upon the secrecy with which it is carried on, and the welfare of the society of free-masons, which in its institutions may vie with the best established republic... so the society of free-masons has flourished during so long a time by secrecy alone..."[1]

Whether or not Bostonian sea Captain Zebina Sears had by 1817 read the 1762 pamphlet *A FREE-MASON'S ANSWER TO THE Suspected AUTHOR of a Pamphlet, ENTITLED JACHIN and BOAZ; or, an authentic Key to Free-Masonry* quoted above, freemasonry, secrecy and the establishment of new republics led him on a real-life odyssey that could vie with the wildest tales of Stevenson, Melville or any weaver of mariners' yarns. Sears, commander of the brig *Neptune*, had captained three privateering voyages in the service of the state of La Plata in the Argentine war of independence. It was in the service of another nascent Latin American nation, Mexico, that Spanish forces captured Captain Sears and imprisoned him on the coast of North Africa. Masonic secrecy and brotherhood with Spanish officials, Moroccan Muslims and a Jewish merchant in Africa were to free him from both the Spanish authorities and Barbary slavery and deliver him safely home to Boston.

Spanish lawyer and anti-Napoleonic guerrilla turned Revolutionary Francisco Xavier Mina had fled to England following a failed coup he had led against King

Ferdinand VII. There he joined South American patriots, determined to continue the fight in the colonies. Mina next sailed to Norfolk, Virginia where he succeeded in raising support for the cause, leaving with a flotilla of three ships which headed south to target Spanish ships from a base on Galveston Island. Seeking further support, Mina went to New Orleans in February, 1817 where he bought two ships, the *Cleopatra* and Captain Sears' *Neptune*. On April 11 this small army landed at Soto la Marina at the mouth of the Santander River with eight ships and 235 men, Zebina Sears and the *Neptune* among them. After several small victories the rebels were routed and captured. Francisco Mina's saga ended by firing squad on November 11, 1817, but Sears and four other Americans landed in Cadiz, news relayed to their countrymen by the *Newburyport Herald* on September 1, 1818, two months after their arrival in Spain. According to the American Minister at Gibraltar Horatio Sprague, Captain Z. Sears of Boston, Mr. T. Weston of Philadelphia and Thomas C. Conklin of Baltimore were confined at Ceuta, though Sears later told family he had been held at Melilla, both penal colonies on the North African Coast.

The tale of Zebina Sears' escape from Spanish captivity and Moroccan slavery is best told in words of descendant Alfred Sears: "Being a mason, the captain received good treatment from the commander of the transport, himself a Mason. By similar fraternal aid, he escaped from Melilla to the Moorish coast and there by the good offices of a Mohometan [sic] Moor, who recognized him as a brother Mason, he was rescued from the hands of the man who, though slavery had been abolished in Morocco, wished to keep him in bondage. The Mahometan escorted Captain Sears to the interior, where he turned him over to a Jewish Mason bound for Fez. There, he was taken in charge by some English merchants and finally reached his home in Boston, after an absence of three years." The *National Intelligencer* reported on his escape, "Gibraltar, July 19, [1819] Capt. Zebina Sears, who has been long a captive of the Spaniard, and confined on the Island of Melillo [sic], on the coast of Barbary, has made his escape, and got among the Moors. It is expected he is now at Tangiers". Ironically, while Zebina suffered brief enslavement in a Moorish merchant's caravan the revolution in Spain had compelled the king to grant amnesty to all political prisoners, including Sears' compatriots. Captain Sears finally sailed into Boston Harbor on the schooner *Eagle* on May 20, 1820.[2]

Sears was saved first by several masonic brothers in the service of the Spanish crown, then by his Moroccan Muslim brother who conducted him to a Jewish freemason who found him a free berth on an English merchant ship by way of Marseille, France. The masonic fraternity was deeply embedded in every facet of Captain Sears's journey. It played a major role in maritime commerce among American, British and Jewish merchants. Freemasonry contributed to the republican revolutionary movements in Spain and Latin America in which Sears had become embroiled, and ubiquitous in the maritime trade of England and well established at Marseille.

Boston, the start and end point of Zebina's adventures, holds distinction as the first and most important port in the spread of freemasonry across the New World and a focal point of the story which follows. The printed word and the merchant seaman combined to create an interconnected masonic movement spanning the Atlantic and beyond. That story will be told alongside the tales of many of Zebina Sears' brother masons, in the pages to come. Much of the story centers around the three grand lodges, two white and one black, in Boston. Saint Domingue served an analogous role in the French Caribbean; and, as the story unfolds, there will be stops in many ports of call spanning the major empires of the Atlantic World.

Beginning in a London tavern exactly one century before Sears's capture, masonic internationalism, ideology, administrative structures and masons' strong sense of shared identity and brotherhood made Sears and his rescuers, in the words of Benjamin Franklin, "Citizens of the Masonic Democracy". The institutions of Franklin's masonic democracy—its constitutions, laws, international diplomacy—were dispersed across every continent Europeans had made landfall upon, so that the Ancient and Honorable society truly "could vie with the best established republic." Indeed, an enlightened 'parallel republic' is perhaps the best way to view the eighteenth century masonic movement in keeping with the identity of its brethren.[3]

In 1717, four lodges of freemasons in London, led by the elite membership of the Horn lodge, agreed to form the Premier Grand Lodge of All England. Though not stated overtly, these highly placed "free and accepted masons", virtually none of whom had any real connection to the building trade, had more in mind than simply obtaining power over a loosely connected group of social clubs and actual "operative" stonemasons. Within a few years they published and publicized the history, constitutions, and laws of their new "ancient and honorable" society, asserting a bold claim as an elite order which had served as the vanguard of progress and civilization throughout the ages beginning in antediluvian antiquity. They courted noble celebrities to serve as grand masters and in other high offices, and used their connections in powerful and influential circles to recruit elite membership. Making skillful use of public pageantry, the vibrant London press, and the intellectual tides of Newtonian science, antiquarianism, club sociability, Whig political ideology and cosmopolitanism which swirled together into the British Enlightenment, they created a multifaceted organization offering multiple levels of appeal to a wide swath of British and Continental society. Carried by merchants and cosmopolitan aristocrats, two decades on the newly revamped society of freemasons had spread from their four London lodges across Europe to the court of Czarist Russia, into North Africa and the Mediterranean, Bengal and India, and from New England to the West Indies. In 1733, the first provincial grand lodge in the Americas appeared in Boston.

The ritual, history, and ideology created by the architects of the grand lodge of England was cohesive enough to imbue the organization with a sense of pride and purpose and to give masons around the world and across ethnic, religious, and political borders a sense of common identity strong enough to erase those boundaries in their dealings with foreign brethren. At the same time, it was flexible enough to adapt to local sensibilities and realities and to appeal to different men in different ways. Although the Premier Grand Lodge of All England has maintained primacy as the wellspring of masonic knowledge and organization, it was never able to exert complete authority over the entirety of the masonic nation it had created. Nor was it able to maintain uncontested control of the invented history or ritual which it had so successfully marketed as the legacy of an ancient order. The claim to having been one part of a venerable, global organization created room for others to claim equal and even more authentic masonic legacies and for intellectuals in and out of the fraternity to debate the true origins and intentions of this "ancient" fraternity. The emphasis on supporting and advancing the progressive socio-political order of Hanoverian England was reinterpreted by radical republicans in both North and South America, Europe, Ireland and even among some Britons to support subversive and even revolutionary movements.

Freemasonry was the first truly global, secular, private organization. Within a few decades of the founding of the grand lodge in 1717 merchant seamen and cosmopolitan elites had spread freemasonry across Europe, the Americas, and Asia and had a foothold in Africa. The global reach of freemasonry crossed borders political, spiritual, racial, and imperial. The travelogue of Maryland doctor Alexander Hamilton records an episode in Philadelphia in which a Barbadian gentleman alleged, among other things, that the fraternity was an "*imperium et imperio*". Dr. Hamilton stated that "though not a mason himself" he considered the fraternity harmless. Within five years of that 1744 conversation the doctor had become the Master of the colony's first lodge, which in turn gained its authority through the most active masonic hotbed of the colonial Americas, Boston.[4]

The nexus of elite London masons who formed the first Grand Lodge in 1717, was actively connected with both the political and the scientific side of the Enlightenment. However, this was not the fraternity's only purpose, and for the average mason probably not its main focus. The Craft offered a combination of sociability with the prospect of social climbing. Doing business was another important objective. In the bustling English port of Bristol, pilots flew masonic flags to attract the attention of brother sea captains putting in to port. Once in port, there were any number of lodges in which a brother might find freemasons involved in commerce or in the many trades servicing the bustling maritime world of the mid-1700s. Freemasons in Saint-Domingue proudly informed the Grand Lodge of Pennsylvania that they sent a brother to the harbor to find any masons who may have arrived on foreign ships and offer them whatever aid they might require. Merchants and planters, their aid was both fraternal and commercial. Captain George Smith reported a similar practice in French ports where British prisoners of war disembarked during the American War of Independence: "during this last war people were employed along the coast to find out who were free-masons among the prisoners of war; and those who were fortunately found to be such, were immediately taken out of confinement, had free liberty to walk in the city where they pleased, and were most generously supplied with every thing they, in their different stations, stood in need of." Stories of the rescue of masonic prisoners of war abound from the 1740s to the Second World War and from Indian country to Zebina Sears escape from Morocco.[5]

Had the English masonic "grand architects" of 1717 lived to see the end of their century they might have been dismayed by many of the novel formulations and interpretations the highly protean society they had created had gone through in its amazing expansion to every inhabited continent. Even so, they would have gloried in seeing Paris's Loge Neuf Souers, a lodge that catered exclusively to scientists, artists, and the nobility, where intellectual lights from across Europe met under the leadership of Benjamin Franklin, America's greatest scientific mind. Whatever they might have thought of the Revolutionary United States, the ubiquicy of their masonic "Craft" among its founders, leaders, and freemen may well have gratified the group's Royal Society Fellows, magistrates, and other London elites who turned an archaic organization of the late Middle Ages into a massively popular international fraternity. At the same time, it was a popular movement of the Enlightenment so resembling an alternate republic, or empire, spanning Europe and her vast imperial holdings around the world that religious and secular authorities across Europe, Ibero-America and ultimately even in the United States sought its extermination.[6]

Contemporary Masonic intellectuals such as Franklin and the anonymous author of *A Freemason's Answer* as well as the fraternity's detractors saw the Craft- as freemasonry came to be called- as a transnational institution binding them to brethren around the world; a parallel republic. Freemasonry had its own system of jurisprudence and diplomacy. Lodges issued certificates which served as passports and maintained and upheld international masonic law through print culture and correspondence that crossed both oceans and national borders. Another part of the enduring mystique of freemasonry was the seemingly uncanny ability of masons to identify brethren and locate lodges in far flung ports of call. An eighteenth-century freemason, be he a common seaman, a merchant captain, a gentleman aristocrat, or even a prisoner of war, was able to navigate the global "republic of masonry" in an age in which communication was slow, literacy far from universal, and when many kinds of information taken for granted in the modern day were often difficult or impossible to obtain. Commercial networks and the remarkable Masonic print culture that sprang up in the 1700s created mental maps of the masonic world that crossed national, imperial, religious, social and geographic boundaries. Moreover, the international masonic community overlapped the major diasporic nations of the Atlantic, the Huguenots, Jews, and the Black Atlantic. Each of these groups adopted and interpreted masonic ideals in their own way and contributed to the development of the international fraternity.

What follows is the first attempt to understand freemasonry's role as a global movement, focusing primarily on the Atlantic world and in particular on the role the craft played in the commerce, politics and cultural development of the colonial Americas. It will trace the overlapping evolution of freemasonry as an intellectual movement supported by a rich print and material culture and its role in European expansion. This tale covers a far wider territory than Brother Sears' great escape, but much of it occurs in ports of call familiar to that republican pirate: Boston, the Caribbean, along the Atlantic trade winds, and in the intellectual worlds of the Enlightenment and the Age of Revolutions. As a work of synthesis, it begin by connecting the important and excellent work of previous scholars on British, European, and early American freemasonry with the original works of eighteenth century freemasons to reinterpret freemasonry as a parallel republic, at least in the minds of the most enthusiastic brethren.

From here, the present work charts new ground by elucidating the importance of the Craft in cross—imperial Atlantic commerce and migration. Traders carried masonry throughout the New World and to the non-European old world. In so doing, they brought a vibrant cultural movement and a sense of shared identity and connection that transcended political and religious division and on a more practical level developed networks of intercontinental business, both legal and illegal, that greatly enhanced the development of the Atlantic economy. Masons used print culture to create a shared sense of identity, what Ben Franklin termed "the Masonic Democracy" and an earlier Boston sermon called the "kingdom of Masonry". By the 1760s Danish Brethren referred to masonry's "Republican freedom," while the Grand Lodge of Austria stated that "every lodge is a democracy". As the eighteenth century progressed into the Age of Revolutions, creoles from Northern New England to Haiti to South America inspired by masonic ideals and practices became the leaders of independence movements and the founders of the new American republics.[7]

A recent story passed on by former Grand Librarian of Massachusetts Cynthia Alcorn illustrates the sustained belief in the freemasonry's connections to utmost antiquity. Several young members of an ultra-orthodox Jewish sect entered the library after having finished a tour of the grand lodge. One politely inquired about the location of the Ark of the Covenant. The Grand Lodge of Massachusetts does contain various masonic 'treasures' including a pistol belonging to Brother John Paul Jones and a lock of Brother George Washington's hair encased in a golden urn crafted by Brother Paul Revere; however, the Ark of the Covenant is not ensconced in any Masonic building in Boston. In another case, the master of a lodge in urban Lynn, Massachusetts related that a candidate entered the fraternity, finished his three degrees of ritual initiation- Entered Apprentice, Fellowcraft and Master Mason- then asked the master to perform an exorcism on his house, which "had spirits". The new master mason was bewildered to find that this is not a service provided by masonic lodges. Widespread among contemporary masons is the belief that the fraternity is a secretive continuation of the Knights Templar, a tale created by eighteenth century French Freemasonry, more recently supported by John Robinson's popular but deeply flawed *Born in Blood: the Lost Secrets of Freemasonry*.

The belief that theirs was not a mere social club but indeed an "ancient society" fit to "vie with the best established republic" deeply impacted Atlantic freemasons' identities and actions. The other unique role of masonic print culture this book elucidates is the widespread publication, reprinting, and distribution of detailed lists of lodges, grand lodges, and masonic officers around the world that allowed a mason cast upon the far shores of an opposing empire to find friends, brothers, and business contacts easily. This print culture existed in many forms, from bestselling books, almanacs, and pamphlets containing listings of masonic meeting times and places around the world to privately printed *Tableaux* and regularly updated lists of lodges, to intentional self-promotion in the colonial press. This last source, particularly rich and yet previously completely unexplored, forms a chapter of the present work unto itself.

The Hubs of New World Freemasonry

Much of the story centers around Boston's three grand lodges: St. John's Grand Lodge (1733), which spread freemasonry along commercial seaways from Northern Canada to Dutch Surinam, including the first lodges in the West Indies and most of the 13 colonies; Massachusetts Grand Lodge (1769), also an intercolonial body that grew out of the Lodge of Saint Andrew's where the core of Boston's revolutionary leadership first came together; and the African American Prince Hall Grand Lodge (1791), an outgrowth of the 1775 African Lodge which would come to form international networks of its own as well as spreading freemasonry throughout African American communities and vitally influencing the development of those communities and their Liberian colonial brethren. Boston offers the oldest and most expansive masonic establishment in the Americas, producing trade networks, correspondence and publications that spanned the masonic globe, and thus served as the most influential masonic port-of-call in the Americas.

Mark Peterson has written extensively on Boston's important beginnings as a largely autonomous, de facto city-state. This "city-state of Boston" achieved hegemony over its New England hinterland and created a stable internal economy integrated into a vigorous Atlantic trade, effectively becoming the "market town" of the British West Indies. Bostonians viewed their city and its dependencies as a republic with active importance in the intellectual world of the Protestant International and as a bulwark of both protestantism and republicanism, as well as an international commercial hub. Boston freemasonry not only echoed but accentuated all of these identities, serving to further Boston and New England's identity and position at home and in the many colonies to which Bostonians carried their Masonic Craft. Freemasonry in other British cominions never attempted to extend itself further than its neighboring colonies, as in the case of New York's grand lodge, locally vibrant yet only extending charters beyond its borders to the nearby colonies of New Jersey and Connecticut. Just as the colonies south of New England were more fully integrated into, accepting of, and dependent on metropolitan authority, so their masonic establishments functioned more as local outposts of the English and Scottish grand lodges.[8]

Boston freemasonry was unique not only in being the first officially chartered, and very possible the first unofficial masonic establishment in the Americas, but also in its aggressive expansionism. Both the Modern and later Ancient grand lodges in Boston held authority for all of North America. Boston Moderns spread freemasonry from Canada to Surinam, claiming to have first established lodges in the Caribbean on Antigua—roughly concurrently with the appearance of lodges on Jamaica, Montserrat and Saint Domingue- and chartered the first lodges in more than half of the 13 colonies. Even in colonies in which masonry arose independent of Boston, Massachusetts sanctioned lodges and provincial grand masters, with masons in other colonies frequently recognizing Boston's authority. Bostonian provincial grand masters saw masonic expansion as an active, ongoing mission of their provincial grand lodges throughout the colonial period. In contrast, provincial grand lodges in other colonies never strayed further than a few lodges in neighboring provinces. Revolutionary leadership in Boston was very tightly intertwined with Masonic leadership. The most active region masonically and in Revolutionary agitation, it is the New England masonic community emanating from Boston that offers the clearest evidence of a strong causal relationship between radical organizing and freemasonry. Moreover, Boston's African lodge took on the expansionist, trans-Atlantic role of Boston freemasonry in the African Atlantic, made masonry an important part of free Black society, and incorporated masonic ideology and history into African American intellectualism and religion.

Departing from Boston, the journey outlined in these pages traverses all of Britain's North American and Caribbean colonies and crosses thence into the French and Dutch empires of the Americas and Africa. In nearly every case, there is a connection to Boston, sometimes causal, sometimes casual. In each, the impact of freemasonry on creole culture, commerce, and politics becomes clearly evident. Virginia's elite masonic lodges boasted many of the nation's earliest leaders. New York had a large trade based masonic establishment in the early colonial period and surviving records as well as circumstantial evidence indicate that it too became embroiled in the patriot cause. This in turn led to the destruction of most of its early records, making it less fertile grounds for study. I's expansive qualities appear to have been limited to nearby colonies; however, what evidence remains does demonstrate connections along trade route to the islands and Canada, mirroring Boston to a degree. Indeed, the surviving papers of New York Provincial Grand Master Francis Goelet and the list of subscribers to a masonic book published in Boston in 1772 demonstrate masonic and professional connections between New York and Boston Masons. Pennsylvania boasts the earliest confirmed masonic lodge records in America. The early grand lodge obtained its charter from Boston and limited itself to a cultural elite within the city. A later "Ancient" Pennsylvania grand lodge extended their authority to French Saint Domingue, a vibrant nest of the fraternity and masonry's point of origin the the French West Indies. Here, vast networks of French lodges formed international trading networks among which circulated such meticulously detailed membership listings as to serve as a virtual yellow pages of masonic traders, planters, artisans and craftsmen from France to the islands and from New Orleans to New York.[9]

Freemasonry reached French Saint Domingue via illicit trade from Jamaica in 1738, the year Boston's provincial grand master Robert Tomlinson introduced the craft to Antigua. In the words of Saint Domingue historian John Garrigus, the island became "one of the most masonically active societies in the world." It served as the New World center for the spread of the distinctive French 'Higher Degrees', an expanded ritual, administrative and intellectual world that served as a foil to British Masonic hegemony. This French masonry spread rapidly throughout the young United States via networks that overlapped those of New England, creating the Scottish Rite freemasonry popular in the U.S. to this day and leading to anti-French masonic conspiracy theories from the 1790s on. They printed and distributed extensive listings on masonic contacts traversing the British, French and Dutch colonies and the French mainland, offering brethren a vast array of commercial and fraternal partners. This work focuses on the expansive networks of Saint Domingue and Martinique's impact on trade and society in the French and British colonies, the fascinating Provincial Grand Lodge of Santo Domingo chartered by Pennsylvania Ancients, and the role of masonry in the transition from white-ruled Saint Domingue to Haiti, both of which maintained considerable masonic connection to the merchants and mariners of Boston.

This data on commercial networks focuses mainly on Boston and Saint Domingue because they are the oldest, largest, and most expansionist hubs of the Atlantic masonic world in the British and French empires respectively, but it is supplemented with studies of two particularly important commercial lodges on the Old World side of the Atlantic. The West India and American lodge in London was a reboot of one of the highly connected lodges that had formed the Premier Grand Lodge of All England in 1717 only to remake itself under the leadership of a creole provincial grand master—a position previously overlooked, the vital role of which also forms an important and original contribution of this study- with vast holdings in the Caribbean. The West India and American served as a meeting place for American creoles and Brittons in the American trade along with British and Continental nobles and notables.

Similarly, the Loge Goede Hoop in Dutch Cape Town boasted a small local membership but was a stopping point for thousands of masons en route to the European East Indies. With ritual performed in English, Dutch, and French—often on the same night—the lodge lived a vibrant life as a social and commercial connection between the masonic establishments of the Indies, Europe, and the African coast. The only masonic lodge on record owning slaves, Good Hope adds a vital masonic node of the Dutch empire. Dutch freemasonry was ubiquitous throughout the empire's colonies in Asia, Africa and the Americas. Dutch St. Eustatius boasted eight lodges under various masonic and national flags. Africa, so important in Atlantic trade and migration, hosted lodges under several European and African American authorities, another important realm explored in the pages to come.

Freemasonry was carried across the sea by merchants and sailors, diplomats and officials, intrepid immigrants, and the many soldiers who participated in military or traveling lodges, a ubiquitous feature of the British military and common in European and American forces as well. By 1751, a faction of aspirational class, largely Irish masons in London calling themselves "Ancient" masons split from their more elite predecessors, whom they termed "Moderns". Where Modern masonry was popular among the nobility and the elite, and at sea mainly among merchants and sea captains, the Ancients initiated common sailors, artisans, and men of more modest means, eventually forming alliances with the grand lodges of Ireland and Scotland. Key to the spread of Ancient masonry in the second British empire was the prominence of Ancient lodges in British military regiments. Jessica Harland-Jacobs and others have assumed, reasonably enough, that the sheer number of military masons who crossed the Atlantic and the fact that they tended to belong to the Ancient faction which eventually became ascendant in England and the United States implies that the military was the primary means by which freemasonry came to the Americas. The evidence does not bear this out. Instead, all the data points to Ancient masonry's having arrived largely with men of the sea and with the migration of aspirational men of middling status, the same men who comprised the rolls of the Ancients in Britain and who elevated their social position in America through active participation in the Revolution (as well as through freemasonry). In rectifying this erroneous assumption, the present work offers a more accurate picture of the roles of both Ancient and Modern freemasonry in trans-Atlantic trade and migration.

Stephen Bullock's *Revolutionary Brotherhood: Freemasonry and the Transformation of the American Social Order 1733–1830* details how the Revolution and the social changes it wrought led to the dominance of Ancient masonry in the early Republic. During the colonial era, however, Modern Masons created lodges that served as hubs of trade and elite sociability. Only in Canada were regimental lodges important in spawning a significant number of lodges, and even here Boston's merchant elite established the craft first. After independence, the protean fraternity shifted its emphasis from maritime to the westward land-based migration, but the utility of masonic citizenship to travelers and men of business never disappeared. In the Caribbean, where masonic lodges dotted the map, it was the English Moderns who dominated prior to the upheavals of the nineteenth century. Rather than a simple social club of elites isolated in their various coastal towns, Modern freemasonry created vast commercial and intellectual webs within a trans-national community. The connections were tenuous, ad hoc and largely dependent on the activities and initiative of individual lodge members. The records of both Boston and Saint Domingue, however, demonstrate that this haphazard system was effective overall in connecting brethren throughout the Atlantic. Nor did this Atlantic commercial aspect of freemasonry end with the American Revolution. Although the main focus of American freemasonry turned inward and westward in step with American society, freemasonry continued to serve as a vibrant web of networks across the continuing realm of Atlantic trade.

The analogy of a masonic "republic" is the best way to truly understand the vast web of masonic networks that connected men, lodges and grand lodges around the Atlantic and Pacific European empires, the Mediterranean and throughout Continental Europe. In the British Empire from which freemasonry originated, these connections tended to be haphazard and ad hoc despite the Premier Grand Lodge of All England's attempts to legislate a coherent system of communication. This is not to say that it was wholly ineffective; on the contrary, masons were able to locate brethren and lodges around the world and to communicate effectively with the metropolis. French and Dutch masonic administration was considerably tighter and more regular than that of Atlantic Brittons. Outside of the officially mandated communication within the grand lodges of each of these imperial powers, cross-imperial masonic connections, particularly at the peripheries of empire and the frontiers of European expansion, were a major factor both in Atlantic trade and in influencing the evolution of the Craft. Indeed, the Craft penetrated Native American society, the Hindu elite and the Muslim world. Before immersing oneself in the overlapping worlds of masonic print and salty colonial sea captains, however, a brief understanding of the singular growth of the Craft and the widespread, sustained backlash against it will prove useful. To fully understand this remarkable global movement, we must pause to understand both the it's medieval roots and the ingenious and intentional creation of this "ancient and honorable society."

Notes

1 *A FREE-MASON'S ANSWER TO THE Suspected AUTHOR of a Pamphlet, ENTITLED JACHIN and BOAZ; or, an authentic Key to Free-Masonry* (London: J. Cooke, 1762), 19–20.

2 Barbara Sears McRae, "Zebina the Privateer, Pirate or Patriot?" *New England Ancestors Magazine* 9, no. 1 (Winter 2008): 35–37, 42.

3 Margaret Jacob, *Living the Enlightenment: Freemasonry and Politics in Eighteenth Century Europe* (New York: Oxford University Press, 1991), 150–1.

4 Dr. Alexander Hamilton, *The Itinerarium of Doctor Alexander Hamilton* (Annapolis, 1744) ebook: https://books.google.com/books?id=c1OIz-UCgmsC&pg=PT211&lpg=PT211&dq=dr+alexander+hamilton+1744+penguin+books&source=bl&ots=AEsuPbHsG-&sig=iVRcH-8lC8BXraZHoRqEJHCUNf0&hl=en&sa=X&ved=0ahUKEwiQ6NysgvHNAhUMPD4KHWRKAXwQ6AEIHDAA#v=onepage&q=dr%20alexander%20hamilton%201744%20penguin%20books&f=false; Reverend William Brogden, *Freedom and Love. A Sermon Preached before the Ancient and Honourable Society of Free and Accepted Masons, in the Parish Church of St Ann in the city of Annapolis on Wednesday, the 27th of December, 1749* (Annapolis: J. Green, 1750). The sermon was dedicated to "the Right Worshipful Alexander Hamilton, M.D. Master" and others.

5 On Bristol, see David Harrison, *The Transformation of Freemasonry* (Suffolk: Arima Publishing, 2010), 1–20; On Saint-Domingue, see Villain, Senior to George Washington / Grand Lodge of Pennsylvania, 1785. MSS Grand Lodge of Pennsylvania Archives, Vol. L, Paquet 72, folio 4; reprinted in Sasche, *Old Masonic Lodges of Pennsylvania Vol. II 1779–1791* (Philadelphia: 1913), 242–4; *Ibid.,* 242–82. Where translations are available in Sasche, I have generally stuck to his English version, as they appear to have been translated accurately and correctly when compared to the originals; Captain George Smith. *On the Uses and Abuses of Freemasonry: a Work of the Greatest Utility to the Brethren of the Society, to Mankind in General, and to the Ladies in Particular* (London: G. Kearsley, 1783), 378–9.

6 Jacob, *Living the Enlightenment,* 150–1; for the term "Grand Architects" I am indebted to Ric Berman's *The Foundations of Modern Freemasonry: The Grand Architects, Political Change and the Scientific Enlightenment, 1717–1740* (Portland: Sussex Academic Press, 2012).

7 Jacobs, *Living the Enlightenment,* 150–1.

8 Mark Peterson, *The City–State of Boston: The Rise and Fall of an Atlantic Power, 1630–1865* (Princeton: Princeton University Press, 2019).

9 Wellins Calcott, *A Candid Disquisition of the Principles and Practices of the Most Antient and Honourable Society of Free and Accepted Masons: Together with some Strictures on the Origin, Nature, and Design of that Institution* (Boston: William M'Alpine, 1772); Ric Berman, *The Grand Lodge of England & Colonial America: America's Grand Masters* (Oxfordshire: The Old Stables Press, 2020), 105–116 contains extracts from Francis Goelet's papers.

2

Global Growth, Politics and Persecution: The Grand Lodge and Universal Freemasonry

John Montagu, 2nd Duke of Montague's mother-in-law Sarah Churchill, Duchess of Marlborough, said of her celebrity son-in-law that, "All his talents lie in things only natural in boys of 15 years old, and he is about 2 and 50; to get people into his garden and wet them with squirts, and to invite people to his country houses and put things in beds to make them itch, and twenty such pretty fancies as these." Rumor has it that the Duke's victims included no less a personage than *philosophe* and freemason Montesquieu, whom he allegedly dunked in a tub of frigid water. Indeed, some literary critics posit that Montagu served as the model for Fielding's "roasting squire," purveyor of obnoxious practical jokes. Such a man might seem well fit to head a more mundane fraternity with less lofty stated goals than the promotion of science and civilization.

Yet Montagu also earned recognition as a man of science, being elected a Fellow of the Royal College of Physicians in 1717, a Knight of the Garter two years later, and a Fellow of the Royal Society in 1725, by which time he had already served as the rand lodge's fourth grand master from 1721 to 22. Indeed, many fellows of the Royal Society at the time were masons, a fact which could only have aided the Duke's election. Other interests Montagu held in common with many of the humbler brethren included Atlantic trade, charity, and racial tolerance. While serving as grand master, Montagu obtained the governorship of

Saint Vincent and St. Lucia, though the French ensured that this would become an expensive losing venture. Some of the earliest mentions of the word "free-mason" in the colonial press involve the Duke's ship *Charles and Free Mason* in Boston's shipping news on January 5, 1719 and again in September, 1721, two months after a visit by the Ship *Free Mason* under the same captain. Montagu funded the education of prominent Black Britton Ignacio Sancho, a baby born on a slave ship who rose to become a founder of the abolition movement, composer, and the first Black man to vote in a Parliamentary election; and may have funded free Jamaican Francis Williams as well. Involved in various other charitable ventures, Duke John was a frequent hero of the celebrity gossip columns of the day, and featured prominently in the British press, making him an excellent figure to launch the grand lodge's massive PR campaign, which soon turned the Craft into the eighteenth century's trendiest, most cosmopolitan social network. The grand lodge celebrated the installation of its first celebrity aristocratic grand master with the first grand masonic procession, a practice that became traditional for the installation of grand masters and provincial grand masters and served as wonderful publicity for the newly revamped Craft.[1]

By 1717, freemasonry was a brotherhood known throughout England and Scotland as possessed of secret recognition signs and possibly occult knowledge patronized by gentlemen with a membership that included both stonemasons and members of the gentry. When the leading members of four London lodges took it on themselves to reinvent the Craft, they did so with an eye towards more than just sociability. Political considerations likely underlay the sudden rebirth of the fraternity. Martha Keith Schuchard has presented a strong case for a powerful Jacobite faction in pre-grand lodge masonry having made use of masonic networks conspiratorially, as well as for simmering conflict between said Jacobites and the pro-Hanoverian masons of the grand lodge. Conversely, Margaret Jacobs and others present some circumstantial evidence for a Whig orientation in at least some lodges going back to the Glorious Revolution. Considering the evidence for these conflicting politically orientations, it appears that internal conflicts over patronage in the Office of Works and influence over the masonic fraternity and the workmen it represented combined with the need to eliminate the potential threat of Jacobite conspiracy and the opportunity to use the effective masonic networks for Whigs' own political networking in the wake of the 1715 Jacobite Rising gave impetus and urgency to the masonic project. If correct, this theory goes a long way to explaining the interest of spymaster Charles Delafaye and his circle. The new Premier Grand Lodge of All England was to be a vehicle for the promotion and protection of the fragile Hanoverian Whig social order and for the propagation of Newtonian scientific rationalism, religious tolerance, and progressive British political ideology. This process of intentional creation is the subject of Ric Berman's *The Foundations of Modern Freemasonry*. In it, he sketches the elite personalities, networks, and aims of those he dubbed "the grand architects" from their institution of the grand lodge until 1740 when the old guard had passed and the craft entered a decade of malaise in England. They embarked on a massive campaign of self—promotion, so that the London press featured over one 1000 articles on the brotherhood during the 1720s men from the nobility to the aspirational classes queued up to take their degrees.[2]

In order to convert the slightly known, somewhat mystical gentlemen's club that existed throughout Britain prior to 1717 into a mass movement of the Enlightenment with its own system of government, history, laws, and citizenship, the grand architects embarked on an ingenious plan. They reworked the centuries-old lodge manuscripts known collectively as the Old Charges, and other operative lodge documents into the *Constitutions of the Freemasons*, published in 1723 two years following the publicity generated by their first noble Grand Master, the extremely popular lord Montagu. Grand lodge successfully courted a constant stream of aristocrats, nobles, gentry and Whig leaders for membership, as well as recruiting in the Royal Society, the Antiquarian Society, and other prestigious intellectual and social networks. Freemasonry was carried across the sea by merchants and sailors, diplomats and officials, and later the many soldiers who participated in military, or traveling lodges, a ubiquitous feature of the British military and common in European and American forces as well.

The *Constitutions* created a mythologized history that both appealed to the widespread antiquarian interest of the times and offered the legitimacy of ancientness. It was multilayered, so that the most credulous in an era which commonly considered the bible to be the literal history of a 5000-year-old world might trace the Craft's origins back to Noah and even Adam. For others, the ancient Egyptians or the Tower of Babel seemed more reasonable. The links to these earliest times were ambiguously framed, with concrete organizational links more clearly asserted first from the era of Solomon's Temple, thence more strongly still from Edwin of York, brother of King Athelstan. For those who found ancient historical claims implausible, the links to medieval England and Scotland offered a more likely point of origination which still shrouded the brotherhood in the mists of time. Indeed, this mythologized history spawned a vibrant masonic print culture which has debated the fraternity's "ancient and honorable" history from 1723 to the present day.

The ideologically charged "history" promoted by artfully recruited noble celebrity grand masters gave masons and the general public the notion that rather than a simple club, they witnessed the re-emergence of a genuinely ancient institution aimed at promoting all that was good in the post-1688 British political and social landscape. The grand lodge recreated the initiatory rituals, the first, second and third degree, and expanded them with elements of Classical mystery religion overlaid with Enlightenment ideology. Early lodges often organized scientific lectures, making the craft an actual force for spreading scientific knowledge. These were practically useful for brethren from the rising industrial class. Combined with more mundane advantages—networking with elite aristocrats and businessmen, and the sociability of club life with drinking, eating, music, and ritual—masonry appealed to a wide cross-section of British male society. There were true believers who felt that they were part of a centuries-old institution promoting human progress and networking social climbers who, even if skeptical of their clubs' antediluvian origins, saw real value in freemasonry's connections and generally in its ideas as well. Others simply wished to be part of the exclusive, trending fad which swept England in the 1720s and 1730s.

Though England in this age boasted many social clubs, by design the Masonic fraternity was distinct from its outset. Traders, diplomats and cosmopolitan Enlightenment elites established lodges across Europe. Freemasonry's path from medieval Scottish and English builders groups to a radically progressive organization of the Enlightenment marks one of history's most truly unique stories. In order to understand how this singular Enlightenment social movement became the most extensive cross-imperial network in the Atlantic world and the effect that it had on that world, it is important to understand how freemasonry emerged from the middle ages to the renaissance to become the vehicle of choice for the grand architects of 1717.

From the Scottish Renaissance to the British Enlightenment

In all ages, major building project, particularly public works funded with government treasure, have been politicized affairs attracting the attention of economic elites. This partial- but only partially- explains the incredible transformation the Masonic fraternity underwent in the 16 and early 1700 hundreds. Prior to 1717, freemasonry functioned as a trade guild and by the 1600s had begun to admit gentlemen who offered patronage to stonemasons as a kind of elite, "accepted" masons. Primary documentation comes mainly from the "Old Charges"- manuscripts dating as early as the 1400s found in both England and Scotland which included a mythological history of the masons back to antediluvian times and a set of charges, or rules, read to the initiate as a catechism. The most complete work on pre-grand lodge freemasonry is David Stevenson's *The Origins of Freemasonry: Scotland's Century, 1590–1710.* The most important conclusions in *Origins* regard the origination of the lodge, the connection of late renaissance occultism with elements already extant in the legends and practices of operative stonemasons made by Scottish Renaissance intellectual and royal overseer of works William Schaw, and the beginning of the practice of taking in gentlemen as 'accepted' masons.[3]

Stevenson explains the origin of the lodge as a temporary structure or settlement where masons from outside a community stayed while working on large building projects. Depending on the scope of the work these could be anything from a transient lean-to or shed to a major structure in which a number of men lived for an extended period. Such lodges developed their own ceremonies, rituals, rules, customs and initiation rights. These lodges worked in conjunction with local masons guilds. Stonemasonry at that time was closely connected with architecture, considered an important science by renaissance intellectuals. Moreover, masons created the permanent edifices of temporal and sacred power which dotted the landscape: the cathedrals, castles, abbeys, and other great stone structures that housed the overlords of church and state. Additionally, the elaborate mythical history included crediting the development of masonic skill in Egypt to the legendary Hermes Trismegistus. In the late renaissance Hermetic philosophy was a popular subject, in vogue with the mystical antiquarians of the time, peaking around 1600. Part of the Hermitic system was the belief that Hermes was a disguise for St. John the Baptist- the patron saint of masons. Moreover, the Old Charges included the mythical connection to Solomon and the building of his temple as the greatest building project in the order's history.[4]

As the sixteenth century drew to a close, the Scottish crown appointed the mystically inclined William Schaw master of works. Stevenson describes Schaw's contribution as follows: "one man saw that some aspects of the traditional heritage of the craft of masonry linked up with a whole series of trends in the thought and culture of the age, and worked to introduce them into the craft." Schaw had traveled in Europe on diplomatic missions and was connected to Giordano Bruno through Bruno's Scottish student and zealous Egyptian Hermeticist Alexander Dickson. Bruno wrote, among other things Hermetic, on the 'Art of Memory'. This was a pneumonic technique used in classical times in which a speaker memorized orations by first memorizing the layout of a great building and then linking his arguments to parts of that building in the order he had passed through it. This art was seen to have occult significance as well as practical intellectual uses applicable in the case of masons to memorizing charges and secrets. The art of memory was also a popular subject at the court of James VI, who had appointed Schaw.[5]

In his position as overseer of the works, Schaw issued two important sets of rules, the first and second Schaw statutes, in 1598 and 1599. The new "Schaw Lodges" seem to have been materially different, more organized and more permanent than those associated with building sites. In Stevenson's words, Schaw "May have built on fragmentary traditions of the craft, but the central theme appears to be innovation rather than continuity." The first Schaw statutes were based on the old charges but altered and expanded in a fashion largely specific to Scottish conditions. They provided, among other things, for a more organized lodge hierarchy with consistent meetings and record keeping. The second Schaw Statutes solidified the system of precedence and the organizational structure of the lodges, and provided for the use of the "art of memorie", the first time that hermetic term appears in masonic instructions. The statues also confirm indirectly that some form of ritual initiation was in place by this time. Schaw struggled to gain royal approval for his new statutes and confronted a hereditary claim on the patronage of the craft masons from William Sinclair of Roslin. Schaw died in 1602, but his innovations took hold among many Scottish masons.[6]

In the seventeenth century lodges in Scotland and England began "accepting" gentleman as a member. Lodge records from the period, the oldest dating from July 31, 1599 at the lodge in Edinburgh, show that this process was sporadic and varied over time and location. Some lodges "accepted" gentlemen masons for a time, then stopped. Others did so only occasionally or not at all, while some came to be dominated by men who had never actually held a tool. The London Masons Company records "Acception" in its earliest account book, dating to the year 1619. These first "Acceptions" were usually men of the company, and it appears they were being inducted into an inner circle. The lodge of Edinburgh minutes first include the admission of three gentlemen on July 3, 1634, the first non-operative masons admitted into a lodge in Scotland. Such "accepted masons" included several founders and other influential Fellows of the Royal Society, members of which played a dominant role in remaking the Craft in 1717. Among the most important "speculative" accepted masons of the seventeenth century was Sir Robert Clayton, Lord Mayor of London. An extremely prominent merchant, banker and ardently Whiggish member of parliament,

Clayton served in the 1690s as master of the first known non-operative lodge of accepted gentlemen. The lodge's membership leaned heavily Whiggish, and had a relationship with the London Company of Masons. If, as Schuchard posits, masonry at the time included a Jacobite faction as well, then political polarization and infighting probably increased in this decade.[7]

An important source on pre-grand lodge freemason is found in Robert Plott's 1686 *Natural History of Staffordshire*. This is the first description of freemasonry in a tome written for the general public. Dr. Plott, an FRS, wrote several paragraphs on the existence of masons lodges in the region which accepted gentlemen and were able to recognize each other throughout the nation using various signs communicated at their initiation. Plott's writing demonstrates that he had access to a manuscript of the Old Charges, and the practices he briefly describes correspond to those adopted at a "General Meeting" in 1663 described in various masonic documents. There are other late sixteenth and early seventeenth century references to the freemasons, their ability to secretly recognize and communicate with each other, and to the "mason's word". These include poet Andrew Marvell's describing, "Those that have the Mason's word" as able to "secretly discern one another." Among the first superstitious reactions to freemasonry's occultism and secrecy is the 1696 case of a group of Scots who considered their freemason neighbor's house to be haunted because when he "took the meason-word" he had "devouted his first child to the Devil." Writing in the *Tatler* in 1710, Richard Steele made reference to Free Masons having "some secret intimation of each other." This was a passing reference which assume the existence of Masonic secret recognition to be public knowledge.[8]

Masonic activity in York in the 1600s included strong links to merchants, tradesmen and local elite families. A mahogany flat rule dated 1663 contains masonic symbols with mention of three local elites. There are apparent references to 'speculative masonry dating to the 1660s, and one 1693 document lists six members of a York lodge. York masonic documents list as 'President' Sir George Tempest, Baronet in 1705, Right Honorable Lord Mayor Robert Benson in 1707, several Ministers of Parliament and a who's who of local elites. Refusing to acknowledge the Premier Grand Lodge, these York masons renamed their group the Grand Lodge of all England Held at York. They claimed continuous existence since Edwin of York's charges of 926, giving them primacy over the Premier Grand Lodge. Trade and politics were interwoven with the York masons from their earliest recorded existence. This schismatic Grand Lodge existed until 1792.[9]

The *Freemason's Calendar, or an Almanac for the Year 1775*, the first in an annual series with a wildly successful run into the 1800s presenting masonic history, news, international lodge directories, and a conventional almanac section heavy on information of use to sea-born traders, offered an essay entitled, "An History of MASONRY in ENGLAND". This essay appeared in subsequent editions and offered a very detailed, almost certainly exaggerated, account of the fraternity's role in every era in British history. The first mention of a grand master is Francis Russell in 1567 and his southern counterpart. As it approaches the present the details ring more plausible and less fantastic, and support the implications of reorganization, politicization and inner conflict from the 1660s on leading to the formation of the Grand Lodge. The English Civil War had greatly disrupted masonry, but "..it began to revive under the patronage of Charles II who had been received into the Order while on his travels. On the 27th Dec. 1663, a general assembly was held, at which Henry Jermyn, earl of St. Albans, was elected Grand Master, who appointed Sir John Denham, kt. His deputy and Mr. (afterwards Sir) Christopher Wren and John Webb his wardens. Several regulations were made at this assembly, and great harmony prevailed among the fraternity." In 1685 Christopher Wren became grand master. Whether this title actually existed at the time is unclear, but the Goose and Gridiron Lodge referred to him as a former master of the lodges in its oldest records. In any case, masonry declined under James II but, "several lodges were occasionally held in different places... At the revolution..[there were] no more than 7 lodges in London and suburbs, only two worthy of notice, the old lodge of St. Paul's over which Wren presided during the building of that structure and a lodge at St. Thomas' hospital southwark over which Sir Robert Clayton, lord mayor of London presided during the building of that hospital."

The story then makes the dubious claim that, "In 1695 king William was privately initiated into masonry. He approved of the choice of Sir Christopher Wren as Grand Master..patronized lodges, particularly one at Hampton court during building the new part of the palace.They built Kensington palace and finished Chelsea hospital." The initiation of King William is likely a Whiggish invention. In any case, the history speaks of a General Assembly in 1697 attended by various nobles, followed by a decline in masonry under the aging Wren. If Wren was indeed a political rival of the grand architects both in general and in masonry, the history the victors had written now blamed age rather than politics for his failings as grand master and the need to remake the fraternity. From 1702, by this account, most lodges had ceased to meet, "... the annual festivals were entirely neglected. The old lodge at St. Pauls, and a few others, continued to meet, but these consisted of few members. It was then resolved that the privileges of Masonry should no longer be limited to architects and operative masons, but that men of different professions might be admitted, who would agree to support the dignity of the Order as an ancient and respectable society."

"On the accession of George I the lodges resolved to cement under a new grand master, to be annually elected as in former times, to revive the communications and festivals of the society, to regulate the ancient usages and customs of the fraternity, and to establish such modes only as might correspond with the practices of the members of which the lodges were now principally composed. Accordingly, on the festival of St. John the Baptist, in 1717, a general assembly of the fraternity was convened. Four lodges attended in form, and a grand lodge was constituted." Accepted masons certainly existed before this point, but the author may be speaking to a redirection toward a fraternity primarily composed of accepted gentlemen. No mention of rival factions appears other than that, according to the *Calendar's* "Remarkable Occurences in Masonry" a timeline of history and news updated in every edition, "A number of valuable manuscripts too rashly burnt by some scrupulous brethren, July 24, 1720." This section has King William's supposed initiation in 1693, and credits the first Grand Master, George Payne, with collecting the documents leading to the *Constitutions*.[10]

Whatever the situation of masonry prior to the Grand Lodge, by 1717, Brittons North and South knew at least something of the brotherhood of Freemasonry. The Craft had already taken on mystical and quite likely political overtones. It had strong connections to the Royal Society, the Whig establishment, and notable figures including Christopher Wren, Sir Robert Clayton, Elias Ashmole, and others. Indeed, it may have had some connection to the Stuart court in exile as well as the Parliamentary supporters of the house of Orange. Yet the remaking of this obscure, exclusive, secretive brotherhood of builders into the vanguard of the British Enlightenment and the trendiest club in the world marked a singularly remarkable undertaking.

The First Twenty Years of Grand Lodge: Freemasonry Goes Global

Merchants, diplomats and the Grand Lodge's remarkable publicity campaign carried the Masonic Craft to all corners of the globe. In Europe, Modern masonry reached France in 1725, and may have already had a nascent presence in its older, pre-Hanoverian Scottish formation among the exiled Stuart court. The Modernized Craft served as a vehicle for British Whig political ideology and Enlightenment ideas, while a rivalry was to emerge between Jacobite and Whig factions, the former influencing the formation of the French Higher degrees with the latter ultimately dominating the masonic scene. French merchants would eventually form large networks of commercially oriented lodges across the Atlantic from London to New Orleans and the Caribbean. Aristocrats carried the new English trend east across Europe where a profusion of lodges, grand lodges, and novel degree systems arose in the decades to come. Around the same time the Duke of Wharton created Madrid Lodge in 1728 and a lodge sprang up in Lisbon in 1735. By 1726 Ireland had formed its own grand lodge, with Boston forming the first American provincial grand lodge in 1733. In response to the success of English masonry under the grand lodge, the Scotts, whose oldest recorded lodges pre-dated their southern neighbors, formed a grand lodge in 1736. All three of these new grand lodges actively spread the Craft.[11]

In the two decades following publication of the *Constitutions*, Masonry established itself in the German states first with the appointment of Fredericus de Thom as Provincial Grand Master in 1729–30. In 1733 England issued a lodge deputation to "11 German Masons, Good Brothers" at Hamburg. In 1738 this lodge initiated the Crown Prince of Prussia, a young Frederick the Great, who opened a private lodge at the castle of Rheinsberg and gave permission for a lodge at Berlin in 1740 which became the Grand National Mother lodge of the Three Globes. Masonry spread throughout the German states quickly from this time. In the Hapsburg domains, the Lodge Three Stars in Prague, born in 1726, became a cultural and intellectual center with Vienna's first lodge opened by 1742. The first Swiss lodge arose in Geneva in 1736, with six lodges in the Cantons by 1745.[12]

In northern Europe, Freemasonry quickly became ensconced in the Dutch Republic from 1731 when Desaguliers initiated the Duke of Lorraine, later Emperor Francis I, by special deputation for a lodge at the Hague. Dutch lodges firmly established the local version of the Craft in the Hague by 1734, with Masonic activity documented in Amsterdam and Rotterdam from the following year. Following a brief suppression, masonry grew exponentially in the Dutch Republic and its overseas empire, with at least 16 colonial lodges in the East and West Indies listed in the 1776 *Freemason's Calendar*. Count Axel Ericson Wrede-Sqarre, initiated in Paris in 1731, spread Masonic light to Sweden, where he opened a lodge in 1735. In 1771 King Gustav III entered the fraternity and became its protector. Less a factor in the Atlantic, the Swedes nonetheless contributed to American masonry with a lodge on the island of St. Bartholemew. Elsewhere in Scandinavia lodges opened in Denmark by 1743 and by 1745 in Norway.[13]

Lodges met in Italy beginning in Florence in 1733 followed by Milan, Verona, Padua, Vicenza, Venice and Naples all by 1735. The Florentine brethren included British intelligence agents, as did the Lisbon lodge, a matter which along with local rivalries led to its suppression and partially prompted the first Papal Bull against the Fraternity. Masonry had also reached Malta by 1738, where the Papal Bull led to suppression but was survived by the Lodge of Secrecy and Harmony. In Eastern Europe, lodges existed in Poland prior to 1739. The Papal Bull of 1738 interrupted Polish masonry, but by 1744 lodges had returned to operation. Freemasonry first entered Russia by 1731–2, when British merchants founded a lodge, in 1740 General James Keith became Provincial Grand Master. In the 1770s Masonry grew exponentially in Russia, to around 140 lodges by 1792, when the Craft faced government suppression. The 1778 *Freemason's Calendar* included, along with extensive essays on masonry in Germany, where all of the grand lodge officers overseeing the 38 listed lodges bore noble titles, and of the Dutch grand lodge with it's 16 colonial outposts in the East and West Indies and Africa, offers an extensive account of the flourishing of Russian masonry. In this country where a lodge was first established by English merchants, many of the nobility had already been initiated. Among noble Russian brethren, "some of them in the year 1772 applied for and obtained a patent from the Grand Lodge of England, appointing his Excellency John Yelaguine, Senator, Privy Councellor (sic) Member of the Cabinet, &c. to Her Imperial Majesty the Empress of Russia, and of the Polish Orders of the White Eagle and St. Stanislaus, Provincial Grand Master for the Empire of Russia. . . the Provincial Grand Lodge of Russia, though so lately established, is at this time, in imitation of our Grand Lodge, building a Hall for the purpose of holding their general assemblies." All of the grand officers bore titles of the nobility, the cabinet, or high military office.[14]

Fraternal expansion extended far beyond Europe in the Craft's first quarter century. George Pomfret, Esq. carried an appointment as Provincial Grand Master to India in 1728 to regularize an already functioning lodge. The British East India Company and later British Regimental lodges practiced freemasonry throughout the subcontinent, expanding the fraternity in tandem with imperial control. As with the much celebrated 1777 initiation of the Nabob of the Carnatic, English masons initiated Indian and Persian rulers and elites. There was a French lodge at Pondicherry under English warrant while the Dutch dotted the Indian Ocean with lodges in Ceylon, Sumatra, Java and Celebes. Under Ottoman rule, lodges sprang up in Smyrna and Aleppo in 1738. By 1736, African masonic activity arose in the form of provincial grand master appointments and possibly an English lodge in Gambia. The members here were most likely merchants involved in the African slave trade, though initiating local elites and commercial contacts would have been in keeping with English masonic practice. Freemasons landed in Botany Bay with the First Fleet in Australia, where military lodges established a transient presence leading up to the first official Australian lodge in 1820. The Catholic empires of Latin America took longer to penetrate, but by the turn of the nineteenth century Freemasonry had penetrated Spanish American and Brazil.[15]

The focal point of our story, the Americas, also saw the rapid dawning of Masonic light. In 1730, Provincial Grand Master for New York, New Jersey and Pennsylvania Daniel Cox spent eight months in America, recording no masonic achievement. The first official charter for North America was that issued to First Lodge and St. John's Grand Lodge in Boston in 1733. Documents from Philadelphia indicate an unofficial lodge there by 1730, while the grand lodge of Massachusetts maintains that it had possessed evidence of a lodge operating in the city as early as 1721 or just thereafter prior to a fire in its previous building. Massachusetts' grand lodge followed England in 1717 and Ireland, 1726, as the third Grand Lodge in the world. The network of 40 plus lodge it created from Canada to South America had important commercial and political implications. Independent of Boston, New York also created a thriving, though apparently more local, Grand Lodge by 1737.

New York's Modern grand lodge was heavily connected to the Patriot establishment, such that of the nine lodges existing there before the British occupation, only one survived and the grand lodge was replaced with an Ancient Tory grand lodge formed from British soldiers and Lodge No. 169 Ancients—the shunned black sheep of Boston's Patriot heavy masonic community. Besides the lack of documents, the original Grand Lodge of New York factors less into the story of Atlantic freemasonry simply because there is no evidence of their having propagated their Craft further than neighboring Connecticut. Massachusetts spread masonry to over half of the North American colonies, including parts of Canada. In addition to New York, independent masonic establishments came to Georgia from that colony's inception—in which masonry played a prominent role; Virginia and North Carolina also featured vibrant masonic communities. From the second half of the 1700s onward, masonry flowered throughout the 13 colonies.

The West Indies sugar islands held far greater importance in European courts than continental North America. Here, where cash crop production, inter-imperial rivalry, smuggling, commerce and warfare all co-existed, freemasonry attained tremendous prominence, with at least a dozen lodges on Jamaica and eight on the tiny smugglers' rock of St. Eustatius. French, English, Dutch and even Swedish islands hosted masonic establishments comprised largely of merchants, planters and colonial officials, with official and unofficial lodges operating and interacting from an early time. British lodges came from the grand lodges of England, Scotland and Ireland, penetrated the Coast of Central America. Again, this expansion began in the 1730s. There is some evidence of masonic activity on the Island of Montserrat as early as 1735–6. Boston introduced freemasonry to Antigua in 1738, from which an active provincial grand master, the governor, spread the craft fervently. That same year, naval Captain William Douglas created a lodge in Jamaica from which illicit traders initiated a clandestine lodge among indigo planters in French Saint Domingue, which in turn became a masonic metropolis as the decades progressed. Also in 1738, French freemasonry landed in Martinique.[16]

England appointed a provincial grand master for South America in the 1730s, a transient merchant who seems to have spent too little time in any one port to create local lodges. On the South American continent, Boston created a lodge in Surinam by 1761, in that same year lodges began to appear in Dutch Guyana. British wood merchants in the 1760s brought their craft to England's Central American holdings. Exiles from Saint Domingue carried the Craft to Cuba. The story of Spanish American and Brazilian freemasonry for the most part begins later, at the close of the eighteenth and dawn of the nineteenth century. The combination of Enlightenment reforms and then of military officers fleeing Napoleonic Europe brought masonry to Iberian America, where masons played leading roles in independence throughout the Spanish colonies as well as in Brazil.

Evangelists and Administrators of Global Freemasonry: Provincial Grand Masters

The exponential success of Freemasonry in its early decades meant that the Grand Lodge officers in London had to create a global structure largely on the fly, often in ad hoc fashion. Masons frequently created lodges independently. These "lodges of St. John" had the right to apply, and pay fees, to the grand lodge for regularization. Otherwise, they were considered "clandestine" and "irregular". Many such lodges arose, some transient, others enduring, some gaining official status after months, years or even decades of operation. It is impossible to even guess at how common these clandestine lodges were, but frequent reference to them in a wide range of masonic sources as well as surviving documents of lodges which became regular indicate that the practice was a major factor in the global spread of freemasonry. Also alluded to in some sources is the holding of lodges aboard ships. Military, or "Traveling" lodges became increasingly common so as to be almost ubiquitous first in British and by the end of the century in many European armies. These traveling lodges, usually holding Ancient warrants and admitting men of lower social rank than most Modern, civilian lodges, played a major role in the spread of Freemasonry in the Second British Empire, though their role in American freemasonry has been exaggerated without foundation by some historians.

In applying the governmental structure of seventeenth century lodges to a new organization which had its own moral codes and an invented history that bound brethren together as members of an ancient society purposed with furthering human spiritual, moral and intellectual progress around the globe, the grand lodge had to adapt on the fly while appearing to be following an age old structure. One means of doing so involved the appointment of provincial grand masters. The grand lodge issued charters requiring annual reporting of initiations, submission of payments for fees and the charity fund, and other bureaucratic requirements. These were followed haphazardly. Masonry did not formalize a system of registration and reporting for its overseas provincial grand masters until 1768, 40 years after George Pomfret, Esq. took the first such commission with him to Bengal were a lodge had been opened in 1728. The next year Capt. Ralph Farwinter took a commission for the East Indies. Some provincial grand masters, such as Captain Farwinter, were merchants and traders. Three of first four overseas provincial grand masters (PGM) were sea captains: Farwinter for the East Indies in 1729, in 1731 Captain John Philips became PGM for "all the Russias", and Captain James Commerford for "the Province of Andalusia in Spain".[17]

In Europe, PGMs were often British diplomats, traders, or local nobles proudly initiated by British masonic evangelists. In the Caribbean, no fewer than four sitting governors served as provincial grand master of four separate jurisdictions, beginning with Governor Matthews of Antigua, initiated by Boston merchant and PGM for North America Robert Tomlinson in 1738. Crown officials such as attorney general of Barbados Thomas Baxter, esq., assigned in 1740 for Barbados and "all of the islands to the Windward of Guardaloup [sic]" also feature prominently in colonial appointments, as the place-men John Hammerton and Peter Leigh (both esquire) who oversaw freemasonry in South Carolina for much of that province's history. Thirty-four of the thirty-six appointments in the Americas and East Indies not listed as Governor or Captain bear the title esquire. Though some of these like Baxter, Leigh and Boston's Jeremy Gridley, PGM "for

North America where no Provincial is appointed" were men of the law, many merchants were also given that title in the provincial lists. The two men not listed as esquire, captain, or governor were the Reverend and Honourable Frances Byam, D.D. for Antigua in 1754–5 and Daniel Cox. Contradicting the idea that military lodges were the primary source of the spread of masonry in the Atlantic, only two military officers featured among all of the provincial grand masters by 1769: Royal Navy Captain William Douglas who founded a single lodge in Jamaica in 1738 and Lieutenant Colonel James Adolphus Oughton assigned sometime between 1747 and 51 for the Island of Minorca.

Merchants made up many of the provincials listed as "esquire". For example, Thomas Marriott Perkins received separate appointments from Lord Carysfort in 1761–2 for the Mosquito Shore and from Lord Blaney in 1764–5 for Jamaica. Perkins was an extremely wealthy and well placed merchant. He also spent part of the early 1760s in London, where he served as master of the West India and American lodge. Originally the Goose and Gridiron, one of the four founding lodges of the Grand Lodge, Perkins converted the lodge into a club for American and West Indian merchants, landowners, creoles and members of the metropolitan gentry. The Mosquito Shore registered its first lodges during his tenure; Jamaica already had an active Masonic community. The records of the West India and American indicate that he spent some time in the provinces under his authority, and the accuracy of the lists for both areas indicate that he carried or received correspondence from them regularly, yet he was often an absentee grand master, as was probably the case for a number of provincials.

Cox was appointed for New Jersey in 1730. Here is another variety of grand master; the appointment given to a mason planning to travel to a new region in the hopes they will spread masonry. Cox had spent time in North America previously and received his appointment while in England prior to what turned out to be only an eight month stay in the Americas. There is no evidence of his having engaged in any Masonic activity during his sojourn in the colonies. Since the activity of PGMs often went unrecorded in England it can be difficult to determine how active a provincial grand master was. Some, like Cox, did little if anything. Others created sprawling networks of lodges, of which all, some or none may have been recorded.

Boston's Modern provincial grand masters, Henry Price, Robert Tomlinson, Thomas Oxnard, Jeremy Gridley and John Rowe, were all, with the exception of Attorney General Gridley, merchants. While Boston's provincial grand masters chartered at least 40 lodges throughout the Americas, only around one-quarter of them managed to return documents and payments to England, allowing them into the official register of lodges and the *Engraved List of Lodge* updated several times a year and circulated widely for circumnavigation of the masonic globe. A similar fraction of the 10 lodges created in South Carolina make the list. There were many lodges in the Americas and elsewhere that never officially entered the British records for the same reason, those of which some record remains are likely not the only such lodges to have existed at the periphery. Furthermore, Henry Price assigned an unknown number of provincial grand masters from his provincial grand lodge in Boston. At least two appointments, for Nova Scotia and North Carolina survive; it appears Jeremy Gridley may have made similar appointments for New Jersey and North Carolina. Who such provincially appointed provincials would have reported to may not have been clear even to them. Thus, there was a considerable amount of masonic activity on the periphery of the European empires of which only a fraction was officially registered.[18]

The growth of such a radical movement, in which men of any race, class, religion, nation or creed might share mysteries, perform arcane rituals, and swear secret, bloody oaths to each other did not go unnoticed. Claims to universality, brotherhood, and sanctity caught the attention of authorities temporal and sacred, as did the profusion of radical British political ideals that migrated into French and other continental minds via the lodges. From Papal bulls to American elections, the century from 1738 to 1840 saw prosecution of freemasons by the Inquisition, Czar, and nearly even in its British homeland.

Politics and Persecution

The reworking of Freemasonry into the pro-Hanoverian grand lodge system created a movement social, intellectual, and political. Ric Berman's *Espionage, Diplomacy and the Lodge* describes both diplomatic maneuvering and intelligence gathering conducted through lodges across Europe. Accusations and conspiracy theories have plagued the Craft from before the time of Grand Lodge to the present day. Papal Bulls rolled forth from the Vatican first in 1738 and 1751 against the organization; the church has repeated its stance many times over in the subsequent centuries. In the 1700s masons faced outright suppression in the Dutch Republic, France, the Italian states, The Hapsburg Empire, Russia, and in Spanish and Portuguese lands. Detractors in England raised suspicions such that the Craft was nearly restricted in 1799 under the Unlawful Societies Act. America's first third-party movement, the Anti-Masonic Party,spearheaded a pogrom that nearly obliterated American Freemasonry in the 1830s. In the twentieth century Soviet and Chinese communists banned the organization, while the Nazis sent masons to concentration camps.

Part of the anti-masonic fervent owed to the organization's secretive nature as well as to its emphasis on religious tolerance and defiance of social class hierarchy and its international image as a nepotistic *imperio in imperium*. Ironically, masonry's structure allowed it to serve as either a bulwark of the establishment or a nest of radical conspiracy, and sometimes both. Mason's and masonry's role in radical and even revolutionary movements during the Age of Revolutions until the failed Revolutions of 1848, and Adam Weishaupt's having utilized freemasonry as the basis of his short-lived Illuminati are also culpable in fueling anti-masonic theories. Since 1717, freemasonry's underlying Whig orientation and Enlightenment political idealism had made the movement a political one both within and beyond the British empire, often taken as supporting much more radical political change than the founding architects had intended. The fraternity's organizational structure offered a template for forming more radical secretive organizations, while its widespread network of like-minded men connected across geographical and social boundaries brought together to practice self government with enlightening aspirations, not to mention the protection of its oaths of secrecy, provided ready made networks of recruitment, communication and coordination for potential radicals. Masonic idealism promoted and validated revolutionary ideas. Masonic networks brought together potential radicals within organizations and in the early United States also connected members of otherwise unconnected groups amenable to being co-opted by the Patriots. Furthermore, it provided experience in running a vast, semi-secret organization to its members as well as a template and recruiting ground for forming similar groups. Taverns hosting lodges, particularly those owned by lodges individual masons, often served as meeting places Revolutionary groups.

Margaret Jacob has written extensively on freemasonry's intellectual impact on the French Revolution and Dutch *Patriotten* movement. Adam Weishaupt used freemasonry as a model and early recruiting ground in forming the Illuminati, as did the Mesmerists and other subversive groups. Her view finds support from Eric Hobsbawm and R.R. Palmer, who also saw masonic influence in the democratic revolutions of the early 1800s in countries including Poland, the German and Swiss states, Italy and Russia. This was most notable in the Italian *Carbonari* movement, which drew on Masonic organizing principles as well as ideology. Historians have noted Masonic involvement, or at least overlap, in the Spanish American Revolutions, including brief mention in the work of Karen Racine, Jaime Rodriguez, John Lynch and Jeremy Adelman; more recently

Roderick Barman has uncovered considerable and direct involvement of Brazil's masonic lodges in that nation's independence movement.

The strongest evidence for causal masonic involvement in forming a widespread, armed revolution comes from Ireland and the Irish Brotherhood, the Volunteers, and other radical groups as described by Jessica Harland-Jacobs. Here, groups based on a masonic model created by masons along with politicized and militarized lodges were a driving force in the unsuccessful 1798 uprising. Stephen Bullock has written extensively on the importance of Ancient freemasonry in creating the new social orders of both the Continental Army and the early American republic. Gordon Wood in his seminal *The Radicalism of the American Revolution*, writes that "It would be difficult to exaggerate the importance of Masonry for the American Revolution. . . Masonry was not only an enlightenment institution; it was a republican one as well." The preponderance of freemasons among America's founders has fed speculation of masonic agency in the nation's birth. Both Jacobs *Pattriotten* and Harland-Jacobs Irish Volunteers made statements indicating a belief that American masons had played a prominent role in their nation's independence. The legends of masonic involvement in organizing resistance to the British crown appear, on analysis, to stem from actual involvement of American lodges, particularly but by no means exclusively in New England, in political action beginning with the Stamp Act Resistance, as we shall see in subsequent chapters.[19]

By 1826, masonry had become such a prominent aspect of the American social and political landscape that many assumed a man had to take his degrees and swear his masonic oaths to rise even in local politics. In some communities, this may well have been true. When former mason William Morgan disappeared under suspicious circumstances after threatening to publish the "secrets" of freemasonry, already widely available in print despite every masons' sworn oath to the contrary, a jury of masons acquitted the men accused of having disappeared him, all masons. This led to the nation's first third party political movement, the Anti-Masonic party, and a nationwide purge of masonry that lasted until around 1840 and left the fraternity a fragmented shell of it's former self. As Bullock astutely points out, this witch hunt focused primarily on the Scottish and York Rites, with their extra mysterious 33 degree systems, and on the white masons able to actually hold power. Some lodges still comprised of Yankee mariners such as Newburyport, Massachusetts' pre-Revolutionary St. John's Lodge, took to sea. Many disappeared. There are even tales of white masons re-learning various rituals from the black brethren whose masonic legitimacy they refused to recognize.

Freemasonry recovered in the decades to come, but it would never be the political or social force that it had been before Morgan's disappearance.[20]

Working Class Irish "Ancients", "Scottish" French Aristocrats and a Global Network

Although the grand architects were remarkably successful in creating their institution's "ancient" credentials, their invention took on a life of its own and ended up outside their exclusive control. In England, Irish immigrants excluded from elite British masonry claimed a more ancient pedigree and a purer form of Masonry and eventually eclipsed their "Modern" rivals with a new "Ancient" form of freemasonry, forming a rival grand lodge in 1751. Scotland and Ireland soon fell into the Ancient camp. The Ancients, led by Lawrence Dermot, Grand Secretary and author of the *Ahimon Rezon,* the Ancients' version of the *Constitutions,* offered a more inclusive, less class conscious, and far more affordable version of Freemasonry. By offering initiation to middling men at reasonable rates while at the same time promoting their brand of masonry as more archaic, authentic, and possessed of secrets, most especially the Royal Arch Degree, which the Moderns had lost, Ancient masonry eclipsed Modern masonry in the half century following its introduction. The "Remarkable Occurrences in Masonry" section of the 1778 *Freemasons' Calendar* states, "Antients' meetings declared to be illegal, March 20, 1755", yet this desperate declaration did nothing to slow the growth of Ancient masonry. In 1813, the faltering Premier Grand Lodge of England merged with the Ancient Grand Lodge, largely on the latter's terms. In Revolutionary America, Modern lodges persisted in states such as New Hampshire and Georgia where the Moderns had been part of the Revolutionary order. In Massachusetts, as in England, the Ancient's overtook the Moderns and the two merged in 1792. In most of the new republic, Ancient masonry came to dominate.

In France and thence throughout the continent, the craft was adapted to Catholic and aristocratic French ideals. This led to the invention of the "higher", or *"Ecossaise"* (Scottish) degrees that evolved into a profusion of new masonic orders across Europe and eventually Scottish Rite freemasonry in the United States. There were highly hierarchical masonic bodies often organized as chivalric orders. They claimed origin largely from two sources: Scotland, acknowledged by the English as having an ancient masonic tradition, and the Knights Templar. Both of these links were largely the work of Chevalier Michael Ramsey, a Scottish émigré to France and crusader enthusiast. This notion of an origin among the

Templars, who had delved into the secrets of the ruins of Solomon's temple, lent credibility to masonic history. To any who might argue that the theory that the craft originated with the sons of Ham was ridiculous, and that the identity of the ancient architects of Solomon's temple was questionable as well, the more recent yet still ancient and similarly secretive Templars served to explain this at first implausible history. French higher degree masonry came to have a major impact on American freemasonry beginning approximately two decades after Ancient freemasonry had begun the transformation of the American Craft, morphing into the 32 degree Scottish Rite system. Scottish Rite, unlike the state by state "Blue Lodge" masonic grand lodges, is divided into Northern and Southern jurisdictions, and as such is the largest single masonic entity in the world. In the early Republic, it was also the source of much of the paranoid fervor that led to the anti-masonic movement.

The misconception that North American and Caribbean freemasonry own their existence mainly to the activity of British military lodges during and after the French and Indian War is widely repeated despite being based on no documentation and on scant, non-causal circumstantial evidence. The argument essential is that British military lodges were a major part of the growth of freemasonry in the Second British empire because so many soldier-masons ended up stationed throughout the empire. Even here, the East India Company and Provincial Grand Masters who were merchants and sea captains had established Indian Freemasonry well before regimental lodges arrived; however, regimental lodges certainly did greatly expand masonic presence. Thus, Harland-Jacob and others have argued in passing that the large number of regimental lodges which crossed the continent during the French and Indian War must have been responsible for the explosion of Ancient freemasonry in the decades following their departure. The argument goes that they initiated Americans as masons, who then sought to form their own lodges.

This argument is problematic on several levels. First, it simply lacks evidence. Only two colonial era lodges can trace their origins to the British military. Of these, Albany boasted a lodge with a small, local membership and little impact outside its rural confines. Boston's African lodge received its warrant from a military lodge, but this appears to have been facilitated by the civilian masonic leadership which claimed jurisdiction over both traveling (military) and local lodges. Deputy Grand Master William Burbeck, a patriot in charge of British military stores (i.e. a spy) likely arranged the military warrant in order to avoid the racially tinged debate over initiating the local Africans. Otherwise, the vast majority of foundational lodges and grand lodge in the Americas had clear commercial origins. This was true for all of New England and New York, Pennsylvania, New Jersey Maryland, the both Carolinas, Virginia and Georgia, essentially for the entire 13 colonies, in all of which masonry was well established long before the Seven Years War.

The explosion of the more egalitarian Ancient brand of freemasonry also had civilian, and frequently commercial links. Largely, it occurred due to the initiation as ancients of so many seafaring men and to the general migration that swelled the free white population from 1.5 million at the moment that Brother Washington brashly initiated war with the French in 1754 to around 2.5 million when New Englanders led by brethren such as Joseph Warren, John Hancock, Paul Revere et al opened the War of Independence. Many of the men who came to the colonies in the two decades in between were artisans or other men of the rising classes who flocked to Ancient masonry. Ex-patriot Scottish merchants formed Ancient lodges in the southern colonies as well.

Had these been the remainder of American masons initiated by British lodges during the French and Indian War, they would likely have appealed directly to British or Irish authorities for their charters, and demographically they would have represented a more random and representative sampling of the men of militia age likely to have served beside British troops. Indeed, since military lodges had the authority to dispense "warrants", early lodges in America, were they military derived, would hold such warrants dating from the war years. This is simply not the case in any of the 13 colonies. Likewise in the Caribbean, where freemasonry reached Antigua through Boston merchants in 1738, the same year that Jamaican merchants established their first local lodges and spread their craft to their partners in illicit inter-imperial trade on Saint Domingue. Based on the correspondence of the Grand Lodge of Massachusetts, these French masons were doing business with Boston no later than 1742, while Grand Master Bediford of Jamaica visited Boston in 1744. Indeed, of the dozens of provincial grand masters active in the 1700s in the Atlantic and Indo-Pacific region, only one bears a military title while the rest are mainly merchants, lawyers, or provincial officials.

Philadelphia's lodge No. 4, which left the Modern Aegis to become lodge No. 1 / Lodge No. 69 on the London Ancient rolls, acts as a case in point. Beginning in 1755, the lodge served the large and growing population of Ancient masons among the seamen and ship's captains of the largest seaport in the colonies. Several high ranking members of the modern establishment joined them. Notable among these were former Grand Master William Ball and Reverend William Smith, who went on to become Grand Secretary of the Ancients, both having come into conflicts with Franklin. The Grand Lodge soon realized that

No. 4 worked as Ancients, and the resultant discord led to the lodge's application to become an Ancient lodge and grand lodge. Their correspondence with the London Ancients' via Cork, Ireland, mentions one member of the lodge having been a member of a military lodge, indicating that he was clearly an exceptional case. In making room for their Grand Lodge, Lodge No. 1 renamed itself lodge No. 2, the membership of which consisted of 16.7 % sea-goers, 66.7 % assorted artisans and craftsman, 12.5 % retailers—whose occupation clearly connected them to artisans and seafarers, with the remaining 4.2 % in agriculture. Agricultural produce featured prominently among Pennsylvania's trade, so that even these probably had commercial links. Cheaper to join and less exclusive, the Ancient Grand Lodge formed in Philadelphia actively spread its brand of masonry to the neighboring colonies, as well as it's aforementioned mercantile connection to Saint Domingue.[21]

Of the 40 or so provincial grand masters assigned by the Moderns to the Americas and the East and West Indies, none bore military titles. The Grand Lodge of Scotland appointed Colonel John Murray as a provincial Grand Master for North America, but his military duties prevented him from achieving anything substantial towards that end; he was succeeded by Boston's Dr. Joseph Warren. The Ancient Grand Lodge of England only began to penetrate the continent in the late 1750s. Prior to this period, however, freemasonry was established in every colony and every island by merchants and other highly placed civilians. In New York Modern masons, men of commerce, had already established nine lodges beginning in the late 1730s. Moreover, the rise of ancient masonry in America did not occur as a massive wave around the time of the Seven Years War, but as a steady current in the massive migration of aspirational craftsmen, settlers, and sailors who migrated to the rapidly developing colonies in the decades that followed, and who made up the bulk of Ancient lodge's membership.

Colonial freemasonry and its American descendants should thus be viewed organically, with the often overlapping contributions of Ancient and Modern, Black and White, Anglophone and Frankish freemasonry all receiving just due. Overall, Ancient masonry took on more involvement in Revolutionary politics and in the social order of the early United States, building on the foundation laid by Modern masons, whose contributions to trans-Atlantic trade and the building of colonial societies have been too often underestimated. Likewise, French-derived higher degree masonry had an equally extensive impact on commerce between French, Dutch and English islands and colonies. It came to greatly influence freemasonry and the public's often negative reaction to it in the early United States. In Latin America, French-derived masonic practice was the ritual of choice among creoles and European migrants who became involved at the highest levels of independence movements from Mexico to the Southern tip of South America. Part II will explore world of shared identity and ideology that bound these disparate brethren of the Enlightenment together.

Notes

1 Sarah Churchill, Duchess of Marlborough, quoted in Martin C. Battestin's "General Introduction" to Henry Fielding's *Joseph Andrews*. (Middleton, Connecticut: Wesleyan University Press, 1967: xxvin); *Boston Weekly Newsletter,* January 5, 1719, September 21, 1721; *Boston Gazette,* July 31, 1721, Shipping News.

2 Martha Keith Schuchard, "Jacobite vs. Hanoverian Claims for Masonic 'Antiquity' and 'Authenticity'" *Heredom: the Transactions of the Scottish Rite Research Society, 18,* 2010, 121–186; Jacobs, *Living the Enlightenment,* 69–70.

3 David Stevenson,*The Origins of Freemasonry: Scotland's Century, 1590–1710* (Cambridge: Cambridge University Press, 1998), 14–25, 75–87; copies of the 'Old Charges' appear in various masonic primary documents, with the most complete collection and analysis in William Hughan, *The Old Charges of British Freemasonry* (London: Simpkin, Marshall and Co., 1872).

4 *Ibid.,* 19–25, 75–87.

5 *Ibid.,* 88–96.

6 *Ibid.,* 35–6, 51–4.

7 *Minutes of the Lodge of Edinburgh, Mary's Chapel, No. 1, 1598–1738.* Transcribed by John R. Dashwood with introduction and notes by Harry Carr. London: Quator Coronati Lodge / F.S. Moore Ltd., 1962 (99–102); Douglas Knoop, G.P. Jones. *The Genesis of Freemasonry: An Account of the Rise and Development of Freemasonry in its Operative, Accepted, and Early Speculative Phase.* London: Q.C. Correspondence Circle Ltd. in association with Quatuor Coronati Lodge, 1978 (146–8); Stevenson, *Origins of Freemasonry,* 168–89; Elias Ashmole, *Memoirs of the Life of That Learned Antiquary, Elias Ashmole, Esq; Drawn up by himself by way of diary. With an APPENDIX of original letters.* (Publish'd by Charles Burman, Esq; London, printed for J. Roberts, near the Oxford-Arms, in Warwick-Lane, 1717), 15–16; Tobias Churton, *The Magus of Freemasonry* (Rochester: Inner Traditions, 2006), 103–4, 196–7; Jacob, *Living,* 70; "Sir Robert Clayton", http://www.historyofparliamentonl ine.org/volume/1660-1690/member/clayton-sir-robert-1629-1707.

8 Stevenson, *Origins,* 125–35.

9 Dr. David Harrison, "The York Grand Lodge", https://dr-david-harrison.com/pap ers-articles-and-essays/the-york-grand-lodge/ Sept. 5, 2015.

10 *"THE FREE-MASONS' CALENDAR: OR, AN ALMANAC, For the Year of CHRIST 1775, and Anno Lucis MMMMMDCCLXXV, being the Third after*

Bissestile, or Leap-Year: CONTAINING, Besides an accurate and useful Calendar of all Remarkable Occurrences for the Year, Many useful and curious Particulars relating to Masonry. Inscribed, with Great Respect, To the Right Honourable Lord Petre, Grand Master. By a Society of the Brethren. Eft (Est) & fideli tuta Silentio Merces. (London: Printed for the Company of Stationers. 1775), 19–22, 39–41.

11 Jacob, *Living the Enlightenment: Freemasonry and Politics in Eighteenth Century Europe* (New York: Oxford University Press, 1991), 3–10, 36–8, 45–47, 80–98, 161–177, 306; Margaret Jacob, *Strangers Nowhere in the World: the Rise of Cosmopolitanism in Early Modern Europe* (Philadelphia: University of Pennsylvania Press, 2006), 96–100; Jacob, *Origins of Freemasonry: Facts and Fictions* (Philadelphia: University of Pennsylvania Press 2007), 118–125; Jessica Harland Jacobs, *Builders of Empire: Freemasonry and British Imperialism 1717–1927* (Chapel Hill: UNC Press, 2007), 1–125; Gould, *History of Freemasonry,* 450–505; Martha Keith Schuchard, *Restoring the Temple of Vision: Cabalistic Freemasonry and Stuart Culture (Brill's Studies in Intellectual History)* (Leiden: Brill, 2002).

12 Gould, *History of Freemasonry,* 450–74, 85, 88.

13 *THE FREE-MASONS' CALENDAR: OR, AN ALMANAC, For the Year of CHRIST 1776, and Anno Lucis MMMMMDCCLXXV, being the Third after Bissestile, or Leap-Year: CONTAINING, Besides an accurate and useful Calendar of all Remarkable Occurences for the Year, Many useful and curious Particulars relating to Masonry. Inscribed, with Great Respect, To the Right Honourable Lord Petre, Grand Master,* By a Society of the Brethren (London: Printed for the Company of Stationers, 1776), Gould 479–481.

14 *Freemason's Calendar, or an Almanac for the Year 1778* (London: Grand Lodge, 1778), 40; Berman, Espionage, Diplomacy and the Lodge, Gould 487, Lucio Artini, Roberto Perticucci, "The English Lodge in Florence, 1732–1737" in *Freemasonry in the Transatlantic World,* ed. John Wade (London: Lewis Masonic, 2019), 203–214; Douglas Smith, *Working the Rough Stone: Freemasonry and Society in Eighteenth-Century Russia* (Dekalb, Ill.: Northern Illinois University Press, 1999), 11–44.

15 Gould 491–2; *Freemason's Calendar;* Smith, *Use and Abuse of Freemasonry;* Freemasons Victoria Library and Museum, https://www.freemasonsvic.net.au/history-and-heritage/.

16 Sharp Documents, Vol. II, "The Story of the Lodge La Parfaite Union on the Island of Martinique", ii–iii, Doc. 19, *Proceedings in Masonry,* 6; John Garrigus, *Before Haiti: Race and Citizenship in French Saint Domingue* (New York: Palgrave MacMillan, 2006), 38; Willem Klooster, personal communication.

17 *THE MINUTES OF THE GRAND LODGE OF FREEMASONS OF ENGLAND, 1723–1739. Illustrated with plates and facsimiles. With introduction and notes by William John Songhurst.* London: Quartuor Coronati Lodge, 1913 (230–7), Calcott, *Candid Disquisition,* 97–103; J. Hugo Tatsch. *Freemasonry in the Thirteen Colonies.* Kessinger Rare Reprints, 1933 (50).

18 Information on PGM appointments taken from Wellins Calcott. *A Candid Disquisition of the Principles and PRactices of the Most Ancient and Honorable Society of Free and Accepted Masons.* London: Brother James Dixwell, 1769 (99–104); on Perkins, from the *Lodge of Antiquity* {CHECK / finish}

19 Jacobs, *Living the Enlightenment*; Palmer, *Age of Democratic Revolutions*; Karen Racine, *Francisco Miranda: A Transatlantic Life in the Age of Revolution* (Lanham, MD: Rowmman & Littlefield, 2002); Neil Safir, "A Courier Between Empires: Hipolito De Costa and the Atlantic World," in *Soundings in Atlantic History: Latent Structures and Intellectual Currents, 1500–1830*, eds. Bernard Balyn / Patricia Denault (Cambridge: Harvard University Press, 2009), 265–293; Harland-Jacobs; *Builders of Empire*; Bullock, *Revolutionary Brotherhood*; Eric Hobsbawm, *The Age of Revolution* (London: Wiedenfeld & Nicholson, 1962); Gordon Wood, *The Radicalism of the American Revolution* (New York: Random House, 1991), 223. Roderick Barman, publication pending.

20 The most comprehensive exploration of the anti-masonic movement is that of Bullock in *Revolutionary Brotherhood.*

21 Norris Barratt, Julius Sasche, *Freemasonry in Pennsylvania, 1727–1907, as Shown by the Records of Lodge No. 2, F. and A.M. of Philadelphia from the Year 1757* (Philadelphia, 1908), 8–24; Bullock, *Revolutionary Brotherhood*, 90–2.

Part II

Print Culture in Creating and Connection Franklin's "Masonic Democracy"

This section elucidates the importance of the vast world of eighteenth-century masonic print culture. The first chapter describes the connections of the founders of grand lodge freemasonry to the scientific Enlightenment and the culmination of their vision in masonic learned societies, scientific journals, books, sermons and speeches internationally. The next chapter focuses on the mythological history created for the society and its effectiveness in promoting freemasonry as a truly ancient order with a higher social purpose. The importance of this fantastic history in formulating a shared masonic identity and its evolution in print over the course of the eighteenth century and beyond form much of this chapter. It will also include the various anti-masonic screeds, exposes and "conspiracy theories" of the eighteenth century and their impact on the fraternity.

Perhaps the most important and groundbreaking chapter in Part I describes how masonic print culture created a unified parallel society which "could vie with the best established republic" not only by spreading the ideals, beliefs, and organizational structures of freemasonry throughout the European dominated parts of the world, but in effectively linking brothers of this mysterious society around the world. The great mystery of masons' ability to locate lodges and brethren on the farthest frontier and in the most alien ports of call perplexed their contemporaries as well as modern scholars. They achieved this largely through printed and widely disseminated lists of lodges providing detailed information on when and where lodges met around the globe. These appear in the many publications described in the preceding chapter- books, pamphlets, masonic almanacs- as well as in stand-alone lodge listings. French masonic lodges also printed annual *tableaux,* with detailed directories of members, officers, and contacts that often included age, occupation, place of birth, and more. Colonial lodges usually gave metropolitan contacts and lists of representatives at lodges in their circle of correspondence. In the hands of avid anti-masons, these *tableaux* came to be held up as proof of an international masonic conspiracy. Though largely British and European in colonial times, printed sources began to appear in the colonies and exploded after independence. Previously unexplored, this mapping of the masonic world in the form of listings carried by sailors, sea captains, immigrants, diplomats and travelers forms an important part of the story of freemasonry in the revolutionary Atlantic World.

The importance of masonic print culture to colonial masons and the world they helped create was so important that it cannot be wholly separated from their story. An important chapter in Part III explores the prominent use of the colonial press in British America to connect masons and spread information on masonic leaders, lodge locations, and events throughout the colonies, including the Caribbean as well as the North American mainland. Again, this is uncharted territory in masonic scholarship, and key to understanding not only American masonry but its impact on the fraternity in the metropolis and on colonial and early American cultural life and society. The importance of science and education to American masons also features prominently throughout the final chapters.

Major masonic works, as well as many minor ones, will gain due attention in the pages that follow. In order to understand the foundations of Masonic intellectualism and print culture, one must begin at the begin, with the Old Charges and *Constitutions.*

The Constitutions of the Freemasons, 1723

The Constitutions of the Freemasons, published in 1723, set the framework of masonic "history" and intellectualism. This work was based on the Old Charges with considerable embellishments and additions. The various versions of the old charges, the eldest of which is the *Regius Manuscript* in the possession of the British museum dated circa 1425, lay out a masonic history which began with Adam or shortly thereafter, and has the Craft patronized by the ancient kings of

Assyria, Babylon, Egypt, and Israel thence to ancient Greece and Rome and finally to France and England, where masons were organized into a grand lodge under Prince Edwin in 926 in York. Berman has argued that though the *Constitutions* is generally ascribed to Scottish Presbyterian minister James Anderson and often referred to as *"Anderson's Constitutions,"* the lead role in its composition was probably taken by Jean Theophilus Desaguliers with Anderson as his subordinate. In addition to Masonic "history" it includes various procedural information which aspiring masons could use to join or form lodges under the aegis of the grand lodge.[1]

Constitutions of the Freemasons expanded on and embellished the 'histories' found in various manuscripts of the old charges, though most of the important elements were present in the charges. It emphasized the links to nobility and included such sweeping statements as that in Rome, Augustus was "believed to have been grand master of the lodge at Rome where he patronized Vesuvius and the craftsmen. . ." Indeed, masons had constructed the seven wonders of the world under Nebuchadnezzar as "Grand Master-Mason" or Moses, the "General Master Mason". The list continues with the second temple of Zerubbabel and the Ptolemaic kings of Egypt, usually referred to as patrons of masons but sometimes as grand or general masters. After Augustus, Rome spread the craft "even as far as Ultima Thule". This leads to English masonry in the reign of Athelstan, whose son Edwin "being taught masonry, and taking upon him the Charges of a MASTER-MASON" obtained a royal charter allowing for yearly general assemblies. He also reformed the constitution based on ancient documents, creating many of the modern institutions of English freemasonry. Here then, we have a clear historical beginning of the current institution, but based on far more ancient usages. The historical statutes briefly suppressing masons under Henry VI are quickly explained away. Anderson and Desaguliers also credit the kings of Scotland as great encouragers of the craft, saying, "the Lodges there kept up without Interruption many hundred Years" and cited James VI and indeed all the Stuart kings except the hated James II as masons along with Inigo Jones, premier architect of their age. Martha Schuchard presents considerable evidence for masonry in the Stuart courts in England and in exile, indicating that this was more than an idle assertion. Of course, masonry also prospered under Whig hero King William of Orange, "who by most is reckoned a free-mason". By 1775 the annual *Freemason's Calendar* asserted that William had been secretly initiated in 1693. Euclid, Pythagoras, Vesuvius and a veritable laundry list of great mathematicians, architects, scientists, and "illustrious cultivators of the mechanical

Arts" of antiquity including obscure figures such as "Kresibius, . . .the inventor of pumps" make the timeline as well.[2]

On the formation of the Grand lodge, Anderson simply explains that "the *Freeborn* BRITISH NATIONS, disentangled from foreign and civil Wars, and enjoying the good Fruits of Peace and Liberty, having of late much indulg'd their happy Genius for Masonry of every sort, and reviv'd the dropping *Lodges of London*,. . . several worthy *particular* lodges have a quarterly *Communication*, and an annual grand Assembly, wherein the *Forms* and *Usages* of the most ancient and worshipful Fraternity are wisely propagated." There is no mention of 1717 as a special event, and the first edition of the *Constitutions* did not even use the term 'grand lodge', although later editions and other masonic histories did. The narrative in the first version of the *Constitutions* concludes, ". . .several *Noblemen* and *Gentlemen* of the best Rank, with Clergymen and learned *Scholars* of most Professions and Denominations, having frankly join'd and submitted to take the *Charges*, and to wear the *Badges of a Free and Accepted Mason*, under our present worthy *Grand-Master, the most Noble* PRINCE *John Duke of* MONTAGUE." The present (and first) noble grand master, John Duke of Montagu, is thus lineally connected to William, Athelstan, Charles Martel, Augustinian, Solomon and Nimrod, among other great noble patrons. There are enough specific edifices, titles, and great personages to awe the simpler reader and enough vagueness and nuance to qualify the less defensible assertions.[3]

The Constitutions of the Freemasons was not the first publication of a book of Masonic constitutions. A year earlier, J. Roberts printed an obscure work entitled, *The Old Constitutions Belonging to the Ancient and Honourable Society of Free and Accepted Masons* which includes the only pre-Anderson published version of the Old Charges. The title page claims the works was "Taken from a Manuscript wrote over Five Hundred Years Since". Since Desaguliers and Anderson were already well into the compilation of the more famous *Constitutions* it seems unlikely that this was created by the Grand Lodge. Rather, an operative group, a lodge not associated with the new Grand Lodge, or an individual connected with the same probably printed it. Whether this was coincidental or in reaction to the growing grand lodge is also impossible to gauge. This work opens with a short description of the seven liberal arts and sciences taught by masonry and the preeminence of geometry among them, referring to masonry as a "science". It further consisted of a mythological history, with several details not found in Anderson that appear in later works, and by far the earliest mention of certificates.[4]

Perhaps the most interesting passage in Roberts is the final section, after the charges, entitled, "Additional Orders and Constitutions made and agreed upon at a General Assembly held at _ _ _ _ _ _ _ _ _ _ _ _ _, on the Eighth Day of December 1663." This section gives the distinct impression that a general refor- mation of the organization of the fraternity as it existed at the time was accom- plished at this date. Among these are the first mention of written certificates decades before they were used by the Grand Lodge. also notable, they use the term "Acception" as well as reference to "the whole company", probably a refer- ence to the London Company of Masons.[5]

The fifth charge states "That for the future the said Society, Company and Fraternity of *Free-Masons,* shall be regulated and governed by one Master, and as many Wardens as the said Company shall think fit to chuse at every Yearly General *Assembly."* The wording of these statutes implies that they were recent innovations aimed at a change in the fraternity occurring at that time. It is inter- esting to consider that this was the same year that many prominent seventeenth- century freemasons, including Christopher Wren, Robert Moray, and Elias Ashmole, were involved in the formation of the Royal Society, and that the ref- ormation of the fraternity may have been related to increasing and codifying the Acception of more learned gentlemen or simply to many high level masons having come together in organizing the Royal Society and applying some of their time and organizational energy to their other fraternity.

Masonic literature created a mythologized history presenting the fraternity as an ancient order which for centuries had quietly erected humanity's most won- drous monuments and driven social, political, spiritual and scientific progress. Volumes might be filled with the evolving 'history' of the order, from Adam to Noah to Solomon to King Athelstan to the knights Templar to the druids to ancient Egypt—few great societies of antiquity were not at some point deemed the origin or product of freemasonry. What is most important to consider is that this faux history separated freemasonry from the many clubs of eighteenth- century England. A critical mass of brethren and outside observers believed that it was truly an ancient global order with a vital higher purpose, deeply inter- twined with the rational, scientific Enlightenment and yet deeply spiritual. The other key point is that this body of print culture both connected masons by presenting listings of lodges, grand lodges and important masons with detailed contact information around the world, and that it unified the fraternity with procedural instructions, legalities, and masonic news.

With a history that claimed Adam or Noah as the first mason, masonic intel- lectuals over the course of the century following the foundation of the Premier Grand Lodge concocted a number of origin myths for the craft. Many traced the society to King Solomon, under whom Hiram Abiff, protagonist of the third degree's mystery religion derived drama, labored. Others examined hidden masonic references in both testaments of the Bible, one especially persistent strain claiming St. Paul as a secret mason. With the onset of the French higher degrees and their rapid spread through Europe many came to believe freemasonry the hidden continuation of the knights templar, an idea which has lasted to the present day among modern-day freemasons. Some connected the Templars to Solomon, assuming they had uncovered lost Masonic secrets of the Ancient Hebrews, whilst others believed that freemasonry originated from the druids. By the end of the century there were many Deistic masonic thinkers, Franklin and Paine among the most notable, a natural extension of the Craft's Enlightenment principles. Brethren included christians, Jews, Blacks, Muslims, Hindus and even Native Americans, highlighting masonry's claim to unite brethren in "that religion in which all men agree" and opening the lines of masonic discourse to new perspectives. Interestingly, the Craft's detractors rarely attacked its claims to antiquity but rather bolstered them by framing the order as an ancient and sinister conspiracy, a position strengthened by clerical and governmental attacks on Masonry across the Catholic world.

In the masonic mind of the 1700s, the relationship between the ancient world and scientific progress remained intimately intertwined. In order to understand the importance of these two important aspects of masonic identity, however, it is easiest to consider them separately. The following chapter tells the story of freemasonry's intimate links to the scientific Enlightenment, beginning with the founding members of England's Royal Society. Later chapters will illustrate how this scientific bent migrated across the Atlantic and blossomed in the early American Republic.

Notes

1 James Anderson, *The Constitutions of the Freemasons* (London, 1723), 7–47.
2 *Ibid.*, 34–44; *Freemason's Calendar for the Year 1775,* 39–41; Berman; Martha Keith Schuchard, *The "Ancient" Stuart Roots of Bonnie Prince Charlie's role as Hidden Grand Master* (Middletown: Gauthier Pierozak, 2019).
3 *Ibid.,* 43–4.
4 *The Old Constitutions Belonging to the Free and Accepted Masons. Taken from a Manuscript Wrote Five Hundred Years Since.* London: J. Roberts, 1722, 2–3. Reprinted in *The Old Constitutions of Freemasonry Being a Reprint.With a Foreword by Joseph Fort Newton.* Anamosa, IA: The National Masonic Research Society, 1917. This rare work includes a photostat of the original.
5 *Ibid.,* 23–5.

3

"Lovers of the Liberal Arts and Sciences": Freemasonry and the Scientific Enlightenment

In 1779 American Minister to France Benjamin Franklin and presiding master of the prestigious Parisian Masonic lodge of the Nine Sister addressed his assembled brethren as, "Citizens of the masonic democracy". The *Loge des Neuf Soeurs* represented freemasonry at its most ideal, its membership rolls a veritable who's who of European and American scientists, thinkers, artists and aristocrats which included from the New World Franklin and his grandson, Thomas Jefferson, Thomas Paine, John Paul Jones, and Boston Son of Liberty-turned-loyalist Dr. John Jeffries. Other members were prominent European masons and reformers from England, France, the German States, the Italian Peninsula, Spain, Poland, and Russia. Overtly and actively politicized in supporting the American and later the French Revolution- in the years prior to 1789 its membership came to include revolutionary republicans such as Sieyes, Danton, Desmoulins, Condorcet, Petion,and Mirabeau- the *Neuf Soeurs* was an active creator of learned, charitable and artistic societies for the masses, and a precocious grandchild of the highly politicized Grand Lodge of England created just over six decades prior.[1]

Newtonian rationalism and the search for the lost learning of the classical world were both hallmarks of Enlightenment intellectualism. Many of the founders and early members of the Grand Lodge of England were members of the Royal Society and members of the Society of Antiquaries and the related Spalding Gentlemen's Society, an antiquarian and later a scientific club. Both societies were major recruiting grounds for early grand lodge freemasonry, and the society was designed to appeal to the overlapping scientific and antiquarian intellectualism of the day. More important than the quantity, however, is the quality of overlapping members. They included William Stukeley, founding secretary of the Antiquaries, and three noble grand masters: the first noble grand master, Lord Montagu; the Duke of Richmond, and Lord Coleraine, who also served as vice-president of the society. William Cowper, the first grand secretary and later deputy grand master, two key positions in the direction of grand lodge, was an Antiquary, as were the masters of several early lodges. The antiquarian Gentlemen's Society of Spalding, had approximately 250 members from 1710 until 1740, just under 25 % of whom were masons, including Desaguliers, spymaster Martin Folkes, Lord Coleraine, Earl Dalkeith, Francis Scott, Sir Richard Manningham, Stukeley and Henry Hare.[2]

These two interwoven ideals, of an ancient past and purpose and of scientific education and enlightenment in the lodges, were a major part of the appeal of freemasonry. They reinforced the intent of the grand architects in remaking freemasonry as a bulwark of the Whig social order in England and the spread of British Enlightenment ideals. They led the candidate to believe that he would have access to a scientific education and to the secrets of the past. The multifaceted nature of freemasonry was a large part of its success. Though those with a more practical or social interest probably outranked initiates seeking intellectual or spiritual fulfillment, this latter group of 'true believers' were the most zealous. They wrote essays, lectures and books; created and administered lodges; and took most seriously their obligations to brother masons. These elements were an important aspect of masonic publicity and promotion. They also created a sense of identity and exclusivity. While the average mason may not have been an antiquary or an aspiring Newtonian, they took for granted that, whatever the actual details, this was a very old organization that at some level was connected to enlightened and important men of science and letters, even if most of the lodges were filled with a humbler, less sober sort of brother.

After the Grand Lodge era began in 1717, the craft's self identification with scientific inquiry and knowledge became important elements in its campaign of self-promotion. At least during the 1720s and 1730s, scientific lectures and demonstrations were common in many lodges, a practice that waned but never fully disappeared. Margaret Jacob credits freemasonry with popularizing Newtonian science on the continent, where by the 1770s Paris, Prague and Vienna were home to exceptional lodges, each composed of a transnational intellectual elite which actively promoted and published their members' scientific, philosophical and artistic work. In the Americas such lectures were rare, though not completely unheard of, but masonic sermons did at least pay lip service to the promotion of learning and the importance of scientific achievement and its connection to the fraternity. Benjamin Franklin's masonic status bolstered this claim, as to a lesser extent did that of Drs. Joseph and John Warren and other prominent men of letters. This element of masonic identity was revived in a new form after independence in masonic support for schools and educational programs.

The Royal Society and the Grand Lodge

Robert Moray, Elias Ashmole, and other important seventeenth century freemasons were among the founders of the Royal Society and supplied its officers from its formation. Whatever link existed between the Royal Society and freemasonry from 1660 through 1716, when 4 lodges met in 1717 to form the Grand Lodge of England, two of the lodges, the Horn and the Bedford Head, included at least 13 and 10 fellows of the Royal Society, respectively, many of whom were both important in the Society and instrumental in recreating freemasonry. During the 1720s at least 45 % of the fellows of the Royal Society were masons. Early freemasonry recruited heavily from the Royal Society and also helped expedite the election of masons qualified to become FRS. The most important of the early Royal Society members to join freemasonry, and the most influential in reworking the craft into a massively popular social movement which included among its stated goals the diffusion of light in the form of Newtonian science, was Jean-Theophilus Desaguliers (1683–1744). His Huguenot pastor father had fled to England shortly before his son's birth and obtained a position in the Church of England ministering to French Anglicans.[3]

In 1705 he entered the Christ Church college of Oxford, where he was mentored by lecturer John Keill, one of the first to teach courses on Newton's theories. Keill, a Fellow of the Royal Society, benefitted from Newton's patronage. Using Keill's pedagogical approach of experimentation to validate Newtonian ideas, Desaguliers honed his professional skills and connection to Newton. Desaguliers earned a BA in 1709, was ordained a deacon in 1710, and finished his MA in 1712. By the time he earned his doctorate in 1719 his Masonic work was well under way.[4]

Scientific lectures were becoming popular in England at this time. Desaguliers distinguished himself from other Newtonian lecturers as great teachers often do, by making his experiments and demonstrations engaging and entertaining. Having already connected his brightest pupil to Sir Isaac Newton, Keill also introduced Desaguliers to the Duke of Chandos. A member of the Council of the Royal Society and an aristocrat with strong commercial ties, Chandos was one of the most affluent men in Britain. Desaguliers now had powerful patrons, connections in the Anglican Church, Oxford University, the Royal Society and the Huguenot diaspora. A natural performer and gifted self-promoter, he became the most popular scientist-showman in England. As such, he received sponsorship from the Royal Society's two most influential members, Isaac Newton and Hans Sloane, and became an FRS in July 1714. Desaguliers gave weekly performances at the Royal Society and throughout England, as well as actively publishing both his own works and translations of French scientific texts. He lectured in Paris and The Hague at times as well, and in 1717 performed an experiment for the royal family. Parliament called on him as a hydrological engineering consultant on several occasions starting in 1716 and into the 1730s.[5]

Shortly after moving to London, Desaguliers became a freemason in the Rummer and Grapes lodge, which soon relocated to the Horn, probably through the sponsorship of George Payne, Grand Master in 1718 and 1720. Both were extremely active in remaking and promoting freemasonry. The idea of the lodges as centers of scientific lectures probably came from Desaguliers and Payne. Desaguliers and other lecturers, including other members of the Royal Society and in particular several of Desaguliers' protégés, mixed masonry and business by performing experiments and giving lectures at Masonic lodges throughout England and in exporting the craft and its Newtonian bent to Europe. In Desaguliers' case, this was a two-way street. He found an expanded market for his lectures and publications among the brethren and promoted masonry while on his professional travels. Desaguliers was also the most likely candidate to have facilitated Montesquieu's 1730 initiation into the Horn lodge in London. Freemason and publisher John Senex collaborated with Desaguliers and through him Newton and Desaguliers doctoral advisee and European protege, Willem-Jacob 's Gravesande, in scientific publishing. Gravesande's publications were instrumental in transmitting Newtonian ideas to continental Europe. Freemasonry was, in Larry Stewart's estimation, "the vehicle by which the Newtonianism of Desaguliers and Folkes found its way to the Continent and to the radical circles of Holland" chiefly through the agency of 's Gravesande.[6]

The overlap between high ranking members of the Royal Society and freemasonry included the first noble Grand Master John, Duke of Montagu, Mathematician Martin Folkes, deputy grand Master in 1724 and president of the Royal Society from 1741 to 53. 1741 Deputy grand master Martin Claire was also a fellow. The Earls of Macclesfield and Morton, both masons, served successively as presidents of the society; Henry Hare, Third Baron Coleraine, was a vice-president. Chemist John Brown served on the Council in 1723–5 and free-mason Brook Taylor served as secretary of the society in 1714–18; several other masons held the same position in years to come. 1740 Grand Master the Earl of Morton, Scotland's foremost patron of philosophical associations, published in astronomy and mathematics. Though more a political figure than a scientist, Charles Delafaye was also a Fellow of the Royal Society. Freemasons served on the council of the Royal Society from 1714 to 1770 without interruption, held the presidency from 1741 to 68, and served as either secretary or joint secretary from 1714 to 47. In all, FRS were members of at least 29 different lodges. In at least 39 instances, masons proposed brethren to become members of the Royal Society. Masonic Enthusiasts Martin Folkes, William Jones, William Stukeley and John Machin were the most active in connecting the two societies, proposing 11, 9, 7 and 7 masons to be FRS respectively.[7]

Another active FRS to act as scientific lecturer, masonic proselytizer and associate of Desaguliers was Martin Clare, a member of the Old King's Arms. In addition to his mother lodge, there are records that Clare spoke on scientific topics at a quarterly meeting of the grand lodge in 1735, at the Shakespeare's head Lodge in 1737 and at the Saracen's Head in Lincoln. Apart from scientific sub-jects, Claire also spoke on masonic history. His 1735 "Address Made to the body of Free and Accepted Masons" before the grand lodge emphasized the connection between freemasonry and science and appeared in the *The Pocket Companion and History of Free-Masons* beginning with the 1759 London edition. He appears to have benefited from Masonic patronage in getting his works published.[8]

The extant records of Claire's lodge, the Old King's Arms, beginning in 1733 include a great number of lectures and experiments during the 1730s and 1740s and imply that they were a part of the lodge's activities during the 1720s. Between 1733 and 1743 the lodges enjoyed 36 scientific presentations on a wide variety of topics. The lodge included a number of Fellows of the Royal Society, including the three most frequent lecturers, Martin Claire and physicians William Graeme and Edward Hody. As the frequency of disquisitions declined in the 1740s the lodge added penalties for those who failed to deliver their promised talks. Other lodge records that describe scientific talks given include the Lodge of Friendship

No. 4 beginning in 1729. By 1736 the lodge had moved to the Shakespeare's Head, where Claire spoke in 1737. The minutes list eight lectures in 1738 and two lectures per year in the following three years. Members of Warrington's Lodge of Lights No. 352 formed a dissecting academy in 1755 that most likely hosted scientific discourses as well.

Various lodge records in Northern England and South Wales contain either a definite or probable indication of scientific lectures and experiments being presented in the lodges. According to the records of York lodge dating to 1726, "in most lodges in London, and several other parts of this Kingdom, a lecture on some point of geometry or architecture is given at every meeting." This active scientific and mathematical instruction also occurred in continental lodges, where Jacob cites records from Sluis, Zeeland as evidence that such intellectual activity went on in Dutch lodges outside major urban centers. The importance of continually associating the fraternity with active promotion of science and learning was clear to grand lodge propagandists. Not only did official and overtly promasonic publications such as Smith's 1735 *Freemasons Pocket Companion* direct the brethren to "be a lover of the Arts and Sciences, and to take all Opportunities of improving himself therein," but even the fake masonic exposés put out to confuse the curious in the wake of Samuel Pritchard's massively popular 1730 ritual exposé, *Masonry Dissected*, included exaggerated descriptions of the study a mason was required to undergo in the lodge.[9]

In addition to scientific elements in Masonic publications, there is evidence that Masonic ideals and professional networks among publishers influenced the publication of scientific works by freemasons. Desaguliers, Senex, Keill and 's Gravesande collaborated in translating and publishing each other's scientific works internationally. Senex's former apprentice, freemason Ephraim Chambers, published the very important *Cyclopedia, or, An Universal Dictionary of Arts and Sciences* in two folio volumes in 1728. Margaret Jacob contends that Chambers' *Cyclopedia* was a major force in bringing Newtonian ideas to continental readers. Speaking to the effectiveness of Masonic propaganda, Chambers' definition of freemasonry stated that it could be "found in every country in Europe, and consisting principally of Persons of merit and Consideration." Of its lauded history, he explained that, "As to antiquity, they lay claim to a Standing of some thousand years." Ten years after Chambers' English *Cyclopedia*, the publication of the first French *Encyclopédie* also shows considerable evidence of Masonic involvement. Of the two editors one was definitely and the other quite likely a mason. The idea of such a work had been promoted as early as 1735 by prominent French

Masons including Ramsay, appointed Grand Orateur in 1736. They heightened their efforts in 1738, the year in which the *Encyclopédie* was published.[10]

The emphasis on scientific education may not have been a hallmark of the average lodge after the opening decade of the Grand Lodge, and indeed, it was probably more prevalent in the elite metropolitan lodges than in those which proliferated around the Atlantic and in the East Indies in the years to come. Even so, it formed a key piece of the masonic identity of colonial brethren. Emphasis on freemasonry's connection to "arts and sciences," geometry, architecture, and learning were a consistent strain in Masonic literature of all sorts throughout the century. In addition, there are indications that Masonic lodges may have served as institutional templates and recruiting grounds for philosophical societies in England, as for example the philosophical, literary and scientific societies and debating clubs formed in Newcastle, Bath and Norwich. This pattern continued in the latter city from the formation of Norwich's Masonic lodge in the 1720s through the 1785 formation of the Society of Friars, a group actively involved in scientific and charitable endeavors.[11]

The Fifth Earl Ferrers Washington Shirley, served as Grand Master from 1762 through 1764 after having served as master of the Horn lodge in 1762. The lodge had maintained its elite status and at the time of Ferrers mastership included the Dukes of Gloucester, York and Cumberland and other members of the nobility and ministers of parliament. In 1761 Shirley had been elected a Fellow of the Royal Society for his work in measuring the transit of Venus. The Earl actively patronized philosophical and scientific endeavors in the Derby area during the 1760s and 1770s. His beneficiaries among brother masons included artist Joseph Wright, whose work combined Masonic symbolism and with scientific elements of the Enlightenment, and engineer John Whitehurst. Whitehurst was a correspondent of Benjamin Franklin, who visited him at Derby. Indeed, the various clubs and societies formed by Franklin in both Philadelphia and England, beginning with the Junto, or Leather Apron Club and culminating in the American Philosophical Society have masonic elements both in their organization and objectives. Franklin and Reverend William Smith drew heavily on their masonic networks in founding the Philadelphia Academy which grew to become the present day University of Pennsylvania, the only Ivy League state university.[12]

Lodges and Learned Societies

Franklin's American Philosophical Society was typical of the philosophical societies of Europe in its Masonic influence. Masons on both sides of the Atlantic and the English Channel formed a wide variety of social organizations. They founded various Masonic schools, orphanages, and other charitable associations, and masons also often appear as the founders of a wide range of organizations including political, philosophical, literary, and marine societies, charities, and libraries. These groups frequently showed elements of masonic organization and idealism, and tended to include a number of masons as members and patrons. Strong links existed between the learned societies of Europe and America and freemasonry. Numerous connections existed between the learned societies and masonry both in terms of the members actively responsible for creating and promoting the societies and in their ideology and pedagogical attitudes, particularly in the second half of the century, when many learned societies "often worked in close cooperation with the local lodges." These societies formed transnational and transatlantic intellectual networks- Franklin was a member of no fewer than 20. They created numerous scientific publications and prizes, and promulgated education and learning. Several of the most important and most clearly masonic societies, and of the lodges most involved in forming such societies, deserve particular consideration.[13]

The original vision of Huguenot Desaguliers and his fellow FRS masons was realized most completely in the *Loge des Neuf Soeurs* in Paris as well as in several lodges of Prague and Vienna freemasonry. The lodge included a membership of scientists, philosophers, artists, and other leading intellectuals from across Europe and America. Indeed, its membership was a who's who of Enlightenment thinkers, including Franklin, Voltaire, Quesnay, Mirabeau, Buffon, Sieyès, Lavoisier, Joseph Priestly, Jeremy Bentham, Count Stroganov, Thomas Paine, Thomas Jefferson, and many more leading thinkers. It created social organizations designed to spread enlightened and scientific thinking and published and promoted the works of its members. Largely through Franklin's leadership, the lodge became active in promoting the American cause during the American War of Independence. It was in a speech before the brethren of the *Neuf Soeurs* that Benjamin Franklin referred to masons around the world as "Citizens of the masonic democracy."[14]

Franklin belonged to over 20 learned societies in Europe and America by 1785, making him one of a select group of Enlightenment figures. In like manner, the Academy of Philadelphia from 1776 on admitted many foreign members,

Frenchmen in particular. Franklin's status as a member of both the Royal Society, the French Académie des Sciences, and to a lesser extent the American Philosophical Society gave him credibility that bolstered his status as representative of a new nation not yet recognized by any government in Europe. As political cover, Denmark and other neutral states in their diplomatic dispatches ordered ministers to visit Franklin as a "learned member of many academies" rather than as the plenipotentiary of the United States.[15]

The connection between science and Freemasonry in France began early. Lord Bolinbroke, instrumental in popularizing masonry in France, founded along with l'Abbé Alar the Club de l'Entresol where Montesquieu, Ramsay, d'Argenson, l'abbé de Saint Pierre and the other members talked politics, science and religion. Ramsay as Grand Orateur of the Grand Loge de France in his inaugural address in 1736 claimed that masonry had a duty to spread the arts and sciences. In this speech he mentioned the *Club l'Entresol* and Chambers' *Cyclopedia*. Helvetius joined before going to England in 1764 and then met with leading English masons and FRS. On his return, he, Francois Quesnay and Victor Mirabeau—both future members of the *Loge des Neuf Soeurs*—formed the circle of economists that came to be known as the Physiocrats. Claude Adrien Helvétius and Joseph Jerome de La Lande formed the lodge "Les Sciences" in Paris composed of Freemason scientists. They planned to make the lodge an international center and include artists and other thinkers in addition to scientists, but French masonry was in temporary decline. This and Helvétius' death in 1771 momentarily ended the project.[16]

La Lande was an officer of the Grand Orient and had drafted its 1773 constitution, and was a patron of Madame Helvétius' salon with access to members of the Paris Academy of Sciences and various provincial academies and learned societies at home and abroad by the time he revived the project and founded Les Neuf Soeurs on July 5, 1776. All members had to have published in arts or sciences; the lodge also admitted those of higher ranks in the aristocracy or civil service who promoted culture and learning. Each new member had to present a discourse at the first assembly after his reception and each musician to present an original piece. Neuf Soeurs had a fund for publishing works of the members, which they were to repay after publication. Its constitution stated that it was to recruit masons from throughout Europe and America, making it from its inception a trans-Atlantic intellectual network. It also authorized the lodge to "sponsor ancillary cultural institutions."[17]

Freemasonry in France was again on the ascendant and the lodge quickly affiliated a host of elite brethren. In 1778 it had 180 members including 40 foreigners: Britons, Americans, Italians, Germans, Spaniards, Dutchmen, Russians, and Poles. About 100 more joined from 1779 through 1784. Hans theorizes that if this rate of about 20 new members joining per year continued until the lodge's temporary closure during the Terror, membership would have reached as high as 400 Enlightened thinkers from around the world. La Lande served as the first master, followed by Benjamin Franklin. Franklin received Voltaire into the lodge on April 7, 1778, only weeks before his death on May 30th, with Count Alexander Stroganov of Russia and Giovani Fabroni of Italy assisting. He was elected Venerable May 21, 1779 and reelected the next year. Franklin immediately introduced three Americans—John Paul Jones, Dr. Edward Bancroft, and William Temple Franklin. Jones, an active mason on both sides of the Atlantic, may arguably (though it is a weak argument) have qualified as an expert in navigation; the master's grandson was his secretary but otherwise young and unaccomplished. Franklin also brought in his French banker. Later, Franklin introduced Thomas Jefferson and his secretary William Short. Again, Jefferson may have qualified but Short was a nepotistic appointment—no master other than Franklin made such questionable initiates, and unsurprisingly none of their discourses survive.[18]

During Franklin's tenure the lodge formed several auxiliary organizations under Masonic control but open to non-masons. The Société Apollonienne promoted publications and lectures, as well as a women's auxiliary and two museums: the Musée de Paris, instituted on November 17, 1780, was intended to promote humanities, in response to which brother scientists founded a rival *musée* which opened on December 11, 1781. Lodge members made up a majority of the membership of both, and featured heavily among the lecturers who spoke at them. The ladies' group was largely run by Helvétius' widow, to whom Franklin unsuccessfully proposed. Franklin served two terms and though he declined to stand for a third he continued to participate in all lodge activities. Under his tenure the lodge became an active center of support for the American cause. This support was overt, sustained, and continued after Franklin's departure. In addition to speeches and cultural events in favor of the American war effort, the lodge financed and edited *Affairs l'Angleterre et de l'Amérique* from 1776 through 1780. Thomas Paine joined as a member as well and indeed the French masonic documents he cites in *On the Origins of Freemasonry* likely came from the Neuf Soeurs.[19]

The lodge continued to promote education, founding a school and supporting a wide range of cultural events and publications. There was also a political faction in favor of reforms. It is impossible to say whether the lodge was directly involved in Revolutionary affairs, or simply included many men who were. Nicholas Hans considers the lodge to have been a major supporter of the Revolution, stating that "the influence of the Neuf Soeurs was felt in all three legislative assemblies of the Revolution. Most of the leaders were members of the Lodge." These included Abbe Sieyes, original agitator for the Third Estate to form the National Assembly; Honore Mirabeau, the Marquis de Condorcet, abolitionist and Girondin leader Jacques Brissot, Jerome Petion, Camille Desmoulins and Robespierre's rival for Jacobin leadership Georges Danton. In the new government, "almost all of the educational schemes and laws were initiated by members." It was lodge member J.S. Bailly who in the August 26, 1792 meeting of the National Assembly proposed that 18 foreigners should become French citizens. Most of these were lodge members. Following the fall of the Girondins the lodge ceased to play an active role in the Revolution and despite its support for the new government was shut down by the Jacobin Terror in 1792. Ironically, many of the lodges most prominent revolutionaries met their ends on the device recommended for that purpose by lodge brother Joseph-Ignace Guillotine.

The preeminent role played by so many freemasons, particularly of the Neuf Soeurs, which had been overt in its support of the American Revolution as well, goes a long way to explaining the Abbe Barruel and others' accusations that the entire Revolution was a masonic plot. The Duc D'Orleans, aka Philipe Egalite, who led the first defectors from the Second Estate to the Third, was Grand Master of the Grand Orient. The Marquis d' Lafeyette, who with Neuf Soeurs member Thomas Jefferson wrote the Declaration of Rights of Man and the Citizen, was an active mason probably initiated in a Continental Army lodge. In 1808 the Neouf Souers was revived under Napoleon and continued as a non-political cultural institution until the upheaval caused by the Revolution of 1848 led to its permanent closure.[20]

Interestingly, the influence of the Neuf Soeurs came back to England, from which the ideals it achieved had first issued, not only by way of the many English members of the lodge but also in the founding of a lodge called The Nine Muses in London in March 1777 created by Neuf Soeurs member and surgeon B. Ruspini. Moscow also hosted a lodge Nine Muses. London's Nine Muses included several other members of Neuf Soeurs: notable musicians Abel and Johann Christian Bach, several Italian painters and engravers—Bartolozzi, Carlini, Cipriani and Zoffani, and a number of scientists. Although not as successful as its French parent, it was another example of an English lodge that served as a Learned Society and connected an international intellectual and masonic elite.[21]

Lodges similar to the Neuf Soeurs played important roles in the scientific community and social life of the Habsburg capitals of Prague and Vienna. Though their membership was less international, Czech and Viennese lodges also created scientific publications and included leading names of the eighteenth century, particularly the Austrian composers Haydn and Mozart. The two cities vied for dominance over freemasonry within the empire. Freemasonry reached the Czechs early, with The Three Stars lodge opening in Prague on June 26, 1726. As in England, noble leadership was a major factor in the lodge's success, with Count Franz Anton von Sprock serving as Three Stars' first master. The lodge funded a theater, hospital, orphanage, library and art gallery and made "significant philanthropic and cultural contributions to Prague." Three Stars introduced western ideas and Enlightened thought and ritualistically synthesized them with a more traditional Czech worldview, and performed some scientific experiments and cultural events.[22]

Three Stars hosted active political discussion, leading to dissension between the brethren. Following Sprock's death the lodge splintered into three factions, two supporting either the elector of Bavaria Charles Albert or young Maria Theresa, the third opposed to political involvement. In 1743 the neutrals won out after the Bavarian faction was arrested, tried and pardoned. Under new master Count Kinigl they replaced the old lodge with the Three Crowned Stars Lodge under Strict Observance jurisdiction. Strict Observance was a German derived Masonic rite growing out of the proliferation of French Higher degrees across Europe. Strict Observance became prevalent in Eastern and Central Europe in the 1760–70s. The *Freemason's Calendar* made sure in it's report on German masonry that grand lodge considered Strict Observance irregular, supporting the Prince of Hesse and Darmstadt's rival Grand Lodge of Germany.[23]

Baron von Hund organized a major masonic conference in 1764 through which he successfully popularized Strict Obeservance. As part of his platform, Hund proposed forming nine grand lodges to oversee and promote the new rite from Bavaria to Russia and from Sweden to Greece, staking a claim to Europe west of the powerful grand lodges of England, France, and the Dutch Republic. Attendees from the Three Crowned Stars realized that they could become one of the proposed grand lodges if they recognized the rite. From this point the lodge attracted both Catholics and Protestants with a number of military men, imperial bureaucrats and some intellectuals and enlighteners. Imperial administrators among the membership protected the lodge and saw it as important to the Enlightenment. These included the Governor of Bohemia and other nobles and notables, several of whom lectured on Enlightenment topics. The lodge resumed its social and cultural activities. As the Grand Lodge of the Strict Observance right, between 1765 and 1772 members of the Three Crowned Stars formed lodges in Bohemia, Austria, Hungary, Transylvania and Poland and in 1772 received authority to form new lodges and organizational structures to govern this territory more efficiently. This gave Prague preeminence in Habsburg masonry until the slow disappearance of Strict Observance beginning in the late 1770s.

In Vienna two cosmopolitan lodges had worked in the 1740s, but either closed or disappeared from view. In 1765 three lodges formed under Prague's jurisdiction, performing similar cultural, social and Enlightenment functions, also attracting some reformers. In 1778 they became associated with the new Zinnendorf Rite largely to escape the authority of Prague. This made Vienna the new hub of Habsburg masonry with lodges in Austria, Croatia, Hungary, Transylvania and Silesia. It attracted many intellectuals and reformers, particularly after the 1781 imperial decree which legalized Masonry. This led many reformers to believe that Joseph saw masonry and its Enlightenment ideas as a part of his reform program and a respectable institution. They tended to support state reform and civil religion under monarchy. Viennese lodges grew and included imperial bureaucrats, reformers, professors, aristocrats, intellectuals, literary circles, and the like; sponsored lecturers on science, art, reform, etc. and other cultural events and saw themselves as supporters of Josephinian reforms, going so far as to name a new lodge after him in 1781.

The True Harmony Lodge was intended to serve as a masonic learned society. Born as a political and literary center supporting Josephinian reforms, True Harmony was additionally a music salon with its own orchestra, and was a locus of scientific research. Created in March 1781 by the Austrian Provincial Grand Lodge, its constitution stated that masons connected with this lodge, "were to examine the varying facets of nature, were to promote the study of the arts and sciences, and were to investigate Enlightenment and Masonic teachings." Similarly to the Nine Muses, the lodge had members in Vienna and corresponding members around the Habsburg Empire; it functioned in a similar way to the Nine Muses; and was both a lodge and a center of intellectual activities.

The lodge had two journals—the *Journal für Freymauer* from 1783 until 1786, which published mainly on Masonic and Enlightenment ideas, with some essays and poems on political reforms. The other periodical, *Physikalische Arbeiten der Eintrachtigen Freunde*, was one of the few scientific journals published in Vienna. The most important contribution to Enlightenment science were the many geological articles, as the lodge became an international hub of geological studies. It also featured a group of important physicians who contributed to medical research and reform in Vienna. Reformers in the lodge represented a moderate faction in the Josephinian Party and used the lodge to disseminate propaganda. They were also important in promoting a Masonic philosophy of the Enlightenment that again drew on the mythological roots of freemasonry and connected them to modern enlightenment concepts and masonic ideas.[24]

In 1785, the political climate changed. On December 1, Joseph issued the *Freimauerpatent*, which stipulated that only one lodge was to function in the capital city of each province and dissolved all others. The secret police could inspect the lodges and each lodge had to submit its roster to them every three months. True Harmony closed in 1786, although its journals first published responses to the anti-masonic movement and calls to action by members. In 1787 Strict Observance administrators dissolved the Three Crowned Stars in Prague. The new Lodge of Truth, the only one allowed in Prague, attracted few brothers of the former True Harmony. Prince Dietrichstein, in the Grand Lodge from the beginning, decided to close it in 1788 due to low membership and the secret police routinely observing the rituals. The edict largely ended secret societies among the Hapsburg empire.

In Russia, there were upwards of 140 masonic lodges by 1792, when masonry was suppressed by the state, including the Russian version of the Nine Muses formed in imitation of the famous Parisian lodge. Russian freemasonry created an extensive print culture that included translations of important English masonic works as well as many works by Russian authors led by prominent thinkers including I. P. Turgenev and Nikolai Novikov, the "Enlightener of Russia", a leading mason whose 1792 arrest marked the end of Russia's masonic heyday. This included both original writings such as Turgenev's *Who Can be a Good Citizen and a True Subject* which appeared in French in 1790 followed by three Russian editions in the next 10 years, and a Russian translation of William Hutchinson's *The Spirit of Masonry* under the Russian title, *Dukh masonstva,* that included an appendix added by Russian masons crediting their craft with having taught humanity, "agriculture, architecture, astronomy, Geometry, arithmetic, music, versification, chemistry, the art of ruling and religion" and that they possess "the art to find new arts", and "the art to become good and perfect." Russian masons saw their Craft as a means of westernization as well as self-perfection, and took its ideological side very seriously.[25]

From the Nine Sisters of Paris to the Nine Muses of Moscow, freemasonry played a notable role in the growth of the scientific Enlightenment. Following the English masonic heyday of the 1720–1730s, the Premier Grand Lodge waned for a time. Ancients' masonry led to a resurgence in interest in the Fraternity and in aggressive self promotion in print by both factions supplemented with many publications by independent authors. Characterized at first by ritual exposes and works derivative of the *Constitutions*, Old Charges, and other early Masonic writing, Masonic print grew into far more sophisticated analysis of the fraternity's vaunted heritage and global status. This growth in turn spurred a resurgence in the scientific aspects of British masonry, at least in the intellectual realm of print culture. Not confined to the metropolis, the republic of masonic letters had a distinct impact in America. Nor was influence exclusively one-sided, rather, masonic literature, news and even ritual crossed the Atlantic in several directions, as the chapters to come will demonstrate.

Notes

1 Margaret Jacob, *Living the Enlightenment: Freemasonry and Politics in Eighteenth Century Europe* (New York: Oxford University Press, 1991), 150–1; Nicholas Hans "UNESCO of the Eighteenth Century: *La Loge Des Neuf Soeurs* and its Venerable Master Benjamin Franklin", William Weisburger, " Parisian Masonry, the Lodge of the Nine Sisters, and the French Enlightenment" in *Freemasonry on Both Sides of the Atlantic: Essays Concerning the Craft in the British Isles, Europe, the United States and Mexico* (Boulder: East European Monographs, 2002), 279–98, 299–345; *Tableaux des Freres de la R. L. . . des Neuf Soeurs, a L'O. . . de Paris, 5782* (Paris: Loge des Neuf Soeurs, 1782), *Tableaux des Freres de la R. L. . . des Neuf Soeurs, a L'O. . . de Paris, 1783* (Paris: Loge des Neuf Soeurs, 1783).

2 Berman, *Foundations*, 113–117.

3 Berman, *Foundations,* 40–41; Paul Elliot and Stephen Daniels. " 'The School of True, Useful and Universal Science'? Freemasonry, Natural Philosophy and Scientific Culture in Eighteenth-Century England." *The British Journal for the History of Science* 39, no. 2 (Jun., 2006): 207–229; Berman, *Foundations,* 101–111.

4 *Ibid.,* 42–45.

5 *Ibid.,* 46–51.

6 Ibid., 181, 185–6; William Weisberger. "Parisian Masonry, the Lodge of the Nine Sisters, and the French Enlightenment," in *Freemasonry on Both Sides of the Atlantic,* 299–345; Margaret Jacob, *The Radical Enlightenment Pantheists, Freemasons and Republicans* (Lafayette, LA: Cornerstone Books, 2006), 96; Larry Stewart, "Newtonians, Revolutionaries, and Republicans." *Canadian Journal of History* 17, no. 2 (1982): 314–21.

7 Elliot and Daniels, "The School of True, Useful and Universal Knowledge"; Berman, *Foundations,* 106–9; Trevor Stewart, "English Speculative Freemasonry: Some Possible Origins, Themes and Developments." *AQC Transactions,* 117 (2004), 116–82.

8 Elliot and Daniels, "The School of True, Useful and Universal Knowledge".

9 Alexander Slade. *The Free Mason Examin'd: or, the World Brought out of Darkness into Light. Being, an authentick account of all the secrets of the ancient society of free masons, which have been handed down by oral tradition only, from the institution, to the present time. In which Is particularly described, the whole ceremony used at making masons, as it has been hitherto practised(sic) in all the lodges round the globe; by which any person, who was never made, may introduce himself into a Lodge. With Notes, explanatory, historical, and critical. To which are added, the Author's reasons for the publication hereof, and some remarks on the conduct of the author of a pamphlet, call'd Masonry dissected. With A new and correct lost of all Regular Lodges, under the English constitution, according to their late removals and additions* (London: R. Griffiths, 1754); Elliot and Daniels, "The School of True, Useful and Universal Knowledge"; Berman, *Foundations*, 175–8; Jacob, *The Radical Enlightenment*, 95–7.

10 Bernard Fay, "Learned Societies in Europe and America in the Eighteenth Century," *The American Historical Review* 37, no. 2 (Jan., 1932): 255–66; Jacobs, *Radical Enlightenment*, 95–7; Berman, *Foundations*, 185–6, 280 fn. 157. Quotes from Chambers are taken from Berman.

11 Elliot and Daniels, "The School of True, Useful and Universal Science?".

12 *Ibid.*, Bernard Fay. "Learned Societies in Europe and America in the Eighteenth Century." *The American Historical Review* 37, no. 2 (Jan. 1932): 255–66. Fay generally suffered from a tendency for exaggeration in the conclusions he reached, however, his work on learned societies reveals many actual linkages and synergies; Shawn Eye, "Brother William Smith: Priest, Educator, & Masonic Leader", in *Freemasonry on the Frontier,* ed. John Wade (London: Lewis Masonic 2019), 277–302.

13 Fay, "Learned Societies"

14 *Tableaux des Freres de la R. L. . . des Neuf Soeurs, a L'O. . . de Paris, 5782* (Paris: Loge des Neuf Soeurs, 1782), *Tableaux des Freres de la R. L. . . des Neuf Soeurs, a L'O. . . de Paris, 1783 (*Paris: Loge des Neuf Soeurs, 1783); Hans, Weisberger, in *Freemasonry on Both Sides of the Atlantic.*

15 Fay, "Learned Societies."

16 Hans, "UNESCO of the Eighteenth Century".

17 Weisberger "Lodge of the Nine Sisters"; Hans, "UNESCO of the Eighteenth Century".

18 *Ibid.; Tableaux des Frères de la R. L. . . des Neuf Soeurs, a L'O. . . de Paris, 5782* (Paris: Loge des Neuf Soeurs, 1782), *Tableaux des Frères de la R. L. . . des Neuf Soeurs, a L'O. . . de Paris, 1783* (Paris: Loge des Neuf Soeurs, 1783).

19 *Ibid.*

20 *Ibid.* David Harrison, "Freemasonry and the French Revolution," September 1, 2015, https://dr-david-harrison.com/papers-articles-and-essays/freemasonry-and-the-french-revolution/.

21 *Ibid.*

22 Weisberger, "Prague and Viennese Freemasonry," 375–420.

23 *Ibid.* "An Account of the Grand Lodge of Germany", *Freemason's Calendar for the Year 1778, 28–9.*

24 JFM, II (1785) Part 3, 114–7 (408).

25 Douglas Smith, *Working the Rough Stone: Freemasonry and Society in Eighteenth-Century Russia* (Dekalb, Ill.: Northern Illinois University Press, 1999), 11–44.

4

From Noah to Newton: Creating the History of an Ancient Society

Thomas Paine was one of the most radical thinkers and activists of the Enlightenment. His anti— monarchical *Common Sense* and aggressively deistic *Age of Reason* were a one-two punch at the intellectual, religious, and political foundations of western society. *On the Origin of Free-Masonry,* published posthumously in 1810, applied Paine's skeptical logic to Freemasonry's vaunted history. In France, Paine had been a member of the *Loge des Neuf Soeurs* while Benjamin Franklin served as its master, and later sat in the *Estates General*, then in prison during the Terror. Paine believe in "the absurdity of deriving masonry from the building of Babel", further pointing out the glaring contradictions in a historical timeline which placed Euclid and Solomon as contemporaries. Ever the skeptic, Paine had this to say of the true origins of freemasonry, "Masonry . . . is derived, and is the remains of, the religion of the ancient Druids". The author of *Common Sense* conclude that freemasonry was indeed a purposeful and ancient spiritual order.

Druidism was only one of many antiquarian origins imagined for the Craft. With a history that claimed Adam or Noah as the first mason, masonic intellectuals over the course of the century following the foundation of the first grand lodge concocted a number of origin myths for the craft. Many traced it to King Solomon. Others examined hidden masonic references in both testaments of the

Bible. St. Paul especially was often held up as a secret mason, an idea featured prominently in the first Masonic sermon given in Boston in 1734. With the onset of the French higher degrees and their rapid spread through Europe many came to believe that freemasonry the hidden continuation of the knights templar, an idea which has lasted to the present day among many freemasons. Some connected the Templars to Solomon, assuming they had uncovered lost Masonic secrets of the Ancient Hebrews. The *Calendars* asserted that the Templars had overseen the masons during their time in England. Interestingly, the Craft's detractors rarely attacked its claims to antiquity but rather bolstered them by framing the order as an ancient and sinister conspiracy, a position strengthened by clerical and governmental attacks on Masonry across the Catholic world.

Had Masonic mytho-history focused only on the most ancient times it might have been less effective. Taking the model created by Desaguliers and Anderson, all of the faux historical discourse of masonry made sure to be vague as to whether the connections to Adam and Noah were institutional, or simply the earliest examples of the science of masonry which led to the formation of the modern fraternity. Various sources ascribe Masonic Charges to Babylon, Egypt, Solomon, or as late as Edwin of York or his royal brother Athelstan. This history early establishes the connection to science through Hermes Trismegistus and Pythagoras. As the century progressed and Masons refined their history, more and more detailed accounts of the architectural history of England from the time of St. Alban's, all with titles such as Grand Master ascribed to England's most important architects, nobles, and kings became the mainstay of Masonic histories. These appear more credible and in works from the *Constitutions* to the first edition of the *Freemason's Calendar* in 1775, these histories come up to the founding of Grand Lodge in 1717 and even more recently. This continuity, detail, and connection to actual people, places, and events in the history of actual stone-masonry make for a more believable read which nonetheless gives the fraternity centuries of realistic history. It bears the implication that the older history, if mythologized, is the embellished oral tradition of centuries of real history and implies an earlier period that, if not antediluvian, nevertheless remained quite ancient.

As the eighteenth century progressed, increasingly elaborate and believable Masonic histories appeared in a great number of sources. Many of the pamphlets, exposes, almanacs, and books on masonry simply copied Anderson or each other, sometimes with their own twists, innovations, or analysis. In 1751 Lawrence Dermont published the Ancient's version of the Constitutions, the *Ahiman Rezon*, a title which purported to be Hebrew for "help for a brother". An Irishman living in London, Dermot was the major intellectual and organizational force behind the rise of the Ancients among London's Irish population and beyond. *Ahiman Rezon* dodged the vulnerability of the ancient history by stating that there was no point in writing masonic history, which was not really well known but certainly very ancient, a claim he supports later in the work with various references to masonry in antiquity.

By the end of the century writers such as William Hutchinson and George Smith used the very historical sources around which the fake histories had been created to analyze the rituals and history in order to elucidate the origins of the fraternity, leading to theories of Druids on top of the Templars, Jews and Noachites already implicated. William Preston's 1772 *Illustrations of Masonry* recast the scientific elements of masonic tradition, revitalizing the ritual around the Atlantic Basin, as well as proposing a possible Druidic origin for the craft. Preston's work was picked up by American Thomas Smith Webb, who published *Webb's Masonic Monitor*. Webb's monitor went through a number of editions and was a mainstay of the extensive masonic print culture of the United States, which continued to expand throughout the nineteenth century. A survey of the most important Masonic literature of the period and of the sermons of colonial masons will illustrate how successfully the grand architects created the belief that, whatever the actual story, freemasonry was an ancient institution. The intellectual debate within international masonry about the true origins and meaning of the craft ultimately served to draw in and bind together new members and promote the craft and its Enlightenment ideals.

This literature included books, almanacs, pamphlets and sermons which were often borrowed from each other. A vibrant pamphlet and pocket book literature made up much of Masonic publishing in the middle of the eighteenth century. In the latter decades of the 1700s a new wave of important books and periodicals appeared in England. In the United States both publishing and freemasonry were extremely popular from the federalist period on, and a vast array of masonic works appeared from the new grand lodges as well as from individual masons. The most important books prior to the final three decades of the century were the various editions of the *Constitutions*, official and unofficial, first published in 1723 and the Ancient's answer to it, Dermont's *Ahiman Rezon*, first published in 1756. These works both went through numerous edition on both sides of the Atlantic. *The Unparalleled Sufferings of John Coustos* also went through many editions from its first publication in 1746 into the nineteenth century. This autobiographical tale of the arrest and torture by the inquisition of lapidary and freemason John Coustos, master of the lodge in Lisbon raided by

Portuguese authorities, was an inspiring story of one mason's devotion to keeping the secrets of freemasonry in the face of the persecution inflicted by the ignorance and bigotry of the Inquisition. To masons around the world, but particularly in the Protestant sphere, it was a warning against the dark forces of the Catholic empires. If, as Berman postulates, Coustos' had connections to British intelligence which the Inquisition caught wind of, his autobiography makes no mention thereof.

Masonic Almanacs appeared no later than the 1750s containing lodge listings, international masonic news, and short historical and philosophical essays on the craft. Similar but expanded contents appeared in a group of related books published throughout the British Isles under the title *Freemason's Pocket Companion*. The first work bearing this name appeared in 1735, but they became far more common from the 1750s through the end of the eighteenth century. Among this family of tomes there were editions which plagiarized or borrowed from each other, as well as others that were largely original. They included masonic speeches, essays, and material from around the world. From the 1750s on, Boston's Reverend Charles' Brockwell's sermon preached in Boston's Christ Church in celebration of the December 1749 Feast of St. John was a mainstay of *Pocket Companions* published in England, Scotland and Ireland.

Cheap, widely available and short enough to be accessible and appealing to the masses, masonic tomes underwent sustained print runs and traversed the Atlantic, serving as quick primers on masonic history, ritual, procedure, and songs and guiding traveling masons to lodges across the globe. One striking element is the extent to which these works reprinted, expanded and expounded upon the fantastical history of freemasonry. Indeed, it formed the centerpiece of many such works such as E. Lyon's 1752 *An Antique History of the Orders of Freemasonry from the Assyrian Monarchy Down to the Present Times, with an Appendix by way of Admonition*. Lyon expanded the ancient aspects of the history and its institutional links to contemporary freemasonry, including many details found in Roberts 1722 *Constitution*. The medieval English history is also more detailed than that of Anderson, giving particular attention to masonry as the origin of knighthood and chivalry. He also emphasizes masonry's allowing men to rise through merit, an important ideal in eighteenth century thought, and references science in several passages.[1]

Over the following decades the focus in Masonic histories slowly began to shift to an emphasis on medieval architects and monuments and more elaborate intellectual analysis of the more ancient roots of the fraternity deemphasizing Adam and Noah in favor of various Egyptian, Greek, Druidic or Crusader origins. The publication of Dermot's *Ahiman Rezon* in 1756 led to a spate of refutations, exposes of Ancients' ritual, and a generally expanded masonic print culture. Several of these pieces offer a glimpse into the Ancient-Modern conflict, ultimately supporting the idea that Irish ethnicity and class were the primary motivations behind the split.

Conspiracy Theories, Gormogons and the Scald Miserable Masons: Early Exposes and Attacks

The *Constitutions* and the mass appeal of freemasonry in the 1720s led to a few attempted exposes or mildly anti-masonic pieces. These included "A Mason's Examination" featured in "The Flying Post or Post Master" on April 11 & 13, 1723, probably the first masonic screed. The following year saw *The Grand Mystery of Freemasons Discovered* and *TheSecret History of Freemasonry.* These were proceeded in 1725 by *The Whole Institution of Free-Masons Opened* and *Grand Mysteries of the Free Masons Discover'd, Wherein are the Several Questions Put to Them at Their Meetings and Installations, also Their Oath, Health, Signs, Points to Know Each Other By, etc.* With one more in 1726, *The Grand Mystery Laid Open, or the Free Masons Signs and Words Discovered.* All printed anonymously in London, they don't appear to have had a great impact on the fraternity. The first exposure certain to have crossed the Atlantic was an article from the August 15 & 18, 1730 "Daily Journal of London" called "The Mystery of Freemasonry" which yet to be initiated future Grand Master Benjamin Franklin reprinted in the *Pennsylvania Gazette* of Dec. 5–8 that year.[2]

A few minor works questioned the fraternity's grandiose claims as an ancient order responsible for human progress from the time of Genesis. 1724's *The Grand Mystery of Free-Masons Discover'd. Wherein are the Several Questions put to them at their Meetings and Installations: as also their Oaths, Health, Signs, and Points, to Know each other by. As they were Found in the Custody of a Free—Mason who Dyed Suddenly. And now Publish'd for the Information of the Publick,* was probably the first such exposé. It also included a 10-page masonic catechism. The next year, *"Two Letters to a Friend. The First, Concerning the Society of Free-Masons. The Second, Giving an Account of the Most Ancient Order of Gormogons, In its Original Institution, Excellency, and Design: its Rules and Orders, and the Manner of its Introduction into Great Britain. With an Intire Collection of all that has been Made Publick on that Occasion. Together with the Supposed Reason of their Excluding the Free-Masons, now First set forth for the Satisfaction and Emolument of the Publick."*

attacked the fraternity on the grounds that its stories and mysteries were ridiculous and that the institution was silly, presenting the fictional Gormogons as the true "ancient society" being imitated by the upstart masons. For the most part, however, the early masons were able to promote their view of masonry's history and purpose without facing much skepticism in the press.[3]

There were a few other anti-Masonic or anti-grand lodge titles published in the 1720s. Though they seem to have had a very limited impact, they open a window into public perceptions of the craft at a time when its popularity was growing exponentially. One particularly interesting piece, *The Secret History of the Free-Masons Being an Accidental Discovery, of the Ceremonie Made use of inn the Several Lodges, upon the Admittance of a Brother as a Free and Accepted MASON. With the Charge, Oath, and private Articles, given to him at the Time of his Admittance,* also published in 1724, appears to have been an attack on the new Grand Lodge by freemasons not connected to it, possibly a member of the London Company of Masons or one of the various independent lodges resisting grand lodge authority. The title page advertises that the *Secret History* was "[p]rinted from the old original record of the society; with some observations, reflections, and critical remarks on the new constitution book of the free-masons, written by James Anderson, A.M. and dedicated to the Duke of Montague, by J.T. Desaguliers, L.L.D. Deputy Grand Master." Apparently based on a version of the Old Charges, this work attacks the minutiae of the *Constitutions'* history from Genesis on, not to refute it, but to present it 'correctly'. It then questions the legitimacy of the new Grand Lodge's authority.[4]

One other pamphlet of the 1720s sought to debate its more contemporary uses among the aspirational classes. The 1726 treatise, *THE FREEMASONS ACCUSATION AND DEFENCE. In Six Genuine LETTERS. Between a GENTLEMAN in the Country, and his SON a Student in the Temple. WHEREIN The Whole Affair of MASONRY is fairly debated, and all the Arguments for and against that FRATERNITY are curiously and impartially handled,* laid out the arguments for and against freemasonry in a rather inconclusive fashion which nonetheless offers some interesting insight into public perceptions of the fraternity. The fictive letters between a son who considered joining a lodge and his alarmed father lay out a debate on the utility of the organization. The opportunities to hear scientific lectures and network among the upper class are contrasted with various accusations of frivolity and, echoing Dr. Robert Plott's 1686 *Natural History of Shropshire,* the poor reputation of freemasons in the countryside as idle drunkards. In the end, the son manages to refute his father's arguments but declines the invitation to join the masons out of filial respect. His conclusion essentially states that the society is harmless and not deserving of the suspicion it has engendered, but at the same time is essentially trivial and ineffective as a means of social climbing.

The most successful early Masonic exposé, Samuel Pritchard's *Masonry Dissected,* caused the Grand Lodge far greater consternation than any of the minor attacks it suffered in its first decade. It appeared in 1730 and continued in print consistently at least into the 1820s. *Masonry Dissected* does not dispute the ancientness of the institution, but rather disparages the value of its modern incarnation. According to *Masonry Dissected*, some vague sort of association of operative masons has existed from the time of Babel and was transmitted through a direct line which included Euclid, Hiram at Solomon's Temple, and French King Charles Martel to the England of Athelstan, who organized simple assemblies and practical charges for working stonemasons. Only in 1691 had the new Free and Accepted masonry with charters and quarterly communications appeared. Pritchard then explained the rituals of the three degrees and the secret words and handshakes that accompanied them. *Masonry Dissected* supported to an extent the claims of antiquity laid out by the *Constitutions*. However, the revealing of masonry's mysteries and disparagement of their value were a serious blow to the fraternity.[5]

Pritchard's work appeared in English, French and Dutch and German; its popularity alarmed the grand lodge and inspired imitators. In answer, Masonic grandee Martin Clare anonymously published the far less successful *Defense of Masonry*. Pritchard's expose continued to be printed for the rest of the century; in Newport, Rhode Island in 1749 the brother of one of America's most prominent masons, James Franklin, released an edition. *Masonry Dissected* forced the grand lodge to alter some aspects of the ritual and recognition techniques because its widespread popularity had given so many non-initiates the secrets of freemasonry.[6]

Several lesser known works from the 1730s attempted to cash in on the fraternity. *The Beginning and First Foundation of the Most Worthy Craft of Masonry, with the Charges thereto Belonging* published in 1739 included, besides the faux history and ritual another unique but highly similar set of the Old Charges. Pritchard also put out another piece called, *The Secrets of Masonry Made Known to All Men* in 1737, a year which also saw two anonymous works, *The Mystery of Masonry* and *The Mysterious Receptions of the Celebrated Society of Freemasons* printed in London.[7]

Unauthorized exposes were the worst threat English freemasons faced in the 1730s, but in Europe genuine persecution of the freemasons had begun. In

England, where anti-masonic accusations had focused on drunkenness and frivolity, the first strong accusation of masonry as a conspiracy to overthrow the government appeared in the April 16, 1737 volume of *The Craftsman*. The author, rather than ridiculing their history, considers it a serious mark against them, arguing that "[t]hey derive their original, as I am inform'd, from the building of Babel, which every body knows was an audacious attempt against heaven; insomuch that God himself thought fit to defeat their design". Ironically, the whiggish *Craftsman* accused this order revamped in part to protect the Whig regime with militant Catholicism, and in a twisted interpretation of the Crafts' inclusivity, of admitting "Turks, Jews, Infidels, . . . even Jacobites, Nonjurors, and Papists themselves." Citing the actions of authorities in France and the Netherlands, the author calls for a prohibition or an additional tax to be laid on the order, which he considered a conspiracy against the government.[8]

This was reprinted along with reports of persecutions in France, Holland, and Florence in *MASONRY farther DISSECTED; OR, MORE SECRETS Of that Mysterious SOCIETY REVEAL'D. Faithfully Englished from the French Original just published at Paris, by the Permission and Privilege of M. DE HARRAUT, Lieutenant-General of Police. With Explanatory NOTES (both serious and comical) by the TRANSLATOR.* Mainly a translation of the French police reports on masonry, it was not particularly damning as Herrault had in the end urged that masonry was no threat and surveilling it a waste of his time. The publisher pointed out that *Masonry Dissected* "may be had" at his establishment, clearly hoping to cash in on masonic conspiracy theorists.[9]

Several anti-masonic tracts also appeared in France and Geneva following the papal Bull against the fraternity in 1738. Among the most interesting of these was the obscure French *Almanach des Cocus*, published from 1740 to 44. This included a purported speech of Grand Orateur of the Grand Lodge of France Chevalier Michael Ramsay with radical themes including that "masonry was meant to unite all nations into a peaceful family with France at the Center and that masonry sprang from the Crusades." Here then, both a version of invented masonic history and the idea of Masonry as an international political organization received serious consideration in a non-masonic source. Ramsay's speech would feature in future anti-masonic screeds during the French Revolution and it's aftermath.[10]

Nor did anti-masons confined their activities to the realm of print. The *London Daily Post,* March 20, 1741 reported on the spectacular satirical procession of the Scald Miserable Masons:

Yesterday, some mock Freemasons marched through Pall Mall and the Strand as far as Temple Bar in procession, first went fellows on jackasses, with cows' horns in their hands, then a kettle drummer on a jackass having two butter firkins for kettle-drums; then followed two carts drawn by jackasses, having in them the stewards with several badges of their Order; then came a mourning-coach drawn by six horses, each of a different color and size, in which were the Grand Master and Wardens; the whole attended by a vast mob. They stayed without Temple Bar till the Masons came by, and paid their compliments to them, who returned the same with an agreeable humor that possibly disappointed the witty contriver of this mock Scene. . .

In response to Pritchard and the public humiliations of the Scald Miserable Masons, as well as the general malaise the grand lodge underwent in the 1740s, English Masonry reduced its self-promotional efforts and public presence for much of the decade. By the 1750s and particularly with the emergence of the rival Ancients, Modern freemasonry moved back to aggressive self-promotion. From this time a flurry of Masonic exposés, generally positive or neutral in tone, as well as several anti-masonic works appeared along with direct responses to Pritchard from members of the grand lodge. The spate of pamphlets, pocket companions and almanacs that poured from the printing presses of London, Dublin, Edinburgh, Amsterdam continued to feature the idea of masonry's mythologized history as fact. That they were able to do so with such considerable success speaks to its appeal.

Enter the Ancients

Lawrence Dermot's, *Ahiman Rezon* first appeared in 1756 and went through a number of new editions in and after his lifetime. From the 1790s on, many grand lodges in the United States put out versions of the book. It was very important in drawing the battle lines between Ancient and Modern Freemasonry, and in promoting the spread of the Ancients' brand. Dermot made skillful use of discourse in his assessment of masonic history. The book opens with a parody of Masonic histories on the grounds that connecting freemasonry to every notable figure in history is simply pretension. He reinforced the claim that it was very old and that the term free masons had been applied to the fraternity at the building of Solomon's Temple, while at the same time distancing himself from and even discrediting many of the more fantastic or historically questionable claims.

In so doing, Dermot discredited the authority of the Moderns and their *Constitutions* while at the same time asserting the view that freemasonry was very old without any outrageous or easily disputable specifics. He sneaks in a few such claims further along, such as the assertion that "[t]he greatest Monarchs in all Ages, as well as Asian and Africa as of Europe, have been Encouragers of the Royal Art; and many of them have presided as Grand-Masters over the Masons in their respective Territories." Working Genesis back into his story, Dermot even states the masons' first name was the Noachidae, or "Sons of Noah", and in his sixth charge, he references "the old Regulation of King Ahasuerus". Later, Dermot includes a prayer "used by Jewish Freemasons" followed by "A PRAYER used among the primitive Christian Masons".[11]

Dermot maintains the association of masonry with science and learning, albeit largely in passing, stating of a freemason that, "at his leisure hours he is required to study the Arts and Sciences with a diligent Mind. . ." Catering to the maritime nature of the membership, he explains that "being beyond the sea" is a reason for the Senior Grand Warden to step into the Grand Master's role. Though the *Ahiman Rezon* includes an explanation of the Royal Arch degree- itself probably a version of a French higher degree which had crossed the channel, and which has traditionally been seen as the main difference between it and the modern degrees, it is a minor passage. Rather than focusing on the esoteric, most of *Ahiman Rezon* is concerned with the practicalities of founding, administering and connecting new lodges and grand lodges and for the regulation of charity funds. Dermot's work was a brilliant means of promoting his brand of masonry. It even included regulations for bringing clandestine lodges and brethren into the new Ancient Grand Lodge fold.[12]

The next major edition, that of 1764, was far more vehement in its attacks on the Moderns, going so far as to glory in the deaths of authors of pamphlets on masonry which in his view shouldn't have been written. Most of this nasti- ness focuses on the author of *Three Distinct Knocks*, a pamphlet that exposed the Ancient ritual, describing the Ancients as Irish masons who were essentially out to collect money from new brothers. Dermot doesn't mention the work by name, and calls its anonymous author "Daniel Tadpole". Dermot claims that a Jew whom Tadpole had betrayed sent to have him arrested. Tadpole hid in a ditch in which he was inadvertently smothered by more than four tons of human ordure unwittingly dumped on him. There follows a long story of Tadpole's funeral. His next piece of vitriol begins by gloating over the international spread of his brand of masonry, which was beginning to outstrip his Modern rivals. "CEVERAL (sic) eminent craftsmen residing in Scotland, Ireland, America and other parts both abroad and at home, have greatly importuned me, to give them some account of what is called modern masonry in London."[13]

His explanation of the differences begins equitably enough, explaining that he means no offense—the insincerity of this claim soon becomes clear—and that most modern masons he has met are "good fellows". However, according to Dermot, the Moderns have a limited knowledge of masonry which is not "universal". He says that this is not their fault, as Modern masonry was created in the reign of George I and "delivered as orthodox to the present members." This, of course, is essentially true as regards the creation of Grand Lodge in 1717. This superiority of the ancients means that Moderns lack the knowledge necessary to be made Royal Arch masons without first passing through the Ancient degrees. The effectiveness of this ploy around the Masonic world will be seen in the records of Boston's Lodge of St. Andrews' which from its inception included many members of the Modern 1st and 2nd lodges who had begun their Masonic lives as Moderns. Both St. Andrew's and its daughter Tyrian lodge in Gloucester, Massachusetts contain instances in their minutes of moderns receiving the Ancient degrees. Dramatically, just 36 hours before delivering his 1778 address before Brother Washington and over 30 years after helping to found Pennsylvania's Ancient Grand Lodge, Reverend William Allen, founding Provost of the College and Academy of Philadelphia and former Grand Secretary underwent similar "healing", repeating the second and third degrees as an Ancient.[14]

Further bolstering the legitimacy of the Ancients, Dermot exaggeratedly claims that they outnumber the moderns 39 to 1. Structuring his rhetoric skillfully to drive home the idea of global dominance, he prefaces his next semi-satirical attack on the Moderns by saying, "In order to satisfy the importunities of my good Brethren (particularly the Right worshipful and very worthy Gentlemen of America, who for their charitable disposition, prudent choice of members, and good conduct in general, deserve the unanimous thanks and applause of the masonical world)". Ancient masonry had begun to grow in the Americas at this point, but even so this is likely pretense. His laudatory description of American masonry seems intended to present the international scope of the Ancients and advertise Ancient freemasonry to Americans.[15]

His undermining explanation of the origins of Modern masonry is based closely enough on the actual events leading to the formation of the Grand Lodge of All England and harmonizes closely enough with the accounts in the Modern's own histories to have a certain ring of credibility. Echoing Plott and the 1726 *Freemasons' Accusation and Defense* as to the existence of masonry in 'the country' independent of the elites who came together to form grand lodge, he reverses their positions, so that rather than drunken troublemakers, the country masons continued the purer tradition of masonry while in London, citing Anderson himself, Dermot explains that "the mistreatment of Christopher Wren caused the masons of London to deteriorate to meet under his successor, so that they went into decline." Following this decline "About the year 1717" some "very rusty" London Fellowcrafts resolved to form a new lodge and that since none of them knew the Master's part they "made up a new composition". Meanwhile, in the country, "particularly Scotland and at York", masons kept up their ancient formalities, customs and usages. Thus, only Ancients had the full Master Masons degree and the Royal Arch.[16]

This evolves into a satirical explanation of the ridiculous practices these new masons devised in order to differentiate themselves from actual working masons, intended to demonstrate that they were elites who wished to set themselves above their working class compatriots. This class difference spoke to the real distinction between Moderns and Ancients. Dermot also states that at this formation of grand lodge, "It was also thought expedient to abolish the old custom of studying Geometry in the lodge, and some of the younger brethren made it appear, that a good knife and fork in the hands of a dexterous brother (over proper materials) would give greater satisfaction. . ." By this point, the practice of holding scientific lectures had waned in the Modern lodges. Dermot held this up as a sign of their masonic decay and to poke fun at that common criticism of masonry, that it was simply an excuse to overeat, again laying the blame for such practices at the feet of the Modern masons. The combination of recruiting men of rising aspirational class status with the idea of a purer, more "ancient" form of masonry sold the Ancient's fraternity quite well.[17]

Neither Dermot's book nor the Ancient's alarming spread could go without answer from the Modern grand lodge. This answer came in a short book probably composed by Grand Secretary Samuel Spencer in 1765, *A DEFENCE OF FREE-MASONRY, as Practiced in the REGULAR LODGES, both FOREIGN and DOMESTIC, Under the Constitution of the ENGLISH GRAND-MASTER.* That the Ancients were viewed by their enemies as low caste Irish immigrants is made quite clear by the *Defence*, which is saturated with mocking references to the flaws of Hibernians, including a racist and classist imagined funeral for Dermot in imitation of his funeral of Daniel Tadpole. Affirming the legitimacy of masonic history and refuting Dermot on this and many other points, then differentiating the "Ancient or York Masons" from the legitimate masons of Ireland and Scotland, the *Defence* describes the Ancients thus:

Though there are several persons of character and ability among the Ancient Masons, the greater part of them are a set of illeterate[sic] and mean persons, such as chairmen, porters, walking poulterers, and the like, chiefly natives of Ireland; who finding it not convenient to stay in their own country, have fled hither to get an honest livelihood; they herd together at Hedge-alehouses, and because they know the English grand –lodge will not authorize their illicit and ignorant proceedings, and that the grand –master of Ireland will not countenance them here, they have, with the assistance of some honest Yorkshire-men, who have come to London on the same account, trumpt up what they call Ancient or York Masonry, and under the specious pretence of being the most Ancient, have drawn in several well meaning and worthy persons, by whose assistance and application, a noble peer has condescended to permit them to make use of his name as their Grand-master, though . . . he seldom, if ever, presides in any of their assemblies.[18]

The author describes his attendance at an Ancient meeting with the Master's speech transcribed in comical Irish dialect, and the mass described as low quality Irish immigrants drunk on porter. Though it did little to slow the Ancients' juggernaut, *Defence of Masonry* is an important document in demonstrating that the true nature of the Ancient—Modern schism was a matter of class and ethnicity, as well as demonstrating that promoting the literal true of the Biblical era masonic history was a matter of importance to the intellectuals and publicists of the Grand Lodge in the second half of the eighteenth century.[19]

Other answers to Dermot's work entered the pamphlet literature as well. In Ireland, an exposé of the New Ancients' Ritual, *The Master Key to Freemasonry*, had inspired, *The Three Distinct Knocks; or the Door of the Most Ancient Free Masonry: Opening to All Men, Neither Naked nor Clothed, Bare-Footed nor Shod, &c. Being an Universal Description of all its Branches, from its First Rise to this Present Time, as it is Delivered in All Lodges.* This work, which came in and out of print in Dublin into the next century, claimed that *The Master Key* was neither complete nor accurate, and offered an expose of the ancients ritual by an author who claimed to be versed in both Modern and Ancient ritual. It describes the Ancient lodges as Irish, and accused them of forcible charity collection and constant money grubbing in general, supporting the view of the split as a conflict between London Irish and the English Elite.

Several other authors joined in this debate. *The Freemasons Advocate. Or, Falsehood Detected. Being A Full Refutation of a Scandalous Libel, Entitled, A Master-Key to Free-Masonry* applauds Dermot's *Ahiman Rezon* while another booklet entitled *Wou'd—Be's Reason: or, an Impartial Review of the Principal Arguments for and Against the Antient Society of Free and Accepted Masons. Advanced in two late pamphlets on that Subject,* attacks both Dermot and the *Master Key.* Irish freemasonry included a vibrant press which released original works and reprints of British originals. While they differ in their views of Dermot, both Irishmen attacked the *Master Key's* assertion that Freemasonry, though originally founded with an eye to rebuilding Solomon's Temple, was now entirely allegorical. They insist on the accuracy of even the more fanciful aspects of the history. The latter also debunked Dermot's assertion that there was no point in writing masonic history. They clearly took this history quite seriously and considered the authority of its authors and the antiquity of the documents it was based on sufficient proof of its validity.[20]

Resurgence and Evolution of Masonic Literature

The next important spate of Masonic books began to appear in the 1770s, when the craft's claims to scientific aspiration and moral authority were reasserted and the more primitive antiquarianism of the first quarter of the century recast in a more analytical and intellectual manner suitable for the tastes and sensibilities of the times. Among the most important and successful masonic works of the second half of the eighteenth century were Wellins Calcott's *Candid Disquisition on Freemasonry.* The first London edition of 1769 had a vast list of subscribers, many quite notable. The 1772 Boston edition included subscribers from Quebec and Montreal to North Carolina and the West Indies. It included expanded history, numerous moral essays, songs, and procedural information. Calcott, an active mason and author who entered masonry as an Ancient but shifted into the Modern aegis, particularly focused on the social advantages offered by masonry and the bonds that connected masonic brothers around the world. His history is a detailed version extending from biblical times to the present. *Candid Disquisition* also included a timeline of provincial grand masters appointments which highlighted the global spread of masonry.[21]

   Probably the single most important work from this period was William Preston's *Illustrations of Masonry.* This 1772 book rehabilitated the scientific and educational claims of the fraternity to the extent that Preston's lectures were officially incorporated into improved degree rituals in England and later the United States; after the *Constitutions* it was probably the most commonly owned book among lodges in England. George Smith's *Use and Abuse of Freemasonry* and William Hutchinson's *Spirit of Masonry* were both more modern in tone and more analytical. George Smith's *Use and Abuse of Freemasonry* strongly reinforced masonic internationalism with descriptions of the state of masonry around the world as well as treatises on masonry's moral and social importance.

More than perhaps any other book of the period, Smith's creates a sense of masonry as a parallel society spanning the globe, a true masonic republic. It gave an extensive review of the international extent of the fraternity, as well as casting the history, scientific aspirations, and moral claims in a more readable and believable manner. Smith's chapter on America and the West Indies makes the New World out to be a centerpiece of the Masonic community. His history of masonry in the Americas begins with Boston in 1733, and gives a list of American locales From Montreal to Demerary in which lodges existed under English, Scottish, France, and Dutch grand lodges, concluding that "lodges are almost as numerous on the great continent of America, and her islands, as in England". Smith's assessment was that "Masonry flourishes in America in a very singular manner. They are far more hospitable and more extensive in their charity than the lodges in England." This section on America and the West Indies finishes his region by region history, which is replete with detailed news and information on Masonry across Europe, the New World, and European colonies in India, east Asia and to a lesser extent Africa, including a probably exaggerated count of lodges and masons around the world: 1247 regular lodges in Europe, 187 in America, 76 in Asia and 13 in Africa. Estimating an average of 30 members per lodge with 1523 lodges worldwide, *On the Use and Abuse of Freemasonry* proposes a total of 45,690 masons across the globe. To Smith's credit, his figure appears conservative compared with Margaret Jacob's estimate in *Living the Enlightenment* of around 50,000 masons in Europe alone. Whatever the origins of his figures, Smith created a strong picture of a global republic of interconnected lodges and grand lodges ruled and governed by shared principles and practices acting for the betterment of mankind and the advantage of individual masons.[22]

Hutchinson, conversely, gave the densest antiquarian analysis of any Masonic author to that time. His tome was an intricate, scholarly work offering a comparative analysis of freemasonry to every ancient sect and religion and developing the idea that it had in fact evolved in antiquity originally as a speculative, rather than operative, sect. This led to a series of moral lectures, expounding on the ancient moral system hidden within freemasonry. Hutchinson's was a major masonic book which began as a series of lectures given by the master of a lodge. Publication of "sermons", "orations," and "discourses" was a frequent masonic practice, as for example A Discourse upon Masonry. As Spoken by the Author when Master of a Lodge in England, in the year 1772, from the Words of the Prophet Amos, Ch. i. v. 9. In Which Discourse is sent Forth Masonry as it stood in the Days of Noah, and from his Generation down to this Present Time. That it was originally presented as a lecture from a master to his lodge indicates that masons were regularly indoctrinated with Masonic history. The Biblical connection and Biblical-era history of freemasonry still sold well enough for this English sermon to have been reprinted in Dublin. The fact that several masters turned their lectures into books in this decade indicates that lecturing on masonic topics by masters or other speakers was a feature of masonic meetings.[23]

Though masonic histories from the last three decades of the 1700s tended to focus more on the medieval period, several other published sermons indicate that the belief in scriptural evidence of Biblical freemasonry was still popular. For example, William William's *Masonry founded Upon Scripture; in a Sermon Preached before the Lodges of Gravesend. On New Year's Day, 1752: and Published at Their Request,* expounded on a thesis that masonic morals and ethics are identical to and founded on scripture and laments those masons who fail to live up to them. This sermon went through at least three editions in as many decades. The second edition of William's sermon was printed in London in 1764 and the third in Aberdeen in 1771. In one instance, a mason bound these two edition together and listed by hand titles, authors, and locations of publication of masonic works from all over England and Boston, Montreal, and Dublin, demonstrating that Masonic print was a trans-Atlantic phenomenon.[24]

Further evidence that the Biblical connection continued to matter to masons is demonstrated by the several answers published in response to the 1768 anti-masonic screed, *MASONRY THE WAY TO HELL, A SERMON: Wherein is clearly proved, Both from REASON and SCRIPTURE, That all who profess these MYSTERIES are in a state of DAMNATION.* The author had determined that the Biblical whore of Babylon was in fact a reference to freemasonry. This London pamphlet provoked a response from a Dubliner, *Masonry the Turn-Pike Road to Happiness in this Life, and Eternal Happiness Hereafter.* The anonymous Irish author countered that Masonry is "a bulwark of the Lutheran and Calvinist doctrine", and that the author of *Masonry the Way to Hell* must therefore be a papist. In brushing aside the arguments of the earlier pamphlet he invokes both free-masonry's connection to science and its antiquity. A further answer appeared in *Masonry Vindicated: A Sermon.* This London author first embarks on a long scriptural essay to prove that masonry is in fact derived from the church and highlighting its charitable work. *Masonry Vindicated* consciously emphasizes the international reach of the fraternity, explaining that, "Besides all this, a good mason, by having a proper certificate from the Lodge he belongs to in England, when abroad in a foreign clime, is sure to meet with good friends and assistance if he wants it, without exposing his calamities to a merciless world. . ." To stress this point he tells the story of a mason shipwrecked in the West Indies and brought to Lisbon by a foreign ship. In Lisbon he was recognized as a mason at which the lodge funded the brother and his three companions' return to England.[25]

These major masonic works, however, were only the tip of the iceberg of masonic print culture. Masonic almanacs, pocket books, pamphlets, and ritual exposes poured from the printing presses of England, France, Amsterdam, the German States, and by the end of the decade even Russia. North American masons published their St. John's Day orations and sermons and reprinted masonic books in addition to the imported British works advertised in numerous colonial newspapers. The case for there having been a great number of masonic "true believers" who took the *Constitutions'* antiquarian claims seriously appears far stronger in light not only of the many authors who produced these shorter, cheaper, more accessible works but their great popularity as evidenced by the numerous editions many of them went through.

More Light: Scientific Resurgence in English Masonry

The final three decades of the eighteenth century saw a resurgence of the connection of science and freemasonry and of Masonic intellectualism in England. This included the tomes of Calcott, Smith and Hutchinson, replete with elaborate antiquarianism, history and cosmopolitanism, among others. The most influential masonic book of this period across the English speaking Atlantic was William Preston's 1772 *Illustrations of Masonry*. Subsequent London editions during the author's lifetime appeared in 1775, 1781, 1788, 1792, 1796, 1801 and 1804; in total *Illustrations of Masonry* has gone through at least 20 edition in England and six in the United States. Translations appeared in a number of other languages across Europe. In addition to containing an expanded and more elaborate history of masonry up to the time of publication and an emphasis on the international scope of freemasonry, this book more than any other revived and expanded upon the importance of education and scientific study in freemasonry. Preston's lectures drawn from the book, and presented in lodges to promote it, revitalized the Modern masonic ritual in England and were so widely adapted into American masonry that they remain a vital part of the degree ceremonies performed in American lodges today.[26]

The importance of *Illustrations of Masonry* in reviving the intellectual credentials of freemasonry and revitalizing the practice of the lodges on both sides of the Atlantic make it one of the most important Masonic books. Preston admitted that seriousness and quality of the membership had declined, calling into question his lofty claims of scientific achievement and the reputation of the fraternity. He calls for masons to "earnestly wish for a reform of these abuses," and optimistically states that, "Of late years it must be acknowledged that our assemblies in general have been better regulated."[27]

Illustrations of Masonry was a major force in turning the simpler, more biblically based mythological history of earlier masonic authors into a historical discourse that was interesting and credible to the readership of the final decades of the eighteenth century. It is probably from Preston that Paine drew his conclusions that Masonry had a Druidic genesis, as Preston suggested this was a strong possibility. The renewed emphasis on scientific study and rationalism as a primary element of the craft ubiquitous to its ritual, history and moral philosophy bolstered the sagging reputation and relevance of the fraternity. Thomas Smith Webb, whose *Freemason's Monitor, or Illustrations of Masonry: In Two Parts* became one of the most influential masonic works in the United States, going through numerous editions and influencing the ritual of both the American blue lodges and the higher degrees which eventually became the York Rite, admitted in the first edition of 1797 that his work was mainly taken from Preston. Though Webb's *Monitors* expanded in future editions, this initial offering was largely just a digested version of the earlier work of Preston.[28]

This resurgence of science in British freemasonry continued as the 1700s came to a close and the new century dawned. As an example, take the *Freemasons's Magazine: or General and Complete Library,* a periodical which included masonic and general articles on history, science, and world events. The first edition, published in June, 1793, included a section called "Notes from America" with entries from Halifax, Philadelphia, Charleston and Boston. It also reprinted Benjamin Franklin's "The Speech of Miss Polly Barker," without, ironically, crediting the actual author, one of the most famous Freemasons to have ever lived. The Second Volume, of January–June 1794, included "A Discourse Delivered before St. John's Lodge, No. II of Newbern, in America, the Festival of St. John the Baptist, June 24, 1789," with patriotic references to Warren, Franklin and Washington.

This was one of a number of Masonic magazines, journals, and other periodicals with an international scope. One example is the London *Freemason's Magazine,* which, 10 years after its 5-year run ended in 1795 led to the German *Magazin für Freimaurer, enthaltend Nachrichten über den Ursprung, Zustand und Fortgang der Freimaurerei im Ausland und vorzüglich in Grossbritannien: nebst dahin gehörigen Abhandlungen,* mainly a compilation of excerpts from the earlier

British periodical translated into German and published in Leipzig. Beginning with Volume 9 in July-December 1797, the *Freemason's Magazine: or General and Complete Library,* changed its name to *The Scientific Magazine, and Freemason's Repository.* This new title reflected the continued identification of freemasonry with science as the nineteenth century dawned.

Masons and masonic historians of the nineteenth century remained convinced of the Craft's antiquity/ The vast array of masonic publications from the 1800s, including the widely read history of Albert Gallatin Mackay and Confederate general Albert Pike's unreadably dense *Morals and Dogma,* continued to debate the true source and era of masonry's origins within the discourse framed in the *Constitutions* and the subsequent additions of French and Jacobite Templar enthusiasts and druid chasing English antiquarians. Easily dismissed at first glance, this fanciful and enthusiastic history derived in large part from the Old Charges of late medieval stonemasons guilds and embellished with elements of the intellectual currents of Whig republicanism, Newtonian science, antiquarianism and late Renaissance mysticism which converged in the opening decades of the 1700s, was highly effective in promoting freemasonry to the world as an ancient and auspicious separate "secret" society unto itself. Even more importantly, it convinced a sufficient number of true believers among the many who flocked to join the masonic movement that they truly represented an ancient order comprising a moral and spiritual elite whose purpose was the furthering of all manner of human progress throughout the world. The identity this belief created was so strong that it bound strangers in peace and enemies in war to act as brothers and to follow a system of laws, traditions and rituals which truly created an alternative republic whose citizens might find a friend and brother wherever his travels might take him.

Notes

1 E. Lyon, *An Antique History of the Orders of Freemasonry from the Assyrian Monarchy Down to the Present Times, with an Appendix by way of Admonition* (London: W. Owen, 1752), 7–8.

2 "A Partial List of the Exposes of Freemasonry" found on web.mit.edu. http://web. mit.edu/dryfoo/Masons/Misc/exposures-list.html accessed April 1–3, 2016. The website lists as its sources Gould's *History of Freemasonry, Vol. 3, 475;* Albert Mackey, *Encyclopedia of Freemasonry*; and "Those Terrible Exposures!", Short Talk Bulletin Series, Masonic Service Association, Vol. XXX, No. 7, July 1952, Washington D.C. as well as "personal collections and the National Union Catalog."

3 *The Grand Mystery of Free-Masons Discover'd. Wherein are the several questions put to them at their meetings and installations: as also their oaths, health, signs, and points, to know each other by. As they were found in the custody of a free –mason who dyed suddenly. And now publish'd for the information of the publick.* (London: Printed for T. Payne near stationer's hall 1724); *Two letters to a friend. The first, concerning the society of free-masons. The second, giving an account of the most ancient order of Gormogons, In its original institution, excellency, and design: its rules and orders, and the manner of its introduction into great Britain. With an intire collection of all that has been made publick on that occasion. Together with the supposed reason of their excluding the free-masons, now first set forth for the satisfaction and emolument of the publick* (London: A. Moore, 1725).

4 Sam Briscoe, J. Jackson, J. Weeks, *The Secret History of the Free-Masons. Being an accidental discovery, of the ceremonie made use of inn the several Lodges, upon the admittance of a Brother as a Free and Accepted MASON. With the Charge, Oath, and private Articles, given to him at the Time of his admittance* (London, 1724).

5 Samuel Pritchard, *Masonry Disected (sic); being a universal and genuine description of all its branches, from the original to this present time. As it is delivered in the Constituted regular lodges both in city and country according to the several degrees of admission. Giving an impartial account of their regular proceedings in initiating their new members in the whole three degrees of masonry.VIZ. I. enter'd'prentic, II. Fellow craft III. Master*
To which is added, the author's vindicaton of himself.
By Samuel Prichard, late member of a Constituted lodge (London: Thomas Nichols, 1730).

6 Samuel Pritchard, *Masonry Dissected. The Fifth Edition* (Edinburgh: William Gray, 1752, Kilmarnock: John Stevenson, 1780; Newport, R.I, 1749). The publisher of the 1749 Newport edition is not listed, a pencil annotation on the copy at the Grand Lodge of Massachusetts library attributes it to Franklin; *Het Vrye Metselaarschap ontleed; in alle deszelfs Deelen, van zynen Oorspronk af tot dezen tyd toe...*(translated by Ingestelde Kamer, Printed by Erven van J. Ratelband en Compagnie, op de hoek van de Kalverstraat, aan den Dam); "A Partial List of the Exposes of Freemasonry" web. mit.edu.

7 A Deceased Brother, for the Benefit of his Widow. *The Beginning and First Foundation of the Most Worthy Craft of Masonry, with the Charges thereto Belonging* (London: Printed for Mrs. Dodd, at the Peacock without Temple-Bar, 1739); "A Partial List of the Exposes of Freemasonry" web.mit.edu.

8 *MASONRY farther DISSECTED; OR, MORE SECRETS Of that Mysterious SOCIETY REVEAL'D. Faithfully Englished from the French Original just published at Paris, by the Permission and Privilege of M. DE HARRAUT, Lieutenant-General of Police. With Explanatory NOTES (both serious and comical) by the TRANSLATOR* (London: J. Wilkes, 1738).

9 *Ibid.,* 25–32.

10 Plez Transou, *Masonic Almanacs and Anti-Masonic Almanacs with Commentary by Plez Transou* (Bloomington: Masonic Book club, 1982), 35.

11 Lawrence Dermot, *Ahiman Rezon, or A Help to a Brother* (London: Brother James Bedford, 1756), v–xii, xiv–xv, 24–35, 44–5.

12 *Ibid., 14–14, 17, 44–45, 57–89.* Samuel Bayard Harrison, Jr. *History of the Supreme Council, 33rd Degree Ancient and Accepted Scottish Rite of Freemasonry Northern Masonic Jurisdiction of the United States and Its Antecedants, Volume 1* (Boston: 1938), 46–60.

13 Lawrence Dermot. *Ahiman Rezon, or a Help to All that are (or would be) Free and Accepted Masons, Containing the Quintessence of All that Has Been Publish'd on the Subject of Free Masonry: With Many Additions, which Renders this Work More Usefull than Any Other Book of Constitutions* (London: Robert Black, 1764), i–xvi, xxiv.

14 *Ibid., xxxiv–vi; Proceedings in Masonry, 445–9*; St. Andrew's Lodge, Minutes and Records. Microfilm, Boston: Grand Lodge of Massachusetts; Tyrian Lodge, Minutes, Book 1. MSS Gloucester, Mass; Eyer, "Brother William Smith, *Freemasons in the Transatlantic World, 293.*

15 *Ibid.,* xxvii.

16 *Ibid.,* xxvii–xxix.

17 *Ibid.*

18 *A Defence of Free -Masonry, 35–7.*

19 *A DEFENCE OF FREE-MASONRY, as Practiced in the REGULAR LODGES, both FOREIGN and DOMESTIC, Under the Constitution of the ENGLISH GRAND-MASTER. In which is contained, A REFUTATION of MR. Dermott's absurd and ridiculous Account of FREE-MASONRY, in his Book, entitled AHIMAN REZON; and the several queries therein, reflecting on the regular MASONS, briefly considered, and answered* (London: W. Flexney, 1765), 5–6, 15–18, 27–34. The copy at the Grand Lodge of Massachusetts includes a handwritten notation that it is one of two existing copies. As it relates strongly to Ric Berman's work, I shared portions with him as a professional courtesy; it is at his suggestion that I attribute the *Defence* to the Modern Grand Secretary.

20 W—-O—V—-n. Member of a Lodge in England at this time. *The Three Distinct Knocks; or the door of the most Ancient Free Masonry: opening to all men, neither naked nor clothed, bare-footed nor shod, &c. Being an universal description of all its branches, from its first rise to this present time, as it is delivered in all lodges* (London: H. Serjeant, 1760), 1–7; *Fifth Edition.* London: H. Serjeant, and Dublin Reprinted, 1762; n.d. Dublin, T. Wilkinson [handwritten note –1765?]; London: J. Limbird, n.d. Limbird began publishing in the 1820s and was active for many years; a handwritten note in one of the Limbird editions in the Grand Lodge of Massachusetts says, "Presented to E.J. Carson of Cincinnati Ohio by Br R Spencer of Lodon England Jun 29, 1849", indicating that it was either printed around that year or that it had been circulating for some time. Willingly Wou'd –Be, Esq. *Wou'd Be's Reason: or, an Impartial Review*

of the Principal Arguments for and Against the Antient Society of Free and Accepted Masons. Advanced in Two Late Pamphlets on that Subject. Dublin: Henry Pepyat, 1760; Richard Lewis. Corrector of the Press. *The Freemasons Advocate. Or, Falsehood Detected. Being A full refutation of a scandalous libel, entitled, A Master-Key to Free-Masonry. With A Defence of the Brotherhood and the Craft, Against all the calumnies and Aspersions, that ever have been, or can be thrown on them, by the weakness of some, and the Wickedness of others* (Dublin: J. Hunter, 1760).

21 Wellins Calcott, *Candid Disquisition.*

22 *Ibid.*, 242–4.

23 William Hutchinson, *The Spirit of Masonry in Moral and Elucidatory Lectures, the Second Edition* (Carlisle: F. Jollie, 1795); *A discourse upon Masonry. As Spoken by the Author when Master of a Lodge in England, in the year 1772, from the Words of the Prophet Amos, Ch. i. v. 9. In Which Discourse is sent Forth Masonry as it stood in the Days of Noah, and from his Generation down to this Present Time. Second Edition* (Dublin: T. Wilkinson, 1772).

24 William Williams, M.A. *Masonry Founded upon Scripture; in a Sermon Preached Before the Lodges of Gravesend. On New Year's Day, 1752: and Published at their Request. The Second Edition* (London: C. Burnett, 1764); *Third Edition* (Aberdeen: James Leslie, 1771).

25 *MASONRY THE WAY TO HELL, A SERMON: Wherein is clearly proved, Both from REASON and SCRIPTURE, That all who profess these MYSTERIES are in a state of DAMNATION* (London: Robinson and Roberts, 1768); *Masonry the Turn-Pike Road to Happiness in this Life, and Eternal Happiness Hereafter* (Dublin: James Hoey, 1768); *Masonry Vindicated: A Sermon. Wherein is Clearly and Demonstratively Proved, that a Sermon, Lately Published, "Intitled Masonry the Way to Hell," is an intire piece of the Utmost Weakness, and Absurdity; at the Same Time Plainly Shewing to all Mankind, that MASONRY, if Properly applied, is of the Greatest Utility, not only to Individuals, but to Society and the Public in General: and is Impartially Recommended to the Perusal, as well as to clear up, and obviate all the Doubts Entertain'd, of those who are not Masons; and to the Fair Sex in Particular* (London: J. Hinton, 1768).

26 Biographical information is taken from the introduction to the online edition of *Illustrations of Masonry* available at http://pictoumasons.org/library/Preston,%20 William%20-%20Illustrations%20of%20Masonry%20%5Bpdf%5D.pdf

27 *Ibid.*, 15, 17–20.

28 Thomas Webb Smith, *The Freemason's Monitor, or Illustrations of Masonry: In Two Parts.* Albany: 1797, v–vi.

5

Navigating the Masonic Globe: Print Culture, Masonic Communication and Connection in the Eighteenth-Century Atlantic and Beyond

On September 2, 1794, St. Peter's, the smaller of two lodges in Newburyport, Massachusetts, received as visitors "two Algerian brethren" named Achmer and Ibrahim. According to the minutes, "they were draped in the Turkish habit, having their Turbans on; they were treated with attention by the lodge and appeared to be very much pleased with their reception." Though very few Algerians had likely heard of Newburyport, Achmer and Ibrahim apparently had no trouble finding St. Peter's. Indeed, one of the most intriguing aspects of eighteenth century masonic records is the cosmopolitan nature of the visitors roles. Masons from around the world were able to consistently locate lodges in far flung ports of call for purposes of networking, commerce, assistance in distress, and sociability. In some cases these connections came through word of mouth or correspondence between lodges or individual masons. Another very important yet previously unstudied resource in mapping the masonic world was the widespread dispersal of printed lists of lodges and other forms of print culture advertising the times and place of meetings of lodges and local masonic contacts created and disseminated on both sides of the Atlantic. This print culture played an important and under appreciated role in spreading freemasonry and connecting masons globally.[1]

Published listings of lodges first appeared with the *Engraved List of Lodges* created by the Grand Lodge of England in 1723 and the "New and Correct List of Regular Lodges" which showed up in grand lodge proceedings and other publications and was readily available from the grand lodge. As the 1700s proceeded, masonic almanacs, books, and other publications appeared in England, Scotland, Ireland, France, the Netherlands, Germany, Sweden, Jamaica, the Americas and after the War of Independence the United States, providing listings of lodges under both the local Grand Lodge and others from around the world. These sources cited each other and sometimes added otherwise unlisted or unofficial lodges based on the personal experience of the authors. As the world of masonic print expanded to include ritual exposes, pro-and anti-masonic pamphlets, and tomes on masonic history and philosophy it became common practice to include lists of lodges in Masonic publications. The masonic news, legend, mytho-history, ritual primers and philosophical essays in such printed works was essential to creating and maintaining a unified, consistent sense of masonic identity among masons throughout the Atlantic and Asian empires of European powers, and in promoting the craft to the wider world. These were often reprinted, plagiarized or reproduced, further disseminating and combining listings of lodges, provincial grand masters, and other important contacts around the masonic world.

Additionally, the French masonic practice of distributing lodge Tableaux with extensive demographic information on a lodge's membership and its circle of correspondence and interaction with other lodges in Europe and the New World provided very exact directories on entire masonic networks spanning Europe, the French Caribbean and North America. These were distributed widely enough that by the end of the eighteenth century they actually fed into fears of a French—Revolutionary—Masonic conspiracy. Moreover, the consistent appearance of Masonic news items in newspapers on both sides of the Atlantic provided up to the minute masonic news and information.[2]

International lodge lists were widely distributed in England beginning with the *Engraved List of Lodges*, produced consistently from 1723 to 1778. Each page was a grid including the date a lodge was established, its number on the rolls, time and place of meeting and a picture of the sign on the tavern where the lodge met. This information was sometimes incomplete in the case of overseas lodges. Several updated editions of the *Engraved Lists* were produced every year and according to the 1756 edition of *Anderson's Constitutions* they were intended to be distributed to all the brethren, implying widespread distribution. Handwritten additions and notes in surviving copies of the *Engraved Lists* indicate that masons actively used them in their travels. By 1770 the Grand Lodge included lists of

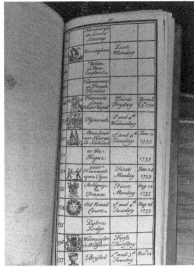

Figure 5.1. The *Engraved List* of 1736. Left: frontispiece and first page; Right: page 10, showing "Boston, in New England", the first lodge in the Americas, at number 126. Later editions included the meeting place, days of meeting and date of establishment. (From the Collection of the Grand Lodge of Massachusetts).

provincial grand masters around the world, a useful set of contacts for the sea-faring mason.

After 1778 the Grand Lodge replaced the *Engraved Lists* with the cheaper to produce and more informative *Freemason's Calendar*, an almanac first produced independently in 1775 and taken over by the Grand Lodge three years later. In addition to lists of English lodges around the world, some editions of the *Calendar* contained listings of Dutch chartered lodges, including those in Africa and the East and West Indies, and lodges of the German Grand Lodge recognized by England. The 1776 *Calendar* stated that their listing was based on the Engraved list, "by W. Cole, Engraver to the Society, No. 109, Newgate-street, where the Public may always be supplied with correct Lists." This demonstrates that the list remained available at any time.

In addition to these engraved lists, printed "New and Correct List of all the Regular Lodges," appeared in the published proceedings and other publications of the grand lodge. The "New and Correct Lists" contained the same information as the *Engraved List*, sans pub sign pictures. These were often broken down into London Lodges, followed by "Town and Country Lodges". More useful to sailors

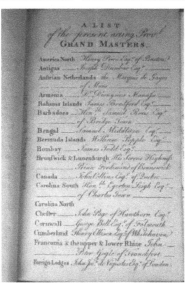

Figure 5.2. On the left, the frontispiece and first page of Benjamin Cole's 1761 list, featuring The West India & American lodge "constituted time immemorial" at number 1. The page in the center features two lodges from the Carolinas at numbers 250 and 251. On the right is the list of Provincial Grand Masters from the final edition, 1778. It begins with "America North Henry Price Esq. of Boston" and features Antigua, Bahama Islands, Barbadoes, Bermuda Islands, Canada, Carolina South and Carolina North in the Americas, with two India entries. More American PGMs featured in the rest of the list. (From the Collection of the Grand Lodge of Massachusetts).

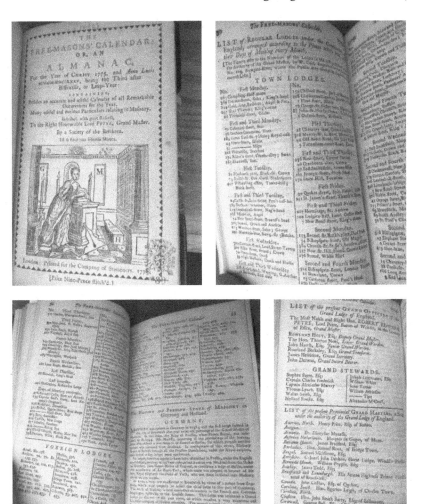

Figure 5.3. The 1775 *Freemason's Calendar*. This was the first, unofficial edition. From left to right: frontispiece; first page of London, or "Town" lodges, listed by day of meeting; the list of foreign lodges; each number represents a lodge in a given location. In this edition the publisher made no attempt to include meeting days for foreign lodges; the first page of the list of provincial grand masters. The list begins with, *"America, North. Henry Price, Esq;* of Boston." Other American entries are identical to those in figure 5.2, right, above. (From the Collection of the Grand Lodge of Massachusetts).

and merchants was the convenient section on foreign lodges arranged geographically after the lists of English lodges. "New and Correct Lists" found their way into any number of secondary publications, those published by the grand lodge and a wide range of books and pamphlets both pro- and anti- masonic, many of which enjoyed long print runs. They were also used by Grand Lodges in other countries in compiling their own lists.

The German source *Alphabetisches verzeichnis aller bekannten freimaurer logen aus oeffentlichen urkunden diefer ehrwurdigen gefellschaft* by Adam Freidr Boehme, published in Leipzig in 1778 cites both the Calendars for 1775 and 1776 and the "New and Correct List" of 1776. This remarkable book compiled a list of 891 lodges from eight cited sources in three languages, including lodges under a number of grand lodges with data on the grand lodge of origin, year of establishment and time and place of meeting. Other German sources for lodge listings included the *Taschenbuch fur Freymaurer, Almanach oder Tashen – Buch fur die Bruder Freymaurer der vereinigten Deutschen Logen,* and *Taschenbuch fur Bruder Freimaurer enthaltend Sammtliche mit der g.u.v. St. Joh. Loge Pforte zur Ewigkeit i. O. v. Hildesheim theils correspondirende, theils derselben Seit 5794.*

Boehme also cites the *Almanac des Franc Masons* for the years 1776 and 1777. This almanacs entered print in Amsterdam in French beginning no later than 1757. The *Almanac des Franc Masons* contained extensive listings of lodges in Europe and the English, Dutch, and French colonies. These include the Scottish lodge at Aleppo and other Middle Eastern lodges, lodges in the North American colonies, a lodge on the Danish Isle of St. Croix, and lodges in India and Batavia. They explain that lodges existed in European factories in Africa, but can't specifically name any. The content of the *Alamanac* was very similar to that of British Masonic publications of the time in terms of the history, philosophy and international news, demonstrating the ideological and intellectual continuity of the movement.[3]

Perhaps the most meticulous Masonic records were keep by the French, a prime example of which is the Grand Orient's annual, *ETAT DU G..O... DE FRANCE.* The *ETAT DU G..O... DE FRANCE TOME TROISIEME. PREMIERE PARTIE 1779,* which offered a richly detailed, highly organized list of lodges and masonic contacts throughout France and the French empire. These included lodge officers with their professions and contact information; in the case of colonial lodges in the Americas, Africa and India many listings included a European contact for the lodge. Other European grand lodges published works with listings of lodges as well. The German *Almanach oder taschenbuch fur die bruder freymaurer 1776–8,* has extensive listings of lodges in the

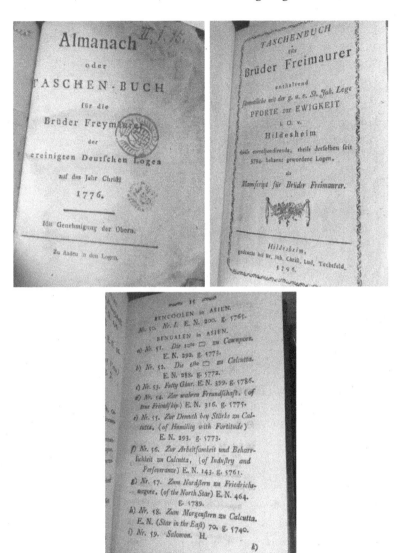

Figure 5.4. German sources for lodge listings. Top Row: Title pages of various German masonic publications dating from 1776 to 1801. This is not a conclusive listing. Bottom Row: selected pages from the 1796 *Taschenbuch fur Druder Freimaurer.* Left: the list of English provincial Grand Masters, beginning with *"America – Nord,* H. Price, *Esq.* en Boston". Center: this page begins with a complete listing of lodges in St. Christoph (St. Kitts), followed alphabetically by listings in India, England, and Germany. Right: Indian lodge listings for Bencoolen and Bengal. (From the Collection of the Grand Lodge of Massachusetts).

Figure 5.5. The title page of Adam Boehme's *Alphabetisches verzeichnis aller bekannten-freimaurer logen aus oeffentlichen urkunden dieser ehrwurdigen gesellschaft* and the pages listing the first six of eight sources he cited in compiling his list of 903 lodges around the world. (From the Collection of the Grand Lodge of Massachusetts).

German states, Russian, Scandinavia, the Baltic regions and Eastern Europe. By 1796 its listings had expanded to include English, Swedish and Dutch grand lodge lodges. It also included a bibliography of 209 masonic titles in various languages, with the *Constitutions* at number one. The Grand Lodge of Sweden in 1798 published the *Almanac Portaif Pour L'Annee 1798 a L'usage des Societes, Qui s'assemblent dans L'Hotel des Franc-Macons au Riddarholm a Stockholm*. This first edition included information only on Swedish lodges, including the lodge on the Swedish Caribbean island of St. Bartholemy with a list of officers. Within a few years the lists came to include lodges of various foreign grand lodges.[4]

There are also lists of lodges from the English Ancients grand lodge and the grand lodges of Scotland and Ireland. Lists of lodges from all three were reprinted in other sources. One copy of Downes' 1804 Dublin edition of Lawrence Dermot's *Ahiman Rezon* at the library of the Grand Lodge of Massachusetts has

Figure 5.6. the frontispiece of the 1767 *Almanac des Franc Masons* and its listings for Asia, Africa, and the Americas. (From the Collection of the Grand Lodge of Massachusetts).

several pamphlets bound into it with lists of Irish, Scottish, and English Ancient lodges and partially listings for the United States, most extensively for the Grand Lodge of Pennsylvania. Separate formatting and page numbering indicates that these listings are copies of independent pamphlets and lists inserted into Downes' book, proving the independent availability of such directories. Downes did not include the pamphlets in his edition; they are bound into a single copy after handwritten records from an Irish lodge dated 1806. The lists begin with a pamphlet of Downes, dated 1804, with contents indicating a list of Irish lodges: "to which has been added the others"; different formatting and page numbering indicates that the non-Irish data came from an original which Downes added to his Irish lists and released as a new pamphlet. Lists of Scott's lodges featured in various works often have a similar format indicating a common source. Harper's 1807 London printing of the *Ahiman Rezon* also included English Antient's lists and a list of military lodges.

Following independence, American publishers and Grand Lodges published numerous listings in diverse formats. An excellent example is *THE*

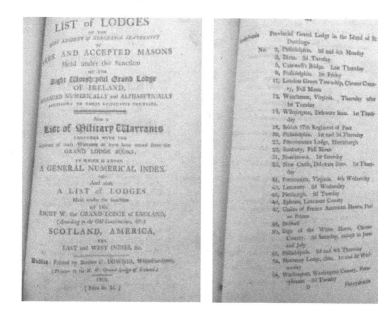

Figure 5.7. Downes Dublin pamphlet of 1804 with lists of lodges under the English Ancients, the Grand Lodges of Ireland and Scotland and extensive lists for many American States. Right: a page from the lengthy list of Pennsylvania lodges features those under Pennsylvania's Provincial Grand Lodge of Santo Domingo in Saint Domingue. (From the Collection of the Grand Lodge of Massachusetts).

FREEMASON'S CALENDAR, AND ALMANAC; for the YEAR of our LORD 1793: CONTAINING, Astronomical calculations,—An account of the Ancient and Honorable Society of Free Masons, with other things necessary for an Almanac. By the Hon. Samuel Stearns LLD. A few copies of his 1793 Almanac are all that remain of the series so it is impossible to known how many years Stearns printed the almanac. In 1793 he offered a list of English lodges which, based on the numbering, must have come from the 1792 *Freemason's Calendar,* followed by a digested list of English chartered lodges in the Americas. It then included haphazard information on lodges and lodge and Grand Lodge officers for Rhode Island, New York, North Carolina, Massachusetts and New Hampshire. Other masonic contents include a history of masonry in America, detailing the chartering of Boston's Modern Grand Lodge and their having granted Benjamin Franklin a charter for Philadelphia, "Thus sprang masonry in America." Stearns also lists prominent masons in the American army and offers a conservative figure of "no less than 575 regular lodges in the world today."

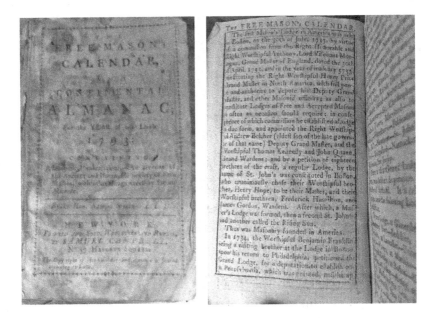

Figure 5.8. Samuel Stearns 1793 *Freemason's Calendar and* Continental *Almanac.* Right: the first page of the almanac's history of masonry in America beginning with Boston's First Lodge. The almanac also included lists of lodges in the Americas under English authority and listings of lodges in many US states, as well as a reprinting of the English *Calendar's* "Remarkable Occurrences in Masonry". (From the Collection of the Grand Lodge of Massachusetts).

Both the achievements and the limitations of these published lists have much to tell us about connection and communication in the Masonic world. For example, though St. John's Provincial Grand Lodge, located in Boston and claiming jurisdiction for all of North America, chartered around 40 lodges from Canada to Surinam, including lodges in all but two of the future US States, and claimed to have introduced freemasonry to both Canada and the Caribbean, only 10 of these lodges appear in the *Engraved Lists* or the *Calendar*. Several of these weren't listed until years after their foundation. Correspondence between Provincial Grand Master Henry Price and the grand lodge indicate that this was due to a combination of inconsistent communication and to the grand lodge's only listing lodges which had paid for their constitutions. Though the appointment of provincial grand masters and other sources confirm that Freemasonry was active in the Caribbean no later than 1738 and perhaps as early as 1736, no lodges there are listed until the *Engraved List* of 1740, with their backdated founding dates. Hughan's facsimile for the list of 1740 includes handwritten additions of Kingston Jamaica with meeting times and St. Michael's Lodge in Barbadoes and three English lodges. In some cases the lists were renumbered to account for foreign lodges, while in others they appear out of sequence. Thus, the extensive activity of provincial grand masters, lodge's of St. John formed by traveling masons, and clandestine lodges were often unknown to the metropolis.

A traveling mason might find such lodges through word of mouth, or in some cases in local publications. For example, while only one of the nine lodges active in New York prior to the American Revolution appears in the *Engraved List*, the contents of Merry Andrew's Almanack for the Year of our Lord 1774 included "A List of all the regular constituted lodges of the most ancient and honorable society of free and accepted masons, in the city of New York, and the time when, and the place where they assemble." *Fleet's Pocket Almanac and Massachusetts Register*, published by freemason Thomas Fleet beginning in 1779, listed 19 Ancient lodges and stated that St. John's had chartered about 30 lodges but that a list was unavailable due to the loss of their records during the war; the African lodge received mention as well. William M'Alpine' 1772 Boston printing of Wellins Calcott's *Candid Disquisition on Freemasonry* included lodge and grand lodge officers, times, and places of meeting for both Moderns and Ancients in Boston and a list of subscribers from several colonies, with non-masons listed separately. Though the *Engraved Lists* had fairly complete listings of lodges in Jamaica, including times and places of meeting for many lodges, *The Elements of Freemasonry Delineated* published in Kingston by Brother William Moore in 1782, offered detailed listings of lodge and provincial grand lodge officers and meeting information with an extensive subscribers list. Colonial newspapers also offered valuable information on local lodges and masonic officers.[5]

The engraving above, *Les Free- Massons*, was the first international printing of the *Engraved Lists* and is among the earliest reproductions in any format other than the original. That it originated in France is testament to the international reach of freemasonry and of the widespread distribution of the *Engraved Lists* of Lodges. The engraving was originally part of the sixth of seven volumes of Jean— Frederic Bernard and Bernard Picart's enormously influential *Ceremonies et coutumes religieusis de tous les peuples du monde,* which remained in print in multiple languages for nearly a century. This particular piece was probably completed by Picart's student Louis Fabricius Dubourg after the former's passing in 1733. It is taken from the *Engraved List,* with the individual entries turned into discreet posters and arranged along a great wall, each of which contains the tavern sign

Figure 5.9. Bernard Picart and Claude Du Bois' Les Free Massons, 1735; the first international reproduction of the English *Engraved List of Lodges*. Boston appears at number 126. (From the Collection of the Grand Lodge of Massachusetts).

and verbatim entry from the list. The first American lodge is number 126: Boston in New England.[6]

The seven volumes were published in France between 1723 and 1737; the first English translation was engraver Claude du Bosc's version, *Ceremonies and Religious Customs of the Several Nations of the Known World*, released in installments from 1733 to 1739. In the original French freemasonry appears in the volume which dealt with various protestant religious, particularly British ones as well as "Fanatical sects and assemblies". The text contains a reference to the masons stating that, "the Policy of the States [Holland] was then very different from what it now is, since they have lately put a Stop to all the Meetings of a Society [Freemasonry] which is no ways offensive to Religion, good Manners, or political Government, and has, and does still flourish in Great Britain, under the Protection of the greatest Men of that Kingdom, even Princes of the Royal Family." Attached to this piece is a long footnote describing the history of English freemasonry. Here then the intellectual strains promoted in British masonic discourse have all become a part of the European intellectual landscape. The footnote in the English edition simple reads, "The Free-Masons are so well known in England, that we need not give our Readers any Account of them: Besides, as it is not a religious Society, it is out of the Sphere of this work: But the ignorant or curious reader may consult the Book of their Constitutions, and the Defense of Masonry, occasioned by a Pamphlet, called Masonry Dissected. The prints here annexed represent Free-Masons." The two works referenced here, *Masonry Dissected* and the answer thereto, also came to be printed in many editions which carried versions of the new and correct list of lodges.[7]

These and other works which reprinted the new and correct lists, or lists based on them, first appeared in the 1730s. As these works spread throughout the Atlantic and were plagiarized or reprinted, various versions of the lists, sometimes outdated, sometimes updated, and sometimes combined with listings from other grand lodges, were printed and distributed. The following is a detailed survey of many of the most important works which reproduced the lists. They of course appeared in *Anderson's Constitutions*. After the first edition in 1723 major new official editions were released in 1738 and 1756. These were frequently pirated throughout the century; Benjamin Franklin's 1734 reprint represent the first American printing of a work on freemasonry.

The books and booklets described in the previous chapter almost invariably include such lists. Take Samuel Pritchard's, *Masonry Dissected*. At least two different printers put out a run of the first edition in 1730; the second edition appeared that same year. By 1739 the work was in its eighth edition. As with most earlier editions, it came with, "A new and exact list of regular lodges according to their seniority and constitutions." This list appeared in the end, after page 24; unlike the rest of the text, the list was unnumbered, and is in smaller, denser type indicating that it was probably a copy of the official lists inserted into Pritchard's pamphlet. The twelfth edition, published in 1747, contains a similar list up to 1745. Various publishers put out runs of *Masonry Dissected* consistently from 1730 until 1826 in London. Editions also appeared in France, Scotland, Ireland, and the United States; these do not always include the lists of English lodges. In response to Pritchard's uncomfortably accurate expose, the grand lodge printed Martin Clare's *Defence of Masonry* and several fake exposes of its own. These included non-sense ritual degrees and modes of recognition along with laudatory retellings of masonic history, essays on masonic philosophy, and other positive pieces. They also included copies of the new and correct list of lodges.

Grand Lodge issued several such works, including Alexander Slade's, *The Free Mason Examin'd: or, the world brought out of darkness into light. Being, an authentick account of all the secrets of the ancient society of free masons, which have been handed down by oral tradition only, from the institution, to the present time. .With A new and correct list of all Regular Lodges, under the English constitution, according to their late removals and additions.* At least four editions of this work appeared in 1754. *The Free Mason Examin'd* includes a personal attack on Pritchard, the mythic history of masonry with many ideas supportive of the fraternity and a set of non-sense degrees. The listing goes up to number 182 with Boston now at 79 and a number of Caribbean and Indian lodges. That it went through at least four editions in one year demonstrates that while not as successful as the piece it was meant to answer, Slade's pamphlet distributed masonic ideas, ideals, and an international directory of lodges in considerable numbers, as well as earning its author a decent sum.

A similar false expose, *The Secrets of the Free-Masons Revealed by a disgusted Brother. Containing An ingenious Account of their Origin, their Practices in the Lodges, Signs and Watch-words; Proceedings at the Making, and the Method used to find a Mason, when in a Foreign Country, &c. &c. as it ever was, and ever will be,* first appeared in 1759. The first edition included a list of lodges going to 1757, the last American lodge being 1755, No. 213 Wilmington on Cape Fear in North Carolina. The six editions printed between 1759 and 1762 served to further distribute the lists of lodges. The disgusted brother offered praise for the institution, a standard history, a description of the intense geometrical studies undertaken in the lodges, and five fake degrees as well as a list of lodges around the world identical to that in the *Engraved List.*[8]

To further emphasize the international scope of this vast diaspora, and to emphasize its interconnectedness, the author makes the following specious claim:

> It was agreed on by the masons, a little before I left them, to have the superb edifices, and spacious domes, erected by all the known lodges in the world, published, with the laborious translations and remarks of each lodge thereon, so soon as they could be procured from abroad, and the plates finished. For which purpose copies of their resolution have been sent all through Europe, to the lodges in Asia, Africa, and America, that they may send their performances to the year 1756, so soon as possible to England, from whence they took their charter. But this must be a work of time.[9]

This postulates not only that the fraternity is actively involved in building grand structures around the world, but also that it is able to communicate effectively enough to undertake such a comprehensive compilation of these many projects in Europe, Asian Africa and America. Taken with the extensive lists of lodges, this strongly promoted the international scope of the Craft.

Although Pritchard's *Masonry Dissected* was the first and most damaging expose of masonic ritual, there were others which remained in print for years and even decades and were widely reprinted. Thomas Wilson's, *SOLOMON in all his GLORY: OR, THE MASTER-MASON. BEING A TRUE GUIDE To the inmost Recesses of FREE-MASONRY, Both ANCIENT and MODERN* is a similarly negative story, which was translated into French as "Le Macon Demiasque, ou le vrai Secret des Francs Macons misaujour." +c 12mo Londres (Paris) n.d. 1751, and was then retranslated. The 1766 London printing by Robinson and Roberts, claimed that the French original was published at Berlin, where it was, "burnt by Order of the King of Prussia, at the Intercession of the Free-Masons." Wherever the first edition was published, Wilson claims to have been an army officer who joined as the result of peer pressure. He described freemasonry as a waste of money chiefly concerned with eating and drinking. The music and songs in the lodges are horrible, the dues exorbitant, the secrets meaningless, and the equality and brotherhood apply only within the lodge, echoing the 1726 *Accusation and Defense*.

The 1766 London edition includes a "New and Correct List" through the end of 1765 on pages 59–66, including Joppa Lodge in Maryland and the Lodge at Beef and Tortola Island chartered in August and December 1765 respectively. A 1772 Belfast edition, in addition to including some of the very songs which so injured Wilson's ears, includes an out of date 1768 version of the English lists along with a list of lodges under the Grand Lodge of Scotland and a list of lodges in Ireland. The Belfast printers didn't obtain an up to date English list. They appear to have used the 1768 London edition with its slightly outdated list and added the Celtic lists from other sources. Scottish editions of the *Freemason's Pocket Companion* encountered similar issues. The Scots list includes lodges in Boston, Virginia, South Carolina, and Jamaica, adding to the range of lodges a mason who picked up the Irish edition en route to the New World might visit.

A 1777 edition described as, "London, printed, and Dublin reprinted for T. Wilkinson No. 40 Winetavern street, where may be had all sorts of Free Masons Books" contains the same lists but with a list of the grand lodge officers of Ireland and of the Ancient grand lodge of England. That Wilkinson carried "all sorts of Free Masons Books" and prominently advertised as much demonstrates the role

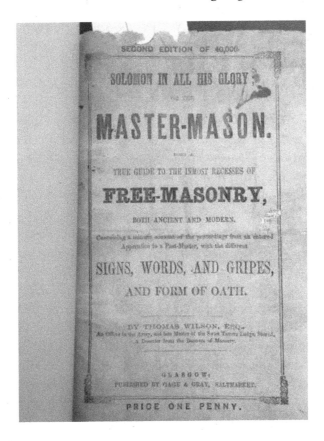

Figure 5.10. The second Glasgow edition of Wilson's anti-masonic pamphlet *Solomon in All His Glory*. A much less successful work than Pritchard's, this edition was nevertheless slated for a pressing of 40,000 (top of page). Pro-masonic pamphlets such as *Hiram, Jachin and Boaz,* and *Mahabone* had more sustained print runs. They spread masonic history, moral claims, ritual and administrative knowledge as well as listings of lodges around the world, serving to promote and connect masonry across the European diaspora. (From the Collection of the Grand Lodge of Massachusetts).

of printed materials in the intellectual and economic realms of masonry. A 1769 edition of *Mahabone* printed by Wilkinson advertised a list of his available publications including a half dozen masonic titles, among which were a copy of the *Ahiman Rezon* with the officers names and meeting days of the lodges in Dublin and the *Free Masons Almanack*. Whether the latter was British or Irish, official or unofficial is not clear, but this ad demonstrates that at least one other series of Masonic almanacs existed. Wilkinson's undated re-printing of Nicholls London edition of Pritchard's *TUBAL-KAIN: Being the Second Part of SOLOMON IN ALL HIS GLORY, OR MASTER MASON: Containing an Universal and Genuine DESCRIPTION OF All its BRANCHES, from the ORIGINAL to the PRESENT TIME... WITH A new and exact LIST of REGULAR LODGES accourding to their Seniority and Constitution...* included the list of lodges ending at lodge number 220, Santa Croix, "A Danish Island in the West Indies, 1756." This edition advertised 21 titles available at Wilkinson's shop, of which the first 12 are masonic. That the 2nd Glasgow edition described itself as a "pressing of 40,000" demonstrates the popularity of masonic print.

There were a number of other exposes which took a more positive tone towards freemasonry while betraying its secrets. Of these, *Jachin and Boaz, Shiboleth,* and *Mahabone* were the most successful. Most extant editions of these widely printed works contain lists of lodges identical to or based on the New and Correct list. *As its title explains, JACHIN AND BOAZ OR, AN AUTHENTIC KEY TO THE DOOR OF FREE-MASONRY, Both ANCIENT and MODERN. Calculated not only for the Instruction of every new-made MASON; but also for the Information of all who intend to become BRETHREN,* at least purported to be intended to aid masons and aspiring masons. First appearing in 1762, the third edition appeared in 1763, also printed by W. Nicoll. Nicoll, like Wilkinson in Dublin, did a considerable business in Masonic books and pamphlets. the author is listed simply as, "a gentleman of London."

The table of contents includes, "A New and Correct LIST of all the English REGULAR LODGES in Europe, Asia, Africa and America accordingly to their seniority and Constitution. By Order of the GRAND MASTER, Brought down to the Year 1763." 1764 saw a fifth edition, with the author now listed as R.S., by the same publisher. In one copy at the Grand Lodge of Massachusetts the list has been removed in its entirety, indicating that it was taken out intentionally for practical use. The list has a different title in the table of contents, being called, "A New and Accurate LIST of all the English regular lodges in the World, according to their seniority, with the dates of each constitution, and days of Meeting," implying that it has been updated. Nicoll's 6th edition in 1765 contained a list complete to April 19, 1765. Wilkinson, still advertising the availability of all sorts of free masons books, published an updated edition in 1776 with a list identical to the 1778 *Engraved List.*

Nicolls continued to print *Jachin and Boaz* for years to come. In 1785, he included a 10 page list of lodges with separate page numbers after the text which appears identical to the *Freemasons Calendar* for that year. A 1795 London edition included a reprint of the entire masonic portion of the *Freemason's Calendar,* renumbered from page 1 as above. E. Newberry's 1797 London edition included the entire masonic section of the 1797 *Calendar*. London editions continued until at least 1828, rivaling *Masonry Dissected* in its longevity. Such success of course inspired imitators. 1765 saw the first edition of *MAHABONE: OR, THE GRAND LODGE DOOR OPEN'D. WHEREIN IS DISCOVERED THE WHOLE SECRETS OF FREE-MASONRY, BOTH ANCIENT AND MODERN* appeared. Written by J***G******, "a regular brother of free-masonry" and published in London by Johnson and Davenport and in Liverpool by J. Gore; these both included up to date versions of, "A compleat list of all the English regular Lodges in the World, according to their Seniority: with the dates of each constitution, and days of meeting." Sections of Mahabone appear to have been directly lifted from *Jachin and Boaz*. Also in 1765, "a Pass'd Master" wrote *Shibboleth: or, Every Man a Free-Mason. Containing An History of the Rise, Progress, and Present Stat of That Ancient and Noble Order* published in London by J. Cooke. Another positive expose and faux history, in contained the list up to April 19, 1765.

Yet another 1764 expose, *Hiram: or the grand master-key to the door of both ancient and modern free-masonry: being an accurate description of every degree of the brotherhood, as authorized and delivered in all good lodges* offered little that the other exposes did not, however, it lists the lodge in a way that presages the early Calendars of the 1770s. It isn't clear whether lodge lists in this format could be had from the grand lodge, or if Hiram gave the later authors the idea; perhaps the similarity is coincidental. However, domestic lodges are now arranged by days of meeting, with locations but no founding dates. Starting on page 94 one finds "Lodges in Foreign Parts". These are roughly alphabetical by location beginning with Amsterdam and Antigua. Boston appears just after Bengal, with South Carolina and Virginia finishing the list. This listing was up to date for the year and contains the same lodges as the other lists. Its arrangement was undoubtedly more convenient for overseas travel. Written by "A Member of Royal Arch" the first edition was printed in London by W. Griffin and in Chelmsford by T. Toft. The advertisement section of the *New York Journal* on September 1, September 22, and November 10, 1768 ran a large display of the entire title and contents page of *Hiram*, "Just published, and to be sold at the Printing-Office, at the Exchange." Masonic works were common among the lists of imported books for sale, as for example Charles Warren's expose, *The Freemason Stripped Naked. . .* advertised with four non-masonic titles in the *New York Gazette* on May 21 and 28. The lists of lodges contained in these works thus quickly crossed the Atlantic, allowing American masons to easily locate lodges in Britain, Europe, the West Indies, the other North American colonies, or even India. The sixth edition of

Freemasons Stripped Naked promised a list of lodges, which also had been removed in the copy in the Grand Lodge of Massachusetts library, indicating that this practice may have been widespread, perhaps among printers plagiarizing listings or traveling masons who kept the lists and passed on the rest of the booklet.

Ritual exposes were a popular genre of masonic literature throughout the 1700s and well into the centuries to come. Also popular were the self affirming books lauding the virtues, antiquity, and moral purpose of the craft produced by masons on both sides of the Atlantic. A number of more or less closely related works went under the title *The Freemasons' Pocket Companion*. This should be viewed as a family of books, as there were several works or versions thereof which went under that name and which reprinted, plagiarized, enlarged upon or differed from each other sufficiently that some represent variations on an original whereas others are essentially new creations. Of the many versions printed from 1735 into the nineteenth century there are several cases in which direct plagiarism resulted in older copies of lists of lodges being promulgated in newer editions. In some cases, notably several Scottish versions, the local grand lodge's roll of lodges was updated while other listings remained static. Irish and Scottish versions tended to include at least their own nation's grand lodge listings and in some cases those of the English as well.

The first book to appear under the title of *Freemasons Pocket Companion*, written by William Smith, "a Freemason", appeared in London no later than 1735. The contents include masonic history, charges, regulations and procedures, masonic songs and prologues and epilogues spoken at the theater, and the list of lodges. This first edition did not include Boston in its lists, but the second edition, published by John Torbuck of London in 1738, had been updated so that Boston and Savannah, Georgia had assumed their places in the lists. Versions of the work were already appearing in Ireland, where lodges unknown to the English were added to the list. A 1735 *Pocket Companion for Freemasons* printed in Dublin which included a listing for an otherwise unknown American lodge, No. 116, held at The Hoop in Water Street, Philadelphia on the first Monday of every month. The 1735 Dublin edition of E. Rider, which has prologues from the theaters in Dublin listed among the contents and "a list of the warranted lodges in Ireland; Great Britain, France, Spain, Germany, East and West Indies, &c." These appear to be those lodges listed in foreign parts under the auspices of the two grand lodges. Since the West Indies had yet to feature in the official English lists, it appears that the Irish were referring to lodges clandestine lodges or possibly short lived lodges under their authority such as Philadelphia's mysterious lodge at the Hoop. That Rider saw fit to emphasize the geographic scope of the craft at such an early time speaks to masonry's having already become a trans-Atlantic phenomenon. James Magee's 1751 Belfast printing of *A Pocket Companion for Freemasons, the third edition*, contained an up to date listing of lodges chartered by the Grand Lodge of Ireland followed by an out of date listing of English lodges. Magee's third edition then was likely put together from an earlier edition in which the English lodges may or may not have been up to date; in any case he had access to updated Irish but not English lists.[10]

A similarly titled but more extensive work, *The Pocket Companion and History of Free-masons, containing their Origine (sic), Progress, and Present State. . .*, with no listed author, emerged from the London press of J. Scott in 1754; this first edition lacked a list of lodges. The second edition, printed in 1759, contained "a list of all the lodges, in a new yet easy method". Those in London are grouped by their meeting days, followed by a listing of 'country lodges'. After this comes the list of Lodges in Foreign parts, which include eight lodges in Jamaica with meeting days for two of them; three in Antigua, four in Barbados, five in India, and one each in the West Indies in Basse Terre, Santacruiz (sic) and St. Eustatius. In North America Boston's First lodge (but not Second Lodge) is listed with its meeting times; Norfolk and Yorktown, Virginia are represented with meeting days; Wilmington on Cape Fear River, North Carolina and Savannah Georgia are listed without days. A number of European lodges appear as well. Later in 1759, an identically titled but more extensive version, with the added moniker, ". . .*The Second Edition. Revised, Corrected, and Greatly Enlarged Throughout, and Continued down to this Time in all its Parts*" was published by R. Baldwin and J. Scott. This contained a much more extensive list of foreign lodges. These included an additional lodge in St. Eustatius and four in Minorca with meeting times listed for several of the Caribbean lodges which had lacked them in the earlier edition and more extensive data on the Indian lodges.[11]

That the *Freemason's Pocket Companion* was distributed across the British Atlantic is illustrated by its advertisement for sale in Colonial Newspapers. For example, the November 30, 1761 *New York Gazette* included an advertisement by James Rivington, New York's premier bookseller with business ranging well beyond the colony of New York, advertised, "This day is published by said JAMES RIVINGTON The POCKET COMPANION AND HISTORY OF FREEMASONS. Containing their Origin, Progress and Present State; an Abstract of their Laws, Constitutions, Customs, Charges, Orders and Regulations, for the instruction of the BRETHREN, As well as for the Information of those who wish to become FREEMASONS. Together with a collection of songs and a list of all the Lodges. The Whole improved beyond the former Edition, and continued down to the Present Time." That it was printed by Rivington and "improved beyond the former edition" implies that he had printed other editions. On October 22, 1764, the same paper advertised among the many titles imported on the Ship *Edward* the *"Freemason's Pocket Companion"*. It appeared among the books and sundry other items to be sold by Nathaniel Bird advertised in Rhode Island's *Newport Mercury* on December 31,1764 and the April 12, 1765 edition of the *New Hampshire Gazette and Historical Chronicle* in a long advertisement for books to be sold at public auction.

In Boston John Mein's London Book Store, according to the *Connecticut Courant* of November 9, 1767, had among many books "just imported" "The Free-Mason's Pocket Companion. Containing the History of Masonry from the Creation to the present time; the Institution of the Grand Lodge; Lists of the grand Lodges of England and Scotland, their Customs, Charges, Constitutions, Orders and Regulations. To which is added, a large Collection of the best Mason's Songs, many of which were never before published." Thus numerous incarnations of the *Freemason's Pocket Companion,* with various lists of lodges, were both imported and in at least one case published throughout the colonies.

Scottish variants began to appear no later than 1752 with W. Cheyne's *Freemasons Pocket Companion.* This was similar to the Earlier English and Irish works but contained an alphabetical list of Scottish lodges as well as an English list current through the year 1737. Like the early 1738 versions, it ends with the response to Pritchard, and appears to be taken from the earlier works with added information related to Scot's masons such as the lists. A more extensive and uniquely Scottish companion soon appeared which was reprinted throughout Scotland for decades. The title, which as with many works from the Era is essentially a list of contents: *The Freemason's Pocket Companion; Containing the Origin, Progress and Present State of that Ancient Fraternity; the Institution of the Grand Lodge of Scotland; Lists of the Grand Masters and Other Officers of the Grand lodges of Scotland and England; Their Customs, Charges, Constitutions, Orders and Regulations; for the Instruction and Conduct of the Brethren. To which is added an Appendix, Act of the Associate Synod Against the Free Masons, with an Impartial Examination of that Act; Charges and Addresses to the Free Masons on Different Occasions; A Complete Collection of Free-Mason Songs, Prologues, Epilogues, &c. with Lists of all the Regular Lodges Both in Scotland and England with Many Other Particulars, for the Use of the Society,* appears no later than 1761 in Edinburgh and continued to be reprinted there as well as in other Scottish cities and in London at least until the 1790s.

The 1761 edition published by Ruddiman, Auld, and company has an extensive history up to the current grand masters of Scotland and England. The list of Scottish lodges appears on pages 109–112; international listings include no. 59, Union Lodge of Drummond Kilwinning from Aleppo; No. 83, Welsh Fuzileers; No. 81 St. Andrew's Lodge at Boston; No. 82 Blandford Lodge, Virginia; No. 98 Union Kilwinning at Charlestoun (sic) South Carolina; and No. 102, Scots Lodge of St. Andrew, in the Parish of St. Thomas, in the East Jamaica. The following eight pages contain the English list through 1737. It appears that they used the English or Irish *Pocket Companion* from 1738, added considerable contents to it, mainly related to Scottish history and grand lodge as well a 1749 Boston masonic sermon found in many pocket companions. In 1765 William Auld worked in partnership with the unfortunately named Smellie, so that the publisher is listed as "Auld and Smellie". Their 1765 edition was considerably longer, and featured an English listing up to May 20, 1761. Auld but no longer Smellie offered an enlarged edition in 1772 in which the Scot's Lodges were updated through 1771 but the English lodges still stopped at 1761. Interestingly, this 1772 Edinburgh printing was plagiarized heavily in *The History of Masonry; or the Free Masons Pocket Companion*, Third Edition, printed in London three years later by John Donaldson. Going by his name, the printer was likely a Scot who had obtained a copy of the Scottish original. Though he might easily have obtained an updated English list in London he didn't bother to do so. Thus, his edition included an almost up to date Scots list and an old, therefore incomplete, English list.

This pattern continued, as in 1792 when John and Peter Wilson of Ayr printed a similarly titled and largely identical work. This edition lists printers in four major Scottish cities, Edinburgh, Glasogow, Ayr, and Stirling, from whence it might have taken ship to any of the ports in the British empire. The information on the Grand Lodge of Scotland only extends through 1760 and the lodge listings are similarly outdated. Since nearly all of the listed lodges still existed this did not render them useless, but rather made them incomplete. It was clearly reprinted from an older edition without any attempt to significantly update the contents, none of the which speak to the intervening decades.

The *Engraved Lists, Pocket Companions* and assorted various pamphlets and exposes were small, cheap and accessible. More extensive books on masonry were also popular and sold well throughout the century. The most important, of course was *Anderson's Constitutions;* the roll of lodges began to appear here by the 1756 edition. Minor works, such as *The Complete Freemason, or Multa Paucis for Lovers of Secrets,* also contain complete or partial lists. This odd book, giving no author, publisher, or date, has lists of lodges in North America, Europe, and the East

Indies but not the Caribbean. The inclusion of Merchants Lodge in Quebec, St. Ann's Lodge in New York, and several of the Later Virginia and South Carolina Lodges indicate a date in the mid—late 1760s.

This pattern continued after the *Engraved List* evolved into the *Freemasons Calendar*. For Example, William Hutchinson's *The Spirit of Masonry in Moral and Elucidatory Lectures* contained a numbered list of lodges taken from the *Calendar*. The second edition, published in 1795, has a list which was current through 1794 along with an up to date list of Scottish lodges. These now included a number of North American, West Indian, and European Lodges. Two years later, *Masonic Miscellanies, in poetry and prose. Containing 1. The Muse of Masonry, comprising one hundred and seventy masonic songs, 11. The Masonic Essayist. III. The Freemason's Vade-Mecum*, By Stephen Jones reprinted not only the list of lodges from the Calendar but the "Extraordinary Happenings in Masonry" section as well. These listings were by now conveniently divided by geographic region and country or colony. The heading, AMERICA included all those lodges in the United States which had been listed prior to the American Revolution plus Boston's African Lodge, which obtained an English charter after the war. The East Indies now includes Sumatra and China, and Africa appears as a heading without entries. The last page consists of the following advertisement, "This day is published, . . . The Free—Mason's pocket Companion and Universal Daily Ledger, for the Year 1798, being the Second after Bissextile or Leap Year, Containing beside 108 rule pages for cast accounts, appointments, memorandums, observations, &c. A complete and correct LIST of all the Regular Lodges and Royal Arch Chapters as well as lodges of instruction in Town and Country, with their places and Times of Meeting; collected from actual enquiry in town, and by communication from the respective lodges &c. in the country. .. London: Printed for Vernor and Hood, No. 31 Poultry. To be continued annually with the necessary alterations."[12]

After *Anderson's Constitutions* the most popular Masonic book of the eighteenth century was the autobiographic *Unparalleled sufferings of John Coustos, Who nine times underwent the most cruel tortures ever invented by man, and sentenced to the galley four years, by command of the Inquisitors at Lisbon, in order to extort from him the secrets of free-masonry; from whence he was released by the gracious interposition of his late majesty, king George II*. First published in 1746, the story of lapidary John Coustos' arrest in Lisbon, where he served as master of a lodge, and subsequent tribulations at the hands of the inquisition made for an exciting tale of persecution and an excellent anti-catholic screed. This tale enjoyed such popularity that it went through many printings, at least until 1821. The original edition did not include lists of lodges, however, subsequent editions often did. An interesting example is the 1790 Birmingham edition of Swinney which included not the list of lodges, but a list of Royal Arch Chapters around the world including Quebec, Antigua, Copenhagen, Christiana, Gibraltar, Genoa and Bengal and "An Oration Delivered at the Dedication of Free-Mason's Hall, at the City of Quebec in Canada" by Alexander Spark. This speaks to the new Canadian orientation of Britain's North Atlantic empire and the prominence of the Ancient's Royal Arch Degree Chapters.

Even more interesting is the 1797 edition published in New York by Jacob Mott. The preface includes a statement on the included lists of lodges, "An original attempt to arrange in order the different domestic lodges, will appear obviously difficult to effect with accuracy; but so far as the subject has admitted, no attention has been withheld. Foreign lodges are enumerated from the latest masons calender (sic) that could be procured." The list of lodges contained on pages 255–82 is reproduced from the 1794 calendar, ending at lodge number 542- apparently the "latest that could be procured." The authors have, however, removed all of the lodges in the United States from the roll. A final note then explains that, "A correct list of Domestic Lodges will, as soon as possible, be printed separately and delivered to the subscribers of this work GRATIS." As with Stearns masonic almanac, this demonstrates that the *Calendar* was a well known resource for American masons. It also shows that American masons saw the importance of creating comprehensive lodge listings for their own country. Whether or not Mott ever completed and distributed his domestic list, it is clear that printing up to date, worldwide lists of lodges was an important factor in navigating the changing landscape of the global masonic nation.

On January 9, 1788, the Modern grand lodge of South Carolina wrote to its counterpart in England. Among the matters they discussed was a request that the English Grand Lodge send them "a list of names of all the lodges in Europe, Asia, Africa and America who acknowledge the jurisdiction of the Grand Lodge of England" Though South Carolina's Modern lodges were on their way to being folded into the Ancient grand lodge and American freemasonry was largely turning its eye to the west, American masons still found these international listings to be important enough to write to their former foes in England to obtain them.[13]

Mapping Masonry in the Early Republic

Just as English and European masonic publications continued to present lists of lodges in the nineteenth century as masonry became a more establishment friendly bulwark of the British empire and continued to play a role in continental sociability, masons in the new America republic continued to include various lists in their publications. In addition to publishers such as Mott who attempted to create universal lists, there were many masonic publications which included regional lodge listings. For instance, the 1807 song book *Free-Mason's Vocal Assistant, and Register of the Lodges of Masons in South Carolina and Georgia* included the times, meeting places, and list of officers for nearly every lodge in South Carolina and slightly less complete information for Georgia, including French expatriate lodges in both states.

Such song books were apparently very popular, as a great number were printed in the 18th and early 19th centuries. In 1802, as announced in its overly long and descriptive title, *The Vocal Companion, and Masonic Register. In two parts. Part I. consisting of original and selected masonic songs, anthems, dirges, prologues, epilogues, toasts, and sentiments, charges prayers, funeral procession, Part II. A concise account of the original of masonry in America; with a list of the lodges in the six Northern states, viz, Massachusetts, New Hampshire, Rhode-Island, Connecticut, New-York & Vermont. With the names of the officers and the number of members of which each lodge consists,* gave extensive information on the lodges of New York and New England. Particularly impressive is that in addition to number of members and names of officers for every lodge in these states, the book also lists subscribers from the lodges. This implies that printer Dunham was able to communicate, either through the grand lodges or directly with the lodges, quickly and effectively enough to compile member information as well as to collect subscriptions from the lodges.[14]

The *Proceedings of the Grand Lodge of North Carolina and Tennessee, for A.L. 5807, A.D* included, in addition to its own lodges, registers for Nova Scotia—both English and provincial, even including the names of three expelled members for the information of masons everywhere. It also included Massachusetts lodges by district (the Grand Lodge of Massachusetts had organized itself into districts by this time) including three "out of the commonwealth, but under the jurisdiction", in Ohio and St. John, Stabroek, Demerara (West Indies). It then listed lodges in New Hampshire, noting two expelled members, followed by Connecticut lodges, with six rejections and two expulsions. There are listings for the grand lodge of New Jersey and Pennsylvania, the later including lodges in Trinidad, New Orleans, and two listed as "West Indies"; Maryland, Virginia, Kentucky and Georgia. For most grand lodges there are rejections and suspensions listed. That this information was being shared nationally implies an attempt at mutual enforcement of discipline and exclusivity by grand lodges throughout the new nation. Interestingly, neighboring South Carolina is one of the few states with established grand lodges not to be included. These are only a few examples of the many masonic books which offered regional or partial national listings of lodges in the new United States. As the focus shifted from the Atlantic to the New Republic, listings for the continent or hemisphere such as Stearns' became a minority to regional works or attempts to create national listings.[15]

French Lodge Tableaux: Masonry's Most Efficient Networking

A final source of print culture connecting masons internationally developed in French freemasonry. French Masonic networks distributed printed *tableaux* with detailed demographic information on lodges, lodge members, and the lodges on both sides of the Atlantic with which they maintained communications. These *tableaux* served as excellent sources of information for the freemason merchant or sea captain, providing an instant network of brotherly business contacts across imperial borders. These networks included French, English, American, Dutch and Spanish American lodges and contacts. They included contacts in Europe as well as Caribbean Jews. One such *tableaux* was held up by Rev. Jedediah Morse as proof of a French Revolutionary conspiracy afoot in America.

The refugee diaspora from Saint Domingue included many masons, among them several lodges chartered by the Grand Lodge of Pennsylvania and the provincial grand lodge it had established on Saint Domingue. As these spread, they maintained their connections, so that a network of French lodges from New Orleans to New York existed which maintained correspondence with each other. This correspondence included the exchange of *tableaux* which served as a directory of merchants, planters, craftsmen, professionals, sea captains and other masons in the Caribbean, the United States, France and other European ports of call. An illustrative case in point is the 1811 Tableaux of Lodge L'Amitie No. 73, meeting in Philadelphia under the Grand Lodge of Pennsylvania but working in French. It lists 66 members with age, place of birth, profession, place of residence and masonic particulars as well as 10 honorary members. Twenty -two, exactly one-third of the non-honorary members were connected to Saint Domingue either by birth or through their Masonic origins. The lodge lists as Affiliated Lodges two lodges in Marseille, three Martinique and one in D'Anvers, New York, New Orleans and Paris. "Lodges in Correspondence" included two French diaspora lodges in Charleston and one in Baltimore in the United States. In the Caribbean they corresponded with French lodges on Guadeloupe, Martinique, Trinidad, Cuba and the lodge on St. Barthelemy which had a mixed French, Swedish and international membership; they also listed seven lodges from various cities in France. Other Tableaux from Saint Domingue, Martinique and French lodges in the United States were similarly detailed. These were created to be distributed to members as well as corresponding lodges and the Grand Lodge, and served as an excellent, if less public, means of connecting masons around the Atlantic.

The regularity with which masonic travelers like the two Algerian brethren Ibrahim and Achmer from around the world found their way into the lodge rooms of even minor lodges such as St. Peter's in the relatively minor city of Newburyport, Massachusetts demonstrates just how effectively masons were able to connect around the world. Print culture was a major factor globalizing freemasonry, spreading masonic philosophy, mythological history, ideology, administrative and ritual framework and a sense of common identity. It was also essential to practical navigation of this Masonic empire which crossed the bounds of national, imperial, racial and geographical borders in the eighteenth century. The dissemination of lists of lodges, both on their own and bound into other publications, as well as the distribution of masonic news in colonial newspapers from the peripheries of empire, the subject of a later chapter, and the exchange of detailed *tableaux* brought together masons and masonic networks from the far flung frontiers of empire to the bustling European metropolises. This vast body of print culture not only served as a travel guide to a mason or aspiring mason on the high seas or the highways, but advertised to the entire reading public the ubiquitousness and importance of freemasonry.

Notes

1 St. Peter's Lodge, Minutes, Book 1, September 2, 1794 (Boston: Grand Lodge of Masons, Grand Secretary's Vault).

2 Jedidiah Morse, *A Sermon Exhibiting the Present Dangers, and Consequent Duties of the Citizens of the United States of America, Delivered at Charlestown, April 25, 1799.* (Charlestown, Massachusetts: Samuel Ethridge, 1799); this booklet includes both the French originals and English translations of the 1798 Tableaux of Loge L'Sagasse of Portsmouth, Virginia and a letter of the lodge which among other masonic matters describes the exchange of Tableaux and the spread of French diasporic lodges, largely composed of refugees from Saint Domingue,to Loge L'Union of New York date May 17th, 1798 .On reporting by English provincial grand masters, see Hugo Tatsch, *Freemasonry in the Thirteen Colonies* (Kessinger Rare Reprints, 1933), 50.

3 *Almanach Des Francs- Macons* (Amsterdam, 1767, 1768), 31.

4 On the Swedish almanac, see, Andreas Onnerfors, "Swedish Freemasonry in the Caribbean: How St. Barthelemy turned into an Island of the IXth Province." *REHMLAC Revista Estudios Historicos De La Masoneria, Latinamericano y Carbena* 1 (1): 18–41.

5 Rivington's New York Gazette, or the Connecticut, New Jersey, Hudson's River and Quebec Weekly Advertiser, December 2, 1773.

6 Bernard Picart, Louis Fabricius Dubourg, Claude du Bosc, Les Free Massons, circa 1735; Boston: Grand Lodge of Massachusetts; Aimee Newell, *Curiosities of the Craft: Treasures from the Grand Lodge of Massachusetts Collection* (Lexington: Museum of Our National Heritage, 2013), 28–9; Lynn Hunt, Margaret Jacob and Wijnand Mijnhart, *The Book That Changed Europe: Picart and Bernard's Religious Ceremonies of the World.* (Cambridge: Belknap Press of Harvard University Press, 2010), 1,3,296.

7 *Ibid.*

8 Anonymous, *The Secrets of the Free-Masons Revealed by a Disgusted Brother. Containing an Ingenious Account of their Origin, their PRactices in the Lodges, Signs and Watch-Words; Proceedings at the Making, and the Method Used to Find a Mason, when in a Foreign Country, &c. &c. as it ever was, and ever will be. The Second Edition.* London: J. Scott, 1759, 1–8; *sixth edition,* London: J. Scott, 1762.

9 *Ibid.,* 8.

10 William Smith, *Freemason's Pocket Companion,* London: John Torbuck, 1st ed. 1735, 2nd ed. 1738, 88–96; William Smith, *A Pocket Companion for Freemasons,* Dublin: E. Rider, 1735, http://www.dublincitypubliclibraries.com/image/wea40-fre emasons. This is probably the same edition as that cited by Lang, though his notes do not make this certain and I have been unable to consult a complete copy of this edition; Ossian Lang, *History of Freemasonry in New York,* New York: The Hamilton Printing C. 1922, 8; *A Pocket Companion for Freemasons,* Belfast: James Magee, 1751, 91–6.

11 *The Pocket Companion and History of Free-masons, containing their Origine* (sic)*, Progress, and Present State: an Abstract of Their Laws, Constitutions, Customs, Charges, Orders and Regulations, for the Instruction and Conduct of the Brethren: a Confutation of Dr. Plot's False Insinuations: an Apology, Occasioned by Their Persecution in the Canton of Berne, and in the Pope's Dominions: and a Select Number of Songs and Other Particulars, for the Use of the Society.* London: J. Scott, 1754 (1st ed.), 2nd ed. 1759, 317–24, 378–80.

12 William Hutchinson, *The Spirit of Masonry in Moral and Elucidatory Lectures, the Second Edition,* Carlisle: F. Jollie, 1795, 334–357; Stephen Jones, *Masonic Miscellanies, in poetry and prose. Containing 1. The Muse of Masonry, comprising one hundred and seventy masonic songs, 11. The Masonic Essayist. III. The Freemason's Vade-Mecum,* London: Vernor and Hood, 1797, 273–5, 325–8.

13 Berman, *Loyalists and Malcontents,* 161–2.

14 *Free-Mason's Vocal Assistant, and Register of the Lodges of Masons in South Carolina and Georgia* (Charleston: Brother J.J. Negrin, 1807), 209–255; *The Vocal Companion, and Masonic Register. In two parts. Part I. consisting of original and selected masonic songs, anthems, dirges, prologues, epilogues, toasts, and sentiments, charges prayers, funeral procession, Part II. A concise account of the original of masonry in America; with a list of the lodges in the six Northern states, viz, Massachusetts, New Hampshire, Rhode-Island, Connecticut, New-York & Vermont. With the names of the officers and the number of members of which each lodge consists* (Boston: Brother John Dunham, 1802), 181–294.

15 Grand Lodge of North Carolina and Tennessee, *Proceedings of the Grand Lodge of North Carolina and Tennessee, for A.L. 5807* (Raleigh: Wm. Boyan, 1808), 17–28.

Part III

New World Networks: The Craft from Puritan New England to the Sugar Isles

The place of Freemasonry in colonial Boston and Saint Domingue accords with recent scholarship on the development of both of those key Atlantic societies. From its 1733 inception onward, Boston's St. John's Grand Lodge mirrored its city-state's aspirations and political behaviors across the Atlantic. Bostonians had taken an expansive view of the authority and autonomy granted in their charter, and often conflated "Boston" and "New England" following the 1643 formation of the United Colonies of New England. Boston's St. John's Grand Lodge acted likewise, interchangeably stating its authority to include "Boston", "New England", or all of "North America". In correspondence to the grand lodge in London they argued consistently, vociferously and successfully that the 1733 charter creating both a lodge and grand lodge in Boston and London's early correspondence had granted the Bostonians dominion over the entire continent. Within New England, freemasons replicated the hegemony of the city state of Boston by forming a tightly woven network of lodges throughout the colonies. Boston's North Atlantic masonic empire expanded into Canada with the growth of New England's commercial and political influence there as well.

The merchant elite and sea captains who formed the bulk of the brotherhood carried their fraternity along with the less esoteric cargos of fish, lumber and sundry other goods, introducing masonic brotherhood to much of the British

Caribbean before it arrived from the metropolis. Here, freemasonry not only greased the wheels of legal and illicit trade from island to island and across imperial borders, but also aided the developing island societies "to imitate the Manners of the City of London," as the *American Weekly Mercury* on December 24, 1734 explained. Freemasonry not only closely followed Boston's commercial and political expansion, but added to its cultural and social impact and legitimacy by serving as the wellspring of the popular Masonic movement with its connections to metropolitan elite society and association with the ascendant protestant—Whig order, Enlightenment ideals, and all important trading networks.

In the close of the colonial period, Boston's younger and more radical 1769 Massachusetts Grand Lodge not only exemplified but actively drove the Boston city-state's resistance to crown authority as a great many of the leaders and most active members of its independence movement first came together in lodge and co-opted their fraternity and its Mason's Arms Tavern—better known as the Green Dragon- to take leading roles in the independence movement. Granted continental authority by the Grand Lodge of Scotland, their leadership mirrored that of the Patriot movement.

At the same time, Boston's Prince Hall led aspiring Black masons to create the first lodge and soon grand lodge within the African Atlantic diaspora, another independent masonic realm which arguably became more expansive and influential than its white parents in that it established freemasonry as an intellectual force, source of identity, and organizational structure throughout free African American communities and in the African colonial nation of Liberia as the American republic expanded. African lodge's leadership also led the struggle for Black civil rights, helping to make Boston a stronghold of the Abolition movement and creating strategies that would be utilized by civil rights activists for over a century and influencing the development of African American culture and religion. Freemasonry at the point of origin of the African diaspora, the continent of Africa, existed in trading stations along the coast and was particularly vibrant in the Dutch colony at the Cape of Good Hope.

In Saint Domingue, freemasonry also echoed and enhanced the island society's development from sugar colony connected with illicit trade to a booming Atlantic colony aspiring to greater autonomy and cosmopolitan bona fides, to the first independent African— descended society of the New World which embraced chosen cultural aspects of the European world and sought its continued commerce even while rejecting white rule. First established among white creoles by Jamaican smugglers in 1738, within a few years the early brethren were corresponding with the grand lodge in Boston, with whose merchants the island carried on a brisk clandestine trade. In *Before Haiti*, John Garrigus describes Saint Domingue as among the most masonically active societies in the world during the island's booming decades in the later half of the 1700s. Saint Domingue sought to both emulate the cultured cosmopolitanism of the metropolis and to achieve greater freedom in trade and self-government. Freemasonry enhanced both of those elements; the former through its association with the cosmopolitan Enlightenment and the latter through its connection to trade and its role as a parallel pseudo-republic.

Soon, metropolitan merchants brought the rich world of French higher degree masonry to the island. From this central colony in the French West Indies, merchants and planters formed extensive networks which included active, formalized connections to lodges throughout the Caribbean empires, in the European Metropolis, and later in the young United States. Not only did masonic networks extend from Saint Domingue, Dominguan masons solicited the grand lodge of Pennsylvania to create a network of lodges free of European authority with a vast network that survived the revolution and carried French masonic practice into the Spanish Empire and into American cities from New York to New Orleans. Lodges of French merchants already existed on both sides of the Anglo-Atlantic from Boston to New Orleans and across to London. When white masons fled Saint Domingue, they bolstered the membership and strengthened the links between this already vibrant network. Saint Domingue exported French higher degree systems to the United States, profoundly affecting not only American freemasonry to the present day but feeding into fears of French revolutionary conspiracy in the early Republic.

Though much of the story of American Freemasonry springs from the Bostonian Grand Masters and their Ancient counterparts beginning with Dr. Joseph Warren, we will first examine the case of Thomas Marriot Perkins, Provincial Grand Master of the Mosquito Shore and Jamaica and master of a London lodge whose intense involvement in American commerce illustrates how freemasonry purposefully brought together far flung trading networks in the small space of the lodge room.

Brother Perkins and the West India and American Lodge

The Goose and Gridiron was one of the original four lodges which formed the Grand Lodge of All England in 1717. The lodge moved to the Queen's Arms Tavern at some point, and was alternately referred to as the Queen's Arms or the

Goose & Gridiron held at the Queen's Arms in St Paul's Church Yard, until July 24, 1759, when it officially became the West India & American Lodge. Reading between the lines, the records imply that the lodge had reached a lull in terms of membership and activity by the end of the 1750s. Conversely, due to a falling out between the Grand Lodge and the Horn, it had taken over the latter's number one spot on the official roll of lodges. The extant records indicate that the lodge had already begun to attract Americans and trans-Atlantic traders. On July 10, the visitors included Bro. Pirkins (sic) of Steward's Lodge. The lodge formed a committee, "to consider some particular affairs." Perkins, former Grand Steward, became a member of the lodge along with 12 other visiting brethren. Among the 12 was one Captain John Scott; in all likelihood the Captain Scott who was a member of Boston's First Lodge and sailed for John Hancock. Apart from printer Philip Lucombe there is no information available about the other 12, however, based on what unfolded in the following minutes it seems likely that they were American Creoles or connected with Atlantic trade. Two of these 13 each proposed two new members, including another sea Captain.[1]

The entry continues: "Our New admitted Bror. Perkins Read some by Laws for the future regulation of the Lodge which were agreed to." Perkins and the dwindling membership had agreed to reinvent the lodge through his personal contacts and influence as a Masonic space for creoles, planters, and gentlemen likely to have an interest in the Americas. Perkins' position as a former Grand Steward in 1756 meant that he was well-connected at Grand Lodge. From 1761 to 2 on he served as Provincial Grand Master of the Mosquito Coast and from 1763 for Jamaica concurrently. Lodges first appeared in the former officially in the *Engraved Lists of Lodges* the year following Perkin's assuming responsibility for the area: "Lodge no. 300 the Lodge of Regularity at St. John Hall Black River Musqueta Shore 1st. & 3d. Tuesday, Mar. 8, 1763; 309 The Lodge of Amity at the Haul = Over up the River Belise in the Bay of Honduras, 1st & 3d. Tuesd. Sep 21 1763". The records at one point refer to Perkins as "of Barbadoes", which, implies that he had connections there as well. The *Engraved List* entries for the above lodges are highly detailed, indicating a clear path of communication from them to Grand Lodge.[2]

On August 8 Perkins presented the lodge a printed book of the new bylaws and members rolls. The lodge had, "...the honor of having the Provintial (sic) Grand of Pensilvania [and] his Son the Gd. Secretary", none other than Benjamin and William Franklin, who also visited grand lodge on November 17th, 1760. The Franklins were excused from paying fees; less prominent visitors, who paid for dinner, were "two of the Stewards Lodge & two Seafaring members." Two sea captains were admitted as members (along with two whose names are missing) at the recommendation of Humphreys, the Master who had also recommended all 13 of the earlier affiliates including Perkins.[3]

The new bylaws drawn up by Perkins delineated the reorientation of the lodge. Article XI dictated that only creoles, noblemen or masons connected to the Americans—those who have "crossed the equinoctial line"—may be admitted new members henceforth:

> The Members of this LODGE, who were not made Masons in it, are not Noblemen, nor have the Honour to wear a BLUE APRON, and are neither NATIVES of, or have never been to either of the WEST –INDIA, SUMMER, BAHAMA, or AMERICAN ISLANDS, or any Part of the CONTINENT OF AMERICA, or have never crossed the EQUINOCTIAL LINE, shall never, on any Account or Pretence (sic) whatever, exceed the number of FIFTEEN, that is, exclusive of those Brethren who are the oldest Members of the Lodge, and have signed these BYE-LAWS before Brother THOMAS-MARRIOTT PERKINS, of *Barbadoes*, but *none* of the above-mentioned *oldest Members* shall ever be replaced when they are no longer Members thereof.

The previous members of the Goose and Gridiron could stay on, but new members were either to be connected to the Americas or noblemen. The latter class were clearly advantageous as brethren to the former. Noblemen might be inclined to invest in or purchase for trade the commodities of the New World. That a small number, up to 15 others might be admitted allowed for flexibility in selecting some useful or desirable local brethren, but would never grant them a controlling block in lodge affairs. The "blue apron" allowed for those well placed in Grand Lodge. That the lodge was open to those who had "crossed the equinoctial line" made clear that the members would mainly be Brittons with business in the Americas and Americans with business in Britain.

As with many lodges' bylaws, seafaring or abroad members were excused from paying dues while out of the country. Unlike many lodges where certificates were issued upon request, Perkins' new rules stipulated that all members, "shall be presented a GRAND CERTIFICATE on Parchment at the Lodge's expense." Affiliated members had to pay an additional fee for the certificate. Certificates served as passports when traversing the masonic globe; that all members were issued one on entry implies that they were expected to travel frequently. Indeed, the new bylaws created an exclusive network within freemasonry. The assumed mobility and expected extended absences of the members was reinforced by article XIV, which stated that members would continue to be considered such indefinitely unless they resigned or were expelled from the lodge.[4]

Beginning with the meeting of July 24, 1759, the minutes refer to the lodge as "The West India & America Lodge late the Goose & Gridiron held at the Queen's Arms in St Pauls Church Yard." Holding the first spot in the engraved and "New and Correct Lists of Regular Lodges"-lists available from grand lodge widely reprinted in Masonic literature- meant that this small node of trans-Atlantic fraternity and commerce was the first lodge a mason anywhere in the world reading the lists would encounter. Immediately, a number of new members gained initiation or affiliation from Barbados, Bermuda, and elsewhere in the Americas. On November 8, 1759 for example, "Being a private lodge night Ja. Maycock Esq. & his Brother Mr. Willm Dottin Maycock of Barbadoes were made Masons. . ..Some other candidates were also proposed, most of them being of Barbadoes or Bermuda." The large number of Barbadians entering the lodge indicates a strong link with that island. The minutes are incomplete, but those that exist show an actively growing lodge. No minutes exist for the masters lodge, but both the *Engraved Lists* and the bylaws state that such was also held regularly. By April 9, 1760, Perkins sat in the masters chair. On June 1, 1761 he was elected to a third term.

The lodge continued to attract the desired creole and seaborne membership. Noblemen also sought admission, for example Sir Richard Glynn, raised in the West Indian and America Lodge on March 11, 1761 by Perkins. Glynn had served as a sheriff in 1752, the year he was knighted, and risen to become Lord Mayor of London in 1758, being created a baronet the following year. In 1762, the lodge's connections to Grand Lodge were strengthened through Brother Dynes, Grand Steward. American members were not limited to the Caribbean; on October 12, 1763 merchant Nathaniel White "of Stanton in New England" was given all three degrees at once since he was "going abroad". In June of that year Brother Thomson of the Port Royal lodge in Jamaica brought a gift of 10 guineas from that lodge for the charitable fund. Since the minutes are highly incomplete and the lodge catered to a mobile and transient membership it is impossible to analyze the membership demographics completely. Many members of the lodge only appear in the minutes on the occasion of their entry. However, it is clear that the lodge received members and visitors from throughout the British Americas, Europe, and the upper reaches of London society.[5]

Perkins continued as master while seeing to his holdings in the West Indies. The minutes of February 10, 1762 state that RWM Perkins "being gone abroad to the West Indies" the senior warden Isaac Pearce presided over the lodge. That night Dr. Joseph Powers proposed that Brother Lucas Tatischeff, secretary to Prince Galitzen, be raised to the degree of master mason. The noble connections of the lodge thus extended onto the continent as well as across the Atlantic. On June 9, "a letter from Bror. Wells Grand Master of Carolina to Bror. Perkins was in his absence read in open Lodge. . . recommending to his & the Lodges particular notice Bror. Mickie & Bror. Elliot as worthy Masons. . ." That the letter was addressed to Perkins personally demonstrates the reach of the latter's personal contacts throughout the Americas. Members such as Perkins, Dr. Powers, and the noblemen, captains, and merchants who made up the lodge brought together a far-ranging web of connections. That night the lodge drank to the health of Brother Perkins, "in full bumpers & also Bror. Wells & all the Lodges in Carolina. . ."[6]

In the final meeting of 1762 the lodge replaced Thomas Marriott Perkins with a new master. Perkins had been actively involved in the lodge for only a few years. The next year he became Provincial Grand Master of Jamaica while still serving in the same capacity for the Mosquito Shore. In 1770 Jamaican masons requested a new grand master, for though he had warranted three new lodges and the brethren considered him "an expert mason" he was also "such a transient Provincial Grand Master", being always at sea. He retained jurisdiction over the Mosquito Shore, trading in hardwoods to his great profit. His importance to trade on both sides of the pond is evidenced by the unique jewel the Sea Captains Lodge in Sunderland-by-the-Sea had awarded Perkins in 1757. The lodge continued to function as a hub of trans-Atlantic commerce until November of 1768. The transition seems to have unfolded as a gradual shift from the strong group of Americans who joined with Perkins to a more conventional membership over a period of several years. On January 28, 1767, two Barbadians, one a surgeon, joined the lodge. From September 23, 1767, the minutes become more regular. On June 8, 1768 two members of Boston chartered Solomon's Lodge in Charleston, South Carolina visited.[7]

As of November 23, 1768 however, the lodge changed both its tavern and its name, now calling itself the Lodge of Antiquity—the name it has born up to the present day. The association with trans-Atlantic commerce did not end with the change of name. Indeed, three weeks later they received a visitor from St. John's Lodge, Barbados, from whence so many of the members made in the past eight years hailed, and made a member of a surgeon bound for sea. Gentleman and Europeans still attended the lodge from time to time, as on May 3, 1769 when the visitors' rolls included the Baron de Gidon and one Pomeresche of Concordia Lodge in Stralsund in Pomerania. Nonetheless, the members roles indicate a shift to a more sustainable, local membership. Trans-Atlantic links lingered on for some time, but they were no longer the lodge's primary demographic and intercontinental networking was no longer its primary purpose. The Lodge of Antiquity, whose master continued to preside with the gavel tradition claims dated back to Sir Christopher Wren, was able to remake itself yet again and to maintain an elite position in freemasonry and to an extent in the position of its most elite members.[8]

Notes

1 W. Harry Rylands, F.S.A. Last Master,*Records of the Lodge of Antiquity No. 2 Vol. I*, London: Harrison and sons LTD., Printers in ordinary to his majesty, 1928, 1–4, 7, 19; Ryland's *Records* is essentially a private publication of most of the extant original minutes and records of the lodge with commentary and explanation. The records prior to 1767 are highly incomplete, but sufficient to provide significant data nonetheless; *Proceedings in Masonry*, 407. This excerpt from John Rowe's diary lists both a Joseph Scott and a Captain Scott, the latter likely the Capt. Scott mentioned in various letters of freemason William Palfrey, Clerk to John Hancock [Palfrey Papers, MSS, Boston: Harvard University] in attendance at the Feast of St. John in December, 1760.

2 *Ibid.*, 197–8; Calcott, *Candid Disquisition*, 102; *Engraved List of Lodges 1764*, 26.

3 *Ibid.*, 197–9; For Benjamin Franklin's masonic connection to Boston's Henry Price see *Proceedings in Masonry*, 4.

4 *Ibid.*, 220–6. The printed work includes a reproduction of the original printed bylaws; the above quoted by-laws appear on pages 14 and 17–19 of the original.

5 *Ibid.*, 225–6, 231–5.

6 *Ibid.*, 230–1.

7 *Ibid.*, 239–40; Jackie Ranston, "The Multifaceted Freemasons of Jamaica", in ed. Wade, 163.

8 *Ibid.*, 250–5.

St. John's Grand Lodge Boston: "Masonry in British America has Wholely Originated from Us."

On August 20, 1737, the *St. James Evening Post* of London reprinted an item from Boston dated June 27, on Boston's Feast of St. John's Day procession, "it being the the first procession in America". Masons among the posts' readers could feel gratified at the Craft's intercontinental reach. Those whose business carried them to New England or who wished to correspond with their brethren there now had the names of all of the grand officers and the tavern at which they met. All readers, masons or otherwise, would be impressed by the membership of the colonial governor. In all, three grand lodges formed in Boston. St. John's Grand Lodge (1733) ranks third in the world after England and Ireland. It was a center of commerce and of elite merchants. The second, Massachusetts Grand Lodge (1769), grew out of the Ancient movement which began in Boston with the Lodge of St. Andrews. With a warrant from the Grand Lodge of Scotland, the Massachusetts Grand Lodge and its Green Dragon Tavern deeply overlapped the radical patriot movement. Finally, just weeks before the outbreak of hostilities with Britain largely brought on by the actions of members of St. Andrew's and their associates, a group of Black Bostonians led by Prince Hall received a warrant for African Lodge from an Irish military lodge. In 1784 they became a Grand Lodge, the point of origin of masonry in the African diaspora. Prince Hall freemasonry has played a major role in African American history since its foundation.

On the primacy of the Ancients, Bullock points out that "Massachusetts Moderns chartered approximately forty subordinate groups, but their warrants went primarily to seaports in other colonies," with only five Massachusetts lodges outside Boston. In contrast, the younger Ancient grand lodge formed far more lodges within the state by 1792 when the largely moribund Moderns merged with the Ancients, mostly on the latter's terms. Bullock's *Revolutionary Brotherhood* correctly interprets this as a prime example of the primacy of Ancient masonry and its role in the social order of the new United States. Considering freemasonry as a transnational *imperio in imperium* in the period preceding the Revolutionary era, however, the network of 40 lodges connecting men of commerce from Quebec to Suriname with stops in nearly every British colony in between and correspondence and visitations that crossed the borders of empire takes on far greater significance. The commercial nature of the Caribbean end of this masonic network is reinforced when taking the dates of newly formed lodges into account, as it follows the spread of New England traders across the islands: Antigua in 1738, Saint Domingue by the early 1740s, St. Christophers, Barbadoes, and finally by 1761 reaching Surinam.[1]

Though Ancient freemasonry swept through the continent beginning in the closing decades of the colonial period and accelerating during and after the War of Independence, Boston's St. John's Grand Lodge, acting with authority for all of North America, introduced or expanded freemasonry into Canada, most of the North American colonies, and the Caribbean. In New York and Georgia, where Massachusetts had no lodges, Modern grand lodges closely connected to the colonial elite and to merchants British, Colonial, and Jewish, introduced the Craft and interacted with the wider nexus originating from Boston. The network of Jewish mason-merchants led by Moses Michael Hayes who held masonic office in New York, Rhode Island and Massachusetts with business connections which undoubtedly profited from the rich masonic establishments of the West Indies is a prime example of how these Modern grand lodges, though communicating only haphazardly, effectively connected cross-colonial and cross-imperial trading networks over vast distances.

Boston was the first major city in British North America, and it played a disproportionate role in trade, politics, warfare and revolutionary agitation throughout the Atlantic period. A town of 16,000 when local patriots initiated the Age of Atlantic Revolutions in 1775, many Bostonians lived on the Atlantic as much as in the cramped peninsula extending into Massachusetts Bay. As in the "profane"—or non-masonic—British empire, so it was in the republic of masonry that Boston was the earliest and most influential hub of freemasonry during the

Atlantic period. Surviving documents clearly demonstrate that while St. John's Grand Lodge and lodge may have been on the periphery of the British Atlantic, the members were often in the imperial and masonic metropolis. They attended lodges and even grand lodge quarterly meetings in England, Scotland, and in other colonies, notably in the 1730s when freemasonry was still going through a period of growth and scientific lectures or related intellectual pursuits were common in British lodges. Whether or not they were able to carry on the same level of intellectual discourse in the colonial lodges, American masons were well aware of the more elevated aspects of English masonic culture, and many of the brethren experienced the heyday of English freemasonry firsthand while others doubtlessly were aware of it through their compatriots.

St. John's Lodge and Grand Lodge in Boston officially received their charter from England in 1733, hand delivered by newly installed Provincial Grand Master Henry Price. Half of the 18 masons named on the charter had been "made in Boston" indicating ongoing masonic activity. The Grand Lodge of Massachusetts claims the existence of documents from a lodge operating at King's Chapel dating as early as 1720 or 1721 which burned up with the Grand Lodge building in 1864. This appears plausible based on the nine brethren initiated in Boston, and the common practice for masons to congregate informal "lodges of St. John", as First Lodge was also called. Moreover, many of the early members were actively involved in King's Chapel.

The merchant elite and sea captains who comprised most of the lodge's membership carried masonry along the Atlantic sea lanes plied by New England's expanding trade. In addition to being the first officially chartered lodge and grand lodge in the New World, Price and his brethren expanded masonry from Canada to South America. In North America, Boston's St. John's chartered the first lodges in Massachusetts, New Hampshire, South Carolina, Rhode Island, Connecticut and Maryland as well as creating two of the first three lodges in New Jersey and adding lodges to Virginia and North Carolina's masonic establishment. Benjamin Franklin and Henry Price met en route home from England, leading to Price's issuing an official charter in 1734 to the previously irregular lodge meeting in Philadelphia. Thus, Boston issued the first regular charters in seven of the 13 colonies. They chartered the first lodges and provincial grand masters in Canada, creating lodges in Nova Scotia, Cape Breton, Newfoundland, Louisbourgh and Quebec and at least two colonial military lodges and several among regular regiments. The masters of Boston's First, Second and Third lodges stated in an Oct. 7, 1751 letter to the Grand Lodge of England, "Masonry in British America has Wholely Originated from Us."[2]

The stories of several of the early brethren are illustrative of the cosmopolitan nature of the fraternity. Governor Jonathan Belcher was the first North American to be made a mason as early as 1704, before the formation of the grand lodge. In a 1741 letter to the lodge written after he had left Massachusetts to serve as governor of New Jersey, Belcher stated that it had been 37 years since he had become a mason. Born in Boston in 1681, Belcher graduated from Harvard in 1699 and spent the following six years abroad. A successful merchant, Jonathan Belcher served on the governor's council from 1722 through 1727, and in 1728 went to London on public business. He was remarkably successful in negotiating London's patronage, returning with a commission as governor of the colony in August, 1730. With the sitting governor as a founding member and his son as the first deputy grand master, the lodge began its life at the top of the local and imperial elite. Belcher served as governor of Massachusetts until 1741. On September 16, 1744 the former governor was present at the Devil Tavern in London when the Earl of Strathmore presided as grand master, at which meeting he paid a guinea to the charity fund on behalf of the lodge in Boston. Belcher returned to the colonies as governor of New Jersey from 1747 until his death 10 years later, maintaining an active correspondence with his Boston brethren. Their attempts to court Belcher's replacement, William Shirley, were less successful, as he politely declined their offer of initiation.[3]

Merchant tailor Henry Price was a particularly energetic character, who served as grand master off and on for decades and finally died at 83 not from senescence, but by accidentally wounding himself in the abdomen splitting rails with an axe. Born in London in 1697, Price first came to Boston in 1723. In 1730 his name appeared in the records of the English grand lodge as a member of Lodge no. 75, Rainbow Coffee House. Price carried the petition for a charter to London and returned with the warrant empowering him as provincial grand master. Much of the lodge and grand lodge's surviving correspondence with the grand lodge of England is that of Henry Price, who served as grand master on and off during several interim periods following the deaths of his successors. Price's letters indicate that he considered himself to have retained authority over North America even after installing his successor Robert Tomlinson as provincial grand master for New England, and acted on that authority to grant charters and appoint provincial grand masters. His name continued to appear in the *Freemasons' Calendar* as provincial grand master of North America until 1805, long after his death.[4]

According to correspondence delivered to the grand lodge of England by Senior Grand Warden Benjamin Barons in 1736, the lodge by that time included

58 members. This letter is likely the source of the information which subsequently appeared in the *Engraved List of Lodges* reproduced in Picard's European best seller listing Boston's lodge at the Royal Exchange meeting on the 1st & 3rd Wednesday. Seventeen were listed as sea captains, four as "esquire", and one colonel, not to mention His Excellence Governor Belcher. In the colonial period, merchants comprised an overwhelming 66 % of the membership, with a further 9.3 listed as "seagoing". As merchants in this era generally took to sea themselves, this would have over three quarters of the Modern masons in Boston sojourning throughout the Atlantic world. The surviving correspondence and records of the lodge demonstrate how the masonic connections of individual members came together in the lodge to create a loose and ad hoc but nonetheless effective means of long-range networking through freemasonry with masonic and commercial implications.[5]

A first-hand account of the relationships of the members of the lodge to each other and the Atlantic sea lanes may be found in the brief autobiographical manuscript of founding secretary and Price's business partner Francis Beteilhe. Beteilhe's story reads as an early version of the immigrant seeking the American dream. It opens on Christmas Eve, 1720, when 22 year old Francis' father passed after going bankrupt in the South Sea Bubble. Francis for a time stayed with relations in France, returning to England, in 1723. The French connections-including "Cousin Morin" in New York and Rev. Roux, who gave him a letter of introduction en route to Boston- indicate that like many influential early masons he was probably of Huguenot descent. Beteihle obtained employment as clerk to Captain Main of the HMS *Biddeford*. They landed in Virginia, then New York where Francis quit, hoping to find work through a cousin. When that failed he resolved to go to Boston, arriving August 1, 1728.[6]

The earliest documents of the lodge, in Beteilhe's handwriting, name him as lodge secretary and Grand Secretary. He appears in the list of brothers made in Boston among the charter members. Beteilhe from August 1728 until April 1737 kept the shop and books of merchant tailor Henry Laughton. Whether Price met Beteilhe first in professional or Masonic circles, they worked together as grand master and grand secretary for the better part of four years before going into an equal partnership on April 27, 1737, 12 days after Beteilhe quit Laughton's service, when he and Price entered into a commercial venture as tailor and woolen draper. It stands to reason that it was in anticipation of opening this new business that Price resigned his commission as grand master at the end of 1736. According to Beteihle, "Att our setting up, thro. the great regard Sundry Merchants & other friends had for me, within One Week's Time we took in to the Value of £5400".

Many of these "sundry merchants and other friends" were certainly masons. Brothers Price and Beteihle decided that it would be to their benefit to "settle a Correspondancy [sic] in England" and agreed that Beteihle should take ship for London.

As Grand Secretary, Beteihle was personally responsible for handling the Grand Lodge's correspondence with England, and was therefore known to highly placed men among the fraternity. Perhaps the most interesting aspect of this journey, however, is that Beteihle intentionally took a circuitous route for purely masonic reasons, "The Reason I did not Embark directly from Boston for London is as follows. Capn Underdown, in Consideration of the Brotherhood insisted I should go with him, and for a further Encouragement, would take of Us, but Ten guyneas for my passage & laying from Boston to London, whereupon, with thanks, we Agree to." Captain James Underdown had become a mason in First Lodge on September 26, 1738. That he offered to take a trifling fare to carry the grand secretary from Boston to London on personal business "in consideration of the Brotherhood" demonstrates how masonic ties benefitted merchants in the Atlantic trade. Underdown was bound first to Charlestown, where a group of Boston masons had a few years before established freemasonry. Beteihle and Underwood's hosts included a list of prominent merchants and political leaders, all likely masons. The diary ends with the departure from Charlestown yet it seems quite certain that the Beteihle took advantage of masonic connections formed not only in Boston but possibly in Charleston and London as well.

Francis Beteihle's lodge brothers also extended First Lodge's transatlantic connections on their commercial voyages. From 1736 to 37, newly made brother Patrick Robertson carried letters introducing the the lodge in Boston to Glasgow-Kilwinning Lodge and Edinburgh Lodge in Scotland, returning replies from the Scottish brethren. Robertson became a mason in Boston; Pelham's 1751 list has him entering on May 12, 1736. He soon departed for Scotland, where the records of Glasgow—Kilwinning lodge meeting at the Old Coffee House record his visit with a letter from Boston in the following manner, ". . .at this Meeting the following being presented by our trusty & well beloved Brother Patrick Robertson of New England, Merchant from our Sister Lodge in Boston, this Lodge unanimously agreed and ordered the said letter to be engross'd in the book and also judge it proper that an answer thereto may be transmitted by the hands of the above Brother James Montgomerie. . ."

According to a letter received from Glasgow-Kilwinning Lodge dated February 22, 1737 and delivered by Glasgow-Kilwinning member Captain Robert Paisley, Robertson had delivered a letter of dated September 1 informing the Scots of the existence and activities of the lodge in Boston. Robertson had carried a letter to at least one other Scottish lodge, Edinburgh, who replied on January 28, 1737. Based on the content of Edinburgh's letter it is apparent that Boston had initiated the correspondence by informing the Scots that there was a lodge present in Boston. It is conceivable that Robertson may have carried letters to other Scottish lodges which did not return an answer or whose answers have disappeared.[7]

The most interesting manuscript from the earliest years of the St. John's Grand Lodge in Boston is "A Dissertation Upon Masonry 1734", which places Boston's early lodge members firmly within the Protestant International described by Peterson while elucidating how First Lodge's brethren viewed the historical and religious claims of their *Constitutions*. The author is unknown. David Walker has incorrectly attributed the sermon to Rev. Charles Brockwell, however, Brockwell was not connected with either the lodge or the church in Boston until a decade or so later. It is possible that Henry Price gave the oration as grand master; if so it is the only such piece that survived among his papers. The "Dissertation" has a number of references to St. Paul as a mason and builds on the assumption of hidden masonic teachings embedded in scripture, both tropes found in early British and Irish masonic writings.[8]

The "Dissertation" referred to the "Kingdom of Masonry" promoting the idea of the Craft as a separate, purer society among the "profane" nations of the earth. That the speaker refers to the instruction of the younger brethren of the lodge implies that the lodge had been functioning for some time. In terms of belief in masonic history, the "Dissertation" expounds on the experiences of St. Paul found in the Bible having in fact been masonic initiation, and similar allusions, even referring back to the building of the Tower of Babel. The speaker also claimed that there remained at least some remnant of a universal language preserved among masons, who had the opportunity and right to learn it, though many did not for lack of capacity or industry. Overall, this piece of oratory tells us much about early freemasonry in Boston. Some sort of lecture or instruction on masonry occurred beyond simple sociability. The author of the dissertation clearly believed in the connection of the craft to both New Testament and Old Testament biblical history and saw the fraternity as a "kingdom" unto itself, as distinct from the everyday world around it as that world was from the scriptural "paradise guarded by the flaming blade". Reverend William Allen's 1778 sermon preached in Philadelphia at the Feast of St. John celebration attended by no less a masonic luminary that General Washington, is highly derivative of this earlier Boston work.[9]

Two years following the 1737 celebration reported in the London papers, the most elaborate celebration of the Feast of St. John on record in the New World was that held in Boston in June, 1739. The brethren first proceeded in their regalia and "preceded by a compleat [sic] band of Musick, consisting of Trumpets, Kettle Drums, etc." from the house of Brother John Wagborn to Governor Belcher's, where they were "elegantly entertained." From there, they walked in procession with Gov. Belcher to the house of Brother Stephen Deblois, "where they were entertain'd with a fine concert of Musick." They then marched to the Royal Exchange, "...where a sumptuous supper was provided, to which were invited many Gentlemen of Distinction, Civil and Military." The ship Hallowell commanded by Brother Alexander French, "discharged 21 great guns three times, viz at Five, Six, and Seven O'clock in the Evening." According to the *Boston Evening Post*, the event had been sufficient to bring the entire town to a halt as spectators crowded around to watch the festivities. "A vast concourse of people attended to see this Procession, insomuch that almost all occupation ceas'd, the streets were crowded; Window's, Balcony's, and Battlements of Churches and Houses were full of Spectators, who were highly pleased with an appearance of so many Gentlemen..." An anonymous brother even set the account to verse and published it as a broadside, "that children may more easily commit it to and retain it in their memory":[10]

First Brother Wagborn was their choice,
Wagborn of founding fame and voice,
At three they to his house repair,
and having staid a little there,
Proceeded onward through the Streat,
Unto his excellency's seat,
For as this Wagborn was a brother,
His excellency was another.
Here having drank and giv'n the sign,
By which he was oblig'd to joyn;
From hence in Leather APRON durst,
With tinsel ribbons on their breast,

Girls left their needles, Boys their book;
And crouded in the street to look,
and if from laughing we guess right,
they were much pleased with the sight,
all this by land,
now follow's after;
the Gallant show upon the water.

The long poem describes the dinner at the Royal Exchange as consisting of "every dainty fare, tongues, hams, and lamb, green pease . . ." Once aboard ship, "they drink'd and smoak'd like any mad". Whether or not any children saw the need to commit this piece of doggerel to memory is questionable, but the level of self-promotion was impressive. Both the press and an independently distributed broadside promoted the grandeur of a provincial grand lodge which could bring all work to a halt and entertain the busy seaport of Boston with three twenty-one gun salutes, several bands, and a series of parades with the colonial governor at their head, all dressed in the exotic aprons and jewels of their society. This was meant not only for the Bostonian reader who had likely seen the processions and heard the cannons, but for readers in the southern colonies and the islands as well. By this time St. John's had issued charters for lodges in Nova Scotia, Portsmouth, Philadelphia, Charleston, and Antigua. Lodge members had active business connections in these cities and both the *Boston Evening Post* and the broadside were expected to reach them. The brethren, whose business took them to England as well, must have hoped that their grand celebration might also receive some notice back in England.[11]

Just at the pomp and circumstance of Masonic processions in England had resulted in backlash in the form of the Scald Miserable Masons, the celebration of the Feast of St. John in Boston 10 years after the grand event immortalized in verse above led to the publication of a less friendly piece of doggerel in the form of Joseph Green's *Entertainment For a Winter's Evening*. This was the festival wherein Reverend Charles Brockwell preached his lauded sermon, "Brotherly Love Recommended", which was to roll from printing presses on both sides of the Atlantic. The *Boston Evening Post* and *Boston Post Boy* both carried short pieces on the "elegant entertainment" and "excellent sermon"; the latter even proclaimed, "We hear the sermon will be printed" and two weeks later carried an advertisement for Draper's published version.[12]

Green, a Harvard graduate, described an event in which brotherly love led to the brethren eating like slobs then engaging in a drunken brawl:

Quarrels oft times don't they delight in, And now and then a little fighting?

Did there not (for the secret's out) in the last Lodge arise a rout?

M----- with a fist of brass

laid T-----'s nose level with his face

And scarcely had he let his hand go

When he received from T_____a d----d blow

Now parson when a nose is broken

Pray, is it friendly sign or token? . . . .

Tis love sure cements the whole

love of the bottle and the bowl. . .[13]

Unlike the far more effective mockery of the scald miserable masons, neither *Entertainment for a Winter's Evening* nor Green's 1755 *The Grand Arcanum Detec*ted: or, A W*onderful Phaenomenon Explained, Which has baffled the scrutiny of many Ages. By ME, Phil. Arcanos, Gent. Student in Astrology* had much impact on the Craft in Boston, though it must have irked the brethren. The latter, like the former, included personal attacks on the appearance and character of several of the members and a mockery of Masonic decorum, describing a brawl over an election of officers, by a group that eats, drinks, smokes, and sweats too much. The Provincial Grand Master for North America and his brethren took little notice of Green's verses. In 1752, they were able to publish to the world their own piece of aristocratic celebrity news when at the June Feast of St. John, "The Right Honourable the Lord COLVILL took the chair as Deputy-Grand-Master of North America. . ." While Colville was in Boston the Brethren made much of this famous brother just as they had Governor Jonathan Belcher.[14]

"From Which Sprang Masonry in Those Parts": Continental Authority and Expansion

Henry Price served as grand master off and on for decades until his death at 83. Following the death of Grand Master Jeremiah Gridley, the elite and well connected Attorney General of Massachusetts, Price briefly served as interim grand master again. His correspondence with London explained that he had never relinquished his authority over North America even while seeing others installed in the chair in New England, and that he had authorized various lodges and provincial grand masters, the records of which are incomplete. The figure of 40 lodges derived from Boston generally includes those described in records from the 1760s and 1770s, yet in a letter of August 6, 1755 Price told the Grand Lodge of England he had already chartered upwards of 40 lodges. Unfortunately, he also stated that many of the more sensitive details would be reserved for personal communication on a planned voyage to England.[15]

In a later letter to the Grand Lodge, Henry Price explained that he had received instruction to spread masonry throughout North America in 1735, a task he began in earnest with St. John's Lodge in Portsmouth, New Hampshire. Portsmouth's St. John's claims a continuous existence since 1736, with Massachusetts proceedings claiming to have issued its charter in 1735. The lodge also included many merchants of Portsmouth and counted a steady stream of British naval and military members among its ranks until the incident at Fort William and Mary, in which lodge members among the Patriot leadership dispossessed their brother, the fort's commander, of his cannons. The ascendancy of the Patriot faction led to a rapid expansion of the lodge during the American Revolution, during which it hosted John Paul Jones and several French officers shortly before they entered U.S. service. There was consistent cross membership between the lodges, including Edmond Quincy and other prominent businessmen, and visitors from Boston show up frequently in St. John's Portsmouth's records and vice versa.[16]

According to the *Proceedings of St. John's Grand Lodge* for *December 27, 1735*, "About this time sundry Brethren going to South Carolina met with some Masons in Charlestown who thereupon went to work, from which sprang Masonry in those parts." The Charleston lodge received a provincial grand master from England, from which time it operated on its own and doesn't seem to have considered itself to be under Boston's authority, though Boston listed it as "not represented" in quarterly communications and as among its lodges in communications sent to England. This despite the visit to Master's Lodge on June 6, 1755 of "Collo. Peter Leigh, late Grand Master SO Carolina".[17]

In 1738 Grand Master Robert Tomlinson "went to England via Antigua, where finding some old Boston masons, he went to work and made the Governor and sundry other gentlemen of distinction Masons". The proceedings claim that thereby "from our Lodge sprang Masonry in the West Indies." Merchant Tomlinson had considerable property in Antigua. Like Tomlinson, these old Boston masons must have been traders, probably with holdings of their own. In 1737 a provincial grand master was assigned for Montserrat, but there is no record of a lodge there until decades later, when a backdated lodge finally appears in the English rolls. Yet by 1740 English roles included lodges on Barbados, St. John's, St. Christophers, Jamaica, and several on Antigua backdated as far as

1738. Provincial Grand Master Captain William Douglas had established the Jamaican lodge, however, Douglas did not visit any other island or provide charters for any lodge other than Kingston. Gov. Matthews in 1738–9 received an appointed as PGM for Antigua and the Leeward Isles. Jamaican and Saint Domingue lodges were connected to Boston by the 1740s. Tomlinson, along with the new PGM for South Carolina, appeared at a communication of the grand lodge in London on January 31, 1739 and returned to Boston that May. From this time onward, Governor Matthews, whom Tomlinson had initiated, served as provincial grand master of the Leeward Islands. Several letters between Antigua and Boston describe the foundation and growth of masonry on the island.[18]

On Wednesday, August 8, 1739, while Tomlinson was in England, the lodge received a letter delivered by the hand of brother mason Major John Murray, senior warden of "one of our lodges" on Antigua. The letter was addressed from the "Grand Lodge Holden at Antigua" under his Excellency William Matthews. The letter explains that the brethren "take kindly our Dear Brethrens offer of a friendly correspondence" but had been waiting for an opportunity to reply to Boston's letter of "the fourth of April last" until they could find a mason bound for Boston to deliver it. This letter had contained the First Lodge's "hearty congratulations upon the Establishment of Masonry in this our Island." The letter was signed "From the Grand Lodge held at the Court House in St. John's the 27th June A.L. 5739". Court House lodge in Antigua and the First Lodge in Boston had thus established a correspondence well before the West Indian lodge appeared in English Grand Lodge's *Engraved List* for the first time in 1740.

Considering the commercial links between Boston and Antigua, having a correspondence with the names and locations of lodges and officers including no less than the governor himself whose brotherly bonds might be called on by a mason arriving in St. John's could be quite advantageous. It seems that the documents and payments for these lodges traveled to England with Tomlinson, whose appearance in Grand Lodge in London following his masonic work in Antigua resulted in Matthews' appointment. The *Freemason's Calendar's* "remarkable Occurrences in Masonry" from 1775 on reported that, "Free-masons at Antigua build a large hall, with other conveniences in that island, and apply to the Grand Lodge to be styled the Great Lodge of St. John's in Antigua, which is granted, April 4, 1744." Antigua had grown, and saw fit to communicate directly with the metropolis. Boston continued to list the island among it's daughter lodges regardless.[19]

The next Masonic news to arrive in Boston from the island was of a more somber nature. On August 21, 1740 the *Boston Weekly News-Letter* conveyed the "sorrowful News from Antigua of the Death of Mr. Robert Tomlinson, Merchant, after Five Days Illness." The short obituary explained that Tomlinson, "was Grand Master of the Lodge of Free and Accepted Masons, in this Town." Tomlinson had, as the *Boston Evening Post* explained on October 20, made out his will "touching his estate in the West Indies" on July 15th, making Benjamin Hallowell, a member of the lodge, his executor. A final notice regarding settlements of Tomlinson's accounts by Hallowell appeared in the same paper in November. Brother Hallowell, born in England, served with distinction in the colonial assaults on Canada as captain of a vessel and held several high offices under the crown government. In his later years his loyalty to the crown would see him driven from the continent. For decades, however, his commercial, governmental and masonic connections served his brethren well.[20]

Boston was not finished chartering lodges in the West Indies. The Grand Lodge's proceedings for April 24, 1767 gives the most complete list of Lodges chartered by St. John's Grand Lodge. Caribbean lodges with Boston charters include Surinam Lodge, St. Christopher's Lodge and Barbadoes [sic] lodge. Surinam is first mentioned as an extant lodge on April 8, 1761. This is very likely the first lodge constituted in South America. The 1776 *Freemasons' Calendar* lists three Dutch constituted lodges in Surinam—1762, 1767 and 1768. The 1762 lodge may be identical to or a daughter of Boston's earlier lodge. Though a transient merchant received appointment as PGM for South America in 1735, England recorded no lodges there prior to Boston's Surinam lodge. According to Paul Revere's wastebooks, Capt. Caleb Hopkins commissioned a plate for engraving summonses from him for Surinam lodge in 1762. Both were members of Boston's Ancient St. Andrew's Lodge.

The records do not include any information on Barbados and St. Christopher's lodges. The *Engraved List of Lodges* of 1740, the first to include West Indian lodges, lists lodges on St. Christopher and Barbadoes, and the *Boston Gazette* on August 11, 1740, included a detailed description of the celebration on June 24 of the Feast of St. John the Baptist by St. Michael's Lodge at Bridgetown. Thus, these two early lodges may have been those created by Boston masons. Conversely, the lodges listed in the 1767 records which can be dated appear in chronological order, implying that the rest may have been chronologically ordered. If this is the case, then St. Christopher's and Barbadoes would have dated between April 1761 and July 1762.

Whatever the connection, the Brethren in Boston were certainly aware of the lodge at St. Michaels, as the *Boston Gazette* on August 11, 1740, included a detailed description of the celebration on June 24 of that year of the Feast of St. John the Baptist by St. Michael's Lodge at Bridgetown. The procession included "a most excellent sermon suitable to the occasion, preached by their Reverend Brother Huxley, Rector of St. Michael's" with the service performed by "Reverend Brother Rose, Rector of St. Thomas's". The procession "took up the whole compass of the town," and included the master and past master, indicating that the lodge had been in operation for some time before the 1740 date given in the lists. The master, brethren and other gentlemen attended on His Excellency the governor, all of whom attended a great ball with "the sisters, and other Ladies and Gentlemen to whom tickets had been given." The report closed by explaining that, "The like was never seen before in this Part of the World, the Town was crowded with People for all Parts of the Island to see the Solemnity." Thus, the brethren of Boston and of the Caribbean were well-apprised of each other's whereabouts and activities through personal and institutional correspondence and the press.

On November 14, 1744, Brother B. Bediford Grand Master of Jamaica visited the lodge. The connections of First Lodge to the West Indies extended beyond the borders of the English colonies. The records of Wednesday, March 24, 1742 record a gift of wine from, "..our Bro. Burnet of Cape Francois" in French Saint-Domingue. Gifts of alcohol flowed across the Atlantic from east to west as well as from north to south. On, August 24, 1743 ". . .Bror: Hall presented a Letter from the Lodge in Minorca,. . . when a Letter in answer was ordered to be wrote and sent by the hands of Bror: Hall which was done accordingly with a Token of 10 Galls: of Rum." This despite the fact that the first mention of Minorca in the English *Engraved Lists* is in 1761. On October 6, 1767 the Grand Lodge published the notice of Price's resumption of the Grand Mastership in all the Boston papers for the information "of all the fraternity in North America and the West Indies under this jurisdiction."

Boston also chartered the first lodges in Canada and over half of the 13 colonies. Canso served as the base of seasonal fishing operations for about 2000 New Englanders and from its capture in 1710 until around 1750, Annapolis Royal and Boston had close political, commercial, social and military connections. The council for Nova Scotia was comprised almost entirely of Boston men who, like the founders of First Lodge, were closely connected with King's Chapel. Masonry, politics and business overlapped to bring the craft from Boston to Canada.[21]

The *Proceedings of St. John's Grand Lodge* include a note dated simply, "5740" stating, "Omitted in place that Our. Rt. Worshl Grand Master Mr. Price Granted a Deputation at ye Petition of sundry Brethren, at Annapolis in Nova Scotia to hold a Lodge there, and Appointed Majr. Erasms Jas Philipps D.G.M. . .."

Philipps had become a mason in Boston on November 14, 1737. At the time Major Philipps was in Boston with Col. Otho Hamilton, William Sheriff and Dr. William Skene as commissioners to establish the Massachusetts—Rhode Island border. Hamilton may have been the member of First Lodge listed by surname only. William Skene had resided continuously in Annapolis from 1715 until his arrival in Boston, and as he was immediately associated with the lodge in Annapolis must have been made a mason in one of those two cities. The *Boston Gazette* of March 13, 1738 included a notice that Henry Price had appointed Major Philipps to be Provincial Grand Master for Nova Scotia. Major Philipps returned to Annapolis in 1738 with a deputation to form a lodge there; he next visited Boston in April 1739 as PGM for Nova Scotia. The 1740 note in the proceedings recorded that he had in that capacity, "...at ye Request of sundry Brethren at Halifax, Granted a Constitution to hold a Lodge there, and appointed the Rt Worshl His Excellency [Governor] Edwd Cornwallis Esqr their First Master.".[22]

Nor was London completely unaware of its cold North Atlantic brethren. In 1738 the Grand Master of England appointed Captain Robert Comins[sic] as provincial grand master for Cape Breton and Louisburg, the latter still under French rule. New England trading magnates and masons Peter and Benjamin Faneuil, who may have employed Cummins, were highly active there, as were many lesser Bostonian merchants. Captain Cummins (or Comyns) was a New England trader connected with First Lodge; he officially affiliated as a First Lodge member on January 14, 1747, but began his Masonic career in either England or Annapolis Royal. Cummins' appointment was thrice renewed. First in 1738, with the stipulation, "excepting such places where a Provincial Grand Master is already appointed." This indicates that the English Grand Lodge was aware of the commission issued to Major Philipps by Boston and respected its validity. Second, in January, 1746, during the occupation of Louisburg, which had surrendered to the New Englanders on June 17, 1745. The sudden need to confirm Comyns appointment eight years after it had last been issued indicates masonic activity in the region. That Cummins affiliated with Boston's First Lodge shortly before he was reappointed provincial grand master of "Cape Breton and ye Town of Louisbourg" indicates a connection between the two regional grand lodges. The appointment was reaffirmed in 1749. Another charter issued to a Canadian lodge at Newfoundland had come from Boston on December 24, 1746. Masonic historian Robert Gould speculates that this may have been a military lodge in the 40th Regiment stationed there, a plausible but inconclusive guess.[23]

Masonry in King George's War

King George's's War (1744–48), led to the initiation of several French prisoners held in Boston. The Siege of Louisburg, the first victory of American militia over European regulars, included a number of masons from Massachusetts and its New Hampshire daughter lodge. Notable among these was newly initiated Brother Richard Gridley, whose skill as an artillery commander led to New England troops' victory on June 17, 1745. When the victors returned home there was a wave of new charters issued to lodges in Canada, Rhode Island and Connecticut. These included Newport, Rhode Island and Halifax Lodges in 1749. Notable among these was the New Haven Lodge chartered on August 12, 1750 with Connecticut military hero David Wooster as its first master. The early 1750s saw a third Boston lodge, two more Connecticut lodges in 1753, two Nova Scotian lodges which paid for their charters in January of that year. The masons petitioning for these lodges included a number of Louisburg veterans. All this indicates the strong probability of masonic activity during the siege and occupation. The French and Indian War saw further Canadian Lodges chartered at Crown Point, a colonial military lodge, and at Louisburg, Quebec and St. John's Newfoundland.

The most celebrated French prisoner brought to Boston was notorious privateer captain Louis 'Doloboratz' (alternately spelled, Lewis 'Delabraz'). After some initial successes, he was captured after a five-hour running fight with the Massachusetts ship Prince of Orange. While a prisoner, Henry Price proposed on October 10, 1744 that 'Delabraz', who had recently been cruising the sea for Boston shipping, be made a mason in First Lodge and furthermore, that he be made gratis. The lodge expedited his degrees in anticipation of his impending freedom and gave him a certificate. The minutes record that Price suggested his initiation on the ground that the Frenchmen, "might be serviceable, [when at home] to any Brother whom Providence might cast in his way". They expected that once a mason he would aid any American or British prisoners should it be in his power to do so. On August 14, 1745, the lodge initiated Anthony de la Bouladerie, son of the Chevalier de la Bouladerie, grantee of Boularie Island in Cape Breton and commander of the earlier French raid on Canso, along with his compatriot Philip Charles St. Paul. Both had been captured in the first French sortie against the raid on Louisburg. They were recommended by Price and Brother Audibert; either of whom plausibly may have done business with them in times of peace.[24]

There is considerable circumstantial evidence for Masonic activity during the occupation of Louisburg. A great number of officers in the Massachusetts and New Hampshire forces were members of the St. John's Lodges of Boston and Portsmouth; several of the New Hampshire officers were also members of Boston's First Lodge, and there were members of the Annapolis Royal lodge present as well. Following the siege a number of colonial veterans and British military personnel became masons in Boston and Portsmouth. Many others were among the forces who remained to occupy the town, these were joined by an influx of brethren in the British regular forces. There were no lodges but many masons among the regiments that joined the occupation.

The boredom of occupation and growing prominence of masonry in British military culture, as well as the presence of high ranking masons among the colonial occupiers and possibly the occupied may explain the need to reappoint Cummins. That lodges were commissioned through him explains why they are no longer recorded. Connecticut freemasonry began with charters from Boston largely by veteran officers of the siege for whom no previous masonic records exist shortly after their return home. The earliest masonic records from Rhode Island also include men who had served at Louisbourg. Veterans of the siege appear as masons in Canadian records shortly thereafter. The same is true of English troops on their return home. It is even plausible that Captain Cadwallader Blayney, who served with both colonial and English regiments, became a mason at this time. Blayney, from 1761 the 7th Earl Blayney and from 1765 a major general, also served as grand master of England in 1764 and Ireland in 1768.[25]

The most notable First Lodge members among the many serving in the New England forces or as captains of New England ships included several whose positions demonstrate the overlapping commercial, political and military prominence of the brethren. John Osbourne was the business partner of Thomas Oxnard, master of the lodge when Osbourne joined in January 1736. Oxnard, a merchant, had migrated to Boston from Durham, England. Osbourne occupied the junior warden's chair that same year and in the following year sat as junior grand warden. During the Louisbourg campaign he served as Chairman of the Committee of War, one of many public offices he held over the years. On returning from London where he had served as the Agent of Massachusetts in London in 1743, Thomas Kilby served as senior grand warden under Oxnard, who had ascended to grand master on the death of Robert Tomlinson. In his capacity in London, Kilby's masonic connections would have been very useful. After returning he was also elected master of First Lodge. That this requires considerable knowledge of masonic ritual and procedure is further evidence that Kilby had been active in

London freemasonry. It also provided a serving master capable of running a lodge among the occupying troops. Kilby died at Louisbourg on August 23, 1746. Mason Robert Glover, adjutant general, affiliated with First Lodge January 23, 1745 and was raised in the Masters lodge on March 22. Dr. Edward Ellis served as surgeon general. Years later he married the widow of wealthy lodge brother Andrew Halliburton.

A member of the Massachusetts forces initiated in the lodge at Annapolis Royal, where he was a lieutenant in Philipps' 40th regiment, was Colonel John Bradstreet. William Pepperrell, overall commander of colonial forces, credited Bradstreet with having first proposed the expedition. Bradstreet had been in Louisbourg frequently from 1725 when he first went there carrying letters to its governor. Following the siege Bradstreet ascended to governor of Placentia, Newfoundland and distinguished himself in the following war as well. There were at least four captains, an ensign and an adjutant from the lodge among the Massachusetts regiments. The New Hampshire regiment boasted three captains, a lieutenant, two ensigns, and an adjutant from the lodge among its officers. These included the senior warden and treasurer. In addition to Lt. Colonel Richard Gridley and William Burbeck, the artillery train included two lieutenants from First Lodge and Captain Abraham Reller, member of the Portsmouth lodge and affiliate member of First lodge. He and Lieutenant Holbrook had affiliated in Boston together on January 11, 1744. Several masons commanded ships as well. Over a dozen officers, a number of veteran soldiers, and several British troopers became masons in the lodges in Boston and Portsmouth on returning from the initial siege and in the years of occupation, including overall commander of New Hampshire troops, Col. Samuel Moore. There is also an unconfirmed tradition that William Wentworth, a member of the Portsmouth lodge since 1740 and future governor of New Hampshire was present at Louisbourg, though he does not appear in regimental records.[26]

Connecticut troops also returned home with a newfound interest in freemasonry. Most notably David Wooster, senior Captain of the Connecticut forces, Nathan Whiting, a customs official at New Haven who served as an ensign in the Connecticut regiment, and Joseph Goldthwaite a Boston Goldsmith and merchant, previously a captain in the artillery company and an adjutant in the first Massachusetts regiment at Louisbourg and landowner in New Haven. Bostonian Arch McNeil, future master of Boston's Master's Lodge, joined them. The three were among the petitioners to Boston's grand lodge for a charter for New Haven's Hiram Lodge No. 1, the first lodge in that colony, granted August 12, 1750, with Wooster as Master and Whiting as junior warden. All three were in Louisbourg from 1747 to 1749; Wooster had also gone to England accompanying the French prisoners. It is possible he may have become a mason in his two months there, but unlikely that he would have learned the masters' ritual. His two compatriots were in Louisbourg continuously until its return to the French. On April 12, 1754, Grand Master Oxnard issued a charter for a lodge at Middletown, Connecticut, with Jehosophat Starr as its first master. Star, "an old and experienced mason. . . more than seven years of age" had served at Louisbourg through 1747, placing his initiation during his time there.[27]

The first Rhode Island charter was granted to Newport on December 27, 1749. The original membership is unknown, so the proximity to the end of the Louisbourg occupation may or may not be meaningful. However, when taking into consideration that two more lodges formed in Boston, the Second and Third Lodge, in February and March 1750, with Hiram Lodge in Connecticut chartered in August, it appears that the end of the occupation of Louisbourg and the return of New England troops resulted in an influx of returning masons. Third Lodge made its last appearance in the records at the quarterly meeting of January 12, 1753. It is reasonable to assume that the boom in returning masons necessitated the two further lodges, but that as things stabilized there was only room for the first two lodges, both of which continued to grow.[28]

Also, represented at the January meeting were Newport and Nova Scotia Lodges No. 1 and 2, which paid for their constitutions. At that meeting Oxnard issued a charter for a third Connecticut lodge at New London. Masons from Rhode Island, Connecticut, and Nova Scotia were all present in Boston for the meeting. Henry Price paid two dollars charity for New London in April, indicating personal connections there. No records of the lodge exist but according to Connecticut masonic historian James Case it was composed mostly of "crown officers in customs". The value of its members to colonial merchants, most of whom did everything in their power to avoid paying customs duties, is obvious.[29]

Thirteen Masonic Colonies

Boston's masonic influence in the American colonies was pivotal. In addition to lodges throughout New England and Canada and the aforementioned lodge in Charlestown, Boston issued charters to lodges in Pennsylvania, Maryland, New Jersey, Virginia, and North Carolina. The lodge in Annapolis in Maryland Received its charter August 12, 1750 with the travelogue author Dr. Alexander Hamilton, who had visited Boston in his peregrinations, as the first master. Boston chartered the second and third lodges in New Jersey, Elizabeth Town Lodge on July 28, 1762 and Prince Town New Jersey first mentioned on September 24, 1765. Though a New York chartered lodge was functioning in Newark as of May 13, 1761 the applicants from Elizabeth Town asked to be counted as No. 1 in the colony, indicating either that they were unaware of the Newark lodge or had been working as a lodge of St. John since an earlier date. The lodge in Pitt County North Carolina created in 1762 or 1764 by Jeremiah Gridley successfully asked for the appointment of a provincial grand master of their own by Price in 1767.[30]

Masons in Philadelphia had been operating as an unofficial 'lodge of St. John' since at least 1730. According to the Massachusetts *Proceedings* dated June 24, 5734 (1734), "About this time our Worshipl Bror Mr. Benjamin Franklin from Philadelphia became acquainted with Our Rt Worl Grand Master Mr. Price, who further instructed him in the Royal Art." Franklin then returned to Philadelphia, convened the lodge, and sent back to Boston for a charter from Price, who granted it, "having this Year Red Orders from the Grand Lodge in England to Establish Masonry in all North America," with Franklin as the first official master. In fact, though they paid Boston for the charter years later, in April of 1752, the lodge never appeared in the English rolls. Virginia lodge, chartered sometime prior to 1761, is a mystery. As much of Virginia's masonic history is known it is possible that this lodge was located in Falmouth, a seaport frequented by Boston traders that is believed to have had a strong masonic presence which disappeared, along with its records, when the city was burned in the American Revolution.[31]

The initiations of celebrity noblemen were a common publicity piece for freemasons in England. In 1750, Boston's Master's lodge had the opportunity, if not to enter a member of the gentry as a mason, at least to raise one as a master. Lord Alexander Colvill, commander of the 20 gun New England station ship *HMS Success,* was in Boston from 1749 until 1752. He endeared himself to the merchants of the city in no small part due to particularly effective supervision of the annual salt trade convoy from the West Indies, so that the town officially thanked him at the end of his term. He became an affiliate member of First Lodge on October 14, 1750, by which time he had already been raised in the Masters Lodge in advance of his January 11, 1750 assumption of the mastership of Second Lodge. As of June 24, 1752 Oxnard appointed Colvill Deputy Grand Master, in which capacity he presided over the grand lodge several times in Oxnard's absence. On Friday, October 12, 1753, Brothers Brockwell, Jeremy Gridley and the grand secretary John Leverett were appointed a committee to write to the departed Colvill. Though a minor nobleman, Alexander was the 7th

Baron Colvill, a source of pride to the brethren and in his official position no doubt a useful connection as well.[32]

The French and Indian War led to several more lodges being formed among both colonial and imperial military units as well as the Merchant's Lodge in the vanquished city of Quebec in which John Hancock entered freemasonry. While brethren like Richard Gridley, Abraham Savage, and many others performed battlefield heroics, merchants among the brethren such as then Deputy Grand Master and future Grand Master John Rowe benefitted financially from a wartime economic boom. This masonic activity began before the North American French and Indian War had morphed into the global Seven Years' War. Emulating the British military masonic connection, on May 13, 1755 "The Right Worshipful Grand Master authorized, by his charter of deputation, dated May 13, the Right Worshipful Richard Gridley, Esq. to congregate all Free and Accepted Masons in the present expedition against Crown Point, and form them into one or more Lodges as he should think fit, and to appoint Wardens and other officers to a Lodge appertaining." This and later lodges among the colonial forces provided an opportunity for the less affluent and connected among the colonial troops to enter Boston's Modern masons.

The French and Indian War brought a far greater British military and masonic presence to North America. Grand Treasurer and future Grand Master John Rowe's Letter Book for the war years includes a substantial number of masons, both colonial and British, including no less a figure than General Amherst, among his debtors. Many of Rowe's associates were freemasons, including James Otis, William Molyneux, the (advantageously) corrupt customs collector Benjamin Barons, and Hancock as well as at least several of his foreign contacts. Since commercial networks like Rowe's were constructed through a wide range of business, kinship, and personal contacts it is not possible to ascertain the extent to which Rowe's vaulted position in the fraternity aided in his business dealings, though the fact that one of his main trading ships was called the *Freemason* demonstrates the importance of masonry both to Rowe personally and in advertising the owner's masonic credentials.

At the Feast of St. John on December 27, 1757, Rowe ascended to senior grand warden. The visitors included the Right Honorable and Most Worshipful John, Earl of Loudon, late Grand Master of Masons in England, His Excellency Charles Lawrence, Governor of Halifax, the officers and members of the three lodges in Boston, "and an unusual concourse of respectable Brethren." The war effort had brought colonial and British military leaders to Boston. That the members of the local lodges were distinct from the 'unusual concourse of respectable masons' implies that the latter were not local. Bringing these men together socially in the lodge offered serious benefits to any member hoping to make a name for himself in military service or a fortune in war related business, as well as simply to connect with well-placed masons from both sides of the British Atlantic. Prior to the year-end Feast of St. John, several prominent Englishmen had sought Masonic initiation in the lodge. On January 31, Grand Master Jeremy Gridley called a special meeting and appointed his brother Richard, the war hero charged with creating at least one military lodge at Crown Point, to initiate five Englishmen "who came to town from Marblehead with Bro. Lowell on purpose to be made a Mason": Captain Harry Charters, Captain Gilbert M. Adams, aid de camp Doctor Richard Huch, Mr. John Appy, Secretary to the Earl of Loudon and Mr. John Melvill [sic].

Boston's Grand Lodge issued wartime constitutions to British regimental lodges and colonial forces. On November 18, 1758 the Right Worshipful Edward Huntingford received a deputation to hold a lodge in his majesty's 28th regiment stationed at Louisburg. Brother Richard Gridley, hero of the first siege of Louisburg, had assisted Brother General Wolfe in taking the fortress a second time, again with Brother William Burbeck at his side and a number of masons under his command. There were ample English masons already among the British forces, however, Huntingford clearly deemed it more expedient to apply for a deputation to Boston. That Gridley himself was the primary contact is evidenced by his appearing for and paying charity from Louisburg Lodge before the Grand Lodge in Boston on December 27, 1758. Richard Gridley was not the only colonial commander empowered to spread masonry in the army. On April 13, 1759, Abraham Savage, a past master connected to both First and Second Lodge and the Grand Lodge, was authorized, "to congregate all Free and Accepted Masons in the expedition intended against Canada, at Lake George or elsewhere, into one or more Lodges, as he shall think fit, and appoint proper officers, &c." Connecticut's Israel Putnam, future Revolutionary general was rescued by a French mason during the war.[33]

Boston's Moderns & Masonic Intellectualism

After the war, John Rowe continued to gain prominence in business, politics and freemasonry. He was installed as grand master on November 23, 1768, a ceremony which created quite a spectacle, with a grand procession of masons in their regalia, a sermon preached by Newburyport mason Reverend Edward Bass, and a sumptuous dinner at the Concert Hall during which a full band played. Among the 128 brethren who took part in the procession were 20 strangers. Of these, four were from nearby Newbury, including Reverend Bass, and three, two surnamed Frazier, had no named place of origin. Eight assorted officers from six different ships, a customs officer, a mason from Georgia and a brother from England all participated. Five officers of Newburyport's lodge attended as well. Six more masons including James Otis skipped the installation ceremony but attended dinner.[34]

The lodge at Portsmouth sent few members because, as secretary John Marsh informed Abraham Savage, there were few members present in lodge when his letter was read. Not only was weather and travel a problem in New Hampshire in November but, "the great Hurry of our Brethren in the Mercantile way, in dispatching their Ships to the West Indies" kept them from lodge. Here then is further evidence of the connection of masons in even the furthest northern seaports in British North American to those in the Caribbean. That the Inspector of Military hospitals in Saint-Domingue and Martinique, a St. George of Rouen, visited the lodge in 1774 after having first attended the Feast of St John the Baptist held in Gloucester, Massachusetts- at which the Patriot leadership of Boston and several seaport communities dined in 1773- further illustrates the connection of provincial New England masons to the well-placed brethren on Saint-Domingue.[35]

The charge bestowed by Henry Price on his latest successor again spoke to a continuity of the Craft's intellectual emphasis on antiquity and scientific aspiration. Alluding in the opening stanza to the temple of Apollo, Price soon moved from classical to Biblical history. He described the Bible as "the Grand Archive of Masonry, and all the most eminent Virtues, Moral and Divine relative thereto." This echoed the very earliest masonic sermon given in the Americas in Boston in 1734, at which Price was certainly present, in forwarding the idea that Masonic secrets were encoded into scripture. The Scriptures, "had been delivered to us by Moses. . .Grand Master of the Lodge of Israel." This repositioning of Moses as a masonic grand master, which appears in several of the Old Charges based pamphlets on Masonic history circulating about the Atlantic, was to be repeated in the Oration given at the Feast of St. John the Baptist on 1783 by Boston Ancient Christopher Gore.

In conferring the ritualistic collar and jewel upon Rowe, Price exhorted that, "The compass extended on it, sheweth, that his Dimensions and Influences are within the Compass of Science, of which you are to be the Patron." The elder Grand Master had received his masonic initiation in England sometime in the

1720s and had attended grand lodge no later than 1733, the era during which the practice of presenting scientific lectures and experiments in Masonic lodges was at its heyday. This experience of freemasonry as a learned society was transmitted by Price and other brothers with masonic experience in England to the lodge. That the new grand master was to be the patron of science and held a position once occupied by Moses demonstrates the effective transference of the intellectual side of freemasonry across the Atlantic.[36]

Nor was the Hub the only site of learned lectures among Boston Freemasonry. A Dec. 28, 1774 letter from Union Lodge on Nantucket informed the Grand Lodge that the previous day brother Zebulon Butler expounded upon "the Beauties of Masonry, the infinite Profit & Advantage of Brotherly Love and Unity." Records for Marblehead Lodge (1760) and St. John's, Newburyport from colonial times are lost, but the memberships reconstructed from both include many town leaders, prominent merchants, and many leading local patriots and likely included similar instruction. Boston's intellectual influence was far from local. In addition to Brockwell's *Brotherly Love Recommended* having featured prominently in many British variants of *The Freemason's Pocket Companion,* the earlier "Dissertation Upon Masonry" influenced American masons in the decades to come. Pennsylvanian William Smith's December 28, 1778 prayer at Christ Church in Philadelphia, attended by no less a mason than George Washington, included elements found in the 1734 "Dissertation", namely, the idea of the lodge as paradise defended by the flaming sword, an image which occurred in other masonic sermons on both sides of the Atlantic as well, though the "Dissertation" seems to be the earliest example. Smith's 1795 Sermon also focused on St. Paul with identical and seemingly derivative passages. That it was apparently plagiarized decades later in the presence of General Washington and the masons of the Continental Army speaks to a lasting influence.[37]

The importance of science and education to masons had appeared in colonial and revolutionary era orations in Boston. During the colonial period New England masons were largely men of commerce, and many were involved in the Marine Societies of Boston, Salem and Newburyport. These societies provided professional networking and relief, but also served to disseminate knowledge of the world and of the sea useful to mariners, serving a function which had scientific elements relevant to its members. Masons were among the founders and leaders of the Marine Societies of these three communities, and their organization shows Masonic influence at the very least. In Boston Grand Master Jeremiah Gridley and St. Andrew's member Jonathan Snelling served as the society's president for many years. Members voted in a Masonic style ballot box wit the same white balls

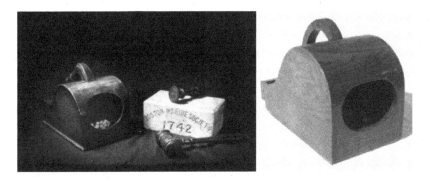

Figure 6.1. Original ballot box of the Boston Marine society next to a standard masonic ballot box. Note the white balls and black cubes, used to elect or reject candidates. (Courtesy Boston Marine Society).

and black cubes. The Newburyport Marine Society formed a company for the Revolutionary militia with many masons as members.[38]

In 1772 the new Ancient lodge in Newburyport, St. Peter's, also heard a lecture on architecture delivered by the master. By 1783 when Christopher Gore sermonized on Moses' role as grand master, the rise of ancient masonry and the American Revolution altered the Britain's transatlantic political and masonic empires. Before turning to the rise of Ancient masonry and the role of both Bostonian Grand Lodges in the Revolution, however, we will delve more deeply into St. John's Grand Lodge's role in the transatlantic empire of Freemasonry.[39]

Notes

1 Bullock, *Revolutionary Brotherhood,* 102; *Proceedings in Masonry,* 105.

2 First Lodge Minutes and Bylaws 1738–1754, Charter of St. John's Lodge July 30, 1733, Microfilm: Boston, Grand Lodge of Massachusetts; Grand Lodge of Massachusetts, *Proceedings in Masonry: St. John's Grand Lodge 1733–1792, Massachusetts Grand Lodge 1769–1792. With an Appendix, Containing Copies of Many Ancient Documents, and a Table of Lodges* (Boston: Grand Lodge of Massachusetts, 1894), 1–4; Melvin M. Johnson, *The Beginnings of Freemasonry in America: Containing a Reference to All that is Known of Freemasonry in the Western Hemisphere Prior to 1750, and Short Sketches of the Lives of some of the Provincial Grand Masters* (Kingsport, TN.: Southern Publishers, Masonic Publications Division, 1924), 1–12, 380.

3 St. John's, Minutes; Harvey Newton Sheppard, *Freemasonry in North America: St. John's Lodge A.F. & A.M. 1733–1916* (Boston: Seaver-Howland Press, 1917), 8–9.

4 *Ibid., Freemasons Calendar or Almanac for the Year 1800–1805.*

5 Francis Beitheile, *The Beitheile Manuscripts*, ed. Muriel Davis Taylor (Boston: Grand Lodge of Massachusetts, n.d.). This volume contains a transcript of the Beitheile MSS, which is identical to the original, and several related documents including the Barons letter; Bullock, *Revolutionary Brotherhood, Freemasonry and the Transformation of the American Social Order, 1730–1840* (Chapel Hill: UNC Press, 1996), 93–5.

6 Francis Beteihle. *Autobiography*. Beteihle Manuscripts, MSS. Boston: Grand Lodge of Masons. A full reprint of Beteihle's manuscripts, which include his autobiography and early minutes and correspondence of the First Lodge, were also fully reprinted with commentary in the *Transactions of the American Lodge of Research* cited above, which also includes the 1736 Benjamin Barons letter.

7 Both letters are reproduced in Sheppard, *Freemasonry in North America*, 29–31.

8 Shawn Eyer, FPS. C.W. Moore M.S.: A Dissertation Upon Masonry 1734, with Commentary and Notes." *Philalethes, The Journal of Masonic Research & Letters* 68, no. 2 (Spring 2015): 62–76. This article includes the entire original text, the original manuscript is held at the Grand Lodge of Massachusetts.

9 *Ibid.;* comparison of the 1734 and 1778 sermons in Eyer, "Brother William Allen", *Freemasonry in the Translatlantic World*, 291–302.

10 *Boston Evening Post,* July 2, 1739; "A True and Exact Account of the Celebration of the Festival of Saint John the Baptist by the Ancient and Honourable Society of Free and Accepted Masons, at Boston in New England, on June the 26, 1739. Taken from the Boston Gazette and Rendered into metre, that Children may more easily commit it to and retain it in their Memory," Lexington: Museum of our National Heritage.

11 Anonymous, "A True and Exact Account of the Celebration of the Festival of Saint John the Baptist by the Ancient and Honourable Society of Free and Accepted Masons, at Boston in New England, on June the 26, 1739. Taken from the Boston Gazette and Rendered into metre, that Children may more easily commit it to and retain it in their Memory." Lexington: Museum of our National Heritage.

12 Boston Evening Post, January 1, 1750; Boston Post -Boy,January 1, 1750, January 15, 1750.

13 Joseph Green, *Entertainment for a Winter's Evening: Being a Full and True Account of a very Strange and Wonderful Sight seen in Boston on the Twenty-Seventh of December 1749 at Noon-Day, the Truth of which can be attested by a Great Number of People, who actually saw the same with their Own Eyes, by Me, the Honble B.B. Esq; by Joseph Green of Boston.* Boston: G. Rogers, 1750; 11.

14 Boston Post-Boy, June 29, 1752.

15 *Freemasons Calendar or Almanac for the Year[s] 1800–1805.(*London: Grand Lodge of England) The *Freemason's Calendar* was an annual publication that appeared independently in 1775 and was taken over by the Grand Lodge beginning in 1776, replacing *A List of Regular Lodges / Engraved List of Lodges* printed annually from

1723 –1778; extant original copies: London: John Pine, 1725 (facsimile), 1736, 1737, 1738; London: Benjamin Cole, 1761, 1764, 1766, 1766, 1768, 1770, 1778; reproduced in Hughan, William, ed . *A List of Regular Lodges A.D. 1734.* London: 1907, 1729, 1734, 1735, 1739, 1740, 1744, 1745, 1754. *Proceedings*, 407–417; Johnson, *Beginnings*, 1–12.

16 St. John's Lodge, Portsmouth, *Records and Minutes, Book 1.* MSS, Portsmouth, NH; St. John's Portsmouth, *Membership Database; Gerald Foss, Three Centuries of Freemasonry in New Hampshire* (Somersworth, NH: The New Hampshire Publishing Company, 1972 (3–99).

17 *Proceedings*, 4–6; Master Lodge Minutes of Meetings 1755–1768, Microfilm (Boston: Grand Lodge of Massachusetts).

18 John Garrigus, *Before Haiti: Race and Citizenship in French Saint-Domingue* (New York: Palgrave-MacMillan, 2006), 38 details Saint Domingue Freemasonry; Jackie Ranston, *The Multifaceted Freemasons of Jamaica*, present volume.

19 Grand Lodge of Antigua to Grand Lodge of Boston, June 27, 1739, reprinted in Sheppard, *Freemasonry in North America*, 31–2; *Freemason's Calendar 1775*, "Remarkable Occurrences in Masonry", 39–41 and in subsequent editions annually.

20 "Captain Benjamin Hallowell Homestead", *Boston Daily Globe*, December 29, 1901 retrieved from: https://www.jphs.org/colonial-era/capt-benjamin-hallowell-homestead.html.

21 Robert Freke Gould, *History of Freemasonry around the World, Vol. IV* (New York: Charles Scribner's Sons, 1936 (29).

22 *Ibid.,* 29–30; First Lodge, Minutes; *Proceedings*, 6–7.

23 First Lodge, Minutes; *Proceedings*, 6–7, Reginald Harris, P.G.M Nova Scotia, A.J.B. Milborne, Grand Historian, G.L. of Quebec, Col James R. Case, Grand Historian, G.L. of Connecticut. "Freemasonry at the Two Sieges of Louisbourg 1745 and 1758". The Papers of the Canadian Masonic Research Association, 1949–1976, Vol. 2, paper 46. May 13, 1958. Accessed online: http://pictoumasons.org/library/CDN%20Masonic%20Research%20-%20Freemasonry%20at%20Louisbourg%20[pdf].pdf.

24 *Ibid.,* 32; St. John's Lodge, Minutes; Proceedings, 209–11.

25 Harris et al. "Freemasonry at the Two Sieges of Louisbourg"; St. John's Lodge Portsmouth, Minutes and Records; St. John's Lodge Portsmouth, Membership Database; First Lodge, Minutes.

26 Harris, et al.; First Lodge, Minutes, St. John's Portsmouth, minutes.

27 *Proceedings in Masonry*, 12, 30–31; Harris, et al."Freemasonry at the Two Sieges of Louisbourg"; *Hiram Lodge No 1, Ancient Free and Accepted Masons* 1750–1916 (New Haven, John J Corbett Press, 1916), 81–114.

28 *Ibid.,* 9–24.

29 *Ibid.,* 24–5; James R. Case. *Connecticut Masons in the American Revolution.* Hartford: Grand Lodge of Connecticut A.F. & A.M, 1976, 3–4.

30 *Proceedings*, 78–9, 98–9, 110–112;Reverend William Brogden, *Freedom and Love. A Sermon Preached before the Ancient and Honourable Society of Free and Accepted Masons, in the Parish Church of St Ann in the city of Annapolis on Wednesday, the 27th of December, 1749* (Annapolis: J. Green, 1750). The sermon was dedicated to "the Right Worshipful Alexander Hamilton, M.D. Master" and others; Tatsch, 50–1.

31 *Proceedings*, 19–20;

32 *Proceedings*, 13–28; Sheppard, 17–18; http://www.biographi.ca/en/bio/colvill_alexander_3E.html, accessed April, 18, 2016.

33 *Proceedings*, 59–63 contains copies of these letters; Leslie Choquette, *Frenchmen into Peasants* (Cambridge: Harvard Historical Studies, 1997), 68.

34 *Ibid.*, 156–60.

35 *Ibid.*, 141; St. John's Portsmouth, Records and Minutes; Tyrian Lodge, Minutes.

36 *Ibid.*, 154–6.

37 Eyer, "Brother William Allen", *Freemasonry in the Transatlantic World*, 297–302.

38 Boston Marine Society, Salem Marine Society, Evans Fiche; St Andrew's Minutes, St Peter's Minutes.

39 Nantucket Lodge to Grand Lodge, Decmber 28, 1774, in *Proceedings in Masonry*, 219; St. Peter's Lodge, Records and Minutes Book I, MSS. Grand Ldoge of Massachusetts.

7

The Grand Lodges' Correspondence: Communication and Connection in the British Masonic Atlantic

En route to England, merchant and future Deputy Grand Master Brother Robert Jenkins carried a June 24, 1749 'letter of introduction or certificate' addressed to "The Rt Woshl [worshipful] Master Wardens and Brethren of any Regular Lodge in London". According to the letter, Jenkins expected to visit the grand lodge. It referred the reader to the bearer "for a particular account of the Propagation of Masonry in N. England." If, as the author of *The Three Distinct Knocks* claimed, the masons of England enjoyed hearing "how masonry proceeds in foreign countries" then Jenkins had plenty of material to entertain them. Much of the wording is very close to that of the letter of introduction William Jackson carried with him in 1768, indicating that it was a common formulation, likely repeated a number of times as merchants leaving Massachusetts sought credentials introducing them to brethren in their intended ports of call.[1]

The correspondence between the masons of Boston and their brethren in Britain, Antigua, Minorca, and Saint-Domingue demonstrates how the trading networks of individual masons routinely formed connections between those masons' lodges, allowing any of their brethren on either end the opportunity to widen their own circle across the sea. Likewise, the extant communications between the grand lodges of England and Scotland and their provincial grand lodges in Massachusetts and between St. John's Grand Lodge and its daughter lodges in the Americas allows us insight into Masonic connections and communications. It also demonstrates how the jurisprudence and procedural rules laid out in the *Constitutions* functioned internationally. The picture which emerges is that this connection was partially effective, and that masons made sufficient efforts to adhere to proper masonic diplomacy such that an imperfect, loose, yet functional chain of communication existed between grand lodges and provincial grand lodges, with sporadic communication between Boston's provincial grand lodge and its far flung progeny.

Unfortunately, the fragmentary nature of the records makes it impossible to know how consistently the brethren maintained these communications. In addition to the serious gaps in the minutes of Boston's lodges at times the Grand Master simply issued lodge charters on his own authority and did not announce these actions at the Quarterly meetings, so that they frequently went unrecorded in the proceedings. Even so, there remains a considerable correspondence between the grand lodges in Boston and London and between Boston and her subordinate lodges. Even if they were unable to forward annual returns as stipulated in their charter, the grand lodge did attempt to obtain paperwork and payments from its daughter lodges and to forward the same to England at least sporadically. When emergency such as the passing of a provincial grand master necessitated it, they were able to communicate with London and receive replies within a short time, indicating rapid activation of communication channels along the flow of shipping between the two sides of the ocean. The provincials consistently and successfully pressed for confirmation of an expansive jurisdiction over North America, which later led to emulation by the Ancients lodge of St. Andrew's in obtaining the same from the Grand Lodge of Scotland.

Freemasonry was indeed a thriving international empire, a parallel republic with a world all its own by October 7, 1751 when Boston's First, Second, Third and Masters lodges sent an important letter to the grand master of England which demonstrates how seriously they viewed masonic constitutionality and jurisprudence. Signed by the masters and wardens of all of the lodges, including Rev. Charles Brockwell and Lord Colvill for the First and Second Lodge, they made it clear that their three successive grand masters "have each in their respective Commissions been Distinguish'd under the Title of PROVINCIAL GRAND MASTERS of North America". The letter asks for clarification as to whether this designation means that other grand masters in North America are subordinate to him and "therefore from him and him only or his Deputy should solicit or Receive their Deputations which some lodges have not observed" or whether his authority extended only to "the province in which he resides". Clearly they are making a case for the former . They state that if the second reading is correct then "our Grand Masters have Exceeded in Granting Deputations to Distant Provinces as Philadelphia, Carolina, Antigua in the West Indies &c. which has prom[ot]ed so Considerably ye Interest of Masonry in North America." They assure the grand lodge that restraining their authority "must have prov'd detrimental to the whole Craft". They therefore ask the grand master to accede in their view "as Masonry in British America has wholly Originated from us".

Building on this slightly exaggerated claim, Boston's lodges ask that Oxnard and his successors be granted "a Full and Plenary Commission to act as Grand Master" over "Massachusetts Bay, New Hampshire, Connecticut, Rhode Island and Providence, New York, New Jerseys [sic], Pensilvania, May Land, Virginia, North and South Carolina's, Georgia, Newfound Land, and Nova Scotia, all of which Provinces are Generally Distinguish'd under the Name of North America." The letter explains that this will allow better compliance with grand lodge's own bureaucratic requirements. To this end they explain that if all of the lodges in North America are required to "Communicate and Correspond with the Grand Lodge in North America thus constituted, that from thence an Account of their several Proceedings may be Transmitted Annually to the GRAND LODGE IN ENGLAND, and as is now done by us, and to which we Refer you." This petition was accompanied by a list of all the masons made or accepted in the First Lodge. These included the date that they were initiated or affiliated from July 30, 1733 to August 28, 1751. A list of all those raised in or affiliated with the Masters lodge since 1738 was also included.

That London did not wish to limit its own authority to appoint provincial grand masters is clear from Henry Price's letter of August 6, 1755 informing the Grand Lodge of the death of Thomas Oxnard, the constitutional reversion of the provincial grand mastership to himself, and the brethren's desire that Jeremy Gridley, Esq. be appointed in his stead with a renewable three-year term. This letter is particularly interesting in so far as it gives glimpses into the connection between masons in distant colonies, communication across the Atlantic and unrecorded Masonic activity carried out by Price. Price began that he had seen "with the utmost pleasure" the deputation they had granted to Peter Leigh "whom I have had the pleasure of seeing in our Lodges in Boston" as grand master of South Carolina. Price informed the English Grand Master that his 1733 deputation had given him jurisdiction over North America. Though it may have been implied, Price did not state that Leigh's appointment was an infringement on his authority. He did, however, explain that it had been "all the brethren in

North America" who had chosen Gridley. He punctuated this with a reminder that "we are the oldest (or first constituted) Regular Lodge in America."

Price also explained that they had sent their application with three guineas for Gridley's appointment the previous December through Captain John Phillips, who had forwarded it to Reverend Brother Entick, Minister at Stepney. This chain of communication was less direct than previous and latter cases in which a Boston merchant such as Benjamin Barons or William Jackson carried documents directly to the grand lodge in London. Price asked the Grand Lodge to contact Entick and enquire after the money, and informed grand lodge that Captain Phillips had a receipt from Entick and that Phillips "using the London Trade may be now found at the New England Coffee House at Change Time." Apparently a favorite of Boston masons and merchants, the New England Coffee House is also mentioned in a later letter of Ancient grand secretary William Palfrey. The haunts of New England merchants in London thus served as nodes of international Masonic communication as well as commerce.

Pressing home his point, the Grand Master for North America informed the grand lodge boastfully that "masonry has had as great Success in America since my Settling here as in any part of the World (except England). Here is not less that Forty Lodges sprung from my First Lodge in Boston." The number 40 is interesting, because while St. John's Grand Lodge did charter around 40 lodges over the course of its existence, there are not nearly so many lodges recorded by 1755. This may have been at least partly exaggeration on Price's part, however, as it was also the case that grand masters in Boston issued charters on their own authority and did not always enter them into grand lodge proceedings, and as a number of the lodges we do know of sprung into the records suddenly when record keeping was given renewed zeal in the 1760s, it is quite feasible that he had created more lodges lost to the records. These lodges may include some of those in the Caribbean and the colonies whose origin stories remain unknown.

Price's closing adds a personal note, giving further insight into channels of transatlantic communication. He told the grand secretary that he "shall be Glad of a few lines from you . . .as I shall have sundry things to Communicate to you from Time to Time and cannot do it but by Letter to you, most of my old acquaintance of Masons being either Dead or Remov'd from London." Though Jeremy Gridley was to be appointed the fourth grand master for New England, Price still anticipated needing to communicate masonic matters with the grand lodge, reiterating that he considered his own masonic authority valid and continued to act upon it. Earlier in the letter he had stipulated that the brethren had chosen Gridley "with my consent" and in several of his letters Price is quick to point out that he was responsible for bringing masonry to North America.

As a mason made in London who had in the past had close personal connections and had sat in the grand lodge during the heyday of the 'grand architects', he had a more intimate knowledge of London freemasonry and would have commanded more immediate respect and acceptance therein than a provincial mason made in Boston might. He closed this epistle by informing the grand secretary that he harbored, "some remote thouts[sic] of once more seeing London with all my Brethren in the Grand Lodge after Twenty Two years absence." That his business had not otherwise taken him back to London implies that Price's 1733 journey likely was made for the purpose of obtaining his deputation. If, so then it speaks to the high importance head and his brehtren placed on freemasonry.[2]

Jeremy Gridley, "the father of the Boston bar", was extremely well-placed in Boston society. As the attorney general of the province, it was he who argued the writs of assistance case against brother mason James Otis. He also served as president of the Marine Society and colonel of the first regiment of militia, though his younger natal and masonic brother Richard saw more actual combat. Gridley sent a written summons to the master and wardens of each of his lodges late in 1757. The masters and wardens updated regulations for the charity fund, included with the letter. These opened with the explanation that "...the number of Free and Accepted Masons in North America are daily increasing". Among other things, these regulations specified that "As the lodges at New Hampshire, Newport, Connecticut and Nova Scotia within our district may contribute to the universal Charity they are always intitled as if Present in Boston". While any sojourning mason in the city might receive aid, the brethren of these lodges could apply to Boston through their master or wardens since these lodges were contributing and communicating with Boston regularly.[3]

Emulating London's meticulous emphasis on the charity fund demonstrates the provincials' awareness of goings on at the mother grand lodge and their view that they were to play an equivalent role on their side of the Atlantic. The importance of proper adherence to grand lodge protocol under Gridley is even clearer in a letter sent to all of the lodges within under his jurisdiction, penned by Deputy Grand Master Robert Jenkins. Jenkins informed the master of each lodge that Gridley had received orders from the deputy grand master of England to "return a list of all the Lodges in his district." Jenkins asked each master to send forthwith an account of their lodge including "when constituted, where held, what number of Brethren made since the Constitution with their Names," the names of the current members and officers and the meeting night, "so that they may be registered in the Grand Lodge of England." Jenkins further explained that each lodge must include three guineas to be sent to England, or else they "cannot expect to find your Lodge on said List." According to Jenkins all of the lists and funds would be forwarded together by the grand master "by the first Opportunity after all the List[s] are Collected." He admonished the masters to concur as soon as possible. The grand lodge in England was attempting to keep its provincial records and payments up-to-date, and the grand master of North America, as Boston's provincials styled themselves, attempted to comply .[4]

Henry Price's correspondence with the Grand Lodge of England from the time following grand master Jeremy Gridley's death, in which Price briefly acted as Grand Master for the third time, is very informative about the nature of Masonic communication, and refers to now lost correspondence and events not recorded in the proceedings or minutes. Among the most important missing correspondence is the instruction from the grand lodge of England to Price to use his position to spread freemasonry throughout the Americas. Several of the requests from Boston for new grand masters cite this as having been issued in 1734, while Price's letters sent to London over 30 years after the fact date the order to 1735. The English had lost all documents relating to Boston prior to Tomlinson's 1736 appointment, but took Boston's claim as genuine. It also confirms that the reason most of Boston's daughter lodges were not listed in the *Engraved Lists* was not due to lack of reporting of their existence, but rather due to non-payment of fees for their constitutions and that those which did appear were listed because those payments had eventually been forwarded on their behalf. This shows that London was informally aware of provincial lodges which it refused to officially list for this reason.

All of the authorizations from London, beginning with Montague's charter to Price issued in 1733, contained more or less the same stipulations, generally with the same formal wording. These included that lodges only be opened to regular masons and that their practices conformed to those laid out in the constitutions and any other orders given them from the grand lodge in England. Moreover, Price, was enjoined, "To send to us [the Grand Secretary] or Our Deputy Grand Master and to the Grand Master of England or his Deputy for the time being annually, an accot[sic] in Writing of the number of Lodges so Constituted with the Names of the several Members of each Particular Lodge, together with such other Matters & things as he or they shall think fit to Communicate for the Prosperity of the Craft." The later deputations to Robert Tomlinson in 1736, Thomas Oxnard in 1743, Jeremiah Gridley in 1755 and John Rowe in 1768 all requested that the information sent on newly constituted lodges include their time and place of meeting, as well as a payment for their constitution which was to go to the Grand Charity and "other expenses". The charters issued by Boston that still exist, to the lodges in Connecticut, Rhode Island, Pitt County North Carolina, and the military lodges of the French and Indian War, and the latest Massachusetts lodges of the 1760s and 1770s all include similar provisions in similar and in some cases identical wording. The deputation to Pitt County even asked for the place of abode of each member, data generally only included in French and French influenced Masonic *tableaux*.

The incompleteness of Grand Lodge records on both sides of the Atlantic makes it difficult to determine precisely how effective this communication was. England's polite reprimand to Price during his final grand mastership that Boston had been remiss in its communications indicates an inattention to transmission of both records and dues. Robert Tomlinson constituted the lodge in Antigua en route to England, and it is clear from his presence at grand lodge with the newly appointed PGM for South Carolina and the subsequent appointment of his initiate Governor Matthews as the provincial grand master for Antigua and the Leeward Islands that he carried news of, and documents and payments for those lodges to England and likely gave at least oral reports on his work in Boston. Whenever the Bostonians needed to confirm a new grand master they were able to carry their petition to England and receive a reply within a matter of months. The correspondence that remains from Antigua implied that with the appointment of Governor Matthews as provincial grand master the islands no longer felt obligated to report to Boston, as was the case in South Carolina. Likewise, Boston's daughter lodges remitted payments in many cases years later, and visited or corresponded irregularly and in the case of New England lodges were often represented by proxies who were members of the grand lodge, generally merchants connected to members of the subordinate lodge.

For example, Pitt County North Carolina's lodge, chartered in 1762, did remit dues payments and member lists in 1767. One of the lodge's prominent members, Col. John Simpson, appeared in Boston occasionally along with three other North Carolinians among the subscribers to William M'Alpine's Boston 1772 printing of Calcott's *Candid Disquisition*. Their January 23, 1767 letter was personally delivered by master Thomas Cooper, merchant. Doubtless his Boston connections and visits resulted in the transfer of information on the lodge not included in the few detailed letters which remain. The petition for the appointment of John Rowe as grand master, carried to England by merchant William Jackson along with a personal letter from Henry Price, included payments for four lodges, Second Lodge in Boston, New Haven in Connecticut, Providence,

Rhode Island, and Marblehead. It also provided foundation dates for all of the lodges with meeting places for Second and New Haven and meeting times for Second and Providence lodge. All of this information appeared subsequently in the *Engraved Lists*. Though previous requests for renewed grand masters' deputations included similar lists (such as the October 11, 1754 petition, drafted at the Quarterly meeting attended by Benjamin Franklin) the request for a deputation for Jeremiah Gridley included a list of 14 lodges by location and year of foundation, none of which were added to the lists.

Jonathan Hampton's July 28, 1762 letter to Jeremy Gridley requesting a charter for Temple Lodge in Elizabeth Town New Jersey is highly informative. The opening line, "I had the honor of receiving both your Letters by the Post," shows that there was earlier correspondence between the two. Gridley had apparently indicated that he was uncertain of issuing a charter due to the earlier warrant to Daniel Cox for Hampton's home colony, to which Hampton responds that he had inquired and found no information of Cox. Gridley's query seems to have included New Jersey and Maryland as potentially under Cox's authority, as Hampton wrote that he had inquired from a Brother in Philadelphia who had explained that the lodge at Annapolis had been warranted from Boston—a fact of which the grand master in Boston seems to have been unaware! The text of Hampton's response implies that there were a number of specifics involved in Gridley's questions regarding Cox's deputation. Hampton had determined that "Cox Died before 1754 the Time you mention." The New Jersey brethren therefore desired, as promised, a "Deputation" for Hampton to serve as the "first Master of the Temple Lodge in Elizabeth Town No. 1. if you think proper to give it that name." They further petitioned for Gridley to appoint a deputy grand master for New Jersey if he deemed it appropriate. That Gridley was aware of the abortive 1730 Cox deputation not only reveals a local knowledge of masonry, but also some awareness of transatlantic masonic politics.

The chain of connection and communication between the lodges is also enlightening. Hampton's closing line states that he, "is very well known by Govr. Bernard." though not a mason, Bernard would certainly have made a fine character reference. Hampton asked that they send the deputation "under Cover to Mr. John Hunt, Post Master in Elizabeth Town, and then it will be not only free of Postage but Safe: unless our Parson (Chandler) should be in Boston, which I expect he is." Thus, there were multiple connections already between the Boston and Elizabeth masons. Post Master Hunt's membership and willingness to waive the postage speaks to the privileged nature of the craft in New Jersey. Hampton also assured Gridley that he would pay any required charges, "by the Post with the thanks of the Lodge."

Another interesting indication of the level of informal communication between lodges appeared in the June 21, 1759 subscription for the masons in Newport Rhode Island to hold a lottery to fund the construction of a Masons Hall. The connection of the Newport masons to the upper echelons of local society is evident not only in the attached lists of masons in Newport and Providence but in the intended use of the hall, for public and governmental functions. the petition opens by stating, "That the Town of Newport having no Building sufficiently Large and Commodious, for Publick Entertainments, where at any time the Governor or General Assembly, might at the Elections, or Other Occasions Assemble and Dine, & where any of his Majesty's Governors or Other Officers, Civil or Military, may Occassionally be publickly Entertained.." the mason intended to build their Mason's Hall to be suitably large to accommodate the above purposes, as well as for the use of the lodge. As a further inducement to the local authorities, the petition stated that "[t]hey can assure this Honble[sic] Assembly they have it in their power to Dispose of the Chief of the Tickets among the Fraternity in other Governments." Their request was granted, on which they sent a copy of the petition and the act of the Newport assembly approving it to Grand Master Jeremiah Gridley in Boston. They stated quite candidly in their letter that, "A Chief motive with the General Assembly for granting so great a favr to the Masons, was the Assurance we gave them, that the chief of the Tickets would be disposed of by and among our Fraternity in the neighboring Colonies." Rhode Island masons benefited from their dependence on and close connections with the dominant Boston establishment.[5]

When On October 26, 1767, Henry Price reclaimed his position for the third time following the death of Jeremiah Gridley, a matter which the grand lodge publicized in all of the Boston papers for the information of "all the Fraternity in North American and the West Indies, under this Jurisdiction", he began a correspondence with London and with his subordinate lodges which is highly informative regarding the nature of masonic information transfer. Among his first acts was to send a letter to the lodge in Pitt County, North Carolina. Though chartered by Gridley in 1762, or "Before Dec. 10, 1764," the lodge is first listed in Massachusetts quarterly minutes in January, 1767. Thomas Cooper had delivered a list of members and officers, dated June 24, 1767, which stated that, "For any further Particulars, we shall refer you to the Worshipful Mr. Thomas Cooper, Master, who will Personally deliver this". On December 30 of that year, Price sent the lodge a letter nominating Cooper provincial grand master. Referring to

Cooper by his profession, merchant, Price states that since obtaining the warrant from his predecessor, Cooper, "did... represent to our said Predecessor, that by reason of the great Distance of some of the Brethren's abode, from the Place of their usual Assembling in Pitt county Aforesaid, their Attendance on Lodges was very inconvenient and troublesome to those Members. . ."

In order to remedy this, Price officially deputed Cooper as provincial grand master, thereby allowing him to constitute lodges wherever they were convenient to the brethren. The wording is quite similar, in many places taken directly from, those he had received from England, stipulating all of the same important points including adherence to the printed constitutions, establishing a charity fund, et al. He also ordered annual lists of lodges and members be transmitted, and that for each new lodge the provincial grand lodge remit to Boston three and a half guineas, "two of which is for Registering them in London, and the rest for the general Fund of Charity." Thus, freemasons sought uniformity in organizational practice from grand lodge to provincial grand lodge to provincial grand lodges thereof.[6]

Most interesting is Price's correspondence with England at the time. His first letter, dated January 27, 1768, was sent along with the petition of the grand lodge for the grand mastership to ascend to deputy grand master John Rowe, another wealthy and politically prominent merchant, payments for the four lodges mentioned above, a copy of Price's original deputation, and a letter of introduction for William Jackson, the merchant who carried the communications. The letter of introduction included Jackson's masonic curriculum vitae as a former junior and senior warden. This last letter, signed by all of the grand officers, explained that Jackson would deliver orally, "a particular Account of the Propagation of Masonry in America." They trusted that the Grand Lodge would be convinced "by his Masonal Abilities, that we have a due esteem for the Honourable Craft." For merchant Jackson, such a letter addressed to "all our Rt Worshipful Brethren in England" and meant both as an introduction to the Grand Lodge and as a general masonic passport, served as an excellent tool in gaining entry to many lodges of merchants and sea captains and introductions to well-placed men of commerce in the metropolis.

In his letter to the grand lodge, Price opens by explaining that the money for the four lodges "would have been paid long before, but some unforeseen Accidents prevented, therefore I hope the said Lodges will not be denied their Rank among the Lodges, according to the Time of their Constitution, notwithstanding the above Omission." Price also informed the English that "Several other Lodges have been Constituted by the Grand Lodge here, in different parts of America, who have not yet Transmitted to us the Stated Fees for their Constitution, but as soon as it comes to hand, it shall be remitted to You, hopeing[sic] at the same Time that they will likewise be Registered among other Regular Constituted Lodges". Though Philadelphia had finally paid Boston for its charter some 20 years after it Price issued it, they never appeared in English records—it seems their payment never crossed the ocean!

On matters of masonic legality and record keeping, Price's letter explained that he had been appointed provincial grand master of New England in 1733 by Lord Anthony Brown, Viscount Montacute, and that "in the Year 1735, said Commission to me was extended over all North America" by Grand Master Lord Cranstoun. "But upon enquiry, I find that said Deputations were never Registered, though I my self paid three Guineas therefor, to Thomas BatsomnEsqr. then Deputy Grand Master, who with the Grand Wardens then in being, signed my Deputation." Whether the 'enquiry' that led Price to this unhappy discovery refers to a lost piece of correspondence or verbally information, it speaks to both the importance of masonic bureaucracy to provincial masons and the level of unrecorded communication ongoing. The stipulation that he had paid the three guinea fee also confirms that it was receipt of outstanding payments that made such deputations official.

The rest of the letter says enough about the seriousness with which the legalities of the republic of masonry were endowed by its members that it bears quoting in full:

> This deputation was the first that the Grand Lodge ever issued to any Part of America, and stands so now in all Lodges on the Continent, Other. Deputations have since been given to different Provinces, but they cannot according to Rule take Rank of mine. So, would submitt it to your Wisdom and Justice, whether said Deputations should not be Registered in their proper Place, without any further Consideration therefore, and the Grand Lodge here have Rank according to Date, as it has (by Virtue of said Deputations) been the foundation of Masonry in America, and, I the Founder. Wherefore Rt Worshipful Brethren, I beg that enquiry may be made into the Premises, and that Things may be set right...

Following his signature was a post script explaining that he had included "An Attested Copy of my said Deputation as Registered in the Grand Lodge Book of this Place, under the Hand of our Grand Secretary, whose signature you may depend upon as Genuine." Price's entreaties were apparently quite effective, as he was from then on included in the *Engraved List of Lodges* and subsequently from

1778 *Freemasons' Calendar* as provincial grand master for North America until 1805, 22 years following his death.

Jackson returned to Boston on September 30, 1768 with Rowe's deputation. This led to a flurry of letters back and forth from all of the New England lodges, most of which—except for Salem, which simply confirmed that it no longer existed as a lodge—sent delegates to attend Rowe's installation. However, the illness of English grand secretary Samuel Spenser and his subsequent replacement by Thomas French led to confusion as to whether Price's January 27th letter had been answered, so that French sent Price a second communication on November 29th. This letter and Price's reply of June 3rd, 1769 shed some interesting light on the state of masonry in the two cities, though Price's desire to communicate certain matters in person in a planned trip to London leaves some questions unanswered. French confirmed that the payments of the four lodges had been received and the lodges registered, and requested that in future Price sent an account of each newly constituted lodge immediate, "otherwise it is not to be expected they can rank in their order of precedency." Also, the lax record keeping of the grand lodge had led to Price's commission having been forgotten, with Tomlinson's 1736 deputation being the first on record "for any part of America." As any good bureaucrat might be expected to do, French politely blamed Price, chastising him for the fact that "[t]hese mistakes might have been long since rectified, if you had kept up, according to your Charter a regular annual Correspondence with the Grand Lodge."

French's next line betrayed the disorganized state of England's records, however, by stating that according to "some loose papers" in his possession Price had resigned in favor of John Rowe. As the loose papers would almost certainly have been the recent letter carried by Jackson in response to which Rowe had received his deputation, it appears that the transition in Grand Secretaries and Spenser's incapacitation had compromised the Grand Lodge's books. The status of the grand mastership was a point on which the grand master, Henry Somerset, Duke of Beaufort himself had instructed French to obtain clarification, including the date of Rowe's warrant, which they had sent only months before! They also clarified somewhat diplomatically that no deputation since granted could infringe Price's authority since they would apply only to "provinces where no other Provincial Grand Master is appointed," which did not actually confirm Price's authority over such later deputations. Price's reply to the question of Rowe's authority was highly interesting, and goes some way in explaining the number of deputations issued by him which don't appear in the proceedings of the provincial grand lodge. Price explained that "it would be tedious to explain the Matter of my resigning as Provincial Grand Master" of New England, for which position he had recommended Rowe as his successor, but that, "you cannot find that I ever gave up my own Appointment over all North America."

Unfortunately, rather than explaining this in writing, Price promised that, "this by the Blessings of God I shall explain to you and all our Right Worshipful Brothers face to face in London, sometime in the Fall, as my Business will then call me home." Simply the fact that the letters of French and his successor James Heseltine were addressed and delivered to Price rather than Rowe and/or the grand lodge or First Lodge indicates that the grand secretaries either considered Price's authority intact or lacked a more convenient contact, or both. The state of the grand mastership was one of "diverse things of consequence to advise of relative thereto, which cannot be communicated by the pen as well as in person." Upon meeting face to face, Price proposed that they "may settle the Provincial Grand Masters and Rank the Lodges in order." Though it is unfortunate that Price did not explain his reasoning or detail these other matters in writing, his explanation makes clear that he had not simply retired from Freemasonry and that he considered his authority over the continent intact 33 years after first giving up his authority over New England. Again, there would appear to be inconsistencies, not least in the requests for the Grand Mastership of New England under Tomlinson, Oxnard and Gridley having been extended at the Bostonian's insistence to include North America, however, the laxity of record keeping and the vagueness inherent in applying the legalities of the 1723 *Constitutions* in practice across the ocean made Price's assertions easier to maintain.[7]

The series of epistles Price exchanged with the grand secretaries conveyed international news. French expressed the pleasure of the grand lodge at learning of the "success of Masonry in America under your patronage" to Price and informed him "In the present eras the Society flourishes all over the world". Their royal highnesses the Dukes of Gloucester and Cumberland had joined the fraternity and "the first Noblemen in Europe, vouchsafe to patronize our mysteries." French also reported an increase in the charity funds of the grand lodge along with the hope that such knowledge would "induce every Lodge in America liberally to contribute towards the support of this excellent Charity." To bolster this assertion, French included the particulars of the account from grand lodge's last quarterly session. This, along with the "money collected by the new Regulations"—probably a reference to the registration system for provincial grand masters created in 1768—as well as listings of the membership of all lodges and their time and place of meeting "that the General List of Lodges may be corrected." The regulations were enclosed in the letter, though the enclosure has not survived. This attempt to more tightly regulate, document and collect revenue from its overseas holdings mirrored England's attitude towards the colonies more generally at the time, and was likely also a response to the pressure placed on the Moderns by the Ancients, who were now expanding across and beyond the Atlantic.

Another important piece of masonic news, first conveyed by French and then again by Heseltine, who enlisted Price's assistance in its disbursement, was the Grand Master's resolution to "revive the ancient splendor of the Order by having it incorporated" under a royal charter. Heseltine sent Price a printed copy of the proceedings relating to the incorporation, having already read in Price's reply to French that the provincial grand lodge had approved the regulations sent by French and that Price intended to forward them "to the other Provincial Grand Lodges on this Continent". Heseltine thus requested that price forward the printed proceedings on incorporation to "the same Lodges in America, except those in Canada, North and South Carolina" to whom the grand secretary had sent the proceedings already. The January 29, 1770 response from Boston informed that Price had "Communicated it to Our Brothers in as Many Distant Lodges as I can According to the Season of the year Whare wee are Burried up with Snow." He did not specify, which lodges he was able to reach.

The Incorporation proceedings themselves are evidence of both the belief placed by the grand master in the medieval history in Masonic literature and of the internationalism of the society. It opened by explaining that Grand Master Beaufort having "determined that the Lodges under the *English* constitution in distant parts, should not only enjoy the common patronage and protection of the Grand Lodge, (as heretofore,) but also be informed of every important transaction therein, has directed the following proceedings to be laid before you." It then explained to the far-flung lodges in "distant parts" that on acceding to office and consulting the annals of the order, the Duke of Beaufort "found, that the fraternity had in former periods, acted under the Sanction of *Royal Charters*; as in the reign of King *Athelstan,* and so lately as that of *Henry* the VIth." Rather than assuming this to have been the last royal charter, he pointed out that the later records had been lost. Beaufort wished to renew the honor of a royal charter of incorporation, as well as raising funds to construct a grand hall for the grand lodge in London. A faction within the Craft had raised opposition to this, and had apparently appealed to the lodges abroad with its dissent.

The grand master hoped, of course, for the support of the lodges around the world for the incorporation and their disdain for any entreaties of the opposing faction. Price's reply, sent via Captain Hood by way of Bristol, informed that after considerable debate the lodge on the 26th had voted in favor of the charter and asked to forward "a copie of the Intended or Compleated Charter to Me as soon as May bie." Price also informed that, "After that, if God Bless Me I intend for London-there I will give the Grand Lodge a true State of Masonry in America." Hesletine, responding to the early letter expressed pleasure on February 15, 1770 that Price approved the incorporation and gave a brief update on its progress.[8]

The plan of incorporation ultimately failed, though Mason's Hall in London was completed in 1776 and stands there to the present day. However, it demonstrates that England saw fit from 1768 on to attempt to regularize communications with its foreign lodges, and that in so doing it enlisted Price's aid in forwarding important communications throughout the New World. Taken with the various requests for new grand masters dispensations, it is clear that while communication was not consistently governed by a standardized institutional structure within the Grand Lodge beyond the initiative of the grand secretary and the provincial brethren, nonetheless the intercontinental masonic republic was able to engage in significant communication sufficient to maintain, regulate, and expand its domains throughout the Atlantic world. The remaining correspondence is fragmentary, but complete enough to paint a picture of connections across seaways, trade networks, and personal, direct connections in the travels of important and zealous masons such as Price and Jackson, so that information too sensitive or tedious to share in an epistle was often relayed orally from one province to another.

Grand Master John Rowe served as a selectman and the moderator of Boston's Town Meeting. According to governor Hutchinson he, along with brother William Molyneux and Solomon Davis, were leaders of popular resistance to the Stamp Act. A moderate Whig, Rowe like many of his brethren participated the early resistance. As we shall see in a later chapter, the divide between moderate and radical Patriots widened in 1768, a year in which the once masonically estranged yet politically active brethren of St. Andrew's voted Rowe an honorary member while he made a donation to their charity fund. That both lodges had participated in Grand Master Gridley's well-attended funeral had also lessened the distance between them. Later that year Rowe was publicly branded an 'incendiary' by other moderates elites, shortly after which he stepped back from politics. Though some Modern masons such as Richard Gridley, who was to command the artillery at Bunker Hill 30 years to the day he first tasted victory at Louisburg, remained ardent in the fight, others such as Samuel Quincy turned loyalist whilst many, like Rowe, retreated from political activity, preferring a seat on the fence.

The changing social order and the vicissitudes of war largely doomed the heretofore thriving Moderns, Brother George Washington's visits to the lodge in 1776 and 1789 notwithstanding. Prominent Tories among the brethren, such as Captain Hallowell and Samuel Quincy, found it necessary to retreat with the British. First Lodge's records absconded with their Tory secretary to Canada, being recovered after the war. More commonly, the brethren suffered through their neutrality, forfeiting their and by extension their lodges' position in the newly independent society. John Rowe's own experience at the April 6, 1776 funeral of his Ancient counterpart, fallen hero Grand Master and General Joseph Warren, best exemplifies the change:

> I went by invitation of Brother Webb to attend the Funerall of the Remains of Dr Warren & went accordingly to the Council chamber with a Design to Attend & Walk in Procession with the Lodges under my Jurisdiction with our Proper Jewels & Cloathing – but to my great Mortification was very much Insulted -by some furios & hot Persons – witho the Least Provocation. One of [the] Brethren thought it most Prudent for Me to Retire. I accordingly did so. This has caused Some Uneasy Reflection in my Mind as I am not Conscious to myself of doing any thing Prejudicial to the Cause of America either by Will, word or deed.[9]

Though Patriot and Brother Richard Gridley helped bear Warren's casket, most of the service was performed by members of the new elite and of the newer, more egalitarian and more Radical Ancient Massachusetts Grand Lodge. By 1792, the two Grand Lodges in the city merged, largely on the Ancients' terms. John Cutler, final Grand Master of St. John's Grand Lodge, was well liked by Massachusetts Grand Lodge's ascendant brethren. They structured the merger so that the older St. John's Grand Lodges' standing as third eldest in the world might be maintained under overwhelmingly Ancient authority. Before turning to the Lodge of Saint Andrew and the Revolutionary period, the next chapter will describe the extensive presence of freemasonry in the colonial press, where it not only impressed itself deeply on the colonial consciousness but spread information on American lodges, masons and on goings on in the global Republic of Masonry.

Notes

1 *Ibid.*, 397–8.
2 *Ibid.*, 402–3.
3 *Ibid.*, 403–5.

4 Ibid., 405–6.
5 *Proceedings,* 466–7.
6 *Ibid.,* 128–30, 483.
7 *Ibid.,* 407–9.
8 *Ibid.,* 7–11.
9 Diary of John Rowe, April 6, 1776, reprinted in *Proceedings in Masonry,* 431; Sheppard, *Freemasonry in North America,* 37.

8

Making Headlines: The Craft in the Colonial Press

On Thursday Evening last at 11 o'clock, departed this Life, the Right Worshipful Jeremy Gridley Esqr. Grand Master of Masons, over all North America, Attorney General for the Province of Massachusetts Bay, A Member of the Great and General Court of said Province, and a Justice throughout the same, Colonel of the first Regiment of Militia, and President of the Marine Society, &c.

His funeral was Attended on Saturday last, with the Respect due to his memory, by the members of his Majesty's Council, and the Judges of the Superior Court in Town, the Gentlemen of the Bar, the Brethren of the Ancient and Honourable Society of free and Accepted Masons, the Officers of his Regiment, the Members of the Marine Society and a great Number of the Gentlemen of the Town.[1]

How Brothers John Hancock and James Otis, members of both Modern and Ancient lodges in town, felt on reading the sad news in the *Boston Post Boy* of September 14, 1767, one can only guess. It carried the obituary of the crown appointed attorney general who had defeated them in the 1761 Writs of Assistance case, costing Hancock a pretty penny yet giving Otis the stage on which he laid out the legal and moral foundations of the case for American Independence. For the rest of the brethren, the loss of the grand master struck a heavy blow. His obituary appeared in the *Newport Mercury* a week later and in the *Connecticut Courant* exactly one week after that. That his role as grand master over all of

North America receives priority over his roles in government, the militia and the marine society speaks to the importance of freemasonry in the colonial social order. Despite their differences, the Ancient brethren of the Lodge of St. Andrew had joined the Moderns of St. John's Grand Lodge in Worshipful Gridley's funeral procession.

Gridley marked the third Grand Master whose death the Boston press had reported. The *Boston Gazette* had conveyed news of Robert Tomlinson's passing in Antigua on August 21, 1740. Fourteen years later, it carried a report on the funeral of, "The Right Worshipful Thomas Oxnard, Grand Master of the Ancient and Honourable Society of Free and Accepted Masons in North America... an experienced merchant, an upright dealer". As with the later funeral of Jeremy Gridley, the masonic procession received a detailed description meant to impress all readers with the solemnity of the occasion.[2]

Following the loss of Grand Master Gridley, however, the Grand Lodge's meeting record minutes of the proceedings of St. John's Grand Lodge of Boston for October 26th, 1767 present the clearest case of colonial masons intentionally communicating across vast distances via the local press. Colonial newspapers frequently reprinted each other's stories as they circulated around the colonies and across the seas, and the brethren clearly expected the Boston papers to make their way to the Caribbean in good time. The minutes record that:

> The following Notification was Published in all the Public News Papers in this Town.

> The Grand Lodge or Quarterly Communication of Free and Accepted Masons, assembled at Boston on Friday the 23d Instt. having taken into consideration their loss in the Death of the late Jeremiah Gridley, Esqr the last Grand Master; Resolved to invite the Right Worshipful HENRY PRICE, Esqr past Grand Master of that Ancient and honourable Society, to Re-assume the Office again, as it Constitutionally reverted to him : He having consented thereto, was with the usual Ceremonies invested, and placed at the Head of Masonry, till another Grand Master is Elected here, and Constituted by the Grand Master of England. Whereof all the Fraternity in North America and the West Indies, under this Jurisdiction, are to take due notice.

> By Order of the Grand Lodge A. Savage Gr. Sec[3]

They specifically intended their published public notice to reach the fraternity in "North America and the West Indies." The death of Gridley and subsequent re-installation of Henry Price was the clearest case in which the minutes expressly state that the press was being used to inform the brethren throughout all of the continent and the West Indies. Clearly, the lodge members assumed that published notices of feasts of St. John, installations of officers and other masonic news would reach the eyes of brethren at the balmy southern extremes of the provincial grand masters' far flung jurisdiction. The minutes further demonstrate the fraternity's consciousness of the need for trans-oceanic spin control.

At a quarterly meeting of January 11, 1751, the lodge came to the following unhappy resolution, "Voted. That Letters be sent to the Several Lodges abroad under our Rt. W: G.M. acquainting them of the scandilous (sic) piece of Ribaldry in T. Fleets paper, and Instructing them by all means to discourage sd paper &c., and it was desir'd of Bro Gridley to form sd Letters which he propos'd so to do." Thomas Fleet was the printer of the *Boston Evening Post*. The *Post* routinely carried notices of masonic feasts, parades, and installations and was generally pro-masonic. On February 5, 1750, Fleet advertised his sale of the *Constitutions of the Freemasons*. A month earlier, on January 1st, the *Post* carried a laudatory account of Brockwell's sermon before the brethren and the procession to an elegant dinner which followed, "at which were several gentlemen of Note, besides the Fraternity." On January 15, Fleet published an advertisement for the sale of said sermon printed by J. Draper; within half a decade, the same sermon was frequently featured in British masonic publications, notably various editions of the *Freemasons Pocket Companion*.

Despite an ongoing cordial relationship with the lodge, however, Mr. Fleet had indeed published a derisive poem, "To Mr. Clio at North-Hampton, In Defence of Masonry. [in verse]" signed simply " a M-s-n". This poem mocked the grandiose poems and accounts of the feast of St. John published by masons on such occasions. That the brethren expected the lodges "abroad" to receive it, and that they might send letters to warn of it in advance, indicates that they took the matter seriously and considered maintaining their image in the press and among the lodges "abroad" under their jurisdiction to be a matter of considerable importance. Whatever came of the immediate event, the *Boston Evening Post* continued to carry masonic advertisements and pro-Masonic pieces. A few years after publishing the "scandilous piece of ribaldry" that had so incensed the grand lodge, Thomas Fleet Jr. succeeded his father as the publisher of the *Post*. The younger Fleet appears as a brother mason in 2nd Lodge from the beginning of the surviving records in 1760. He was one of many printers who were also masons. Colonial masons continued the English masonic practice of initiating printers and putting their presses to good work in sustained publicity efforts.[4]

Front Page News across the Thirteen Colonies

Almost from the beginning of the grand lodge era of freemasonry in 1717 the fraternity actively and aggressively made use of the press to promote their "Ancient and Honorable" society. Prior to 1720, there were very few references to freemasonry in the British papers; from that year until 1735 the freemasons were featured in the British papers nearly 1000 times. The fraternity in England recruited a number of printers and writers. The aristocratic leadership recruited to front the brotherhood initiated a wave of positive celebrity news coverage, with only a few minor negative stories, mainly in the Tory press. This use of the public print culture to promote the newly upgraded ancient society was so effective that, as Berman puts it, "Principally as a function of the far-reaching newspaper coverage generated by its aristocratic leadership, freemasonry's public profile altered fundamentally from the early 1720s." Celebritiy noblemen were as important to selling newspapers in the 1720s as pop culture icons and politicians are today. Berman Continues, "The press became a catalyst for change and the publicity created aspirant interest across London and the provinces, producing the foundations of what became virtually a mass movement among the gentry and the professional classes."[5]

Masonic items from Britain and Europe made it into the colonial press as American printers regularly reprinted stories from the metropolis. The frequent descriptions of processions and observance of masonic feast days, installations of officers, celebrity initiations, and the like in the English press set an example for colonial masons. In the colonies, however, notices of the foundation of lodges, advertisements of lodge meetings and publication of the officers and grand officers serving in a given community served the further purpose of promoting the lodges to traveling masons and connecting masons and would-be masons throughout the Americas. The various reports of new lodges, installations of officers, feasts, and regular lodge meetings from throughout the continent carried in papers which circulate around the colonies and back to the metropolis filled in information on the masonic map missing in metropolitan lists of colonial lodges and provided up to date contacts for masons in the Atlantic world.

A search of the database America's Historical Newspapers from 1717 when Grand Lodge masonry began until the outbreak of the war of independence in 1775, returns 511 distinct items. Of these, 120 are classified as "shipping news", 214 as "advertisements", 155 "news /opinion", 4 letters, 19 pieces of poetry, and 11 as legislative acts (some articles have multiple classifications). Of these 511 pieces, 86 made the front page. This count does not include at least seven articles from the *Pennsylvania Gazette* from before the digitized records begin, or at least five articles from the *Maryland Gazette*, which does not appear in the collection. No digital results are available for New Jersey, Delaware, North or South Carolina, or Maryland, but freemasonry existed in all of these colonies and the *South Carolina Gazette* and *Maryland Gazette* both featured articles on freemasonry in their pages. In the *South Carolina Gazette*, also know as *Timothy's Gazette*, Berman counts at least 14 distinct articles or advertisements; at least one, the notice of the upcoming Feast of St. John, was printed in every paper for a fortnight, doubling the count from this source. All told, freemasonry appeared in the colonial press at least 552 times prior to the American Revolution. This count also does not include Caribbean or Canadian papers, regions in which freemasonry was active from the mid-1700s on.[6]

Broken down by colony, this partial distribution of masonic news stories in this 58 year period is as follows: 139 in Massachusetts, in New Hampshire 14, 34 from Rhode Island, 18 in Connecticut, 204 from New York, where at least nine lodges were active before the arrival of British troops in 1776; in Pennsylvania a digital search returns 84 results, with at least seven more as described above, making a total of 91; in Georgia, where digitized records begin in 1763 but which boasted a masonic lodge since its inception in 1739, the craft was mentioned at least 18 times. Though New York returns more search results overall, this is largely due to advertisements and shipping news. The most sustained and aggressive masonic self promotion was centered in Boston.

Viewed by decade, the results are as follows. In the 13 years from the beginning of Grand Lodge freemasonry until 1730, there were at least five mentions of free masons or freemasonry, all in the Boston press. This consisted of the arrival or departure of ships called *Freemason* and news on masonic happenings reprinted from the London papers. The latter may have happened as a matter of course, but the fact that it seemed noteworthy to Boston printers, and to none elsewhere in the colonies, adds circumstantial support to the existence of a lodge at King's Chapel in the 1720s. In the following decade, masonic items appear in 46 articles, including those from the *South Carolina* and *Pennsylvania Gazettes* not digitized in America's Historic Newspapers.

The 1740s saw a decline in Masonic reportage, with only 28 stories reported. This is most likely due to the retreat from the public eye of English freemasonry in the wake of the public satire of the Scald Miserable Masons—who were reported in the Boston, New York and Philadelphia presses—and the generally stagnant state of the grand lodge in England during this time. The Grand Lodge passed a motion following the mockery of the Scald Miserables barring the proceedings of any lodge from being published in the press from June 1741 on. Though this did not hold up past the end of the decade and was never completely adhered to, it resulted in a considerable drop in the number of masonic news items coming out of London. Berman theorizes, logically, that in South Carolina the close connections between England and Solomon's Lodge in Charleston, South Carolina, explains *Timothy Gazette*'s silence on matters masonic in the 1740s after at least five Masonic articles in 1736–9 and with a resumption of Masonic content in the 1750s.[7]

Moreover, Masonry had received somewhat of a black eye in the colonies due to the death of Evan Rhees, a naive young Philadelphian whose master, not a mason but a prominent doctor, and several friends had proposed to make him a mason. In June 1737, after taking a blasphemous oath, learning fake signs, and kissing one of the false mason's posteriors, Rhees was invited to an initiation ceremony which involved grabbing raisins out of a pan of burning liquor. Dr. Jones either accidentally or intentionally spilled the fiery fluid on his apprentice, who died three days later from the resulting burns. Andrew Bradford, rival of Benjamin Franklin and the first to re-print anti-masonic content from England in a colonial paper, seized the opportunity to attack the fraternity. His father William Bradford was engaged in a professional and political feud with rival printer Peter Zenger and the Country Party, members of which made up New York's masonic lodge. Luckily for the Bradfords, a group of Black burglars who may have undergone a similar faux masonic initiation were making headlines in New York. Several of these same Black thieves were later accused of being involved in the 1741 slave conspiracy. The Bradfords shared their anti-masonic ammunition in what amounted to a coordinated campaign. Franklin and the masons of Pennsylvania put out several pieces in their defense, but promoted themselves much less aggressively in the coming years.[8]

Following the press ban of the Grand Lodge of England, the 1740s masonic content focused mainly on reports of prosecutions abroad, particularly those in Vienna and in Lisbon where John Costous and his brethren faced the persecution which led to Coustos' bestselling book a few years later. Both of these events received reportage in the *Boston Evening Post, Boston Weekly Newsletter, New York Weekly Journal* and the *Pennsylvania American Weekly Mercury*. In each case stories reached Boston first before hitting the press further south either from Britain or from Boston. The persecutions in Holland, France, Florence and Poland and the papal bull against the order had already received several stories in the 1730s and persecution of masons from that time became a staple of metropolitan and colonial Masonic news coverage. Only Boston masons actively promoted themselves, their committee sent to wait on Governor Shirley receiving coverage in the *Boston Gazette* or *Weekly Journal* and being reprinted in the *New York Weekly Journal.*[9]

From 1750 freemasonry featured more prominently in the news again, with 135 stories, advertisements, or other items involving free masons. In 1761–1770 this increased dramatically with 222 masonic items, 93 more appearing from 1771 through 1775 when war altered the face of the Atlantic. This dramatic increase in the final decade and a half of the colonial period may be due in part to the growth of the colonial press, but it was also due to the growth in both American and Atlantic freemasonry. By this time lodges operated in every colony and in most, possibly all, of the islands of the West Indies as well as having permeated Europe and penetrated Asia and Africa. In addition to reprinting standard Masonic items from Europe—aristocratic celebrity initiations, accounts of grand, elaborate masonic processions and stories of persecution by the despots of European church and state—the colonial papers included local items which echoed those from the metropolis. These included reports of Masonic feasts and processions in North America and the West Indies, visits to the theater by lodges, and acts of charity by the local masons. They also included information on the formation of new colonial lodges, appointments of provincial grand masters, advertisements for masonic products and printed works, and stories on the grandiose and important nature of colonial masonry with its links to governors and other elites of the colonial world.

As in Europe, many prominent colonial printers were freemasons. In Boston, Brother J. Draper, printer of the *Weekly Rehearsal*, was the earliest member First Lodge in the newspaper business from the 1730s. Thomas Fleet Jr. succeeded his father as the publisher of the *Boston Evening Post*. The younger Fleet appears as a brother mason in the records of 2nd Lodge from the beginning of the surviving records in 1760. In Boston, Jonathan Edes later joined St. Andrew's lodge and Isaiah Thomas served as Grand Master in 1803–5 and again in 1809. By the time of the American Revolution, all three patriot printers in Connecticut were masons. Benjamin Franklin was the most famous masonic printer in America and often employed other masons in his printing network. Peter Zenger was either a lodge member or closely associated with the masons in New York from the opening of the first lodge there; in South Carolina Peter Timothy, publisher of the *South Carolina Gazette*, was a mason and his father may have been a lodge member briefly before his death in 1738, as the paper had a decidedly pro-masonic stance, reporting on the lodges first meeting on October 28, 1736 and frequently thereafter.

The connection between freemasonry and seaborne commerce led to a number of ships being named *Free Mason*, itself a means of promoting the Craft and advertising the Masonic affiliation of a newly arrived vessel's owner. The first mention of freemasonry in the colonial press was the January 5, 1719 departure of Jacob William and the ship *Charles and Free Mason* for Jamaica in the *Boston Weekly News-Letter*. On July 31, 1721, the *Boston Gazette* reported the arrival of John Peddie's Ship *Free-Mason* from Newcastle. Late the same year on September 21 the *Boston Weekly News-Letter* again featured John Peddie, now on the *Charles & Freemason*. Not mentioned in the report was that the owner of the *Charles & Freemason* was John Montagu, the craft's first noble grand master, whose ship en route from England to Boston to Jamaica carried the first whispers of freemasonry to two future American Masonic hubs. In later years, there were five postings for sales of ships called *Freemason*, or rather, four ships and the hull of a fifth, the latter for sale by mason and future grand master John Rowe. Two sloops, a brig and a schooner *Freemason* were also sold in Rhode Island and Marblehead, Massachusetts.

News of celebrity memberships and initiations made its way to the colonies no later than May 25, 1727 when the *Boston Weekly News Letter* carried a London item from March detailing a masonic meeting at Mercer's Hall in Cheapside, "where there was a great Appearance of the Nobility and Gentry; 3 Dukes, 3 Earls, 4 Barons, 4 Baronetts, and several other Gentlemen of distinction. The entertainment was noble and regular, and the Lord Inchequin was chosen Grand Master for the ensuing Year." The charity of the organization was often featured along with its nobility, as in the next piece of Masonic celebrity news published in the *Boston Gazette* on June 15, 1730 on the recent Quarterly communication "where were present the most Noble his Grace the Duke of Norfolk, Grand Master, with his general officers, the most noble his Grace the Duke of Richmond, the Rt. Hon. The Earl of Inchiquin, the Lord Kingston, the Lord Colerain, and many other Persons of Worth and Quality," and "several large sums" were raised for charitable dispersement to distressed brethren. The following month, on July 27, the *New England Weekly Journal* reported on a meeting at the Horn Tavern Lodge which included the familiar British noble attendees and where four "Foreign Noblemen…were admitted members." All French, these included most notably the *philosophe* Montesquieu.

Masonic celebrity and charity also combined in a report from *Boston's Weekly Rehearsal* of July 24, 1732 which included two masonic items dated April 26 and 28 in London and Hampstead, and reported the attendance of Montague, Desaguliers, and other persons of distinction, the initiation of a blind gentleman and charitable aid for a "Brother in Distress". They also publicized their own celebrity initiates, promoting one of Governor Belcher's lodge appearances in 1734. In 1752, they unveiled to the world their own piece of aristocratic celebrity news when at the June Feast of St. John, "The Right Honourable the Lord COLVILL took the chair as Deputy-Grand-Master of North America. . ." While Colvill was in Boston the Brethren made much of this famous brother just as they had Governor Andrew Belcher.[10]

By 1730 reports of Masonic celebrities and philanthropy had spread beyond Boston. The news of young Montesquieu's initiation into the most prestigious lodge in London was reprinted in Franklin's *Pennsylvania Gazette* on August 13, 1730. A month earlier on July 9, the *Gazette* had reported on the grand lodge of England. Forty-eight years later Franklin initiated another philosophe, Voltaire, into the *Loge des Neuf Souers*. It is only from his *Pennsylvania Gazette* that we learn on December 8, 1730 that there were at that time, "Several Lodges of Free Masons erected in this Province." On February 9, 1732 the *Maryland Gazette* reported on a meeting in Cheapside at which, ". . .in the presence of several Brethren of Distinction, as well Jews and Christians, Mr. Edward Rose, was admitted of the Fraternity, by Mr. Daniel Delvalle, an eminent Jew. . .".

Articles highlighting masonic charity appeared frequently. On the sixth of April the following year, the same paper carried an item dated [London. December 16.] on a "Grand Committee of Free and Accepted *Masons*" who met to raise money "for the *Relief* of their poor *Brethren*, throughout Britain and Ireland." The grand lodge's efforts to raise money for the Trustees of Georgia "to enable them to send over several poor families" to the new colony and thereby contributing to colonization and Empire building, made it into the Boston papers. Colonial lodges made sure to promote their own charity as well, and these reports from England were echoed in stories such as that of the *Connecticut Courant* of April 1, 1765 which reported on premiums to be paid on various articles raised in the county of New Haven by "A lodge of FREE MASONS held at the fountain Tavern in New Haven. . .taking into consideration the unhappy circumstances of the Colony." This was a particularly ambitious piece of Masonic charity for a colonial lodge, as it was actually designed as an economic stimulus for the whole colony and a defiant response to the Stamp Act.[11]

Reports of Masonic happenings in the early stage of Masonic expansion were not limited to England. The *Boston Weekly Rehearsal* reported on the installation of officers of the Grand Lodge of Ireland on September 27, 1731 and October 30, 1732. Both of these installations, as with their English counterparts, included noble grand masters and notable gentlemen. The *Pennsylvania Gazette* on May

13, 1731 included both information on masons and the notice of a meeting in Dublin. That such meeting notices were being reprinted on both sides of the Atlantic served to advertise the lodge internationally. Franklin seems to have had his eyes out for such notices: on July 22, he published an account of a meeting in London and on May 11, 1732 a masonic notice from Dublin. English masonic news was not confined to London; in 1754 the *New York Mercury* reported on the formation of a new lodge of freemasons in Bristol, England.[12]

European Masonic events also appeared in the colonial press. There were stories on the persecution of masons in Holland and the Catholic world as well as positive stories of the cosmopolitan reach of the Craft. For example, in October of 1737 the *Boston Evening Post* relayed from London, "We hear that a deputation from the Society of Free and Accepted Masons of this Kingdom is to be sent to Germany, to congratulate (a Royal brother) the Duke of Lorrain [sic] on his Accession to the Duchy of Tuscany." A few months before the first reports of repression in France in July 1737, the *Boston Gazette* reprinted a British piece proclaiming that "the order of Free-Masons, established long since in England, has become lately much in vogue at PARIS, there being great striving to be admitted. . ." The short article speaks of five lodges and "persons of great distinction" including the Marshal d'Estrées having joined them.[13]

Local printers noted the Craft's penetration into the Muslim world. Thomas Fleet's *Boston Evening Post* of September 18, 1738 reprinted an article on masonry in Florence, Leghorn, and "smyrna Aleppo." Without going into the details of the persecution of Tommaso Crudelli (or the probable espionage of British lodge members) the report happily explained that the lodges there had re-emerged from their short-lived suppression. The same piece continued, "we hear from Constantinople, that the Lodges at Smyrna Aleppo are greatly encreas'd, and that several Turks of Distinction have been admitted into them." Fleet, a provincial New Englander added to this, "*This is false again; the Free Masons sure are Men of too much Honour, Religion and Good-Sense to receive the declar'd Enemies of Jesus Christ into their Society.*" Fleet's personal prejudice aside, this one report told of resilience in the face of Catholic tyranny and the penetration of British Enlightenment culture into the Ottoman Empire in the form of Freemasonry—a useful link for Boston mariners such as Zebina Sears who might run afoul of the Barbary Coast in the decades to come.

Caribbean Freemasonry also entered colonial consciousness through colonial reprints of London press items. The *American Weekly Mercury* on December 24, 1734 reported, "[LONDON. October 1] The Earl of Crawford, Grand Master of the Siciety[sic] of Free-Masons, hath sign'd an Instrument for establishing a

Lodge of Masons in the Island of Montserat[sic]. A playhouse hath been erected at Plymouth Town in that Island, and a Spirit appears among the People there to imitate the Customs and Manners of the City of London." This is the first report of any masonic activity in the islands, pre-dating that recorded by the grand lodges in Boston and London by some four years (assuming the "signed Instrument" led to an active lodge).

On August 11, 1740 the *Boston Gazette* reported on the June 24 celebration in Barbados of the St. Michael's Lodge in Bridge Town. Festivities included "an excellent sermon". The order of the procession, "which took up the whole compass of the town" is given in detail, "...the like was never been before in this Part of the World, the Town was crowded with People for all Parts of the Island to see the Solemnity." A mason reading the *Gazette* whose travels took him to Barbados could now locate St. Michael's lodge in Bridgetown at Mr. Frith's house even though St. Michael's Lodge does not appear in any extant copies of the *Engraved Lists* officially until 1745. The 1740 *Engraved List* at the Grand Lodge of Massachusetts includes a handwritten entry for the lodge. This may be the "Barbadoes" lodge chartered by Boston's provincial grand master or his initiate, Governor Matthews of Antigua.

A similar report from New York several decades later speaks of a lodge not found in the official English lists. Under the heading, "Nassau, New-Providence, Dec. 30" it tells of a celebration during which a brig and a schooner, "decorated with a great variety of colors" moored "opposite the lodge-room at brother Fleming's" provided cannon fire to accompany the lodges procession from the lodge to Christ Church for a sermon by Rev. Brother Carter. More cannons were fired on the way back, and the night, "concluded with a ball and a handsome entertainment for the ladies, who made a very numerous appearance; and was conducted with great decency and regularity." Here is another grand celebration, this time in the Bahamas in a lodge which was not listed in any of the European guidebooks.[14]

Feasts of St. John and public processions were an important part of Masonic news. Over the years there were at least 48 advertisements for feasts of St. John or other special meetings of the fraternity in places that included Boston, Quebec, New Hampshire, Rhode Island, Connecticut, New York, Maryland, and Georgia. In Boston, St. John's often advertised its feast to the brethren and following the receipt of their official paperwork St. Andrew's made this a regular practice. These advertisements were mainly intended to reach the local masons, lodge members and any traveling mason in port during the festivities. Promoting the celebration of Feasts of St. John and the installation of officers carried word of the existence of the lodge far and wide as colonial papers traveled the seaways and dirt roads of the Atlantic world. These ads generally included the names of the lodge secretary, the grand master or master of a given lodge, and brethren from whom tickets might be purchased as well as the name of a tavern connected with the local masons.

The Boston Lodges, especially St. Andrew's, made a regular practice of advertising their feasts, but smaller lodges such as Wallingford and Stratford, Connecticut printed notices as well. So pervasive was this practice that the very first newspaper printed in Canada, the *Quebec Gazette* of June 21, 1764, carried a notice from Merchant's Lodge (the Mother lodge of Boston's John Hancock) advertising their upcoming festival. As there were many, mainly military, lodges in the city as well as masons among the merchant seamen who frequented it the ad stated that, "such strange brethren as have a desire of joining the Merchant's Lodge No. 1, Quebec, may Obtain liberty by applying to Miles Prenties, at the Sun, in St. John's Street".[15]

As in England, the processions and feasts were also items upon which the press reported after the fact, in positive and often glowing terms. Beginning in 1736, this became standard practice in Boston particularly. At the June installation and feast, "...they had an elegant Entertainment, his Excellency the Govornour[sic], the Rev. Mr. Commissary Price, and several other Gentlemen of Distinction being present." In emulation of their English Brethren, the brothers of Boston decided to up the ante as the 1730s proceeded. After listing the grand officers for the year, the Boston Gazette described a procession—"the first of its kind in America" as follows, "...the society attended the G.M. in procession to his Excellency Governour Belcher, & from thence the Governour was attended by the G.M. and the Brotherhood to the Royal Exchange Tavern in King—Street, where they had an elegant Entertainment. It being the first Procession in America, they appeared in the proper Badges of their Order, some Gold, the rest Silver." This news crossed the Atlantic and was featured in the London Press. Six months later the brethren at Boston's daughter lodge in Charleston, "...proceeded, all properly clothed, under the sound of French horns, to wait on James Graeme Esq., PGM, at his house in Broad Street."[16]

Both the newspapers and an independently distributed broadside promoted the grandeur of the provincial grand lodge's ostentatious 1739 procession, described earlier, which could bring all work to a halt and entertain the busy seaport of Boston with three twenty-one gun salutes, several bands, and a series of parades with the colonial governor at their head, all dressed in the exotic aprons and jewels of their society. This was meant not only for the Bostonian reader who had likely seen the processions and heard the cannons, but for readers in the other colonies and the metropolis. At a similarly impressive festival a decade after, Reverend Charles Brockwell preached his lauded sermon, *Brotherly Love Recommended*, which was to roll from printing presses on both sides of the Atlantic. The *Boston Evening Post* and *Boston Post Boy* both carried short pieces on the "elegant entertainment" and "excellent sermon"; the latter even proclaimed, "We hear the sermon will be printed" and two weeks later carried an advertisement for Draper's printed version.[17]

The colonial presses also shared local masonic news. For example, the *Boston Gazette* carried news from Philadelphia of the election of native son Benjamin Franklin in 1734 and the very elegant entertainment which followed, at which, "the Proprietor, the Governor, and several other persons of Distinction honour'd the Society with their presence." The next year news of Franklin's replacement by James Hamilton featured in the *Boston Post Boy*; in 1737 the *Boston News Letter* reported that William Plumstead had acceded to the chair. Similarly, when Joseph Warren received his commission from the Earl of Dalhousie, Grand Master of Scotland, making him "Provincial Grand Master of Ancient Free and Accepted Masons in North America"—of which Boston now boasted two- the glorious news initially featured in the *Boston Gazette* of January 1, 1770. Four days later, on January 5, both the *New Hampshire Gazette* and the *Connecticut Gazette* repeated the story. The Boston and Newport, Rhode Island press carried the story early in 1766 that the lodge in Hartford, Connecticut had prepared and delivered a eulogy on the death of the Duke of Cumberland in January, 1766. New lodges or changes in the place or time of meeting of established lodges publicized the fraternity as well.[18]

In 1738 the *New York Weekly Journal* printed a notice for the brethren that the lodge would henceforth be held at the Montgomeries Arms Tavern on the first and third Wednesday of the month. Notices from out of state were sometimes printed or reprinted, as in the *Boston Post-Boy's* January 1750 recounting that "the first regular Lodge of free and accepted Masons was congregated and held at Newport on Rhode Island; by virtue of a warrant given them by the Grand Master of North America." (who was, of course, located in Boston). That Boston intended its Masonic news to be spread around the entire Masonic world was made clear again in 1772. The *Massachusetts Gazette* and the *Boston Post Boy and Advertiser* announced on September 7 that "The Right Worshipful John Rowe, Esq; Grand Master of MASONS for North America" had "on Friday evening last constituted a New Lodge". The Rising Sun Lodge was to be held at the British coffee House in King street on the first Wednesday under its master,

Dr. Benjamin Church, the patriot who was in a few years' time to betray the Revolutionary cause. The ad finished by saying in no uncertain terms that, ". . . all Regular Lodges in America are to take Notice."[19]

Frequent advertisements for masonic books and items featured in the colonial newspapers speaks to the fraternity's importance in colonial society. The interest in masonic books such as the Constitutions and *Freemason's Pocket Companion* elucidates the intellectual interest in the craft among colonial masons. Overall, the *Constitutions of the Free Masons* is mentioned in eight advertisements in Boston, New York, and Georgia. The first such was an ad in Boston's Weekly Rehearsal of August 19, 1734, published by mason J. Draper. The most widely advertised masonic publications were various versions of the *Freemason's Pocket Companion*. This work is listed in at least 16 advertisements In Rhode Island, Connecticut, New York, and Georgia. All but one are "imported", James Rivington also advertised an edition of his own printing in 1761. Ads for the *Pocket Companion* first appeared in 1752; the last was printed 20 years later in 1772. The owner of a *Freemason's Pocket Companion* had all the means necessary to start a lodge of St. John based on the constitutional and legal information in the *Companion* as well as the contact information necessary to seek legitimacy from the Grand Lodge.[20]

Other masonic works were prominently advertised as well. The *New York Journal* on September 1, September 22, and November 10, 1768 ran a large display of the entire title and contents page of *Hiram: Or the Grand Master – Key To the Door of both Ancient and Modern Free – Masonry. . .* Regarding the publisher, it simply says, "Just published, and to be sold at the Printing-Office, at the Exchange" this and the prominence of its advertisement imply that it was a locally reprinted version. The *New York Gazette* of May 21 and May 28, 1770 included a long display add with full titles for five works. The fourth was Charles Warren's *The Freemason Stripped Naked. . .* These last two works, prominently advertised, included full exposes of Masonic ritual along with the standard fare found in other works of Masonic print.

Draper continued to profit by Masonic print culture, publishing Brockwell's *Brotherly Love Recommended in a Sermon Preached Before the Ancient and Honourable Society of Free and Accepted Masons, in Christ -Church, Boston, on Wednesday the 27th of December, 1749. By Charles Brockwell, A.M. His Majesty's Chaplain in Boston.* Draper advertised this pamphlet in the *Boston Post Boy* on January 15, 1750. Draper's printed version of his sermon most likely explains the sermon's being featured in British versions of *Pocket Companion*. The last Masonic printed work to be advertised along with several other works by the same printer was William M'Alpine's reprint of Wellins Calcott's *Candid Disquisition on the*

Principle's of the Antient and Honourable Society of Free Masons printed in Boston in 1772.

The variety of masonic items listed for sale, as well as those described as lost or stolen in colonial newspapers speaks to the economics of the republic of masonry. Though his name does not appear in any lodge records, Boston's John Dabney "Mathematical Instrument Maker from London" advertised his ability to "Make and Mend all sorts of Mathematical Instruments," including "...Free Masons Jewels..." Dabney's advertisements appeared in the Boston Evening Post in 1739 and again in 1740. That he sold Masonic "Jewels" along with practical and experimental mathematical tools speaks to both the association of freemasonry with the dawning scientific culture of the Enlightenment and its profitability to a craftsman able to produce items for the Masonic enthusiast. Engravers and instrument makers continued to profit from freemasonry throughout the colonial period, for example Henry Pursell, engraver of New York advertising "Free Masons Medals" among his wares in June of 1775 while the brethren in Boston were already hard at war. There were at least 34 advertisements for "Free Mason Glasses" including "Double Flint Freemason Glasses", "Half Pint Tumblers" and "Free Mason Wine Glasses". Moses Judah, father of ubiquitous Jewish Freemason Moses Michael Hayes, offered "Free Masons and other snuff boxes" on at least eight occasions from 1765 to 1775. Freemason William Jackson of Boston also ran three ads for masonic snuff boxes in 1765. Isaac Noble, liquor seller of New York, on six occasions listed among his wares "Free-Mason's Cordial". Items lost or stolen included masonic certificates, pocket watches, and various other masonic implements such as the "silver set Freemason Broach, with a square and compass marked on it, or a square Piece of Silver, engrav'd on it a Freemason's Coat of Arms, by a Person who 'tis suppos'd did not know the use of it."[21]

In New York, the use of a tavern by masons was advertised in the sale of the house. The steady patronage of a masonic lodge made the profitability of buying a tavern more easily assured, as in this advertisement, which appeared twice in 1767, "noted tavern, having the sign of the Free-Mason's Arms... to be sold at public vendue." There were several ads in Massachusetts, New York and Pennsylvania for products unrelated to freemasonry which referred to the local Masons Arms in directing patrons to their stores. That this was so demonstrates the prominent establishment of publicly declared Masonic houses in local geography and in turning the ideal of a republic of Masonry into a physical reality by establishing Masonic outposts throughout the "profane" world. Taverns bearing the name "Mason's Arms" as most famously in the case of the meeting place of the Lodge of St. Andrew's (better known as the Green Dragon), were generally owned by lodges or masons connected to the lodge. In other cases the owner of the house was usually initiated if a non-mason or else the house was selected due to its proprietor being a brother. This added another lucrative element to masonic involvement for those able to host a lodge in a public house. Not only was copious consumption a hallmark of eighteenth century masonic meetings and feasts, but lodge members were likely to become regular customers as well. Notices of the feast of St. John celebration at lodges in Stratford and Wallingford, Connecticut have the feasts happening the Mason's Arms in those towns demonstrating how common Mason's Arms were in communities hosting lodges.[22]

Cultural events were another important means of showing that freemasonry was connected with the arts and sciences. Masons sometimes advertised plans to attend the theater together, especially when they were sponsoring a play either for the public or exclusively for the lodge. The *New York Gazette* or the *Weekly Post Boy* on March 27, 1769 informed of a performance of two plays, "By command of his Excellency the GOVERNOR. For the Entertainment of the Right Worshipful the Grand Master, the Masters, Wardens, and Brethren of the Ancient and Honourable Society of Free and Accepted Masons". The performance also included "several masons songs". Hugh Gaine, printer of the *New York Mercury* was one of two contacts listed for "Tickets for the Boxes and Gallery," indicating that this some what lukewarm patriot printer was also a mason. Pitt tickets were delivered for the brethren to Mr. Burns', where "The Company of all the Brethren in Town, is earnestly requested, to meet . . ., at five o'clock on the Day of Performance, and walk from thence in Procession, to the Theatre."

As with the processions on Feasts of St. John and the newspaper reports recounting them, this advertisement not only told the brethren when and where to assemble but announced to the newspaper-reading New Yorker that they might view this spectacle, in itself a display of the prominence and standing of the local masons. That the brethren were a group which might "by command of the governor" enjoy a private showing at the theater spoke to the culture and exclusivity of the group. The first such command performance was probably "The Recruiting Officer" described in the *South Carolina Gazette* on May 28, 1737 ". . .acted for the entertainment of the Honourable and Ancient Society of Free and Accepted Masons. . . A proper prologue and epilogue were spoken and the Entered Apprentice's and Master's song sung upon the stage which were joined in chorus by the Masons in the Pit to the satisfaction and entertainment of the whole audience. . ." The masons came and went to the theater in procession; though not reported by name, the lodge included many colonial officials, merchants, and planters.[23]

Masonic theater going appears from time to time in the colonial press. Interesting as well are the references to freemasonry in theater promotions aimed at the general public. Among the many wonders described as part of a performance advertised in the *Pennsylvania Chronicle* of August 15–22, 1772 was a "sea fight" between two ships, one bearing the masonic square and compasses and the other the emblem of the Star and Garter. This latter is mentioned briefly in the first degree of freemasonry, as less ancient and honorable than that order which a mason has just joined. That freemasonry was an important part of the colonial social order and a bulwark of the patriot establishment implies a political meaning, as the masonic ship faced off against an enemy representing an order loyal to king and parliament. A similar ad from New York states "Between the Acts, several Free Masons Songs." Since most masonic books and pamphlets included songs, these might have been performed by masons or non-masons; either way, they advertised the fraternity and were considered a draw to theater goers. The description of a book on King's Chapel notes that some parts of it may have been "the work of Free Masons", demonstrating the penetration into broader public culture of the fantastic history created in masonic literature. Finally, the *New York Magazine* and the *New York Gazette* of 1763 describes two horse races, the "Free-Mason's Purse" and the "Elizabeth-Town Free Masons Plate" held in New York and New Jersey that year.[24]

Freemasonry's featuring at least 552 times in the colonial press demonstrates clearly that it was an organization of considerable importance to colonial Americans. Masonic goods, services and books made up a lucrative economy of their own. Much masonic business was done through the lodges and through personal networks, as with that of Paul Revere, approximately half of who's known customers were masons, who often bought masonic items for themselves or their lodges. Masonic glasses, snuff boxes, and jewels appeared frequently in newspaper advertisements. The colonial press featured news from England and Europe on noble masonic initiations, grand masonic processions, continental persecutions, and generous charity; however, the reprinting of these items in the American papers was more than just a part of the reprinting of metropolitan news in general. Reprinted items show up most frequently and consistently in cities with the largest and most active Masonic establishments: Boston, New York, and Philadelphia. Colonial masons emulated these acts and the publication of them and actively courted and when possible initiated local printers. Again, they did so most aggressively in the expansionist masonic Atlantic hub of Boston, but also in other colonies including New York and the deep southern colonies of South Carolina and Georgia.[25]

The Masonic press campaigns of American lodges and grand lodges not only served to establish the colonial masons' standing as good brethren and a vibrant part of the global republic of masonry, but created a map of that republic, filling in many spaces which remained terra incognito to the compilers and engravers of the "New and Correct" and *Engraved Lists* of lodges. The North American press carried reports of West Indian and American lodges not to be found in any British or European directory. They gave the times and places of meetings and the names of local masonic officers and grand officers to whom a newly arrived brother might apply for a meal ticket, charity, or to take their next degree. The pervasiveness of the Masonic society in the press of even backwater colonies confirmed to the maritime world and to the metropolis just how important and ubiquitous this society truly was. Indeed, the dreams of the architects of 1717 to spread the British Enlightenment and Whig values had succeeded in the New World far beyond what Desaguliers and his brothers had likely hoped or envisioned.

Notes

1 *Ibid.,* 117; Boston Post Boy, September 14, 1767; Newport Mercury, September 21, 1767; Connecticut Courant September 28, 1767.
2 *Ibid.,* 33, *Boston Gazette,* July 1, 1754.
3 Grand Lodge of Massachusetts, *Proceedings*, 127.
4 Grand Lodge, *Proceedings*, 13–4; Berman, *Loyalists and Malcontents; MSS proof copy;* James R. Case, *Connecticut Masons in the American Revolution.* (Grand Lodge A.F.&A.M of Connecticut, 1976), 5.
5 Berman, *Foundations of Modern Freemasonry,* 76, 121–4.
6 *Maryland* Gazette February 9, 1732, April 6, 1733; Data on additional Pennsylvania articles is taken from Johnson, *Freemasonry in North America, 59–66;* Berman, *Loyalists and Malcontents.*
7 Berman, *Loyalists and Malcontents* (pre-publication proof MSS).
8 *Boston News-Letter,* "Philadelphia, FEb. 7, 1737," March 9, 1738; Bullock, *Revolutionary Brotherhood,* 50–1; Jill Lepore, *New York Burning, 99–102, 138–45.* The newspaper wars between Zenger and the Bradford's are covered in detail in a proceeding chapter on masonry in the African Atlantic, and thus receive only a summary account in the present chapter.
9 *Boston Gazette or Weekly Journal,* April 25, 1737, February 16–23, 1738, November 3, 1741, *New York Weekly Journal,* November 23, 1741, *Boston Evening Post,* April 26, 1736 "From the Political State, January, 1736," July 11, 1737, August 28, 1738, September 11, 1738, September 18, 1738, June 6, 1743, June 20, 1743; *Boston*

Weekly News Letter, June 21–28, 1739, June 23, 1743; *Pennsylvania American Weekly Journal*, June 30–July 7, 1743; *New York Weekly Journal*, July 25, 1743.

10 Boston Post-Boy, June 29, 1752; *Boston Gazette*, April 1, 1734.

11 *Connecticut Courant*, April 1, 1765, "At a Lodge of FREE-MASONS, held at the Fountain Tavern, in New-Haven, Tuesday, 19th March, 1765."; *Boston Weekly Newsletter*, March 30 –April 5, 1733.

12 Johnson, *Freemasonry in North America*, 59–66; *New York Mercury*, February 4, 1754, "Bristol, October 27". This appears to have been a headline for Bristol, England, not Connecticut, based on the lack of any record or reference to a lodge in Bristol, Connecticut at this time and the time lag between the original news and the New York reporting thereof. Also, the article speaks of a "greet meeting" and a deputation from the grand master of England; no such direct warrant was issued for Bristol, Connecticut, whereas they were common in Bristol, England.

13 *Boston Evening Post*, October 23, 1737, July 11, 1737, September 18, 1738; *Boston Gazette*, April 25, 1737.

14 *New York Gazette*, March 3, 1762, "Nassau, New Providence, Dec. 30."

15 *Connecticut Journal*, June 1, 1770, December 3, 1772, June 18, 1773; *Quebec Gazette*, June 21, 1764, quoted in John Hamilton Graham, *Outline of the History of Freemasonry in the Province of Quebec* (Montreal: 1892); 42.

16 Boston Evening Post, June 28, 1736; Boston Gazette, June 27, 1737; *South Carolina Gazette*, December 29, 1737, quoted in Berman, *Loyalists and Malcontents*.

17 *Boston Evening Post*, January 1, 1750; *Boston Post-Boy*, January 1, 1750, January 15, 1750.

18 *Boston Gazette*, July 8–15, 1734, January 1, 1770; *Boston Post-Boy*, July 14, 1735; *Boston News-Letter*, July 14, 1737; *New Hampshire Gazette*, January 5, 1770, *Connecticut Gazette*, January 5, 1770; *Boston Evening Post*, "At a Lodge of Free and Accepted Masons Held at Hartford," January 24, 1766; *Newport Mercury*, "At a Lodge of Free and Accepted Masons Held at Hartford," March 3–10, 1766.

19 *Boston Gazette*, April 1, 1734; *New York Weekly Journal*, "Wednesday January 17. 1738/9," January 22, 1738; *Boston Post-Boy*, January 15, 1750 "Newport, RI"; *Massachusetts Gazette and the Boston Post Boy and Advertiser*, September 7, 1772.

20 *Boston Weekly Rehearsal*, August 19, 1734; *Boston Evening Post*, February 5, 1750; *New York Magazine*, October 24, 1763; *Georgia Gazette*, November 10, 1763; *New York Mercury*, November 20, 1752, November 27, 1752, November 8, 1764; *New York Gazette*, October 26, 1761, November 2, 1761, November 30, 1761, November 8, 1764, November 22, 1764, November 29, 1764; *Newport Mercury*, December 31, 1764; *New Hampshire Gazette*, April 12, 1765; *Connecticut Courant*, July 27, 1767, July 28, 1772, August 3, 1772, *Georgia Gazette*, April 7, 1763.

21 *New York Mercury*, April 19, 1756, April 26, 1756, May 3, 1756, May 10, 1756, August 3, 1761, November 14, 1761; "advertisements", "Moses Judah," September 28; May 4, 1767, June 3, 1775; *New York Gazette*, June 6, 1751; June 17, 1751, July 8, 1751,

July 15, 1751, May 13, 1765, May 20, 1765, June 3, 1765, June 15–26, 1767, June 29 –July 6, 1767, July 6 –July 13, 1767, September 7 –September 14, 1767, March 7, 1768, March 21, 1768, April 4, 1768, April 18, 1768, April 25, 1768, May 2, 1768; *Pennsylvania Gazette,* October 3, 1754, October 17, 1754, November 21, 1754; *Boston Post Boy* November 11, 1762, February 3, 1766, April 4, 1766, November 23, 1772, December 2, 1772, December 12, 1772, January 14, 1773; *Boston Evening Post,* August 19, 1765, August 26, 1765, September 2, 1765, April 7, 1766; *Pennsylvania Chronicle,* June 26 1769, July 3, 1769, July 1 –8, 1771, July 8–15, 1771, July 15–22 1771, July 22–29, 1771; *Norwich Packet and the Connecticut, Massachusetts, New Hampshire and Rhode Island Advertiser,* April 21–28, 1774, *Boston Gazette and Country Journal,* February 6, 1769;; Newell, *Curiosities of the Craft, 38–39*; *Boston Evening Post,* October 8, 1739, June 8, 1741; *New York Gazette,* June 26, 1775.

22 *New York Journal,* December 10, 1767, December 17, 1767; *Boston Evening Post,* May 10, 1756; *Newport Mercury,* September 12, 1763; *Boston Gazette and Country Journal,* December 7, 1763; *Essex Gazette,* January 16–23, 1769; *Connecticut Journal,* June 1, 1770, December 3, 1772, June 18, 1773; *Boston News Letter,* October 6, 1768, October 10, 1768, April 2, 1769; *New York Mercury,* June 11, 1764; *Pennsylvania Gazette,* August 22, 1745, September 5, 1745.

23 *South Carolina Gazette,* May 28, 1737, quoted in Berman, *Loyalists and Malcontents.*

24 *New York Gazette,* December 28, 1761, March 7 1763, March 21, 1763, March 28, 1763, April 18, 1763, August 8, 1763; *New York Magazine,* December 28, 1761; March 21, 1763, March 28, 1763; *New York Journal,* August 8, 1771.

25 Steblecki, *Paul Revere and Freemasonry,* 92–120.

9

The Lodge of St. Andrew: "Headquarters of the Revolution"

On July 4th, 1795, Paul Revere joined Governor Samuel Adams in an elaborate ceremony to lay the cornerstone of the new state house. He did so not as an honored revolutionary hero or leading local artisan, but as grand master of Masons in Massachusetts. The image of the masonic grand master anointing the stone with corn, wine, and oil evokes a neo-pagan feel out of keeping with the professed Christianity of the early republic. The stone was laid with an inscribed silver plate, a piece of the grand master's handiwork, and copper, silver and gold coins. The conclusion to Revere's brief address was filled with republican ideology and masonic symbolism, "May we, my brethren, so Square our Actions thro(sic) life as to shew to the World of Mankind, that we mean to live within the Compass of Good Citizens that we wish to Stand upon a Level with them that when we part we may be admitted into that Temple where Reigns Silence & Peace."

Masonic cornerstone layings were a common spectacle in the early Republic. The event brought together Revere's political, professional, and masonic life. Once masonic brother Amos Lincoln had finished erecting the building its dome was covered in copper rolled by Revere. For Worshipful Revere, as for men throughout the Atlantic world, freemasonry was closely intertwined with business networking, political ideology, and the internal world represented by the pseudo–religious symbols of the order. On June 17, 2015 over 1100 Massachusetts masons made the short march from the grand lodge to the statehouse to rededicate the cornerstone, temporarily removed due to water damage, adding new items to the coins, newspapers and silver plate laid by Grand Master Revere.[1]

Paul Revere served as grand master of the Grand Lodge of Massachusetts, formed in 1792 with the merger of the moribund Modern St. John's Grand Lodge and the dominant Ancient Massachusetts Grand Lodge. Massachusetts Grand Lodge had come out of the Lodge of St. Andrew's where Revere had entered freemasonry in 1760. The lodge of St. Andrew's hold a particularly important place in history because its membership came to be largely identical with that of the Patriot movement. In 1764, the lodge purchased the Green Dragon Tavern, famous as the "Headquarters of the Revolution", where most of Boston's radical groups met. The lodge has even claimed to have originated the idea for the Boston Tea Party. There is considerable evidence that the lodge of St. Andrew was actively involved in radical politics, particularly in connection to the Sons of Liberty and the Boston Tea Party.

Saint Andrew's Lodge and the royal arch chapter connected to it seem to have formed largely due to genuine enthusiasm for the supposed authenticity and "ancientness" of Ancient masonry. In clandestine existence since 1754, the lodge obtained a Scottish warrant in 1760. Among the founders figured eight members of First Lodge, one from Marblehead, two from Providence, one from Portsmouth, one from Second Lodge, two each from West Indies, Scotland, England and Quebec, and one each from the lodges at Louisbourgh and Seconto in Nova Scotia. The lodge obtained a charter through Isaac DeCoster, a mason connected to Halifax, Nova Scotia. He communicated through James Logan of Falkirk to the Grand Lodge of Scotland in Edinburg. Boston merchant James Anderson carried many of these letters. St. Andrew's appear in Scottish lists form the 1760s on. James Otis joined First Lodge March 11, 1752 and affiliated with St. Andrew's January 4, 1754, that year holding the position of Senior Warden in both lodges. St. Andrew's had no official charter in 1754, and their membership records for the period are incomplete. John Hancock was raised in the St. John's Chartered Merchants lodge at Quebec, making him a member of St. John's, affiliating in 1762 with St. Andrew's.[2]

Many of the most important Patriots joined between 1760 and 62, often with the dates of their initiatory degrees overlapping or with some future patriot leaders performing masonic rituals for others. Such members included Paul Revere, Joseph Warren, John Hancock, William Palfrey, Moses Deshon, Jonathan Snelling, Thomas Crafts of the Loyal Nine, Joseph Webb (also a member of 1st lodge) Samuel Barrett- tea party participant and 2nd lodge and Rising Sun cross-member; Ezra Collins, Adam Colson (who shouted "Boston Harbor a Tea Party tonight" at end of the pre-party town meeting) and other, less well-known future Sons of Liberty. Earlier members included James Otis, William Burbeck, John Pulling, officially a member of Marblehead lodge who closely associated with St Andrew's and hung the lanterns in the Old North Church on the night of Paul Revere's ride, future Patriot leaders who were cross members with the local Modern Masonic lodges. In all, 26 of the Lodge of St. Andrew's confirmed Sons of Liberty were masons prior to the beginning of the Stamp Act Crisis; Lawyer and clerk to John Hancock John Lowell being among the last pre-stamp initiates early in 1764.

James Otis and John Hancock, two of the earliest and most influential patriot leaders, were both Modern masons and St. Andrew's members. They had already shown opposition to Britain in fighting the Writs of Assistance case in 1761. Though Hancock attended the lodge only infrequently, he did attend and his clerks William Palfrey and John Lowell were heavily involved in the lodge. Otis attended lodge even less frequently, but was in charge of its legal dealings and remained in communication with the brethren. In the immediate prelude to the Stamp Act the most radical political leaders in Boston mixed with the future Sons of Liberty, Tea Party Indians, Caucus members and militiamen of the Revolutionary movement. In effect, the lodge formed key relationships between the the future leaders, lieutenants, and active followers of Boston's radical movement in the years just before that movement began. Moreover, it did so in an environment charged with the political overtones of eighteenth century freemasonry.[3]

Wishing to emulate the continental authority of their Modern rivals, on January 11, 1769 St. Andrew's along with three British military lodges sent a petition asking for a grand mastership over North America. They explained that the modern grand lodge in Boston had authority to create lodges anywhere in America where no other grand master was appointed, and that "if there was in America an Authority to Constitute and appt. Lodges of Ancient Masons, Great numbers would speedily apply for Deputations for erecting of Lodges in different Parts of this Continent: some in this Province have signified their Inclination so to do, but by Reason of the Great Difficulty attending an immediate Application to the Grand Lodge of Scotland have been oblige'd to take Deputations from the Modern Gd Master here." In response, Scotland issued authority within a 100 mile radius of New England to the new Grand Lodge. In 1771, it extended this jurisdiction to the entire continent. Ironically the masonic political schism between Ancients and Moderns meant that the patriot leadership had masonic authority over the British regimental lodges in the city. This created some tension, but also offered the opportunity for intelligence gathering, particularly by Deputy Grand Master William Burbeck, in charge of supplies at Castle William.[4]

In the event, they created only three new lodges, all in Massachusetts, prior to the outbreak of the revolution. Once the war began, however, following a lapse during the siege of Boston, they set to work chartering many lodges throughout New England. Their continental authority was in reality to be more regional; however, as the patriotic members of the lodge ranked highly among the leaders of the new state, they soon came to greatly surpass the older grand lodge in membership and importance. As the focus shifted from the Atlantic and the networks of imperial and cross imperial commerce to the rising productive classes and democratic politicians of the new republic with its active state governments, the inclusive, republican nature of Ancient freemasonry won out over the merchants of First Lodge.

Business, Brotherhood, and the Independence Movement

Though less international than St. John's, connections formed in the Lodge of Saint Andrew's led to significant business opportunities at home and abroad. Overall, the membership held less elite status, but still had widespread maritime and commercial interests. The demographics of the lodge included 25 % merchants as opposed to 66 % of St. John's. With the exception of John Hancock, St. Andrew's merchant members owned less capital, under one-third the merchandise and factorage carried by their Modern brethren. Sea captains made up 36 % of the lodge, as opposed to just under 10 % of First Lodge. Thus, just over 50 % of St. Andrew's members took to the sea. Another 8.3 % plied trades related to maritime commerce. This web of connections soon took on political utility as the leaders of the lodge became leaders of revolution. This is most clearly exemplified in the careers of several of its members, notably silversmith Paul Revere, merchant William Palfrey, and William Burbeck the deputy grand master conveniently in charge of stores in British occupied Castle William. Dr. Joseph Warren served among the very top ranks of Patriot leadership along with the likes of Hancock, Otis, and Samuel Adams. In addition to his official positions in Massachusetts government, Warren undertook much of the organizing of subversive activity, including an extensive spy network. Warren served as master of Saint Andrew's beginning in 1768–9 and as Grand Master from 1769 until his death at the battle of Bunker Hill on June 16th, 1775.[5]

Revere was initiated into St. Andrew's Lodge on September 4, 1760, shortly after the formerly clandestine lodge received official sanction from Scotland. Revere's masonic business affords one of the clearest pictures of the advantages of freemasonry to a skilled craftsman. He created items specifically for masonic purposes, including Jewels for lodge officers, medals, punchbowls and ladles and plates for printing certificates and summonses. He also supplied more mundane goods to a wide range of customer, including a disproportionate number of freemasons. His wastebooks record their first order for a masonic item, a freemasons' medal for James Graham, in January of 1761. Among the masonic items crafted by Revere in the following year was a plate for cutting notifications for John Pulling. Pulling was a founding member of Marblehead Lodge as well as the friend called up by Revere to hang the lanterns in the Old North Church. Revere sold most of his masonic items to customers in Massachusetts, however, freemasonry brought him into the commerce of the greater Atlantic, most notably the 1762 order by Capt. Caleb Hopkins of a copper plate for engraving notifications for a lodge in Suriname.[6]

Most of his masonic business came from closer to home. He kept a plate in his silver shop for printing certificates for masons initiated by the various lodges in the city, essentially guaranteeing that each new mason in Boston had to visit his shop at least once. Prior to the outbreak of the War of Independence Revere crafted a variety of items for the grand lodge, St. Andrews, and all of the lodges chartered by the Ancient's grand lodge before the onset of hostilities. Revere had a hand in the founding and organization of all three of these lodges, including Tyrian in Gloucester and St. Peter's in Newburyport. Masons from both of these outlying communities subsequently show up among Revere's customers.[7]

The wastebooks are by no means an all-inclusive record of Revere's business but they do describe a substantial portion of the orders he received. Of the 309 customers described between 1761 and 1797, 146 can be positively identified as freemasons. Considering that freemasons made up a relatively small proportion of the total population yet made up nearly 50 % of Revere's recorded customers the logical conclusion must be that freemasons preferentially patronized Revere's shop. The proliferation of masonic lodges following independence resulted in a boom in masonic business for Revere. The last distinctly masonic item created by Revere was a golden urn commissioned by the grand lodge to hold a lock of the late Brother George Washington's hair.

Figure 9.1. Summons engraved by Paul Revere for St. Andrew's (1772), St. Peter's, Newburyport (1772), and Tyrian (Gloucester, 1773) lodges in Massachusetts. (Courtesy American Antiquarian Society).

Paul Revere's heavy involvement in the running of St. Andrew's Lodge and, from its foundation in 1769 Massachusetts Grand Lodge, indicates that he took the fraternity very seriously apart from its business potential. Revere held offices in 1762, 1764, and 1765. He served as secretary in 1768–9 and as master in 1771 and again in 1778, 1779, 1781, and 1782. Revere also served as senior grand deacon of the Massachusetts Grand Lodge from 1769 to 1774 under Grand Master Joseph Warren. Between 1777 and 1783 he rose from the fourth highest office in the grand lodge (junior grand warden) to deputy grand master. From 1784 to 5 he served as either master or treasurer then from 1786 to 93 Master of the new Rising States Lodge culminating in his term as grand master of Massachusetts from 1794 to 1797. During this time he also served on a number of committees and attended lodge regularly. This represents a substantial commitment of time and energy, more than was necessary to use the craft as a springboard for his silver business. In his farewell speech as grand master, Revere reminded the brethren that, "the cause we are engaged in is the Cause of Humanity, of Masons and of Man." The Masonic writings that he left, like the speech given at the cornerstone laying and the farewell address, indicate that Paul Revere took the high-minded rhetoric of freemasonry seriously and identified the craft and his role in it as more than simply a networking device. He was not the only craftsman to benefit from the masonic economy. Like the earlier John Dabney, mathematical instrument maker from London, Revere's competitors, fraternal and masonic brothers Benjamin and Nathanial Hurd, also engraved masonic summonses, with extant certificates from 1764 and 1780, and a 1752 seal for the grand lodge.[8]

Paul Revere had taken his third degree on January 27, 1761 along with several other young men including William Palfrey. Future secretary of the Sons of Liberty then Paymaster of the Continental Army. Palfrey, like Revere, was a consummate networker and was very active in Boston's radical political circles.

Figure 9.2. Receipt from Paul Revere to Tyrian Lodge bearing Revere's signature dated Boston February 13, 1770 for instruments delivered to the hand of Epes Sargent Jr., property of Tyrian Lodge, Gloucester, Massachusetts (Courtesy Tyrian Lodge).

His correspondence is extensive and varied; a single letter might jump from the price of whale oil to the liberties of the colonies or from official army business to grand lodge administration to personal matters. The heavy presence of identifiable masons among his professional and political contacts gives a strong impression that the fraternity was an important part of his financial success. His letters also clearly demonstrate that he was a 'true believer' who took the esoteric side of freemasonry very seriously. Analyzing Palfrey's masonic career and the more revealing references in his correspondence demonstrates Palfrey's zeal for freemasonry and his ability to use masonic connections in business.

At the time of their initiation the 20 year-old Palfrey was a clerk for Nathaniel Wheelwright, after Thomas Hancock the most successful merchant in Boston. Both St. Andrew's and Second Lodge list a Bro. Wheelwright with no first name. As the Modern Second Lodge was the province of elite merchants and as Brother Wheelwright first enters the records of St. Andrew's on the night of Palfrey's third degree it appears likely that this was Nathaniel Wheelwright. In 1764 Palfrey jumped from the house of Wheelwright to that of Hancock. Whether he had met John Hancock in the course of business before or not, the two had first attended lodge together from May 14, 1761. Palfrey became secretary of the lodge immediately after entering, so that his ability in handling the business of the lodge would have been known to his new employer. Another of Hancock's clerks and future Massachusetts politico, John Lowell, entered the lodge in 1764. Palfrey acted as a clerk to Hancock but with the stipulation that he could conduct his own business as well, making him as much junior partner as employee. They often employed Captain's Scott and Hall as masters of their vessels. Both men were masons who rarely attended lodge but made use of the craft connections in Atlantic commerce, as in Captain Scott's attendance at the West India and American Lodge in London.[9]

Palfrey visited every New England lodge for which pre-war records exist. His letters to Ancients founder Lawrence Dermot state that he also attended lodges in London. He traveled to the southern colonies on business on several occasions and it seems likely that he would have visited lodges there as well. He, like Revere, served in a number of offices in both lodge and grand lodge, including grand secretary under Grand Master Joseph Warren and as the first master of Massachusetts Lodge in 1770.

Prior to this time, however, a series of letters the young Palfrey exchanged with Moses Brown of Providence demonstrates both the usefulness of masonic affiliation to a young businessman and the mutual enthusiasm of the two for freemasonry. Their letters indicate that Palfrey met Brown and at least one of his brothers, probably John, as well as Dr. Jabez Bowen, a prominent member of the community and later of Providence's Sons of Liberty, in the lodge. The Brown's all were active freemasons, not to mention members of one of Rhode Island's dominant merchant houses. The lodge in Providence included other notable such as William Ellery, who was to serve as clerk of the Rhode Island assembly and then as a representative of Rhode Island to sign the declaration of independence, initiated in First Lodge while studying at Harvard, and other movers and shakers in colonial commerce and Revolutionary politics.[10]

Most of the letters between Brown and Palfrey were concerned with the latter's failed courtship of Providence beauty Polly Olney, a friend of Brown's. As it turned out, Palfrey made the mistake of taking the young lady's initial 'no' as a final answer. Ms. Olney later informed Brown that she had expected William to persist, and intended to give in eventually. By the time he realized his mistake, however, he had become more interested in his future wife, Suzana Cazneau. The letters teem with Masonic references evincing the enthusiasm of young men with a newfound interest. The two refer to each other and to their mutual acquaintances as 'brother' frequently. On February 19, 1761 Palfrey states, "...give my Love to your Brother and Dr. Bowen, we have nothing new stirring here at present save that I was made a Royal Arch this Week." On March 26 he wrote, "I have inclos'd you two small cutts, one for your Brother, the other please to accept of Yourself & hope they'll be agreeable, should have sent one for the Doctor, but could not get but those two, please to give my Love to the two Brethren abovemention'd..." The 'cutts' were apparently Masonic engravings of some sort. Palfrey's other new brother, Paul Revere, was the only mason in St. Andrew's who listed engraver among his professions, making it highly plausible that these trinkets came from his shop.

Their letters further demonstrate the utility of masonic connections. Palfrey's letter of April 13 closes with an introduction of another young brother, "The bearer of this, Doctr Jackson, a very intimate Friend of mine & a brother of ours..." There is no Dr. Jackson listed among the members of St. Andrew's, Palfrey's lodge, but Second lodge includes several Jacksons; most of whom were merchants. Whoever Dr. Jackson was, he was a friend of Palfrey's previously unknown to Brown but their mutual masonic membership instantly made him Brown's 'brother'. In a world as dependent on credit and on maintaining a creditworthy reputation as that of the commercial Atlantic this instant brotherhood was invaluable. As the courtship was beginning to unravel Palfrey wrote on August 17, "Remember me to the fraternity and all other acquaintances & believe me Your Affectionate Bror." His wishing to be remembered to the entire fraternity indicates that he had become acquainted with the lodge there; what he lost in love he at least partially made up for in business connections. In addition to the Browns and Jabez Bowen, Jewish masons connected to Moses Michael Hayes were actively involved in Rhode Island freemasonry. Among these was Aaron Lopez, who later appears among Palfrey's many business correspondents.

Palfrey's later letters to Lawrence Dermot, the most prominent figure in the creation and spread of the Ancient brand of freemasonry, indicate that his zeal for freemasonry had not abated with age. His first letter, dated simply 1771, indicates that he had been barred from attending the installation of Grand Lodge officers for arcane procedural reasons that he considered constitutionally invalid. Palfrey's normally artistic calligraphy had deteriorated into a shaky, angry scrawl. He was clearly both insulted and disappointed over the matter. Though Dermot's reply no longer exists it was apparently quite conciliatory, as Palfrey's letter of March 17, 1771 nearly gushes over the opportunity to meet the guru of Ancient freemasonry, "I confess your superiority in the knowledge of the constitution of the Craft.- Ancient Masonry is yet but in its infancy in New England and as I have it much at heart I would willingly acquire a greater knowledge of it than my scanty opportunities have yet afforded. It is partly for that purpose, & partly for the esteem I have for Brother Dermot as a social companion that I solicit a further acquaintance and as my stay in England is now but very short I would willingly improve it to the best advantage_ Therefore Sir I should be glad to meet you at Brother William's or any other place you shall please to appoint previous to the meeting of the Lodge next Friday Evening." Not only was he attending lodge for its social and professional benefits, but he took the esoteric and constitutional aspects of freemasonry quite seriously.[11]

Both Paul Revere and William Palfrey were active in the Patriot cause; Scottish printer William M'Alpine, who joined the lodge shortly after Revere and Palfrey on March 12, 1761, was not. He attended the lodge with some regularity until July 14, 1763 and then disappears for nine years, returning on November 14, 1771 by which time he had achieved a degree of unpopularity throughout the Whig community that made up the bulk of the lodge's membership. Scots printers and booksellers in Boston had an antagonistic relationship with the established local industry and were noted Tories. The most infamous was John Mein, whose attacks on John Hancock resulted in Mein's financial ruin and exile. Mein's business partner John Fleeming occasionally collaborated with M'Alpine and guilt by association had seriously hindered the latter's business by 1772. Ironically, in that year M'Alpine achieved one of his most successful publishing ventures ever, selling a number of books to his political enemies.

Originally published in England, Calcott's work on masonic philosophy and pseudo-history was among the most popular books about freemasonry of the eighteenth—century. The edition printed in Boston in 1772 by William M'Alpine contains a subscribers list including separate sections for Massachusetts, New York, Nova Scotia, and Connecticut. Individual subscribers' locations ranged from Quebec and Montreal to Barbados. This is surprising in that, while some colonial booksellers had formed widespread professional networks covering such vast areas, those in Boston generally did not take part in them until Isaiah Thomas following the War of Independence. Furthermore, M'Alpine was a minor local publisher whose other works show only limited, local distribution. M'Alpine averaged around 5 % of Boston's printing business in most years from the time he began publishing with the exception of 1765 and 1767 when he achieved 15 % and 18 %, respectively. Furthermore, M'Alpine had been in a long running feud with many of the established printers, in town, notably freemason Thomas Fleet, over printing of the popular *Ames Almanac*.[12]

That notwithstanding, a number of Patriot leaders and rank and file who were freemasons bought his edition of the Calcott book, as did masons among the British military. Many of his buyers also appear on the one existing list of the Sons of Liberty in Boston and / or as participants in the Boston Tea Party. On the title page the publisher listed himself as Brother William M'Alpine. Subscribers included Joseph Warren, Paul Revere, John Lowell, William Palfrey, William Moylneux, Benjamin Church, Richard Gridley, William Burbeck, Thomas Urann, John Gray, Caleb Hopkins and even professional rival Thomas Fleet, as well as a number of Boston Sons of Liberty, Tea Party Mohawks, and patriot leaders from Newburyport, Gloucester, Portsmouth and throughout New England. The men who subscribed to M'Alpine's edition took the Craft seriously enough that they would put aside political, professional, and personal grievances and prejudices in order to obtain a work they believed would further their understanding of Freemasonry, and to actively promote the printer's work so their brethren could do so. This shows one more moment in which freemasonry brought together men who were otherwise enemies and illustrates how important Masonry was to its eighteenth—century brethren. Lodge records and the book's subscribers list illustrate how a few visits to lodge could market a brother printer's wares from Canada to the Caribbean.

On November 14, 1771 M'Alpine attended lodge for the first time in nine years in order to promote his plan to print the book. Among the visitors that night was James Frederick Gersdorf, who appears among the subscribers for Massachusetts listed as 'Lieut. in his majesty's Sweedish(sic) navy'. In addition to several other Europeans, the lodge roll for the night included visitors from various lodges: Thomas Newell, Capt. Peter Hussey, Nathaniel Tucker and Francis Shaw, all of whom appear among the Boston subscribers. So does William Codner who was among the first officers of the Massachusetts Lodge formed out of St. Andrew's in 1772. A number of its officers appear among the list of book subscribers. William Johnson also sat in lodge that night; he is listed among the subscribers as the secretary of Union Lodge, Nantucket. Other members of Union lodge subscribed as well. John Tyler of Portsmouth, New Hampshire was there and although he did not end up buying a book other members of his lodge did.[13]

In 1771 Boston included St. Andrew's, Massachusetts, First and Second lodges. Both First and Second Lodge were closely associated with a new lodge, Rising Sun, which formed in 1772. McAlpine visited St. Andrew's again on February 13, 1772. Visitors that night from other Boston lodges were present, including two members of Second Lodge, one of whom subscribed for a book. Though he never visited Second Lodge his former partner, John Fleeming, became active there early in 1772 and may have used his membership as a Modern to promote the book in the three Modern lodges in the city.[14]

M'Alpine's last visit came on June 24, 1772, the Feast of St. John. Many visitors were present, though most were listed by last name only, making them difficult to positively identify with subscribers on the list. One visitor present bore the name Duguid- among the subscribers listed in Massachusetts are William and Thomas Duguid of Windsor in North Carolina. Two other North Carolinians, both named Simpson, subscribed. It is possible that the Duguid mentioned was William Duguid, with no location appended to his name; assuming that he was related to Thomas Duguid he may have ordered books for the other North Carolinians on the list. It is also plausible that they were all traveling through the area and only one attended the lodge.

A final page lists additional subscribers from Tyrian Lodge in Gloucester. Members of Tyrian attended the feast on the 24th and apparently collected subscriptions in Tyrian then returned them to M'Alpine. He never visited the lodge in Gloucester, and did not attend St. Andrew's again, so it seems that he probably printed the book shortly after June 1772. Gersdorf returned to Boston and attended St. Andrew's in September, October and November then disappeared again. In addition to picking up his own copy he could have carried other copies with him in whichever direction he sailed. More likely to have done so are any of the many sea captains and merchants among the subscribers who appear intermittently in the time between M'Alpine's first appearance at lodge in late 1771 and the feast in June 1772. Nor would they had to have been in lodge on the same night; once he made it known that he was taking subscriptions the Masonic grapevine clearly brought in a great number of subscribers.

In Massachusetts, including Falmouth Lodge in what is now Maine and several subscribers from Quebec- where masons from Massachusetts had established Merchant's Lodge after the French and Indian War- plus a captain from Barbados and four North Carolinians, 253 subscribers bought 368 books. It appears that the subscriptions in other colonies came through personal connections from Boston. New York City boasted nine lodges and Connecticut 12 at the time. The only non-New Yorkers listed are the deputy grand master of Quebec and a mason from a lodge in Montreal who may have been in New York at the time. In sum, the 79 New York subscribers purchased a total of 91 books. Only four of the city's nine pre-war lodges are listed by name, indicating that the city might have been canvassed more thoroughly.

Of particular note is Captain John Harris Cruger, junior grand warden of the Grand Lodge of New York. Cruger had extensive business connections with mason John Hancock and his clerk William Palfrey. Palfrey was a subscriber as well as the grand secretary of the Massachusetts Grand Lodge. He was a close friend and business associate of Cruger's and in fact traveled on business in New York and Connecticut in 1772 and could have been involved in collecting subscriptions or delivering books there. All 24 Connecticut subscribers were from two lodges, one in Hartford and one in Stratford. The Hartford lodge had received its charter from Massachusetts and boasted many members connected with both King George's and the French and Indian War and involved in Patriot politics, all of which would have brought them into association with members of the lodges in Massachusetts.[15]

Massachusetts chartered lodges in Nova Scotia and trade connected the two regions. Though originally established by St. John's, Nova Scotia's Masonic establishment had become closely connected to the British military. M'Alpine's Massachusetts subscribers included members of military lodges present in Boston and many military men appear among the 68 masons and 5 non–masons listed in Nova Scotia, who altogether bought 71 books. Two subscribers came from Louisburg, the rest are listed either as Halifax or by regiment, or without a location given. Halifax is the only community listing non-masons.

By this time the military masons in Boston and the members of St. Andrew's tended to be on poor terms, however, as a loyalist M'Alpine would have had better standing with the soldiers than he did in his mother lodge. Moreover, not all Boston masons were patriots; a minority were loyalists and some were apolitical. Among the subscribers were two highly placed freemasons with military connections. Richard Gridley, past master of Second Lodge, had overseen the Siege of Louisburg in 1745 and besieged the same city again with General Wolf in 1758; he was a half-pay British officer for life. His second in command William Burbeck was past master of St. Andrew's and a Son of Liberty. He was in charge of stores at Castle William and lived there alongside the British garrison. Both men served on the patriot side during the War of Independence. It has been speculated that either, particularly Burbeck, connected as he was with the administration of the garrison and believed to have attended regimental lodges before fighting against the British, may have used their connections for espionage. We must now ask, did they also use their proximity to the enemy to sell books?[16]

Interestingly, with the exception of Montreal all of the far—flung subscribers appearing from Massachusetts or New York hailed from regions with a Massachusetts chartered lodge— Quebec, Barbados, Louisburg, and North Carolina. Neither of the Grand Lodges in Boston appear to have assisted in the marketing of the book as there is no mention of it in the *Proceedings* and the sporadic dispersal of lodges in New York and Connecticut indicate that there was no systematic effort to canvass the entire colony in either case. This demonstrates that informal Masonic networks were far reaching and highly effective. Brother M'alpine was sent home by a Patriot army, a number of whom owned his edition of Calcott. General and Grand Master Warren had purchased six copies. William M'Alpine died in Glasgow in 1788, exiled along with the rest of the Scots printers. The copy of *Candid Disquisition* at the AAS includes on the inside front cover a stamp from Isaiah Thomas' press marking it as his personal copy. Thomas served as Grand Master of Masons in Massachusetts from 1803 to 5 and again in 1809, while revolutionizing American printing.

Ancients' Intellectualism in Republican Boston

Before examining Boston Freemasonry's connection to American Independence more deeply, let us place St. Andrews in the cosmopolitan world of transatlantic masonic intellectual culture. St. Peter's lodge in Newburyport, chartered by Warren in 1772, included one lecture on architecture by the master in that year. Several wartime sermons and orations printed by St. Andrew's Lodge in the years to come echoed the same themes Price had eloquently spoken to at John Rowe's 1768 installation. In a 1782 charge delivered on the Festival of St. John the Baptist, John Warren, senior grand warden and soon to be master of the Ancient's now ascendant Massachusetts Grand Lodge, echoed the earliest masonic histories in referring to Noah's family's masonic character and made Newtonian references to gravity and to the mechanical arts and sciences. At Warren's installation as Grand Master, a chair formerly held by his late brother and Patriot martyr Joseph Warren, exactly one year later, Christopher Gore expounded not only on these ancient Masonic themes but gave considerable insight into colonial masonic practice and masonic internationalism as well. This sentiment is merged with Patriotic themes, as Boston's Ancient Brethren heavily overlapped Boston's Patriot elite.[17]

The first 11 pages of Gore's 13-page address revisit the mythological history including the family of Noah, the Assyrians and ancient Egypt. Echoing Price, he names, "Moses, that benevolent Grand Master of Israel". Archimedes is also credited with having sat in the masonic east as grand master. Of the persecution of masons in ancient and modern times, Gore explains that: "True it is, that in days of ignorance and bigotry, the Masonic institution has been branded, as inimical to government, and the lodge has been accused, as a mere scene of cabal and intrigue against the laws of the land, where it resided. But this suggestion has found place only in the breasts of base and gloomy tyrants." As a successful rebel against such a "gloomy tyrant" speaking to many who had shared in this now victorious struggle, these lines would have offered deep emotional gratification and affirmation of their achievement.[18]

Affirming this connection, he shifted from the ancient world to the immediate present, reminding his brothers that, "The history of the American army, affords innumerable instances of sublime patriotism, exalted and enlarged by Masonic virtue. Foremost among these, stands the late illustrious WARREN, Major-General in the army of Freemen, Most Worshipful Grand Master of all the Ancient Lodges in North America." He next reminded those assembled, many having sat with Warren in lodge and stood with him in war, "with what solemn piety his funereal obsequies were performed in this sacred temple." In reminding the brethren of the virtues of their fallen grand master, Gore referred to the quality of the lectures given by Warren, a Harvard-educated physician and radically forward thinking man of the Enlightenment.

Gore's oration reminded the fraternity that "There are many among you, my beloved brethren, who have heard him, from the chair of Solomon, inculcating with irresistible eloquence the doctrines of the benevolent and social. Not a few of you have illustrated, by your conduct, the efficacy of his lectures." This answers several important questions about colonial freemasonry. First, it shows that Warren was indeed a true believer who took freemasonry and his role at its head very seriously; more generally, it demonstrates that lecturers were given in American masonic lodges. Though none of the laconic records of St. Andrew's

Lodge or Massachusetts Grand Lodge refer to Warren's lectures, Gore offers first hand evidence of their being delivered in Boston's Ancient lodges. The oration finished on a high note, celebrating the newly won peace and the installation of "another plant from the same godly stock".[19]

The brethren were further treated that day to a charge delivered by John Elliot A.M. The learned Elliot's charge included classical references to Horace and the lessons taught at the school of Pythagoras. He spoke of the proverbs of Solomon and the writings of St. John the Evangelist, closing his speech with a verse of Drake. On the importance of science and learning, Elliot offered an illuminating passage which addressed the gap between the aspirational and actual intellectual abilities of the brethren and admonished them to study to the best of their abilities, and that should they be unable to excel intellectually nonetheless to do so morally, echoing the gap between the first and second degrees:

> All that I have now to recommend you is, that you be diligent in your studies--- and not rest contented with *superficial enquiries after truth*. Sensible, that it is not every one who hath the capacity of a Pythagoras, or a Locke, and *that one star differeth from another in luster*, we cannot with so much propriety insist upon it that you should all be philosophers, as that you should excel in moral virtue. You may learn, however, much by frequenting lodges-by attending to the instructions of them who are appointed to unfold the *mysteries of the Craft*, and applying to the work assigned you.[20]

Again, Elliot speaks to unrecorded intellectual activity and instruction within the lodges in admonishing the brethren, even those who lack the capacity of the great philosophers, that they might learn much in the lodge and from those "appointed to unfold the mysteries of the Craft"— the officers and grand officers whose positions required the study of masonic ritual and lore. These lodges were not directly connected to Price, nor did their membership likely recall firsthand the glory days of English Masonic intellectualism decades before, though there were many with experience of Boston's Modern lodges and of contemporary British freemasonry. Yet in the two charges delivered at the installation as grand master of a second Harvard educated Patriot warrior named Warren there is clear evidence that the masonic history, enlightened republicanism, moral philosophy, and scientific aspirations which saturated the literature and formed the identity of transnational masonic society remained intact 50 years after the first American lodge charter had been received in Boston. These ideals were set to take on new significance as the fraternity's association with the victorious patriots carried the masonic movement to the highest levels of social power and prestige in the early decades of the new United States.

Notes

1 Edith Stebecki, *Paul Revere and Freemasonry* (Boston: Paul Revere Memorial Society, 1985), 55–57; https://massfreemasonry.org/news/cornerstone-ceremony-commemoratives/

2 *Proceedings*, 438–441, 447.

3 St. Andrew's, Minutes.

4 *Ibid.*, 449–451.

5 St. Andrew's, Minutes and Records; Bullock, *Revolutionary Brotherhood*, 90–1.

6 Lodge of St Andrew, *Minutes, 1756–1778* (Boston: Grand Lodge of Massachusetts) microfilm; Edith Stebecki, *Paul Revere and Freemasonry*, 70–5, 108–113.

7 St. Peter's Lodge Minutes Book 1, Grand Lodge of Massachusetts, Boston; Tyrian Lodge Minutes Book 1, Tyrian Lodge, Gloucester; Stebliecki, *Paul Revere and Freemasonry*, 70–5, 108–113.

8 St. Andrew's, Minutes and Bylaws; Steblecki, *Paul Revere and Freemasonry*, 102–4; *Boston Evening Post*, October 9, 1739, advertisement; Aimee Newell, *Curiosities of the Craft: Treasures from the Grand Lodge of Massachusetts Collection* (Boston: Grand Lodge of Massachusetts, 2013), 38–9.

9 William Palfrey, Moses Brown, *The Course of True Love in Colonial times Being the Confessions of William Palfrey of Boston and the Friendly Advice of Moses Brown of Providence Concerning Polly Olney* (Boston: The Merrymount Press, 1905), ix. This book contains a series of letters between Palfrey and Brown from the early 1760s.

10 Ronald Heaton, *Masonic Memberships of the Founding Fathers* (Silver Springs: The Masonic Service Association, 1974), 16.

11 Palfrey to Dermot 1171, Palfrey to Dermot, March 17771, Palfrey MSS.

12 Calcott, i–xvi; Mary Ann Yodelis Smith, "William M'Alpine," in, *Boston Printers, Publishers and Booksellers, 1640–1800*, ed. Benjamin V. Franklin (Boston: G.K. Hall & Co., 1980), 358–360.

13 Lodge of St. Andrew, Minutes and Bylaws, 1756–1778, Boston: Grand Lodge of Massachusetts, microfilm.

14 *Ibid.*, Second Lodge, Minutes; Grand Lodge, *Proceedings in Masonry*, 108–9; Calcott, *Candid Disquisition*, i–xvi.

15 James Royal Case, Merele P. Tapley, *A Bicentennial History of the Grand Lodge of Connecticut* (Hartford: Grand Lodge of Connecticut, 1989), 4–33; Hugo J. Tatsch, *Freemasonry in the Thirteen Colonies* (United States: Kessinger Rare Reprints, 1933), 60–72, 176–191; William Palfrey, Letters of William Palfrey to John Harris Cruger, Boston: Harvard University Houghton Library, Palfrey Family Papers bMS 1704.3.

16 Lodge of St. Andrew, Minutes and Bylaws; Jayne E. Triber, *A True Republican: The Life of Paul Revere* (Amherst, Mass.: University of Massachusetts Press, 1998), 111–3.

17 John Warren, Esq. S.G.W. *A Charge Delivered to the Antient and Honourable Fraternity of Free and Accepted Masons, at Boston, on the Festival of St. John the Baptist. A.D. 1782* (Boston: 1782); Christopher Gore, Esq. *An Oration: Delivered at the Chapel, in Boston: Before the Ancient and Honourable Society of Free and Accepted Masons, June 24, 1783* (Boston: Brother William Green, 1783). John Elliot's charge delivered at the same ceremony was included and contiguously numbered in the same bound pamphlet; St. Peter's Lodge, Records and Minutes Book I, MSS (Boston: Grand Lodge of Massachusetts Secretary's vault).

18 Gore, *Oration*, 10.

19 *Ibid.*, 101–13.

20 Elliot / *Ibid.*, 14–22.

10

Revolutionary Boston and Beyond: Freemasonry and the Sons of Liberty

"To improve the most noble art [geometry], to adore the Grand Architect of the Universe, is one of the areanums of Freemasonry. In recommending which to all the Sons of Liberty, I conclude, Sir, Your most humble servant, ARCHEOLOGUS" – "Archeologus", *Timothy's Gazette, March 30, 1752.*[1]

On September 30, 1761 St. Andrew's lodge initiated Joseph Warren, he having been proposed for membership by William Palfrey, future secretary of the Sons of Liberty and paymaster of the Continental Army. Presiding as master that night was William Burbeck, artillery officer in two past wars and in the Revolution to come. That evening, Dr. Warren met Paul Revere, his future subordinate in subversive activities. Senior Warden Joseph Webb, Moses Deshon, John Jenkins, future rebel artillery commander Thomas Crafts, Joseph Tyler as well as Burbeck, Palfrey, Revere and Warren would all become members and leaders of the Sons of Liberty in the years to come. Known future participants in the Boston Tea party meeting that night included Thomas Urann, Samuel Peck, Warren and Revere. Of the 20 members and 14 visitors, a significant number became politically involved in the years to come. During the half decade prior to the Stamp Act crisis which began American resistance to the crown, much of the top, secondary and tertiary leadership as well as rank and file members of the future resistance movement joined St. Andrews. The lodge also purchased the Green

Dragon Tavern, later known as the "headquarters of the revolution" for the number of subversive groups that met there. Governor Thomas Hutchinson referred to the Green Dragon as a "Nest of Sedition".[2]

Freemasonry played a strong contingent role in creating the relationships and directing the organization of the radical movement, beyond its also significant ideological support for the radicals' ideals. It also connected Boston's radicals to their counterparts within New England and beyond. The preponderance of freemasons among the Revolutionary generation and Founding Fathers has long led to speculation as to what freemasonry's connection to revolutionary activity was causal as opposed to coincidental. The evidence which follows supports the case for an active part in influencing the course of the Revolution. Though the data supporting a causal role in dictating the course of the Revolutionary movement, particularly in events such as the formation of the Sons of Liberty and the Boston Tea Party, is strongest in Boston, there is evidence of such involvement in many other colonies as well including New Hampshire, Rhode Island, Connecticut, New York, Philadelphia, Virginia, North Carolina and Georgia.

In Boston, both Moderns and Ancients were actively involved in resistance to the Stamp Act. Prior to the more radical period post-1768, John Rowe led much of the resistance; he became grand master during this time. The overlap between the leadership and membership, as well as much of the organizational structure of Boston freemasonry matches that of the Sons. To the extent that evidence on the Sons in other colonies remains, it seems Boston was not alone in this and in fact freemasonry and the Sons had the same leadership, contact points and communication channels in much of New England. Boston freemasonry and its leadership also overlapped other overtly political organizations such as the North End Caucus, formed by grand master Joseph Warren, and many groups such as the Marine Society, Ancient and Honorable Artillery Club and various fire clubs co-opted for political purposes, not to mention city and colonial government. St. Andrew's masonic networks overlapped those of St. John's, and included cross-visitation and organizational links to Patriot leadership in many seaport communities. Gloucester's Ancient Tyrian Lodge, closely connected to Paul Revere and made up of a who's who of local revolutionaries, shared politically active membership with Newburyport's St. Peter's lodge and St. Andrews. Modern lodges in Marblehead-with members including future vice president and namesake of gerrymandering Elbridge Gerry, General John Glover, and a slew of Continental officers. Lodges in Newburyport, Falmouth (now Maine), Nantucket, Portsmouth (New Hampshire), and in Newport and Providence, Rhode Island all featured a number of patriot leaders, mainly predating the onset of the independence movement and primarily among those most actively connected to lodges in multiple communities, including Boston. Finally, there is considerable evidence that the Lodge of St. Andrew's connection to the Boston Tea Party is more than mere legend.

The Fraternity of the Sons of Liberty

The Sons of Liberty was a set of radical groups that appears to have formed locally in a number of mostly seaport communities in response to the Stamp Act and became connected as unrest unfolded. In Boston, most of the leadership of the Sons had become masons prior to the Stamp Act, as had at least 26 to around 30 % of the membership, with others joining during the Stamp Act Period. Most telling from the perspective of causality is the fact that in both Ancient and Modern Lodges cases the overlap tends to be among men who became masons well before the Stamp Act Period. As noted above, Palfrey, Revere and Warren entered freemasonry together. The first introduced Joseph Warren to the lodge, and thus to Revere, and also through freemasonry became connected to the future leadership of the Sons in Rhode Island; he also held concurrent positions as secretary of the Sons and the Massachusetts Grand Lodge, of which Warren was grand master, Burbeck deputy grand master, and Revere served in various offices. Palfrey also sat in lodge with John Hancock well before entering his employ, and Hancock's clerk and future revolutionary and political leader John Lowell was among the last pre-Stamp Act members to enter the lodge early in 1764. Though he did not attend lodge often, James Otis remained connected to the brethren.

While it is true that St. Andrew's membership included some future tories like William M'Alpine, it is telling that these men rarely if ever attended lodge once the political crisis began. The masters of the lodge were consistently leaders or active members of the Sons and other revolutionary agitation: William Burbeck 1760–65, Joseph Webb 1765–6, Burbeck 1766–7, Joseph Warren 1768–9, Samuel Barrett 1769–70, Paul Revere 1770–1, Jonathan Snelling 1771–2, John Lowell 1773–4, and Edward Proctor 1774–6. Of these, all but Urann is listed as a Son of Liberty; he like Barrett, Revere and Warren participated in the Boston Tea Party and other rebellious actions and it is likely that he simply missed dinner on the one night that the Sons of Liberty took attendance. A similar overlap exists for the wardens, secretaries and treasurers of the lodge.[3]

The Sons of Liberty used secret signs, passwords, and insignia as do Freemasons. The language used by the Sons of Liberty as evidenced by their correspondence and several of the letters of prominent Sons shows marked sim-ilarities with those of freemasonry. For example, freemason and Son of Liberty Robert Treat Paine referred to the Sons as a fraternity. These men occasionally employed other Masonic symbols as well, for example in an April 16, 1766 letter from the Sons in Providence to the Sons in Boston they congratulate their "breth-ren" on their "love and charity;" in Robert Treat Paine's public letter he invokes the Masonic symbolism of the beehive. Thomas Young writing to New York Son of Liberty Hugh Hughes writes "as your Friend William Molyneaux says, truth is a small compasses." Molyneux, a mason, would have been very familiar with the symbolism of the compasses to represent truth. Sons documents also attest to a degree of class leveling in so far as the accusation of a Son of Liberty of any class against a man of higher standing would be taken at the brother's word. Interesting testimony regarding the political nature of Boston Freemasonry is the fact that Samuel Adams, a non-mason, included the Masonic lodges in his rounds of politicking. No record of Adams's visits to any lodge exists in the min-utes of meetings, however, his presence is recorded in the Centennial Memorial of St Andrew's and is attested to in several non-Masonic sources.[4]

Bullock and others support the view that the Ancients of St Andrew's were radicals, while the moderns of St. John's were either neutral or loyalist, with a few notable exceptions. This is a considerable oversimplification. To understand the complex role of the moderns in Revolutionary Boston it is necessary to differen-tiate between the activism of the Stamp Act period and the more severe radical-ization which occurred from 1768 to the onset of hostilities. During the Stamp Act Period the Moderns represented the very people most involved in organizing resistance to Parliament- the merchant elite. It is interesting to note that Andrew Oliver attended Master's Lodge regularly and also visited Second Lodge until January of 1764, after which his name disappears permanently from all records. Clearly, the Stamp commissioner was not welcome among Modern masons.[5]

Like most subversive radicals, the Sons of liberty did their best to keep their identities secret. However, secretary William Palfrey kept a list of the list of Sons of Liberty who dined at Liberty Tree, Dorchester on August 14, 1769. 1769 was an important year for the Sons as, according to a letter from Thomas Young to New York Son Hugh Hughes dated July 30, "The society of the Sons of Liberty after lying sometime inactive have again resumed their former vigor and begin to mediate a renovation of their correspondence thro the Continent." The list includes 355 sons, including seven visitors from Pennsylvania ("Dickinson, brother of the farmer"), 'Jerseys'("Reid, Mr., Secretary to Gov. Franklin"), four Carolinians, and one Virginian. Not included is John Rowe, Grand Master of the Moderns, who had been a leading son until the movement became more radical in 1768. Lt. Governor Hutchinson, writing in 1766, listed as leaders of the radicals John Rowe, William Molyneaux, and Solomon Davis. Rowe was a leader of the Sons until he was publicly branded an "incendiary" by other elites in the British coffee House in 1768, after which he gradually withdrew from the cause. Molyneaux appears as a visitor in Second Lodge, St. Andrew's, and the Massachusetts Grand Lodge. Adding him to the list of known Sons we have a total of 349 names to compare with the records of the lodges.[6]

Of those who can be positively identified as masons, 37 were pre- movement members of St. Andrew's (29 exclusively) not including honorary member John Rowe; 24 exclusive members of second lodge; 10 members of First Lodge who can be positively identified from the records of the 1750s or other sources (making 34 Moderns to 29 Ancients). There were 13 brothers who belonged to both camps; 12 who appear among the visitor roles of either St Andrew's or Second Lodge—primarily the former—and may have been members of First Lodge or brothers unaffiliated with a local lodge. This includes only those masons who appear in lodge records prior to the date of the dinner, the majority first appearing in Masonic records prior to the Stamp Act agitation. Two others may be positively identified from the Wellin's subscribers list, and there are 13 names which represent probable or possible brethren who cannot be definitively identified. In total, between 26 and 29.4 % of known Sons of Liberty were confirmed Freemasons. Considering the incompleteness of the records of First Lodge—the largest lodge in the city members of which tended to be merchants opposed to the Stamp Act- this must be considered an absolute minimum.[7]

Nine members who joined in 1766–67 also appear among the Sons 1769 anniversary dinner. There is no way to reliably determine which organization they entered first, however, their dual affiliations demonstrate the close connection between the two groups. They tend to be less prominent Patriots who for the most part were not involved in political affairs prior to their Masonic affiliations. Of particular interest is the January 8, 1767 initiation of Thomas Chase, a member of the Loyal Nine, the small political club that began anti-stamp activism. A Thomas Chase appears as a visitor to 2nd Lodge twice, in 1762 and 1763. Thomas Chase or Case also visited St Andrew's in 1764. At the time due to the Modern—Ancient schism, Modern masons wishing to join the Ancient Lodge of St. Andrew's were sometimes required to re-take their Masonic degrees. Therefore it is possible that Chase was already a modern mason who had visited the Ancients and simply retook his degrees. Even if we are dealing with two separate Chase's, his prominence among the Loyal Nine and the Sons followed by his Masonic initiation indicate a relationship between those overlapping groups.

Likewise, Modern Masons among the leaders of the Sons all entered masonry prior to the Stamp Act Crisis. Three Moderns present at the dinner deserve special attention. Thomas Fleet, a member of Second Lodge prior to 1760, was the publisher of the seditious *Boston Evening Post*. Richard Gridley, hero of the siege of Louisburg, had commanded the Massachusetts troops on the expedition to Crown Point and fought with distinction on the Plains of Abraham. His accomplishments as an artillery commander and military engineer were so highly esteemed that he was a half-pay officer of the British Army for life, and thus well connected at Castle William, as well as the commanding officer of the Ancient and Honorable Artillery Company. He was also a past master of Second Lodge. William Burbeck was both a Modern and a charter member of St. Andrew's. He had also put up the money for the 1764 purchase of the Green Dragon. At the time of the dinner he was deputy grand master under Joseph Warren. Burbeck was Gridley's second in command of the Ancient and Honorable Artillery Company, which met in the Green Dragon.[8]

The overlap becomes tighter as the known leadership of the Sons of Liberty is considered. The secretary, William Palfrey, was secretary not only of the Merchants Club but also grand secretary of the Massachusetts Grand Lodge. The letters of the Sons of Liberty to John Wilkes instruct Wilkes to direct his correspondence not to Edes and Gill's print shop, the location specified to the Sons in other colonies in their documents later collected by Jeremy Belknap, but to the Whig Coffee House owned by brother John Marston. Masonic networks along maritime trade routes were ideal channels for discrete political communication. Nearly all of the letters exchanged between Boston Sons' secretary William Palfrey, the Sons of Liberty and John Wilkes were delivered by masons: Capt. Hall, Capt. Scott, and Dr. John Jeffries. Scott and Jeffries were confirmed Sons of liberty.[9]

Morgan and Morgan's *Stamp Act Crisis* credits for creating the Sons of Liberty in Boston the Loyal Nine, a smaller group of nine men, including two and possibly three freemasons, who committed some of the first acts of resistance. Their argument for causation is wholly chronological—the Loyal Nine acted then the Sons of Liberty formed, and included the Nine in their initial activities. How a group of nine men, including only one genuine elite, freemason Henry Bass, morphed into a citywide movement under new leadership that soon connected to similar movements across the continent is omitted from Morgan's work. It seems more likely that the nexus for the Sons came out of the lodges, or at least

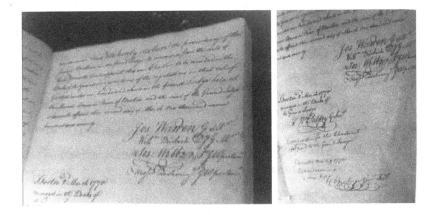

Figure 10.1. March 2, 1770 Minute Books of Gloucester, Massachusetts' Tyrian Lodge Signed by Sons of Liberty Joseph Warren, GM, William Burbeck, DGM, Joseph Webb, SGW, Moses Deshon, JGW, William Palfey, Grand Secretary, three of whom were also North Caucus Members, and Gloucester Selectman, Patriot leader and lodge charter member Epes Sargeant, Jr. (Courtesy Tyrian Lodge).

was closely connected through them, allowing them to draw on freemasonry for membership, physical space in the Green Dragon, and organizational practices. That at least two of the Nine were masons would have made folding this smaller group into the new organization that much easier.

A Network of Networks

Key Patriot freemasons were often involved in multiple political or politicized organizations. Paul Revere was among the leadership of the Sons of Liberty, North End Caucus, Long Room Club (assuming there actually was such a group—no contemporary reference to it exists prior to Drake's 1884 *Tea Leaves*) and carried out the orders of Patriot leaders. Grand master of masons Joseph Warren co-founded the North Caucus, and helped lead the Long Room Club, Sons of Liberty and the Boston Committee of Correspondence. James Otis was also in the Long Room Club (which may simply have been a euphemism for the Sons of Liberty) and Committee of Correspondence and was the radicals' ideological leader from the very beginning. Less well known, Thomas Chase was a member of the Loyal Nine, the North Caucus, the Anti-Stamp Fire Club and participated in the Boston Tea Party. Another North End Caucus member and Tea Party

Mohawk, Thomas Urann, served as master pro temp of St. Andrew's at the special meeting held on the might of the Tea Party. William Molyneux was a member of the North End Caucus and the Boston Committee of Correspondence. He organized women's sowing bees and notoriously raised gangs of youths to tar and feather Tories. Molyneux appeared as a visitor to both St Andrew's and Second Lodge, and at the first Massachusetts Grand Lodge meeting after the Tea Party. At minimum, 30 % of the 60 known members of the North End Caucus were freemasons, mainly from St. Andrew's. Whether or not the Long Room Club was a distinct group or another name for the Sons, it was named for the Green Dragon's long room.[10]

Joseph Warren was among the most prominent political figure in the Patriot cause. He presided over the State House while still leading many of the grassroots organizations of mechanics and agitators and the Massachusetts Grand Lodge. Paul Revere, in addition to the groups already mentioned, had by 1774 become, "one of upwards of thirty, chiefly mechanics, who formed ourselves into a committee for watching the movements of the British soldiers, and gaining every intelligence of the movements of the Tories. . .we held our meetings at the Green Dragon Tavern." The mechanics reported only to Samuel Adams or freemasons Warren or Benjamin Church. William Palfrey, zealous mason and ultra-patriot, dined, drank, and sat in lodge while in England with men such as John Wilkes, George Hailey, and lesser men involved in the Wilkite agitation. Doubtless, both politics and freemasonry (and any overlap between the two) were topics of discussion because the lodges and their members were politically involved. Considering his attendance of lodges throughout New England and in old England, it seems likely that Palfrey, whose Masonic, business, and political networks overlapped heavily, must have attended lodges in New York, Pennsylvania, and the Carolinas when he traveled on business- including the time he traveled on the business of 'the committee' in the months prior to the Boston Tea Party. His last trip to England included intelligence gathering as well.[11]

John Rowe was not the only Son of Liberty to exit the fight as political tensions increased from 1768. No less than 20 of those who dined in Dorchester that August evening in 1769 turned coat. Several other masons who appear on the list of Sons of Liberty—Andrew Cazneau, William Palfrey's beloved brother-in-law, Samuel Quincy of Second Lodge, and Dr. John Jeffries of St. Andrew's who had carried letters from Palfrey to John Wilkes- all became loyalists once the shooting began. It seems that many Modern masons did the same. Jeffries was so well regarded that while in exile he entered the *Neuf Soeurs* during Franklin's tenure and was eventually welcomed back to Boston. His case was an exception. The defection of the less radical sons may in fact have accelerated the radicalization of the movement. The structure had been created and had grown sufficiently strong to stand losing the less committed. At this point more radical leaders including Joseph Warren, Paul Revere, and the radical artisans of the North End, many of whom were members of St Andrew's, replaced the less radical leadership of the elite, many of whom were modern masons and who had helped to create the Sons of Liberty based on the organizational template of freemasonry.[12]

The records of Second Lodge and the known membership of 1772 Rising Sun lodge indicate a political schism among Boston Moderns. In the years preceding Rising Sun, Second Lodge was not only well attended but received as visitors William Molyneux and James Otis— together on one occasion- William Palfrey, and other Whigs. Following the formation of Rising Son, attendance dropped dramatically and was largely Tory or members with no discernible politics. The 18 members of First Lodge who asked for the petition included St. Andrew's members / patriots Samuel Barrett and John Gray, Son of Liberty William Jones and as Master leading Patriot Benjamin Church, Jr. Moderns in Portsmouth, based on their records, and apparently in Newburyport and Marblehead, where Patriots emerged as leaders and reinvigorated the lodge, all underwent power struggles resulting in Patriot control of the lodges. Notably, unlike many Modern lodges, these survived the revolution. In Rhode Island and Georgia, as well as several Connecticut lodges, known members were prominent Patriots from the onset of radical agitation. These Modern lodges also survived the war. This indicates that the revolutionary orientation of a lodge or grand lodge, rather than simply its Ancient-Modern orientation, was a key determinant in its survival in the independent United States.[13]

Masonic Sons of Liberty across the Colonies

Outside Boston the names of the Sons of Liberty are hard to come by, but those who can be identified tended heavily to be masons. In New Hampshire the papers of the Sons of Liberty which comprise Belknap's collection were given to him by St. John's member William Parker, implying that Parker must have played a leading role in the Sons. Many of the documents are marked as being in the handwriting of Colonel Theodore Atkinson, also a prominent member of the lodge. Joseph Bass, the first of seven committee members to sign his name to the correspondence of the Sons was also a mason. Samuel Langdon's description of the Sons as "the leading inhabitants of the town" implies an overlap with the lodge, which also boasted many of the principle inhabitants. Many members of the lodge were prominent in political and military affairs throughout the Revolutionary period.[14]

Masonic documents from Connecticut and Rhode Island are sparse, however again several of the leading Sons of Liberty in both states may be confirmed to have been masons. Freemasonry in Connecticut began with the return of soldiers from the Louisburg campaign of 1745. On their return to Connecticut a number of Louisburg veterans led by Col. David Wooster founded the first lodge in that state, Hiram #1 in New Haven, with a charter from Massachusetts. Wooster died a on the Revolutionary battlefield. Israel Putnam, a leader of the Sons and commander at Bunker Hill, became a mason during the French and Indian War. Samuel Wyllys also numbered among Connecticut's masons who were Sons of Liberty. Important to the Sons of Liberty were printers; masons owned all three of Connecticut's newspapers, and all three were overtly Patriot in their politics.[15]

In Rhode Island, William Ellery was a leading politician and Son of Liberty who had received his Masonic degrees in First Lodge while or after attending Harvard. He was therefore directly connected to a number of Boston Sons. John Brown, Dr. Jabez Bowen, and John Jenkes, all members of the Providence Sons' committee, were masons as well. As the letters between a young William Palfrey and Moses Brown prove, Palfrey first met the Brown brothers, Dr. Bowen, and other future Rhode Island political leaders in the lodge in 1761. Moses Deshon, prominent Boston Patriot, member of St Andrew's, officer of Massachusetts Grand Lodge, visitor to Second Lodge, and Son of Liberty, became a mason in St. John's Lodge Providence prior to 1761. John Brown is generally believed to have led the rebels who stormed the grounded revenue cutter *Gaspee* in 1772, shooting the ship's commander in the leg.[16]

In all four New England colonies the Sons of Liberty were linked by overlapping Masonic connections which predated the Stamp Act period. These links through an organization which provided a structure of governance, intercommunication, mutual trust, secrecy, Enlightenment ideology and an extensive human network provide the most logical explanation for the speed, efficiency, and uniformity with which the Sons of Liberty were able to create themselves and become such a powerful political force.[17]

Sons in New York and Philadelphia

The Grand Lodge of New York disappeared with the arrival of the British and was replaced with a group of Tory refugees from Boston and British officers. Prior to this time nine lodges operated in the city of which only one, St. John's, survived the war, without its records intact. They even tell the story of a Patriot member brought to New York as a prisoner of war who escaped prison and hid in the lodge, which had been taken over by British officers. During a meeting he fell from his hiding place through the ceiling. The brother tavern keeper explained the situation to the surprised English officers, who advised their American brother on the best time to cross the water unseen.

What records were kept during the war, indicate that most of the original members left with the Patriots. Prior to its dissolution, the original Grand Lodge of New York issued a charter to a military lodge for troops traveling to join the Patriots at the Siege of Boston. This and the fact that its membership was scattered and its operations and those of the lodges under its auspices halted with the arrival of the British indicates that the membership was heavily patriot. Prominent pre-war members included Robert Livingston, master of his lodge. The most important New York Son of Liberty who was a confirmed freemason before the birth of the Sons was Isaac Sears. Sears was among the most important leaders of the Sons of Liberty in New York. He affiliated with a Patriot heavy lodge in Connecticut in 1775 after the lodges in New York had been driven out of the city by the British.[18]

Of the 94 signers of the constitution of the Albany New York Sons, only 8 or 9 were members of the local lodge; another two members of the Scottish Rite Ineffable Lodge of Perfection by 1774. Records for this second body are incomplete, and membership was generally for men who were already masons in a standard lodge. Compared to the overlap in other colonies this is a considerably smaller proportion- only between 8.6 and 11.8 %. These include the sometimes master of the lodge, Jeremiah van Rensselaer, whose name is the second on the constitution after that of super patriot Thomas Young. Albany's Sons were the only ones known to have a written constitution. Considering that the freemasons were the one society which had been operating under written constitutions since 1723 at the absolute latest, and the only one of the two societies known to have contributed to the Albany sons which had one, it is highly plausible that the Masonic contingent in the Albany Sons, while a secondary contributor to its overall membership, contributed the idea of writing and signing a constitution. The prominence of the Master of the Lodge's name near the top of that constitution implies a leading role for him, a logical choice since he was accustomed to organizing and operating a secret society.

Pauline Maier credits the local Dutch reformed church with having served as the organizational base for the group here, however as David G. Hackett points out, the leaders and older generation among the church opposed the radicals and the Dutch members were younger men whose activity put them at odds with their faith. Many of these younger Dutchmen joined the Sons, but their church very much against the will of the church. When the Albany Sons made contact with their brethren in New York City they were reorganized on the New York model. Albany was the only local unit which was reorganized when it entered the New York—New England Sons of Liberty network, implying that the others shared a similar and compatible if not identical organizational structure from an early time.[19]

Philadelphia Ancients boasted three lodges prior to the Revolution, Lodge No. 2, which had begun as Modern No. 4 and created the Ancient Grand Lodge, and two newer lodges, No. 3 and No 4. The two younger lodges continued operations as normal through the war, however No. 2 experienced two prolonged interruptions. First, between February 14, 1776 and October 15, 1776, at which time the resume minutes explain:

> The members attendant of the Lodge are extremely unhappy that the present contest (though in favor of Liberty) hath rendered it impossible for them to give that attendance which they would willingly have given to this body. They however hope that the extreme necessity of the times will fully compensate for such deficiency conscious that Brother Masons are so sensible of the advantages of freedom as to accept the apology.

The redcoats apparently considered the lodge "a nest of rebels"- their meetings again ceased from July 21, 1777 to November 6, 1778 during the enemy occupation of the city. The lodge furnished 28 captains, 10 majors, and 16 colonels to the Continental Army. At least two naval captains, Lambert Weeks and James Anderson, joined the lodge on October 15, 1776 and took expedited degrees the following day before going to sea. On February 2, 1779 Worshipful Colonel Thomas Proctor opened the lodge then resigned the chain "on account of particular business regarding his regiment." Following the lodge's struggles the December 28, 1778 St. John's Day procession marked the lodge's triumphant return to their city. It was here that Reverend Smith gave his sermon, derived from that given in Boston 49 years prior, to General Washington in his first public appearance as a mason. Without documents of the Sons of Liberty in Philadelphia it is impossible to know who of Lodge No. 2 belonged to that group specifically, but the lodge was clearly politicized. As the grand lodge, the same brethren chartered a lodge in the Pennsylvania artillery in 1779.[20]

The Sons in the South

The two states with the strongest revolutionary tradition after Massachusetts are Virginia and Pennsylvania; both had correspondingly strong Masonic establishments as well. As Morgan and Morgan point out, the men who led the revolutionary movements, particularly in the two leading colonies of Massachusetts and Virginia, rose to prominence during the Stamp Act crisis. As in Massachusetts, many prominent Virginians including Thomas Adams, John Bannister, Richard Cary, John Fitzgerald, Hugh Mercer, John Muhlenberg, William Woodford and of course, George Washington, were masons. George Washington entered the lodge in Fredericksburg November 4, 1752. The origins of his lodge are unknown, but it worked in Ancient fashion and hosted the region's elite for decades. Though fragmentary, its records include one president, one member of the Continental Congress, 30 officers in the Continental Army and 15 in the militia, one tavern keeper whose house host subversives, as well as seventeen merchants and planters apiece. Again, without specific lists of Sons of Liberty it is impossible to definitively connect the two groups, but much of Virginia freemasonry, particularly in Fredericksburg Lodge, had a decidedly Patriotic bent.[21]

In Virginia there were a number of lodges working under warrants from five European grand lodges: the Modern and Ancient grand lodges of England, the grand lodges of Scotland and Ireland, and the Grant Orient of France. According to the *Proceedings in Masonry, 1733–92* of the Grand Lodge of Massachusetts, there was also a lodge chartered by St John's Grand Lodge somewhere in Virginia on October 24, 1766. This date does not correspond with any of those recorded in Virginia. Most likely it was issued to one of a number of lodges in Norfolk, the largest port in the Commonwealth and the probable birthplace of Virginia freemasonry.[22]

A major port, many Boston masons sailed in and out of Norfolk- until the twentieth century, the only city in America to have a Freemason Street running through it. Freemason Street was so named by 1753 at the latest, possibly a good deal earlier. Unfortunately, all Masonic records from Norfolk were lost in the fire started by Lord Dunmore's bombardment on January 1, 1776; however, various document surviving from Norfolk's early days suggest that several lodges existed in the town at the time. According to Pauline Maier, the Norfolk Sons of Liberty were preparing to join the inter-colonial Sons of Liberty network when the new of the repeal of the Stamp Act arrived. If the Massachusetts chartered Virginia lodge was located in Norfolk- and no other suitable location exists as the origins of the other Virginia lodges are accounted for- it places all of the interconnect Sons of Liberty along lines of Masonic communication.[23]

In North Carolina, The only Sons of Liberty whose identity can be confirmed is the chairman of the Sons, Cornelius Hartnett and Robert Howe. Hartnett led the citizens of Wilmington in demonstrations against the Stamp Act. He also presided as master in Wilmington Lodge and later served as deputy grand maser and grand master during the American Revolution. He has been called 'the Samuel Adams of North Carolina' for his leadership from the Stamp Act until his death in 1780 after escaping rough captivity. Harnett and Masonic brother and future Revolutionary general Robert Howe led the Sons of Liberty who marched in arms to free two ships seized by the customs. North Carolina had masonic ties to St. John's Grand Lodge in Boston as well as extensive ties to the Patriot heavy Virginia masonic world. Pauline Maier demonstrated that the one identifiable group of Sons of Liberty in South Carolina overlapped heavily with a local fire club. The Fire-wardens here, coincidentally or not, were members of the Charleston lodge.[24]

The Sons in North Carolina formed a connection with their counterparts in Savannah Georgia. Members of Savannah's Solomon's Lodge #1 were prominent among the founders of the Sons of Liberty in Georgia. Provincial grand master Noble Wimberley Jones, and brothers Joseph Habersham, George Walton, and John Houstoun were among the Sons of Liberty who threatened Governor Wright and his council. Jones, an assemblyman since 1755 and leader of the Sons of Liberty from the Stamp Act on, also had a role in appointing Benjamin Franklin as the colony's representative. It was largely his continual re-election as speaker of the assembly that led Governor Wright to dissolve that body. Like St. Andrew's Long Room in Boston, freemason and first master in 1774 of Unity Lodge Peter Tondee's Long Room, 'a minor hotbed of revolutionary politics', served as the meeting place of the second provincial congress follow news of the fighting at Lexington and Concord. The composition of the congress was heavily masonic: the president, Archibald Bulloch, was master of Solomon's lodge; congressional secretary George Walton secretary of the lodge; in all 20 masons from three lodges— Solomon's, Unity, and militarily oriented Grenadiers—represented eight communities in the congress. Bulloch served as Georgia's first president and commander-in-chief while Walton signed the Declaration of Independence and went on to become chief justice and later governor. Fifteen of sixteen members of the Committee of Safety and three of five delegates to the second continental congress were masons, as were at least six of the few known Sons of Liberty.

Jewish freemason and Patriot Mordecai Sheftalls served as chairman of the Parochial Committee. The Parochial Committee was a complimentary parallel governing structure which worked in conjunction with the Sons. Governor Wright in 1775 called the rebels, "a Parcel of the Lowest People, chiefly carpenters, shoemakers, blacksmiths etc. with a Jew [Mordecai Sheftalls] at their head". During the war Wright listed Sheftalls as "The Great Rebel" on a list of rebels made after the Britsh re-took Savannah. Sheftall had an extensive business network throughout Pennsylvania, the Caribbean and the Carolinas, and like New England's masonic merchants his fraternal connections must have been useful both in business and in politics in all of these colonies. Interestingly, Sheftall visited Boston's Second Lodge for the October, 1765 meeting, at the height of the Stamp Act Crisis. A Modern mason, it is plausible that he may have visited the more prominent first lodge as well; prominent Sons of Liberty frequented both lodges and it seems unlikely that the topic of resistance to the Stamp Act did not come up over the course of the evening.[25]

St. Andrew's Throws a Tea Party

How much treason was hatched under this roof will never be known, but much was unquestionably concocted within the walls of the Masonic lodge.[26]

The chain of events which led from political resistance to armed revolt began with the Boston Tea Party on December 16, 1773. The Tea Party and its Mohawks had close associations with the Green Dragon and the Lodge of St. Andrew's. It is unlikely that the Lodge of St. Andrew purchased the Green Dragon Tavern in 1764 with the intention of turning it into the "Headquarters of the Revolution," rather it was a sound business decision. The long room was considered the best hall in any tavern in town. The lodge had been meeting in the Green Dragon since its inception, but its acquisition gave them a valuable piece of real estate and an established business. The name was officially changed to the "Freemason's Arms," but Bostonians continued to call it the Green Dragon. It became the meeting place, not only for the Lodge of St. Andrew's and its masonic offspring the Provincial Grand Lodge of Massachusetts (1769) and Massachusetts Lodge

(1770), but for a number of revolutionary groups including the North End Caucus, Loyal Nine, the town selectmen, the Long Room Club (if such a club existed), the Committees of Correspondence, the Sons of Liberty, Ancient and Honorable Artillery Company, and Revere's mechanics. In providing a physical space for so many groups linked with resistance and Revolution, St Andrew's made a major contribution to the Revolution. Furthermore, members of the various groups involved must have become frequenters of the tavern and had ample opportunity to interact officially and unofficially.[27]

Traveling, or military lodges of the British 29th and 64th regiments also met in the Freemason's Arms, at least briefly, offering the opportunity to eavesdrop and interact to Patriot masons. At the time drinks and meals were often served during meetings by tavern staff who were also freemasons. They shifted to meeting on their own at Castle Island. This provided Deputy Grand Master William Burbeck, in charge of stores at the Castle until his defection to the Patriots at the outset of the war, with ample opportunity to interact with enemy brethren. Sgt. John Batt, who initiated Prince Hall's African brethren, likely at Burbeck's request and certainly with his blessing, was probably the same former British sergeant named John Batt to defect and enlist as an American in Henley's Regiment of Continentals in Boston in 1778. So sympathizers as well as careless tongues likely sat in lodge with the deputy grand on Castle Island. Joseph Warren had a number of informants probably including the wife of General Gage, and may have used the traveling lodges as a source of information. Furthermore, it would have made masons in the British military establishment reticent to take action against the tavern.[28]

The Rubicon crossing of American resistance was the Boston Tea Party. This action, as dramatic as it seems, was part of an establishment tradition of resistance based on Whig ideology. Legend has often ascribed the Tea Party to the brethren of St. Andrew's; certainly, the Green Dragon Tavern was a staging point for the "Indians." The list of known Tea Party participants includes members of St. Andrew's Lodge, the North End Caucus, and the Sons of Liberty. Cooper Samuel Peck, active in both St. Andrew's and the North End Caucus, asked in town meeting earlier that day if "tea was misceable in salt water."[29]

William Palfrey took a business trip in the months prior to the tea party. Ostensibly, he was traveling through New York and Philadelphia on business for John Hancock. Not averse to mixing business with politics, Palfrey's real agenda becomes clear in a December 3, 1773 letter addressed simply to "Hon'd Sir." In it Palfrey passes on information on the tea situations in the colonies he has visited to "your committee" or "the committee." He stated that he had met "the committee" of Philadelphia the night before. He goes on to inform the committee that they should proceed with the actions they have planned, indicating that the Boston Tea Party had been devised prior to his departure in early November or late October. He later confirmed the real business of his trip, "My Most respectful salutations & hearty good wishes attend the Gentlemen of the Committee beg leave to assure them that my whole time of absence shall be devoted to their service in the common cause."[30]

A fragment of a song sung as a rallying cry on the night of the Tea Party connects Warren, Revere, and the North Enders to the Tea Party:

Rally Mohawks – bring out your axes!
And tell King George We'll pay no taxes
Then rally boys and hasten on
To meet our chiefs of the Green Dragon
Our WARREN's there, and bold REVERE.[31]

Within St. Andrew's there is a traditional view that the plan was devised in the lodge and its execution committed to the North End Caucus. Brother John Hancock's Cadets stood guard while the Mohawks did their work. In a letter to Samuel Adams, William Palfrey explained that the Cadets disbanded when, in the wake of the tea party, the governor intended to revoke his commission. Brethren acquainted with the 'Mohawks' have offered some corroboration of this story. A speech given in the Lodge of St. Andrew's Centennial Memorial describes the story as told by the late Col. Henry Purkett, "Our brother the Colonel, by what he used to say to us, as well as by what he did not say, declared that the "Boston Tea Party" was got up at the "Green Dragon Tavern," and in St Andrew's Lodge."

Purkett had yet to enter the lodge at the time of the Tea Party. He was apprenticed to Samuel Peck, a lodge member since no later than April 10, 1756. Peck and Purkett both participated in the Tea Party, the master having made his query regarding tea and salt water in Town meeting. Peck apparently told Purkett to stay home that night, but the young apprentice and North End Caucus member disobeyed. Logically then, it seems that Peck was present at the lodge when someone suggested the plan and brought it back to his apprentice, who after distinguished military service joined the lodge in 1795. Francis Drake corroborates the Lodge's version of events, and credits-albeit probably incorrectly- John Rowe with having asked in town meeting, "Who knows how tea will mingle with salt water." While the basis for Drake's claim is difficult to ascertain from either the town records or Rowe's diary, mason Samuel Peck's comment on the misceability of tea does appear in the records. Brother Adam Collson gets credit for yelling, "Boston harbor a teapot tonight!"[32]

Many of the North End Caucus members who were masons were also Sons of Liberty, and the Caucus is generally credited with a leading role in the Tea Party. Their minutes for Oct. 23, 1773 state, "voted- That this body will oppose the vending any Tea, set by the East India Company, to any part of the Continent, with our lives and fortunes." They then voted a committee of Paul Revere, Abiel Ruddock and John Lowell "to correspond with any Committee chosen in any part of the town on this occasion." The group next met on November 2nd at

Figure 10.2. Lodge of St Andrew minutes for December 16, 1773. "Lodge closed (on account of the few brethren present) until tomorrow evening." Thomas Urann served as Master Pro Temp- he is listed among Drake's Tea Party Participants. No other flourishes like those on the bottom of the page occur anywhere in the minutes. (From the Collection of the Grand Lodge of Massachusetts.)

the Green Dragon, the first recorded instance of the Caucus meeting in its new home, and an indication that they meant to be closer to the nexus of resistance. The entire meeting concerns resistance to the tea, including requesting the presence of John Hancock and creating a resolution threatening the owners of the tea. They voted, "That this body are determined that the Tea shipped or to be shipped by the East India company shall not be landed." The Caucus minutes include no other meetings after this one until March 11th when they met at their original venue.

The records of the Lodge of St. Andrew include two interesting entries relating to the tea party: November 30, 1773: "Lodge adjourned on account of the few Brothers present. N.B. consignees of TEA took the brethren's time." The next meeting occurred on December 16. The lodge had already met on the 2nd and the 9th. No business was conducted at the special meeting held "by adjournment" on the 16th. Thomas Urann served as Master pro temp, yet he appears on Drake's list of Tea Party Mohawks that same night. Four other brothers were present. The minutes say only, "Lodge closed (on account of the few brethren present) until tomorrow evening." The Green Dragon must have been busy that night, as

Figure 10.3. John Johnson's 1773 Watercolor of the Green Dragon Tavern, bearing the legend "Where we meet to plan the consignment of a few shiploads of Tea." Clearly visible in the upper left hand corner in the Masonic square, compasses, and letter G. (Courtesy American Antiquarian Society).

it hosted the small lodge meeting and a large contingent of the 'Mohawks' that stormed the tea ships. The next evening the lodge met again, initiating and preparing to initiate a number of new members. The minutes for the meeting of the 16th also contain a set of flourishes resembling letter T's; no other such flourish appears at any point in the minutes. One final tantalizing piece of evidence of the lodges involvement is the 1773 watercolor by John Johnson showing the Green Dragon with the Masonic square, compasses and let G and the caption, "Where we met to plan the consignment of a few shiploads of tea."

Worshipful Brother Paul Revere's Ride

John Pulling and Robert Newman, the two men credited with hanging the lanterns in the Old North Church to warn of the British assault on Lexington were both masons. In reality, this was probably accomplished by Pulling, a vestryman of the church and member of Marblehead Lodge no later than 1760 closely associated with St. Andrew's. Pulling and Revere had served on several Boston committees including the Committee of Correspondence, Inspection, and Safety and a sub-committee "to collect the names of all persons who have in any way acted against or opposed the rights and liberties of this country." He was closely connected to Patriot leaders in Marblehead, most if not all of whom were lodge members. Pulling was moreover a merchant accustomed to climbing ship's rigging and quite capable of ascending the familiar bell tower with a lantern or two on his own.

Paul Revere's account of his ride indicates that he had chosen a friend to hang the lanterns in the Old North Church. The singular is key. Robert Newman's family on the centennial celebration publicly took credit for their ancestor based on his having been questioned by the British on the night of April 19, 1775. Newman, a member of Second Lodge, was a sexton in the church and was questioned by the regulars later that night. He apparently explained that he had given Pulling the keys to the church on the latter's request. Satisfied, the troops left the Newman household unmolested but seized Pulling's property and would have arrested him if not for a daring late night escape across the water. Thus, Newman either turned rat right away or was completely ignorant of Pulling's patriotic activities. Revere and Pulling met through masonry prior to the resistance movement, another case of masonic contingency in the American Revolution. The legend that a British officer who was a mason aided in Paul Revere's release from capture on the night of his famous ride is implied by his account. The officer in question, on hearing that his prisoner's surname was Revere, asked if he was Paul Revere. Receiving an affirmative answer he reassured the prisoner that he would not be harmed.[33]

The Widow's Son's Funeral

St. Andrew's began with masonic enthusiasts who become deeply ensconced in the Patriot cause. These men were representative of much of the rank and file of freemasonry, particularly Ancient freemasonry in America. The funeral oration spoken by Perez Morton at the masonic funeral of Grand Master Joseph Warren, who fell at the battle of Bunker Hill where he was felled by a ball to the head, offers a look into freemasonry's relationship to the struggle in the minds of these Patriots. Perez Morton's, *AN ORATION, Delivered at the King's Chapel in Boston, April 8, 1776, on the Re-interment of the Remains of the late Most Worshipful Grand-Master, Joseph Warren, Esquire, President of the late Congress of this Colony, and Major- General of the Massachusetts forces, who was slain in the Battle of Bunker's Hill, June 17. 1775,* documents the Masonic worldview of American Revolutionaries in a highly politically and ideologically charged address given to an audience of Masons and Patriots shortly after the British evacuation of Boston.

Warren was among the last casualties at the Battle of Bunker Hill, taking a ball to the head defending the hastily-built redoubt atop Breed's Hill while most of the Massachusetts militia was already in retreat. As Morton makes clear, the details of his death fit the story of Hiram Abiff virtually to a tee. In the Third Degree, the candidate undergoes Hiram's murder at the hands of 'ruffians'. Like Warren, Hiram was a 'widow's son'. His body is buried first in the rubbish of the temple and then at the brow of a hill under a sprig of acacia. A repentant ruffian reveals the location, where Hiram's body is identified by a jewel, after which he is reinterred in a place of honor.

Though he probably died instantly when the musket ball entered his brain, Warren's body was bayoneted by vengeful British troops, replicating Hiram's multiple death wounds at the hands of a gang of 'ruffians'. His body was cast into an unmarked mass grave; a loyalist member of the lodge led his brother's to the grave, which like Hiram's was set at the brow of a hill. They identified Warren's body by a 'jewel'—a piece of golden dental work fashioned by silversmith cum dentist Paul Revere, the earliest known case of dental forensics. The assembled masons then raised the grand master's body from the ground and offered him a proper burial. The he raising and multiple burials complete the legend. To men who believed that the legend of Hiram Abiff represented the genuine secret history of a Biblical figure and founder of their order, the parallels must have been deeply meaningful.

Morton dedicated three substantial paragraphs in his *Oration* to Warren as a freemason. Like Hiram Abiff, he had achieved the grand mastership by merit. Morton lauded Warren's wisdom, strength and beauty, virtues symbolically represented by the ancient grand masters as described in the second degree. The oration then expounded upon the deceased's charity. Finally, and most dramatically, Morton described the parallels between the deaths of the two grandmasters.

> The Fates, as though they would reveal, in the person
> of our Grand-Master, those mysteries which have so
> long lain hid from the world, have suffered him, like
> the great master-builder in the temple of old, to fall by
> the hands of ruffians, and be again raised in honor and
> authority. We searched in the field for the murdered
> son of a widow, and we found him, by the turf and the
> twig, buried on the brow of a hill, though not in a decent
> grave. And though we must again commit his
> body to the tomb, yet our breasts shall be the burying
> spot of his Masonic virtues, and there —
>
> An adamantine monument we'll rear,
> With this inscription, < Masonry lies here.' "[34]

Morton does not refer to the aid of a Tory mason, possibly Dr. John Jeffries, in finding the grave 'by turf and twig.' Nonetheless, this also corresponds to the allegory in which the ritual one of Hiram's betrayers, after his capture, reveals the location of the grave. Even so, those similarities would not have been lost on the brethren present that day to see their beloved widow's son raised in honor and authority before being again committed to the tomb. The funeral oration gives a rare illustration of how the assembly brethren saw the causes of freemasonry and liberty to be inseparable.

Freemasonry was not the cause of the American Revolution, but it did bring together many Revolutionary leaders. In the early days of the movement, particularly during the Stamp Act, it served as an organizational support that was co-opted into the movement. Unlike other such societies, it was inter-colonial in scope and offered pre-existing networks, physical meeting spaces, and trustworthy brethren with shared political ideology. It overlapped all of the other, more local groups co-opted in like manner, bringing together both individuals and organizations. Stephen Bullock has described the importance of freemasonry in establishing social hierarchy and shared cultural bonds in the Continental Army. Following the war, freemasonry grew exponentially in the early Republic. In *The Radicalism of the American Revolution* Gordon Wood states offhandedly that, "the importance of freemasonry to the Revolutionary generation cannot be underestimated."

Though much has been made of the role of Boston's Ancients in revolutionary agitation and of Ancient freemasonry in the global spread of the craft, Boston's Modern grand lodge played an essential role not only in creating lodges and provincial grand lodges from Canada to South America, but in establishing the Craft's prestige in the colonial mind and thus paving the way for the explosion of ancient freemasonry in the early Republic. Modern lodges that supported independence generally survived and thrived after the war, save ironically in New York, the stronghold of the British. In Boston, the Modern grand lodge which had done so much to spread the Craft across the hemisphere declined as the old elite it represented was replaced with the new elite ensconced in the Ancient Massachusetts Grand Lodge.

Notes

1 "Archeologus", *Timothy's Gazette*, March 30, 1752; quoted in Albert Gallatin, Mackey, *The History of Freemasonry in South Carolina, from its Origin in the Year 1736 to the Present Time, Written at the Request of the Grand Lodge of Ancient Freemasons of South Carolina by Albert G. Mackey, M.D., Grand Secretary of the Grand Lodge* (Columbia: South Carolinian Steam Power Press, 1861), 24–27.

2 St Andrew's, Minutes and Records; *Tea Leaves: Being a Collection of Letters and Documents Relating to the Shipment of Tea to the American Colonies in the year 1773 by the East India Company* (Boston: A.O. Crane, 1884), 41. William Palfrey, "An Alphabetical List of the Sons of Liberty who Dined at Liberty Tree, Dorchester, Aug. 14, 1769." *Proceedings of the Massachusetts Historical Society 1869–70* (Boston: Mass. Historical Society, 1871), 140–2.

3 St. Andrew's, Minutes; Palfrey "A list of the Sons of Liberty", Drake, *Tea Leaves*.

4 Thomas Young to Hugh Hughes, *Misc bound Documents* (Boston: Massachusetts Historical Society), Fischer, *Paul Revere's Ride*, 22–3; Correspondence of the Portsmouth Sons of Liberty, Belknap Papers,(Boston: Massachusetts Historical Society) microfilm, Box 61; Correspondence of the Providence Sons of Liberty, Peck Collection 63–70 (Providence: Rhode Island Historical Society).; Lodge of St Andrew's, *Centennial Memorial of the Lodge of St Andrew* (Boston: Press of Arthur

W. Locke and Co., 1870), 13; Russell Bourne, *Cradle of Violence* (Hoboken: John Wiley & Sons, 2006), 89; Benjamin Carp, "Fire of Liberty: Firefighters, Urban Voluntary Culture, and the Revolutionary Movement". *William and Mary Quarterly* 58, no. 4 (Oct. 2001): 718–818.

5 Master's Lodge Minutes.

6 Palfrey, "List of the Sons of Liberty;" "Meeting, May 19", 1768, Palfrey MSS; Second Lodge Minutes; St Andrew's Minutes; Morgan and Morgan, *Stamp Act*, 160; Russell Bourne, *Cradle of Violence: How Boston's Waterfront Mobs Ignited the American Revolution* (Hoboken: John Wiley & Sons, 2006), 130. Hutchinson to Pownall March 8 1766 quoted in Morgan, *The Stamp Act Crisis*, 190; Young to Hughes quoted in Benjamin Carp, *Defiance of the Patriots: The Boston Tea Party and the Making of America* (New Haven: Yale University Press, 2010), 46.

7 Palfrey, "List of the Sons of Liberty;" St Andrew's, Minutes; First Lodge, Minutes; Master's Lodge, Minutes; Second Lodge, Minutes; Wellins Calcott,. P.M, *A Candid Disquisition of the Principles and Practices of the Most Ancient and Honorable Society of Free and Accepted Masons; Together with Some Strictures on the Origin, Nature, and Lesson of that Institution* (Marlborough: Brother William MacAlpine, 1772), i–xiii.

8 Jayne E. Triber, *A True Republican: The Life of Paul Revere* (Amherst: University of Mssachusetts, 1998), 111–3. Revere had served as a lieutenant under Gridley at Crown Point. Triber speculates that the personal animosity between Burbeck and Revere hindered the latter's receiving the artillery commission he desired.

9 Correspondence of Palfrey to Wilkes, Wilkes to Palfrey, Sons of Liberty to Wilkes, Wilkes to Sons of Liberty, 1768–1770, Palfrey MSS; St. Andrew's, *Minutes*; First Lodge, *Minutes*; Second Lodge, *Minutes 1760–1778* (Boston: Grand Lodge of Massachusetts) Microfilm,; Francis S. Drake, *Tea Leaves: Being a Collection of Letters and Documents Relating to the Shipment of Tea to the American Colonies in the year 1773 by the East India Company* (Boston: A.O. Crane, 1884), 41. William Palfrey, "An Alphabetical List of the Sons of Liberty who Dined at Liberty Tree, Dorchester, Aug. 14, 1769." *Proceedings of the Massachusetts Historical Society 1869–70* (Boston: Mass. Historical Society, 1871): 140 – 2.

10 First Lodge, *Minutes*; Goss, *Life of Col. Paul Revere*, 635–6; St. Andrew's, Minutes; Bourne, *Cradle of Violence*, 89; St. Andrew's, *Minutes*.
   150th Anniversary of the Lodge of St. Andrew (Boston: Lodge of St. Andrew, 1907), 273–300. Fischer presents partial lists of members St. Andrew's Lodge and five groups known to be involved in revolutionary activities, including a list of known tea part "Indians". Unfortunately, the 1763 list of St. Andrew's member he used does not include patriots who joined the lodge prior to other activities but after 1763. He does not list Masonic affiliations other than St. Andrew's.
   Bullock, *Revolutionary Brotherhood*, 107.

Paul Revere Memorial Association, *Paul Revere – Artisan*, 122; E.H.Goss, E.H. *The Life of Colonel Paul Revere, With Portraits many illustrations facsimiles etc. 3rd ed.* (Boston: Howard W Spurr, 1899), 635–6. Likewise, –not first cite for Goss.

11 *William Palfrey to Unidentified, December 1773, Palfrey MSS;* Paul Revere Memorial Association, *Paul Revere – Artisan*, 129; Paul Revere, "A letter from Col. Paul Revere to the Corresponding Secretary", *Collections of the Maschusetts Historical Society for the year MDCCXCVIII* (Boston: Samuel Hall, No 53, 1798), 106–111.

12 Palfrey to Wilkes 1769–1771, Palfrey MSS; on loyalists, see Maier, *From Resistance to Revolution*, 306–12.

13 Proceedings, 196, St. John's Portsmouth, Minutes and Records, St John's Newburyport, History.

14 Peck MSS, Belknap box 61, Maier, *From Resistance to Revolution*, 306–12, St John's Lodge, Portsmouth New Hampshire, Archival Database.

15 Hiram Lodge #1, *Hiram Lodge No 1, Ancient Free and Accepted masons 1750–1916* (New Haven: John J Corbett Press), 1916: 1–9; St John's database; J. Tatsch, *Freemasonry in the Thirteen Colonies* (United States: Kessinger Rare Reprints, 1933), 168–192; James Royal Case andMerle P. Tapley, *A Bicentennial History of the Grand Lodge of Connecticut* (Hartford: Grand Lodge of Connecticut, 1989), 6–36; Second Lodge Minutes.

16 St. Andrew's, Minutes; William Palfrey, Moses Brown, *The Course of True Love in Colonial times Being the Confessions of William Palfrey of Boston and the Friendly Advice of Moses Brown of Providence Concerning Polly Olney* (Boston: The Merrymount Press, 1905), 3–7.

17 St Andrew's 150th, 269; Peck MSS, Belknap box 61, Tatsch, *Freemasonry in the Thirteen Colonies* (Kessinger Rare Reprints, 1933), 168–176.

18 Ossian Lang, *History of Freemasonry in New York* (New York: The Hamilton Printing C. 1922), 6–65; James R. Case, *Connecticut Masons in the American Revolution* (Grand Lodge A.F.&A.M of Connecticut: 1976), 4–7, 26–42. Grand Lodge of Connecticut, *Connecticut Masons in the Revolution, a Nominal Roll* (New Haven: Grand Lodge of Connecticut, 1974), 55.

19 http://www.nysm.nysed.gov/albany/org/masonic.html#4846. Maier, *From Resistance to Revolution*, 303–4.

20 Barrat, Sache, *Freemasonry in Pennsylvania 1727–1907*, xi–xiv.

21 *The Lodge at Fredericksburg a Digest of the Early Records Abstracted from the Record Book of Minutes, 1752–1771; Lodge Accounts to 1785; with an account of the Members of the Lodge in the American Revolution; and a nominal roll of all names in the Records.* Complied by Ronald Heaton & James Case (Silver Spring: Masonic Service Association of the United States, 1981), 8–9, 26; Morgan, *Stamp Act Crisis*, 295–305; Heaton, *Masonic Memberships of the Founding Fathers,* vi–xxiii.

22 Grand Lodge of MA, *Proceedings,* 482–483.

23 W.S. Morris, *Early Dates in Norfolk Masonry* (Norfolk: William S. Morris, 1928), 4–6.

24 Thomas C. Parramore, *Launching the Craft*, 3–54; Frederick G. Speidel, *North Carolina Masons in the American Revolution* (Raleigh: Press of Oxford Orphanage, 1975), 60–2; Berman, *Loyalists and Malcontents*, pre-publication draft; Maier, *From Resistance to Revolution*, 306–312.

25 William Bordley Clarke, *Early and History Freemasonry of Georgia 1733/4 – 1800* (Grand Lodge of Georgia: 1924), 62–5, 84–5; Wood, *Radicalism of the American Revolution*, 245; Walter J. Fraser, *Savannah in the Old South* (Athens: University of Georgia Press, 1983), 84–6; Berman, *The Grand Lodge & American Freemasonry*, 160–4; Second Lodge Minutes.

26 Drake writing about the Green Dragon, quoted in Mansfield A. Hobbs, *The Contribution of Freemasonry to the Success of the American Revolution* (New York: St. Paul's Conclave No. 12, 1925), 8.

27 Bullock, *Revolutionary Brotherhood*, 113. Hodapp, *Solomon's Builders*, 66. Fischer *Paul Revere's Ride*308; lists alternative meeting sites for the Long Room Club and North Caucus- which began meeting in the Dragon in 1773.

28 Grand Lodge, *Proceedings*, 226–8; Rince Hall, Primus Hall John Batt Reel, Microfilm. Boston: Grand Lodge of Massachusetts.

29 Maier, *From Resistance to Revolution*, 275–8.
   Langley, *American Revolution and the Craft*, 43–4.

30 William Palfrey to unidentified, December 3, 1773, Palfrey MSS.

31 Langley, *Revolution and the Craft*, 43–4. Brother James Gleason recorded the fragment. Gleason was a child during the Revolution and later collected remembrances from his elders. As such it may not be a perfect remembrance.

32 *Ibid.*, 41–4; Palfrey to Samuel Adams, August 25th, 1774, Palfrey MSS.; Lodge of St. Andrew, *Centennial Memorial* (Boston: Press of Arthur W. Locke and Co. 1870), 113. The story is recounted in an oration by W. Bro Hamilton Willis; Francis Drake, *Tea Leaves* (Boston: Smith and Porter, 1884), lxiii, lxvi–lxvii.

33 Paul Revere. *Statement on His Ride and Capture*. 1775. From americanrevolution.org/revere.html; Rev. John Lee Watson, *Paul Revere's Signal: The True Story of the Signal Lanterns in Christ Church, Boston Reprintd from the Collections of the Massachusetts Historical Society* (Cambridge: John Wilson and Son, 1877).

34 *Ibid.*

11

Boston's African Lodge: Hub of the Black Masonic Universe

Freemasonry had both practical and emotional appeal to blacks throughout the Atlantic. On March 6, 1775, 15 free black Bostonians led by Prince Hall, already on his way to a position of leadership in the Black community which comprised approximately 10 % of the city's population, took their degrees in a Irish military lodge under Sergeant John Batt. Boston's 'African' community included creoles, both native Bostonians and migrants from southern and Caribbean colonies, as well as African born Blacks such as Cato Gardner, who raised $1,500 of the $7,700 for the building of the African meeting house in 1806. Boston's African Lodge went on to become a major force in agitating for the rights of Blacks and organizing the leadership of Boston's African American community. The fights they led for voting rights and school integration presaged the Civil Rights movement of the twentieth century and pioneered the legal strategies of later generations of activists. Led largely by masons, Black Bostonians helped make their city a center of the Abolition movement and supported William Lloyd Garrison and other white abolitionists.

As in the white Masonic world, Boston's black brethren formed their own grand lodge and spread the Craft to free Black communities in the northern United States. They drew on masonic mytho- history in creating early Afrocentric and Black nationalist ideas that became ensconced in African American intellectual culture sufficiently to have a continuing influence on these strains of discourse for over a century. The overlapping relationship between the founders of Prince Hall freemasonry and the early Black churches led to a noticeable masonic stamp on the latter.[1]

The Africanist literature produced by the lodge is a direct outgrowth of the masonic history of the *Constitutions* and *Calendars*, and is largely derived from them directly. Combined with Prince Hall's religious writings they paint a clear picture of Hall's intellectual quest to place Africans at the origin of what he saw as the two most ancient and civilizing organizations of the European world—the church and the lodge. The lodges promoted this masonic worldview in *The Columbian Parnassid* and its published sermons, which it sent to the Grand Lodge of England and noble supporters, and actively courted connection with the wider masonic world on both sides of the Atlantic. Indeed, African Lodge was the only American lodge added to the English *Freemason's Calendar* and "New and Correct Lists of Lodges" after American independence. The Lodge provided London with news on New England lodges. There is also some indication that Hall, a leading Black activist in Boston, used masonic connections to prominent whites to influence the language of the 1780 Massachusetts constitution which effectively ended slavery in the state. The lodge they founded in Providence eventually moved to Liberia, the first certain foundation of a Black lodge in Africa.

Traditionally, masonic historians have always claimed that Hall was born in Barbados and came to Boston. There are no documents to confirm this, although Barbados has issued a postage stamp in his honor. An alternative hypothesis posits that he was born in slavery to a Bostonian leatherworker named Hall, who owned a young slave named Prince. Since Prince Hall was a leatherworker and caterer by trade and was about the same age as the slave Prince owned by the white Hall, it seems most likely that these were the same people. This is not conclusive, however, because Prince Hall was a very common name among Afro-Bostonians, no fewer than seven showing up in Revolutionary war records. Hall's fourteen companions remain mysterious. The group certainly included the sailors and dockworkers who comprised the majority of free Blacks in Boston. A servant of white grand master John Rowe also became a brother. Hall may have been behind at least one of the petitions submitted to the Massachusetts legislature in the early 1770s asking for an end to slavery. He and other masons went on to author several petitions, one asking the legislature to aid in returning Blacks to Africa in 1787 to found a colony there, another asking for a school for Black children. The first petition, entitled *To the Honourable at General Court of the Commonwealth of the Massachusetts Bay. The Petition of the Subscribers a number of African Blacks,* is a clear indication of the African identity of the lodge's members.[2]

The previous year, he had offered Governor Bowdoin in writing on behalf of the lodge to assist in suppressing Shay's rebellion. In 1788, Hall led the protests against the kidnapping of three black sailors, including a brother mason, who were returned from the Caribbean. When the white government was not forthcoming in providing a school, it was the lodge and particularly revolutionary veteran Primus Hall who educated the youth of the Black community. They also provided the standard masonic charitable services including funerals and looking after members' widows and orphans. As time progressed, the lodge and its officers and members were heavily involved in community affairs including the Abolition and civil rights movements of antebellum Boston. That Hall and his people asked to be relocated to Africa indicates a strong sense of connection to their ancestral homeland, as does their identifying as "African Blacks".

Among the most important aspects of the African lodge's early years are its writings, which draw on masonic history to create an early version of pan-African ideology over a century before that term came into use; their cultivation of trans-Atlantic contacts, and the use of masonic connections to influence highly placed white masons. Indeed, Hall and Marrant's view of freemasonry as originating in Ancient Africa and spreading civilization to Europe is derived from the faux histories found in the *Constitutions* and the works that followed. There is also a connection between these masonic writings and Hall's religious writing, "The Lives of Some of the Fathers and Learned and Famous divines in the Christian Church from our Lord and Saviour Jesus Christ". Both seek to prove that Africans were the motive force in spreading the two ancient institutions which brought civilization and light to the world, Christianity and freemasonry. African lodge's correspondence with the grand lodge in England and publications in *The Columbian Parnassid* sought to actively assert this new twist on Masonic intellectualism across the wider masonic world.

Foundation of the African Lodge And Grand Lodge

Both the Lodge of St. Andrew's and African Lodge No. 1 maintain a tradition that several members of St. Andrew's were present at and assisted in the installation of African lodge. They further claim that the aspiring black masons, led by Hall who had achieved some standing in the community, approached Grand Master Joseph Warren in hopes of receiving a charter and that he favored the idea but was not able to bring it forward to a grand lodge in which it would likely have met considerable resistance. This oral tradition is plausible based on Warren's progressive attitudes. It does, moreover, seem highly likely that the patriotic Black Bostonians would first have approached the less elite, more radical of the two lodges, which included men known to them through business and in the community, before seeking out an Irish lodge among the hated British regiments.

The African Lodge declared itself a grand lodge in 1791 due to the ongoing difficulty of communication with England. June of 1791, when the African Grand Lodge installed its officers, is the one year in which there is no mention of a Feast of St. John the Baptist in St. Andrew's Lodge records. St. Andrew's lodge historian Winthrop Wetherbee believed this to be due to the lodge, which admitted a very small number of Black members in the early 1800s and thereafter, participating in the installation of African Lodge's officers. He also states, without sourcing the claim, that Modern grand master John Rowe and other white masons visited the lodge prior to the merger of the two white grand lodges in 1792. If any member of Massachusetts Grand Lodge did arrange for African lodge's warrant, it was probably former St. Andrew's master, Modern cross member and Warren's deputy grand master William Burbeck.[3]

Burbeck had served as master of St. Andrew's from 1760 to 1765 and again in 1767. The Son of Liberty and patriot artillery commander was, until the shooting started, the local commander of the fort on Castle Island and remained in charge of stores there once the British regiments took over the castle. He was second in command under brother Richard Gridley of the Ancient and Honorable Artillery company and a veteran artillery officer and Boston's primary maker of fireworks. Burbeck certainly used his position to provide intelligence to the patriots. Attending the regimental lodges at the castle was part of his duty as deputy grand master. Following the outbreak of hostilities Burbeck rowed himself to shore, surrendered, and was immediately commissioned an officer in the Massachusetts forces. According to Wetherbee, Brother Burbeck was present at the original initiation of Prince Hall and his brethren. Directly after this ceremony Prince Hall applied to Grand Master Joseph Warren for a permit for his lodge; Wetherbee speculated based on their archival documents that this was planned through Burbeck and failed only because of the death of Warren at Bunker Hill and subsequent break in Masonic activities until the Siege of Boston lifted. He further argues that Hall used Masonic connections to John Hancock and John Lowell to ensure that the key phrase "all men are born free and equal" was inserted into the Massachusetts constitution. Prince Hall and other lodge members fought at Bunker Hill. Primus Hall's service extended through much of the war.[4]

Following independence white Grand Lodges generally refused to accept Black masons, including those of African Lodge. This led African Lodge to apply to the Modern Grand Lodge of All England for a charter. The "New and Correct Lists" neither added nor erased lodges in the new United States in the decade following the American Revolution with one important exception. In 1785, Boston's African Lodge first appears in the roles at number 459. By listing the African Lodge in the *Calendar*, the Grand Lodge immediately advertised its existence to the Masonic world and opened its doors to visitation from every corner of the republic of masonry. It firmly announced that Africans across the Atlantic had a place in the fraternity. Essentially, African lodge brethren were now free to access the fraternity anywhere but in their own nation. Indeed, as the three Blacks kidnapped from Boston soon found out, masonic brotherhood could be most useful where slavery was most entrenched.

The correspondence between Prince Hall's lodge, William Moody, master of the Perseverance Lodge held at the Fleece, New Police Yard West, and English grand secretary William White was mostly carried by Captain James Scott, a mason and sea captain who frequently commanded John Hancock's vessels. Scott had delivered letters from the Sons of Liberty penned by William Palfrey to British radical and Freemason John Wilkes. He had been a member of first lodge for decades, and appears to have been a member of the West India and American lodge. Scott delivered the lodge's charter issued by the Duke of Cumberland, Grand Master of England, on May 2, 1787, approximately three years after it was composed. That Scott, a white member of Boston's oldest masonic lodge and a long time Hancock associate, went through the effort of carrying correspondence and documents for the African Lodge reinforces the fact that at least some important white masons in Boston supported African Lodge.[5]

Liberal sentiments moved William Moody, Master of London's Fleece Lodge, to assist in obtaining the charter for African lodge and to send the lodge a *Constitution* and *Calendar*, "though a stranger", as Hall stated in his thank you letter to Moody. This provided the African Lodge's members, many of whom were seafarers, with valuable information on the history and current events of the craft and on the location of lodges throughout Europe, the Caribbean, and around the world. Masonic mythological history with its references to Biblical and African monarchs clearly influenced the Africanist ideas in Hall and associate John Marrant's later sermons and tracts, and the references to the Knights of

Malta and other medieval orders found in the "Remarkable Occurrences" in the *Calendar* feature in these writings as well.[6]

The letters between Hall and Grand Secretary William White include a series of communications and remission of payments mostly directed through James Scott. Though not all of the letters have clear dates, they do indicate that communication was difficult. Hall's letter of May 20, 1796 informs the grand secretary that he had sent "six addresses delivered to my African Brethren on the 24 of last June," as well as a "small sum of money as a charity to the grand fund," which was carried by Brother Nero Daves "who died on his way to London last winter." It is unlikely that Hall would have learned of Daves' death quickly since the ship he died on was en route to London and thus by the time the sad news reached Boston he must have been dead for some time. The same letter states that Hall had sent an epistle the previous January 20, and had not received a letter from White since his (Hall's) letter of 1791. That he forwarded so many copies of the sermon implies that he intended White to further disseminate African lodge's Afro-centric interpretation of masonic history.

The contents of one letter are particularly interesting as they relate to the *Calendar* and to England's interest in the Masonic state of affairs in the former colonies. In an undated letter, Hall responds to questions about several of the lodges in New England. This letter appears to be from 1793 based on a reference to a sermon preached on the 25th of June the previous year, such a sermon having been giving on the 25th in 1792, and to the reference in the letter to a merger of several Boston lodges which had happened that year, when the Modern Rising Sun Lodge had merged into First Lodge, which had absorbed the second lodge in 1783, consolidating into one the Modern establishment. Not long after, in 1792, occurred the merger of the grand lodges in the city. Hall's reply is a bit vague but essentially correct. Based on Hall's letter, they had also asked specifically about the two Connecticut Lodges, No 93 in New Haven and No. 145, as well as Boston's Second Lodge and Marblehead Lodge. White had apparently asked about at least some of the New England lodges which were included in the "New and Correct Lists" presented in the *Calendar*. Hall reminded White that, "you wrote to us about the lodge No 2 that yousd(sic) to meet the Royal Exchange. . ." and goes on to explain that they had merged with "one or two more lodges." These were the First Lodge and the Rising Sun Lodge, though Hall did not explicitly state as much. Hall went on to inform White of the death of Henry Price and that John Cutler had become the Grand Master.[7]

Unless White neglected to share this information with the Grand Lodge's printer it would seem to indicate that this letter miscarried, as Price was still listed as the Grand Master and the First and Second Lodges in Boston as distinct entities for years to come in the *Calendar*. Regarding Marblehead, Hall states that, "I can't git no information of them neither they meet or not but I believe they do not for if they did I believe I should have heard of them. . ." Interestingly, this supposition on Hall's part was incorrect, Marblehead lodge having continued until the present day. However, Marblehead had suffered economically during the war to the point that no member of African Lodge would have had reason to go there. On the two Connecticut lodges, Hall explained that, "as for the Lodge No 93 in New Haven in Connecticut I hear they keep a Regular Lodge and I have reason to Believe it: the lodge No 145 do (illegible) the same as sum of them hath veseted(sic) our Lodge." This last piece of intelligence is significant, for it indicates that white masons from outside Massachusetts were aware of and even visited the African Lodge, carrying with them news of other lodges within their circles.

This letter is a very rare glimpse of the way that correspondence between masons, in this case the grand secretary of England and the master of Boston's African Lodge, carried masonic information around the world. In this single letter, Hall conveys the status of five or six lodges, if one includes those which have merged, in four communities in two separate states. This was in response to a lost request for information about several of the lodges so described. The requested intelligence dealt specifically with lodges included on grand lodge rolls which in English minds might still be under their jurisdiction. That Hall had more accurate information about the lodges in Connecticut than the one down the road in Marblehead demonstrates the way the network of personal connections trumped physical geography in the masonic world.[8]

Hall also attempted to give African freemasonry a prominent space in the intellectual world of masonic history and ideology. On May 2, 1787 Boston's *Columbian Centinel* reported African lodge's receipt of its charter. This was the beginning of a sustained publicity campaign by African Lodge. The *Columbian Magazine Volume II, No. 3* published in Philadelphia in August 1788, contains a long poem entitled, "An ORATION delivered before the Grand Master, Wardens, and Brethren of the Most Ancient and Venerable Lodge of AFRICAN MASONS" as well as two pieces of news from Boston. The first carried the news of the death of mason Perez Morton's mistress. Though it doesn't mention Brother Morton by name, the scandal was big news in Boston and its presentation here may have been a swipe at an unbrotherly white mason. The second report, dated July 29, begins, "The three negroes who were kidnapped and carried away from this town last February returned home." After describing the circumstances of their capture, the report states, ". . .they were carried to St. Bartholemew's, in the West-Indies, and offered for sale. A merchant coming on board, found one of them to be a *brother mason*, and having heard his story reported it to the governor." The report happily explained that one of the perpetrators was in prison, then describes the still at large ringleader.

This short piece is important on several levels. First, Hall and African Lodge had led the efforts to free the three sailors, including one of their brothers. They enlisted influential whites, likely through masonic contacts, in successfully petitioning the state government, itself replete with caucasian brethren, to pursue the case. There is a triumphal air to this report, and its description of the perpetrator is an attempt to warn potential victims and perhaps even see him brought to justice. It informs white masons that even a West Indian merchant looking to buy slaves recognized the legitimacy of the victim's masonic membership and came to his aid, and that the highest power in a slave colony acted on the Black brother's behalf. This advertised the utility of the craft to aspiring Black masons. It was a truly Atlantic tale of interracial masonic brotherhood in a venue with a trans-Atlantic circulation- the introduction to the *Columbian* stated that, ". . .a considerable number of those magazines will be sent to different parts of Europe." The lodge thus attained international publicity in two major publication in 1788, the *Columbian Magazine* and the annual *Freemasons Calendar*.

The *Columbian* was an excellent place to advertise the newly chartered African Lodge. It is very plausible that this was where the Black Philadelphia masons who applied to Boston for a charter first learned of No. 459. "An ORATION delivered before the Grand Master, Wardens, and Brethren of the most Ancient and Venerable Lodge of AFRICAN MASONS" draws heavily on Biblical arguments for masonic legitimacy, accepting that both Cain and Ham were blackened via curse—a major argument offered to support black slavery- and that both were progenitors of masonry. It argues for Black masonic legitimacy to white masons, advertises the fraternal enjoyment felt at the lodge to black and white alike. In addition, it connects the lodge, its members, and the craft to Africa, and references covertly the lodge's activism and the Massachusetts constitution.[9]

The issue of attribution bears consideration. As the Oration is credited to a fictional Coromantee speaking African and a merchant translator, the authorship cannot be fixed with certainty. Hall does not appear to have written any other poetry, though the meter is simple enough to have been a good amateur's creation. Peter Hinks, one of the foremost scholars of African American Freemasonry, has suggested that it may have been written for Hall's lodge by Jeremy Belknap or another white author in his circle. Belknap had worked closely with Hall in mobilizing the Massachusetts governed to act in freeing the three kidnapped sailors, and he and his circle were connected to the publishers of the *Columbian*. The only mention of African Lodge related compositions in Belknap's papers, however, is the one cited below in which he attributed authorship of most of John Marrant's important 1789 sermon to Prince Hall. It seems likely that Belknap's literary circle at least arranged for the Boston news and Oration's publication, though it is not possible to say who actually wrote it. In any case, the Oration served as an advertisement to masons around the literary world of the enjoyment and hospitality to be had at African lodge.

The piece opens by informing the reader of the lodge's existence and its being slighted by white masons, "ADVERTISEMENT- Some Readers, perhaps, may need to be informed, that in a certain metropolis, on this continent, there is a fraternity of *Negroes*, who are formed into a LODGE. They celebrate festivals, walk in processions, and wear aprons; but, it is said, are not readily acknowledged as masons by their *white* brethren." Here, the thesis is subtly expanded to include, without stating as much, the African roots of a fictional learned mason, "Their rights and claims are vindicated in this oration, which was spoken in the *Mandingo* language, at a late meeting of their lodge, by a very learned brother, and is now translated into English doggrel by a gentleman, formerly concerned in the African commerce, who is well versed in that ancient, musical, and sonorous language, but is afraid that he has not been able to express all its beauties in our modern, mixed, and imperfect dialect." The African mason who is able to speak on masonic jurisprudence in an African tongue is clearly fictional. The imaginary "gentleman, formerly concerned in the African commerce" implies a white brother who despite involvement in the slave trade visited the Black lodge as a brother. That the English version is less beautiful than the African original is a strong yet subtle statement of African pride.

The next section, "SCENE" speaks to the scientific and antiquarian facets of the craft from an African orientation. "Before the grand master on the table, a model of an Egyptian pyramid in ivory. On one side of the arch, a representation of the antediluvian city built by Cain. . ." Thus the masons of Egypt and of Cain's African metropolis feature among the elegant furnishings of the lodge. Advertising the conviviality of the lodge, the "necessary implements" include not only the standard masonic "trowels, levels, plumb-lines" but also "bottles, bowls, tankards," assuring readers that a visitor to African Lodge would not go thirsty.

Next, our Mandingo speaking mason informs his Black brothers that Africans are not only legitimate masons, but were the first to claim that right.

As thus – – – by universal fame

We blacks are call'd *the seed of* CAIN,

… Now it is clear from text of Moses (Which every brotherhood supposes

the best of books) that this said Cain

Built the FIRST CITY* [Footnote * *Gen.4.v.17*] Ergo, then

This ground we safely rest the case on

That brother Cain was the first mason.

The section on genesis continues, discounting Adam's qualifications as the first (white) mason. "And the first lodge however odd, Was held within the land of NOD." Having glorified and proudly toasted the normally vilified Cain and proven that his African city of Nod invented arts and sciences- with reference to Tubal, who figures in masonic ritual- the poet does the same for "…HAM our second founder, There never was a mason sounder." The Biblical curse of Ham is thus accepted and turned to Black advantage as proof of Black's having founded freemasonry.

From here the author turns to the question of whether a slave may be a mason by referencing the work of Jewish captives in Egypt. Again, we are reminded that masonry throve in a great African civilization, and that the Bible argues in favor of the primacy of the black brethren, as "By this account we clearly see / Men may be masons tho' not free." The stanza continues by boasting of the merits of operative masons and poking fun at the sort of gentlemen likely to shun their Black brothers, "Why should those speculative drones / Claim the sole rights of Hiram's sons, Who never move a tool to work / Unless, perhaps, their knife and fork?" This particular stanza speaks to the class differences which separated the workingmen of African Lodge from many gentleman-laden white lodges, and serves as a counterattack against the masonic legitimacy of the masons most likely to call the African Lodge's regularity into question.

The Oration continues with another toast to the *black* lodges of Nod and Ham "Where students from all quarters came, To hear the scientific lecture, and learn the trade of architecture." African Lodge's Oration adds to the body of literature making these assertions of scientific education. This leads into a stanza that ends with the conclusion, "That SLAVES may be ACCEPTED MASONS."[10]

The next stanza refers to the freedom guaranteed in the Massachusetts constitution:

> But we have need of no such plea,
> Thanks to our country WE ARE FREE.
> Slav'ry that curse, that false pretence
> By government is banish'd hence.
> No slaves in durance here are bound
> Save those on Castle William's ground;
> But "free and equal" are the terms
> By which we hold our lives and farms.
> White, brown, and black, and ev'ry shade
> Have equal "rights" to them convey'd.

This may be more triumphal boasting by Hall, if indeed he had used masonic connections to avail on John Lowell to see the "free and equal" language included in the Massachusetts constitution. In case their freedom and equality are not sufficient qualifications in the eyes of the world, the next stanza lauds England's Grand Master Effingham, who had signed their charter. Skillfully, Hall combines the masonic legitimacy of England with patriotic American sentiment, recounting how Effingham had resigned his post rather than serve in America. The piece concludes with long masonic charge and more calls for the drinking bowl. In the *Columbian Magazine*, Prince Hall and his Masonic brothers advertised African Lodge to white and black masons, aspiring masons, and to non-masons who knew of the fraternity's self-invented ancient history and ideology. The lodge continued to attempt to promote itself in print, publishing sermons presented by John Marrant in 1789 and by Hall in 1792 and 1797.

African Lodge, the African Church and Black Nationalism

Atlantic blacks were less educated and often, like many white's of their day, open to literalist christianity, so it is reasonable that many of African lodge's members were among those masons who took masonry's biblical "history" seriously. Prince Hall, though literate and intelligent, believed deeply in the Bible as fact, as evidenced by his religious writing. Indeed, one defining difference between Prince Hall masonry and standard freemasonry stamped onto the African version of the Craft by its founder is the closely Christian nature of Black masonry. That the

Craft spread with the AME and AMEZ churches and often shared its highest officers with these two sects is not coincidental.

Prince Hall's papers include several religious writings. "Some Remarks on Mr. John Edwards compleat History or Summary of all the Dispensations and Methods of Religion from the Beginning of the World to the Consummation of All Things" is unfortunately illegible, but the title speaks to Hall's spiritual investigations. "The Lives of Some of the Fathers and Learned and Famous divines in the Christian Church from our Lord and Saviour Jesus Christ" is a long handwritten series of biographies of church founders who came from or were educated in Africa. They begin longer and more detailed and towards the end become quite attenuated, indicating that he either lost steam as he went or that he placed the most important and richly detailed of his subjects first. Several of these biographies turn up in his later masonic writings, particularly his 1797 sermon to the lodge. In addition to placing prominent Christians, including those who brought the word to Europe and even Britain, in Africa, Hall also dwells on cases of the oppression of the lowly but righteous Christian, an obvious parallel to his own people. Hall's religious and masonic writing emphasized the African origin and dissemination of christianity and freemasonry.[11]

The first sketch recounts the story of Dionysius Areopagita, an Athenian of eminent family who traveled to Heliopolis, Egypt at the age of 25. Here, Dionysius converted to Christianity and carried the word back to Athens, where he faced resistance and disbelief. The next tale is "The Life of Cyprian who Dyed Anno Christo 269". Cyprian "was born in the ancient city of Carthage in Africa, and being educated in the study of the Liberal Arts, he Profited so much therein, that whilest he was young, he was chosen Professor of Rhetorick." These references to the "liberal arts" including rhetoric overlap those found in masonic literature. The story may have helped to impress Hall with the importance of the liberal arts in which masonry professed to educate its members, rhetoric being the second of the seven. Converted by "a godly Presbyter of Carthage" Cyprian rose to be presbyter and then Bishop of Carthage.

After an unreadable section the story continues, ". . . his fame increased so exceedingly, that he was not so much the Bishop of Carthage, as of all Africk, yea of Spain, the East, West and Northern Churches, yea he was judged the father of all Christians." Hall has Cyprian spreading Christianity from Africa to Europe and even acting as the head of the church there. Finally, he was arrested by the proconsul of Africa for refusing to make sacrifices. Thus, our African evangelist and Bishop of Carthage, "Spain, the East, West, and Northern Churches" stands firm against the oppression of Rome. After a largely illegible passage we find that the Africans Alexander and Athanasius, Bishop of Alexandria, defended true Christianity against the heresies of the Arians.

After several short and mostly unreadable pieces on "The Life of Basil, who Flourished Anno 370" and "The Life of Hierom Who Dyed:422" there is a longer piece on Augustine. The beginning is difficult to read but the word "Africa" clearly appears in the second line. As with Cyprian, Augustine became learned in the liberal arts, ". . .he first taught grammar in his own city where he was born; then Rhetorick in the City of Carthage. . ." After traveling to Rome and Milan and serving as tutor to Valentinian he received baptism. Even before finding the gospel, this African was educating no less a personage than the Caesar of Rome in the liberal arts. On returning to Africa he became a great evangelist. As Athanasius had in his day, Augustine fought the heresies of his epoch.

"The Lives of Some of the Fathers. . ." is undated. It contains no legible overt masonic references but some of the stories appear in Hall's later masonic orations. Prince Hall's interpretation of early church and masonic history with its African roots and the suffering of the church fathers is interesting in light of the fact that it predates the formation of the independent Black church. In fact, considering that an overwhelming number of founders of the several major Black churches were Prince Hall masons exposed to Hall's brand of Afro-centric freemasonry, as well as to his masonic writings and teachings, it is logical to conclude that Hall influenced the intellectual and ideological orientations of the early Black church.

A Sermon Preached on the 24th of June 1789, Being the Festival of St. John the Baptist built on these themes. Though credited to Reverend John Marrant, Jeremy Belknap, wrote that Hall had composed most of the sermon for Marrant to deliver. The thesis accepts the accusation of whites that Africans are the sons of Cain, then cites Gen. iv. 17 in which Cain and his sons built a city on the east of Eden to prove that masonry was originally an African art and that freemasonry is therefore African. Again citing the story of Ham, it continues, "Nimrod the son of Cush, the Son of Ham, first founded the Babylonian monarchy. . .and founded the first great empire at Babylon, and became grand master of all Masons, he built many splendid cities in Shinar, and under him flourished those learned Mathematicians. . ." The sons of Ham are thus recast as the founders of civilization, mathematics and of the sacred Craft of freemasonry. The story continues that the second son of Ham carried masonry into Egypt where he built the city of Heliopolis. The other descendant's of Noah—the progenitors of the non-African races- received masonry from their African cousins, "the descendants of Abram sojourned in Egypt; . . . practiced very little of the art of architecture till about eighty years before their Exodus, when by the overruling hand of providence they were trained up to the building with stone and brick, in order to make them expert Masons before they possessed the promised land." It is through those ref-ugee African masons that all the knowledge of the Near East made its way to Europe.[12]

Having established that Black freemasons founded civilization and science, Marrant spoke to the contemporary situation of Africans around the world, " Ancient history will produce some of the Africans who were truly good, wise, and learned men, and as eloquent as any other nation whatever, though at present many of them in slavery, which is not a just cause of our being despised; for if we search history, we shall not find a nation on earth but has at some period or other of their history been in slavery. . .". Hall, in one of the earliest speeches published by an African American, laid the foundation for many of the ideas of later pan-Africanism and Black Nationalism: that it is from Africa that civilization and science flourished; that it was the African who taught the arts of civilization to the other races of the world; and that many of history's great men were Africans, whose current state of enslavement in no way diminished their greatness.[13]

Hall's correspondence with Grand Secretary White indicate that he sent six printed copies of the sermon to England. He apparently hoped to see his Boston sermon, like Brockwell's 40 years before, included in British masonic publica-tions. The sermons were given before an audience that included not only lodge members but white masons as well. *A Charge Delivered to the Brethren of the African Lodge on the 25th of June, 1792*, Hall's next publication, featured both biblical allusions to Africans civilizing whites and christians standing in the face of oppression. It also drew on masonic histories, likely derived from the *Calendar*. Biblical themes begin with "the compassion of a Black man to a Prophet of the Lord, Ebedmelech. . ." who interceded on Jeremiah's behalf. Hall then stated, "I shall now cite some of our fore-fathers, for our imitation." Drawing on his earlier Biblical work, he tells the story of Tertullian, who defended christians when accused "because of their silent meetings", a notable issue for masons. He repeats the story of Cyprian of Carthage, "Spain, and the east, west and northern churches," finishing with Augustine and Fulgentius. Citing these examples, he rails briefly against the deprivation of education, a matter on which the lodge led in petitioning the city and when unsuccessful took on the duties of teach-ers themselves. Counseling patience, he admonished his listeners to, "Hear what the great Architect of the universal world saith, Aethiopia shall stretch forth her hands unto me."

Hall then offered a history of masonry since the fall of Jerusalem in 70 AD. Wildly anachronistic like many masonic histories, this appears to be based largely on the "Remarkable Occurrences" section of the *Calendar*. A confused timeline leads to the Knights of Malta, a hint of masonic Templarism. Speaking of their wars with the Turks, he poses this question, perhaps intended for white masons as much as Blacks, "Query, whether at that day, when there was an African Church, and perhaps the largest Christian church on earth, whether there was no African of that order; or whether, if they were all whites, they would refuse to accept them as their fellow Christians and brother Masons. . . Sure this was not our conduct in the late war, for then they marched shoulder to shoulder. . ." The author sent copies of this sermon to the grand lodge of England, and to the king and his son the presiding grand master and Prince of Wales.[14]

Hall's *Charge delivered to the African Lodge, June 24, 1797* contains the expected Biblical and masonic allusions but also rails more directly against slavery, prejudice, and Blacks being deprived of education. This speech shows a keen awareness of events in the African Atlantic, admonishing the brethren, "let us remember what a dark day it was with our African brethren six years ago, in the French West Indies" where now, "the scene is changed; they now confess that God hath no respect of persons, and therefore receive them as their friends, and treat them as brothers. Thus doth Ethiopia begin to stretch forth her hand, from a sink of slavery to freedom and equality." He speculates that "the loss of the African traffick..begins to dawn in some of the West-Indie islands." More great Africans from Biblical and masonic history appear, as "Jethro, an Ethiopian" who instructed Moses, his son-in-law. Implying masonic connection, "Jethro understood geometry as well as laws that a Mason may plainly see." These stories culminate in the interracial love of the greatest of masons, Solomon, who ". . .was not asham'd to take the Queen of Sheba by the hand, and lead her into his court, at the hour of high 12, and there converse with her on points of masonry (for if ever there was a female mason in the world she was one)". The charge finishes by encouraging upright masonic virtue and extending brotherhood to masons of all complexions.

These published works all promoted the primacy and legitimacy of African masonry and promoted an African identity among Blacks. This Africanist view, Hall's emigrationist ideas, activist focus, and mixing of freemasonry with evangelical christianity all became defining elements of Black freemasonry and wider Black intellectualism. Hall's direct influence was a major facet therein. The 1787 petition for African repatriation was ignored, but most of African lodge in Providence left for Liberia around 1813. Freemasonry has been an integral part of Liberia's elite and political classes ever since. A locus of African masonry, the Craft in Liberia long shared in the colonial and elitist social aspects of that nation's ruling elite. Prince Saunders was sent from England to Haiti, where Christophe sent him back to England as an envoy. In both countries he used masonic connections to his advantage. Saunders' *Haitian Papers* appeared in England in 1816, and in the U.S. in 1818. A proponent of Haitian emigration, he returned to the island and served as Boyer's attorney general.[15]

Boston's Black community was the most activist in the nation in struggling for abolition and equality. Every activist and leader of that community of note save Robert Morris was an active Prince Hall mason, including notable Black leaders Thomas Dalton and Lewis Hayden, both grand masters, and incendiary writer David Walker. The same was true in Philadelphia. In the antebellum years Prince Hall freemasonry spread largely in tandem with both the AME and AMEZ churches. AME founders Richard Allen, Absolom Jones, and Marrant were all masons, as was AMEZ Bishop and masonic grand master James Walker Hood and a number of other preachers in both churches. In each case, lodges and churches tended to appear more or less simultaneously in new communities. Hall was an intellectual leader whose fusion of christianity, freemasonry, and Africanism influenced the theology of these early black church fathers.[16]

The influence of Hall's pan-African Masonic myth becomes clear in other antebellum Prince Hall speeches. The December 27, 1852 address of Most Worshipful District Deputy Grand Master for the Middle District of the United States Samuel Van Brankle's *Masonic Oration delivered at Bethel Church in Philadelphia* is a prime example. Brankle echoed and expanded on his predecessor's synthesis of biblical and Masonic history. Like Hall, he credited the founding of the Babylonian monarchy to "Nimrod or Belus, the son of Cush, the eldest son of Ham. . . being Grand Master of all Masons". Later, he ascribes the greatest skill in masonry to the descendants of Ham who built Babylon and the pyramids of Egypt. Much of van Brankle's work comes directly from the 1789 sermon, indicating that it or its ideas had remained in circulation. As the highest ranking mason in three states his work had wide influence.[17]

Nor was this connection limited to the lodge room or the church. In 1836 mason Robert Benjamin Lewis published *Light and Truth; Collected from the Bible and Ancient and Modern History, Containing the Universal History of the Colored and Indian Race, from the Creation of the World to the Present Time*. First published by a white publisher then republished in a significantly expanded form by "a Committee of Coloured Gentlemen" including Boston's Prince Hall past grand master Thomas Dalton, both versions contained significant masonic symbolism, language and interpretation. One chapter in particular, "Arts and Sciences" drew on masonic ideology, including a long section on Egyptian architecture. The following chapter was called, "The Explanation of the Five Virtues." The descriptions of the five virtues: truth, justice, temperance, prudence and fortitude, are lifted directly from masonic ritual.[18]

The path of Hall's intellectual influence leads all the way to Harlem over a century after his death. Reverend Absolom Jones served as the first grand master of Pennsylvania, while spreading the influence of the church in that state. Grand master and bishop James Walker Hood founded lodges and churches in tandem in many communities. He had direct Masonic connections to Martin Delany, the "Father of Black Nationalism" whose assertion that masonry was passed down through orders of Egyptian and Ethiopian priesthood were part of the masonic oratory to which Hood was exposed, along with Delany's assertion of the "ancient greatness of the negro race." Major Delaney frequently used Masonic allusions and symbolism and pan-African identity in his writing, including the novel *Blake: or the Huts of America; a Tale of the Mississippi Valley, the Southern United States, and Cuba 1859–1862*.[19]

Edward Blyden, born in St. Thomas, spent most of his life in Africa where he wrote *African Life and Customs;* many consider him "the father of pan-Africanism." Alexander Crummell, one of the earliest pan-African thinkers also traveled to Liberia as an AME minister and tried to get American Blacks to join him, returning to America when he gave up on forming his Black Christian republic. Prince Hall lodges in America and Liberia have maintained a close relationship from the beginning of the Liberian nation, and most prominent members of the Liberian government have been masons. Both freemasons, Blyden and Crummell, particularly the latter, had a strong influence on John Edward Bruce, a high- ranking member of the Prince Hall Grand Lodge of New York, founder of several of the earliest Black Nationalist organizations and an important influence on both Arthur Schomburg and Marcus Garvey. Bruce and grand secretary Arthur Schomburg, the famed Black bibliophile, formed the short lived Loyal Order of the Sons of Africa in 1912, a militant group including African and Caribbean blacks, formed largely through Masonic connections. Garvey also incorporated Masonic elements and pageantry into the UNIA. Prince Hall's intellectual legacy had a lasting impact, therefore, on African American community organization and activism which through Hall are indebted to the masonic "grand architects" who met at the Goose and Gridiron tavern in June of 1717.[20]

Prince Hall freemasonry continues to be a vital force in African American communities to the present day. Immediately recognized as "regular" masonry in Britain and Europe, it was not until the latter half of the twentieth century that most predominantly white American Grand Lodges, beginning with Connecticut

254 | *Freemasonry in the Revolutionary Atlantic World*

and Massachusetts, extended their recognition. Prince Hall and John Marrant's skillful recasting of masonic "history" from an African perspective deeply influenced early African American religious and intellectual culture. Black mason's community building and leadership of the Abolition and Civil Rights movement, counting names such as W.E.B. Dubois and Booker T. Washington, labor leader A. Philip Randolph who devised the 1964 March on Washington at which Martin Luther King delivered his famous "Dream" speech, and a host of other activists and cultural figures, make great contributions to the struggle for Black equality. Indeed, Masonic lodges often hosted Dr. Martin Luther King Jr., while militant pan-African and Black nationalist ideas first flowed from the pens of David Walker and other Prince Hall masons. Yet African Lodge was by no means Atlantic Africans' only experience of freemasonry.

Notes

1 African Lodge, Records, Microfilm; Demographic information on Boston's black community is taken from James Oliver Horton and Lois E. Horton,, *Black Bostonians: Family Life and Community Struggle in the Antebellum North*, revised edition (New York: Holmes & Meier, 1999), 1–14; and www.afroammuseum.org/site14.htm, accessed July 28, 2015.
2 Chernoh Momodu Sesay, Jr., "Freemasons of Color: Prince Hall, Revolutionary Black Boston, and the Origins of Black Freemasonry, 1770–1807," unpublished dissertation, Northwestern University, 2006. Accessed through Proquest dissertations, UMI Number: 3230175.
3 Winthrop Wetherbee / Lodge of St. Andrew's, *Bi-Centennial Memorial* 1756–1956. Boston: Lodge of St. Andrew's, 1958. This information is found in a manuscript copy of a draft of the memorial, which appears in the Grand Lodge of Massachusetts in the Prince Hall files.
4 Winthrop Wetherbee, "Prominent Mason Addresses Banquet," *Prince Hall Masonic Digest* 9, no. 2 (August, September, October 1960): 4–9, 23. Wetherbee was prominent in St. Andrew's, his roles included lodge historian; at the time this speech, Wetherbee had been performing an intensive research project intended to prove the legitimacy of Prince Hall's African lodge to white masons, who at the time still refused recognition and relations to black freemasons. Though a logical and meticulous scholar, Wetherbee was not a professional historian and did not cite his sources as precisely as an academic would. His description makes clear that he had access to internal documents and that he had conducted outside research including contacting descendants of the Burbeck family.

5 African Lodge, Minutes, May 2, 1787, microfilm, Boston: Grand Lodge of Massachusetts; Palfrey, Letters of William Palfrey to John Wilkes and Sons of Liberty to John Wilkes, Palfrey MSS.

6 Prince Hall / African Lodge to William Moody, May 18, 1787.

7 *Prince Hall to William White, n.d.* / *1793*, Microfilm, Boston: Grand Lodge of Massachusetts; Harvey Newton Sheppard, *Freemasonry in North America: St. John's Lodge A.F. & A. M. 1733–1916* (Boston: Seaver-Howland Press, 1917), 1–3. 69.

8 *Prince Hall to William White, n.d.* / *1793*.

9 African Lodge, Records (Boston: Grand Lodge of Massachusetts), microfilm.

10 Paul Elliot, Stephen Daniels, "The 'School of True, Useful and Universal Science'? Freemasonry, Natural Philosophy and Scientific Culture in Eighteenth-Century England." *The British Journal for the History of Science* 39, no. 2 (Jun., 2006): 207–229; Elliot and Daniels describe the presentation of scientific lectures in the lodges and the scientific aspirations of the fraternity.

11 African Lodge, Records and Minutes. Peter Hinks and others were previously aware of *The Lives of Some of the Fathers and Learned and Famous divines in the Christian Church from our Lord and Saviour Jesus Christ"* but were unable to analyze it in detail due to the poor quality of the microfilm. I was able to use special software to digitally enhance the image, making it partially legible. There is one other religious tract, "Some Remarks on Mr. John Edwards compleat History or Summary of all the Dispensations and Methods of Religion from the Beginning of the World to the Consummation of All Things", however, even with digital enhancement only the title is readable.

12 John Marrant, *A Sermon Preached on the 24th Day of June 1789, Being the Festival of St. John the Baptist, at the Request of the Right Worshipful the Grand Master Prince Hall and the Rest of the Brethren of the African Lodge of the Honorable Society of Free and Accepted Masons in Boston, by the Reverend Brother Marrant, Chaplain* (Boston: Bible and Heart, 1789), 12.

13 Marrant, *Sermon*,13–14, 20; Vincent Carretta, "Book Reviews", *Early American Literature* 39, no. 1 (2004): 175–7.

14 Joanna Brooks, *American Lazarus: Religion and the Rise of African-America and Native American Literatures* (New York: Oxford University Press, 2003), 132.

15 Harold van Buren Voorhis, *Negro Masonry in the United States* (New York: Henry Emerson, 1945), 31; Joseph Walkes, *Black Square and Compasses: 200 Years of Prince Hall Freemasonry* (United States: 1979), 33–4.

16 Horton, *Black Bostonians*, 28–40, 73–105; John Ernest, *A Nation Within a Nation: Organizing African American Communities Before the Civil War* (Lanham: Rowman & Littlefield, 2011), 99–101; David G. Hackett, "The Prince Hall Masons and the AFricn American Church: the Labors of Grand Master and Bishop James Walker Hood, 1831–1918," *Church History* 69, no. 4 (Dec. 2000): 770–802.

17 Samuel van Brankle. *Masonic Oration Delivered 27ᵗʰ of December, A.L. 5852, A.D. 1852. At Bethel Church, At Philadelphia, For the Benefit of the Poor of Said Church, By Samuel Van Brankle, Most Worshipful National District Deputy Grand Master, for the Middle District of the United States of America, Comprising the States of Pennsylvania, New Jersey, and Delaware* (Committee of Arrangements: 1852), 8–10.

18 *Ibid.;* Benjamin Lewis, *Light and Truth; Collected from the bible and Ancient and Modern History, Containing the Universal History of the Colored and Indian Race, from the Creation of the World to the Present Time* (Boston: A Committee of Colored Gentlemen, 1844).

19 Ernest, *A Nation Within a Nation*, 103–105; Schomburg Exhibition Curatorial Committee. *The Legacy of Arthur A. Schomburg: A Celebration of the Past, a Vision for the Future* (New York: New York Public Library, Astor, Lenox and Tilden foundations, 1986), 31–41; Hackett, David G. "The Prince Hall Masons and the African American Church: the Labors of Grand Master and Bishop James Walker Hood, 1831–1918." *Church History* 69, no. 4 (Dec. 2000): 770–802.

20 William Seraile. *Bruce Grit: the Black Nationalist Writings of John Edward Bruce* (Knoxville: University of Tennessee Press, 2003), 90–101, 115–17; John Edward Bruce, "Arthur Schomburg the Freemason," *John Edward Bruce Papers, Reel 4.* New York: Schomburg Center, Microfilm; Marcus Garvey et al. *Marcus Garvey and the Universal Negro Improvement Association Papers Vol. I 1826–Aug. 1919* (New York: The New York Public Library), 225, 233.

12

Freemasonry Across the Black Atlantic

Freemasonry identified itself as an ancient, global brotherhood open to good men regardless of race, nation or faith. The Craft did not always live up to this ideal, but neither did it always fall short. Indeed, by the end of the first century of grand lodge masonry, Blacks had obtained citizenship in the republic of masonry on both sides of the Atlantic. Boston's African Lodge, founded in 1775 by Prince Hall and his brethren, was the culmination of decades of exposure of African creoles and even native Africans to the ideas and practices of freemasonry, but it might not even have been the first majority Black lodge in the British Atlantic. Eureka lodge No. 673, founded in Nicaragua at some point during the British occupancy of the Mosquito coast, may have had a largely black membership, though unlike Hall's Boston lodge it was not founded by and for Blacks and did not survive the British empire's exit from the colony. English, Dutch and French masons brought their craft to north and west Africa in the first half of the 1700s, and to South and West Africa by the end of the century.[1]

Masonic ritual and society bore remarkable similarities to West African secret societies, elements of which survived in the Americas. Added to the connection and bonds of brotherhood with otherwise unfriendly white society, this made the craft appealing for African creoles. Slaves labored in, and were therefore exposed to freemasonry in the Cape of Good Hope and probably other Masonic lodges in Africa and the West Indies where masons maintained large halls. There were several slave conspiracies in which Blacks assumed the title of freemasons or were associated with them by nervous whites. Indeed, the potential for organizing revolt was one objection raised to Black freemasonry. On Saint Domingue and elsewhere in the French Caribbean, as in the metropolis, elite free blacks and over time even native Africans achieved lodge membership. Freemasonry assumed an importance among the elite of Haiti almost immediately, and masonic ties to both the Grand Lodge of All England and Boston's Prince Hall masons formed in the early decades of independence. Boston's African Lodge spread its brand of black masonry throughout the United States and into Liberia.

Masonic records other than those of the Dutch and later English lodges in South Africa are more or less nonexistent for the West African coast. We know of Masonic activity there from the appointments of provincial grand masters and references to lodges in Africa in surviving almanacs and books. The records of the lodge *Goede Hoop* include several references to unchartered lodges. It was common practice, particularly in the colonies, to form lodges and then seek official sanction from a European or provincial grand lodge. Such lodges often existed for years without official sanction, if they ever sought and obtained it. This was exacerbated where the transient nature of European settlement and difficulty in communication with the metropolis were the rule such as on the African coast.

Smith's 1783 *Uses and Abuses of Free*masonry states that in Africa ". . .a gloomy sameness almost everywhere prevails, except among the European factories, with whom masonry flourishes." This claim that masonry flourished in European trading posts is confirmed by the *Almanach des Francs-Macons*. The 1767 edition states, "Even though there are various lodges on the coasts of the continent, we are acquainted with one in particular in the isle of Malta, which is called Secret and Harmony." In 1768 the authors echoed this sentiment, saying that, "As we only know of the constant wars of Africa, there are only a very small number of Lodges in cities or there are some in establishments of Europeans, and they are there usually under the protection of the Consuls." *Use and Abuse of Freemasonry* echoed the view that unspecified African lodges existed. Smith asserted that, "Under the auspices of the Earl of Louden Modern masonry extended to Africa, and a lodge was constituted at James Fort, A.D. 1736, by virtue of a patent from England. There is also a lodge at the Cape of Good Hope, constituted from The Hague in 1773. There is a French lodge in the island of Mauritius; a Dutch lodge in the island of Madagascar; and one at St. Helena under a Scotch Constitution." Later, in summarizing his chapter "Freemasonry Around the World," he claimed the existence of 13 lodges in Africa while only describing the five above.[2]

This number cannot be seen as reliable, yet Smith's count may well include knowledge or at least hearsay of clandestine and unofficial lodges. Although no records remain for the lodge chartered in Gambia in 1736, this date matches the appointment of a provincial grand master for the region. In 1735 Richard Hull was appointed provincial grand master for Gambia, and in 1736 David Creighton, M.D. became provincial grand master for Cape Coast in Africa. The next year William Douglas, Esq. received a similar appointment for "the Coast of Africa and Islands of America," the route he patrolled for the Royal Navy. Douglas' jurisdiction is telling as it indicates that freemasonry was spreading along the routes of the slave trade that carried human cargo from Africa to the West Indies. It also indicates that the spread of freemasonry in Africa was roughly simultaneous with its entry into the Islands. Douglas' time in Africa was cut too short to establish masonry by an order to sail to Jamaica where he chartered the island's first lodge. The first provincial grand master in the Caribbean was assigned to the Island of Montserrat in 1737, followed by "Governor Matthews for the Leeward Islands" in 1738, the year the first recorded lodge in the islands was chartered by Boston's provincial grand master Robert Tomlinson, who initiated Matthews. According to Garrigus' *Before Haiti* the first lodge on Saint Domingue was created by English masons, probably indigo smugglers, from Jamaica in 1738. These may have come from the lodge chartered by Douglas. The two islands' relationship involved illicit trade and freemasonry for the rest of the century.[3]

That three provincial grand masters were created in quick succession in the 1730s when the British slave trade was at a high point is telling. During this period British merchants supplied increasing numbers of slaves both legally and illegally to the Spanish Americas. While London merchants controlled the legal trade with the Spanish Isles, having received the *Asiento* after the conclusion of War of the Spanish Succession in 1713, Bristol based slavers carried on a brisk clandestine trade in human laborer with the Spanish through Jamaica. It stands to reason that the Jamaican masons who introduced Freemasonry into Saint Domingue, with its growing sugar industry, were part of this nexus. Bristol, like London, had a bustling Masonic establishment and many of the sea captains plying the African shore from either harbor were masons. The British West Indies were booming with the ever growing sugar industry, and labor was in demand across the Caribbean basin. That the demand for provincial grand masters had occurred in Africa slightly before it did in the Caribbean—but later than it did in India or New England—taken with the appointment for "the coast of Africa and the islands of America" and that Tomlinson had substantial holdings on Antigua and commanded a ship of Boston traders implies that freemasonry followed the trade winds into the Caribbean on merchant ships from every point in the triangle trade.

Loge Goede Hoop: Cosmopolitanism on the Tip of Africa[4]

The Loge Goede Hoop in Dutch South Africa is the best documented colonial African lodge. Though its membership was white, it exposed at least some black Africans -the lodge's slaves- to the Craft, and played a notable role in the commerce of colonial Africa and the East Indies. A node of masonic internationalism similar to the West India and American Lodge and Boston's First Lodge, the Loge of Goede Hoop evolved from Dutch East India Company social club to popular stop for masons en route to the East Indies, and then to a means of assimilating the old Dutch and conquering British elites. This lodge kept a regular correspondence with both Amsterdam and several lodges to the East, including a regular relationship with the French lodge on Mauritius. In 1771 sea captain Abraham van der Weijde, was appointed by the Dutch grand master to begin freemasonry at the Cape of Good Hope. The 1776 *Freemasons Calendar* offered a list of Dutch lodges including 18 colonial lodges, *Goede Hoop* among them.

Van der Weijde's commission may simply have been to make official an already existing masonic establishment. South African tradition maintains that freemasonry began at Kaapstad, a small settlement of the Dutch East India Company with a sparse European population active in the slave trade, as well as among the ships of various nations which landed at the Cape. Captain van der Weijde was a member of the Dutch Lodge Salomon in Bengal, and frequent visitor to the Cape who held a commission as second deputy grand master to visit all lodges abroad. He chartered the lodge with four company employees, two sea captains and several locals. Following an unsuccessful duel he received the first recorded masonic funeral in Africa.

The presence of the lodge of freemasons was better received at sea than on land, and prior to the outbreak of war between the Netherlands and England the lodge hosted and initiated more Londoners, Frenchmen, and Dutch sailors en route to the Indies than it did locals. Goede Hoop performed far more degree work than most lodges while at the same time maintaining a relatively small permanent membership. They explained the dearth of local interest to grand lodge as due to two main causes. Anti-masonic sermonizing by the local clergy had caused wives to prevent their husbands from joining- one member resigned in

February, 1775 "fearing domestic differences." Secondly, the masonic principle of equality was unappealing. As the lodge put it "people in the Indies set great store by rank, persons would not join an Order that put forward equality as one of its maxims..." The membership was composed largely of migrants from Europe working for the company, with most degrees performed for transient sailors.

The lodge's popularity among this latter population was considerable. From its official beginning in 1772 until war caused the lodge to go into hiatus in 1781, the extant records, which represent about seven out of the lodge's nine years of operation, include 188 names. Of these, 41 became members of the lodge at some time. Some of those who did not become members could have been local, but they were overwhelmingly seaborne visitors. In total, the lodge recorded 140 entered apprentices, with only five listed as born in South Africa, 122 fellow craft and 84 master mason degrees. Lodge Historian Rylands calculates that since two out of nine years' worth of records are lost, the total number of degrees performed would have been around 400. The total number of visitors must have been higher as well, using a strictly statistical formulation perhaps over 230. Furthermore, names were recorded inconsistently, so these numbers are likely low.

London was the most common place of origin for degree candidates, with ritual performed in English, French and Dutch. Abraham Chiron served as the first master of the lodge. Chiron had been a mason since at least 1765 when he affiliated to the lodge Zur Einigkeit at Frankfurt am Main. Acting for the lodge in The Hague was Grand Secretary R. van Laak, bookseller. Chiron spoke English and knew the ritual in both languages. After his term as master ended he took the chair on five recorded occasions to perform degree work in English. As there were many English candidates prior to this time it seems he routinely performed English ritual for them as master. A chronological journey through the first nine years of the lodge illustrates just how active and international Good Hope was during this period.

There are records of eight meetings from May through July, 1772 when the Brethren voted to acquire a larger hall. The 1776 *Freemason's Calendar* had this to say of Dutch masonry, "It may be justly remarked of the above lodges, that many of them surpass in elegance and splendor the greater part of the lodges under the English constitution. On their public festivals no expense is spared to support the honor of masonry. Their halls are furnished in the most superb taste...", so the resolution was in keeping with Dutch masonic style. International degree candidates in the first eight meetings included two entered apprentices and two master masons from London, and entered apprentice candidates from Mauritius and France. The lodge had immediately become a convenient place to enter freemasonry or obtain a higher degree. Performing degree work for passing mariners gave the lodge a steady source of income, as well as allowing the brethren sociability and international connections.

The minutes also record that the lodge resolved to meet on the first and third Friday and set different fees for residents and visitors from ships for the first two degrees. This is a further indication that profiting from the visits of masons bound for the East Indies was a major part of the Lodge of Good Hope's financial structure. Goede Hoop held many meetings in addition to the two scheduled monthly meetings, mainly as ships entered the harbor. Masonry was strongly established in all of the European enclaves of the Far East, and brethren en route to or from the orient often stopped at the Cape of Good Hope. Word of mouth as well as the *Alamanach Francs-Macons* and the *Freemason's Calendar* efficiently directed the brethren to the lodge. Thus the need for a dedicated building and staff—both paid and enslaved.

The minutes of February 1774 record that the lodge first decided to buy a slave, instead deciding the following fortnight to hire a young bondsman. Slave ownership shows up in the records in several subsequent instances. In November 1775 the lodge voted to sell its slave. At the subsequent meeting they opted to hire a new thrall from Ceylon for a one month trial. The next May, the lodge purchased two more men. In 1807 the lodge's property included two unfortunates. That the lodge needed slaves speaks to its activity and financial health. It also raises the question of slave ownership by other lodges, clandestine and regular, in Africa. Perhaps more interesting is the parallel with the West Indies where whites were heavily dependent on slave labor and masonry well established with opulent buildings such as the Great Hall on Antigua described in the *Cal*endar. The rapidity with which freemasonry spread among free Blacks throughout the islands beginning in Haiti and then wherever freedom created opportunity, the similarity to West African secret societies and indeed claims of freemasonry among slave conspiracies present tantalizing circumstantial evidence of wider exposure of slaves to freemasonry throughout the slaveholding Atlantic.

The first half of 1774 recorded 13 meetings, generally with at least one and often multiple candidates, mainly non-South Africans. In June the lodge sent the Grand Lodge a list showing 15 effective members and two serving brethren. On February 14, 1775 the records show that Chiron left the East so that the "French Grand Master" Mace de Vallons could take the chair. Vallons initiated two Parisians. Following this, "The master thereafter initiated four other candidates, one of them a French Canadian, and then all five were crafted." French visitors that month included the Registrar and Chief of the Council of Pondicherry, where the *Engraved Lists* describe an English constituted lodge, and a gentleman of Maine, who received his third degree at the Cape.

The lodge held eight meetings in April, a particularly busy month, when a large number of ships put in at the Cape. In all there were 32 meetings in 1775, with 53 degrees conferred. This is an extremely high number for any lodge in any time or place. One meeting included French, English, and Dutch visitors. Though most of the candidates were bound to sea, new members that year included two sea captains and the superintendent of workmen at the new hospital. In 1777 a visitor listed as "Grand Master Andringa" attended the first meeting of the year. Later that year the Baron van Niewenhijm graced the lodge with his noble presence.

March of 1778 was a very busy month for the lodge, which held five meetings. The degree work performed provides an interesting snapshot of the lodge's activity: at the first meeting one each of the first and second degree; two initiations at the second; the third meeting in March included four entered apprentice and six fellow craft degrees; the next lodge night saw five brethren raised as master masons, and the final meeting of the month duplicated the ritual work of the first. All this activity yielded only two new permanent members for the lodge. One of these, however, was a bold and enterprising French naval officer by the name of Francois Reynier Duminy who had entered company service, largely in the slave trade, and married into the Dutch community. This initiate was to save the lodge from extinction in the difficult decade ahead. On St. John's Day the lodge was gratified with the reading of a letter from Loge D'Union de L'Orient thanking them for assistance rendered to a French brother and entertained at the expense of two English visitors who had received the first two degrees in the lodge.

In 1779 the lodge elected Captain M.W. Carel de Lille deputy master to represent them at The Hague. They remitted money to Grand Lodge on an irregular basis, but kept up a reasonably consistent correspondence. On April 30 visitors to the lodge included a Spanish Brother and his candidate, Dennis O'Kelly "Captain of engineers in the Spanish Royal Service." The records contain a gap until January 4, 1780, however, the resumed minutes indicate that the lodge had continued to be quite active. In 1781 records show the lodge regularizing degrees performed in an impromptu lodge held aboard a Dutch East India Company ship. In addition to the Blue Lodge Degrees, some members held French Higher Degree positions.

On February 19th, a French brother took the chair to enter and pass three French candidates. The same guest served as master for the three new brothers' third degree three days later. Another entry demonstrates both the level of communication between lodges in the Indian Ocean and the importance they attached to masonic regularity. A brother had arrived with a certificate from an "unconstituted" lodge on Mauritius in which he had been initiated. The brethren decided to make inquires of the French constituted Lodge Triple Alliance on that island, and in the meantime to allow the brother to visit. This demonstrates that unofficial lodges were functioning in Africa. Meetings included as many as 12 visitors on one occasion; among them a Swedish Baron excused from dues he was unable to pay. The lodge membership dropped to 11 based on the list of those present or absent for the feast of St. John. This diminishing membership hurt the lodge financially despite the robust number of visitors. Owing to diminishing cash balances the lodge debated selling their building and took up a collection to aid a visiting brother en route to Batavia rather than assisting him out of lodge funds.

On March 7, 1781 Master Daniel Brand died, causing Chiron to resume the office of master. Six days later they performed multiple degrees on officers and men aboard the French vessel, *Marianne de Sortine*, eight men in all receiving various degrees. Through April, the ship's officers took 10 degrees over 5 more meetings in March and April. The minutes for this period end on April 24, 1781. With war declared between England and the Netherlands, ships no longer called at the Cape frequently and the lodge entered a hiatus. Sometime after this point the lodge, down to eight active members with the departure of Duminy on urgent business, ceased to meet. Chiron returned its warrant to Holland, and it was officially struck form the roles on October 16, 1785—temporarily, as it turned out. It was to be reborn and take on a new role while retaining vestiges of its former internationalism, much like the lodge of Antiquity had, after a nine year run as an international commercial and social network.

Francois Duminy had left the Cape to carry news of the outbreak of war to company posts in the Dutch East Indies. Duminy returned to the Cape and from around 1790–92 made attempts to revive the lodge. Though the original charter had returned to The Hague with Chiron, Duminy claimed the authority owing to his higher degree status to issue a new one, reestablishing the lodge officially on June 24, 1794. The new warrant contained 13 other names, all Dutch, at least seven of whom were members of the lodge before it suspended its work. From this point on most initiates were native born.

As a result of the war, the Cape became an English colony effective September 16, 1795. From this point on the lodge served as a vital link between its members, some of whom had fought the British, and the new rulers, many of whom were freemasons. On October 19, less than a month after the British take-over, the lodge sent a deputation to invite English Brethren Rear Admiral Sir George Keith Elphinstone and General Craig to the lodge. General Craig attended and was tendered the gavel by Duminy, who solicited his protection as governor of the colony. Craig attended again on November 2, along with John Malcolm, aid de camp to Major General Clarke, who was there made a mason. In the coming weeks the lodge performed degrees for several British officers. Masonry allowed the fraternity's small membership to ingratiate themselves to their former enemies and new rulers.

In June 1797 the brethren applied for approval and protection from new governor and brother, the Earl of Macartney,. Their relationship with the powers that be remained strong from then on. The lodge's biggest problem was that a mixed group of Dutch and English masons had formed a lodge whose legitimacy Goede Hoop did not recognize. The new lodge did not last long, however, it is another example of a colonial provincial grand master creating a transient lodge in Africa. British masons considered Goede Hoop the legitimate masonic authority on the Cape, and troops asked for at least two dispensations to create regimental lodges. Relations with British military lodges and masons continued during the first period of British rule.

When Jacob Abraham De Mist, LL.D, Commissioner of the Batavian Republic, arrived to take over the government of the colony from the British authorities he also brought with him a commission as Deputy Grand Master of Holland and the original charter of Loge de Goede Hoop. De Mist's masonic prominence may have aided in the transition, considering the number of masons among the British administration. He presided at the consecration of the new masonic temple on July 7, 1803, with over 200 masons "of every rank and nationality" and 100 ladies present plus a military guard. This was the beginning of his association with the master of the lodge, Johanness Truter, with whose masonic work he was greatly impressed. De Mist later appointed Truter secretary to the governor's council and on leaving the Cape provincial grand master for all the lodges in "the Batavian Colony at the South Point of Africa". This became official on May 25, 1806 with De Mist's return to the Grand Lodge in Holland.

One more interesting story appears in the records of the lodge from this time that demonstrates the strength of masonic ideology and internationalism. The lodge regularized the three degrees received by William Henry Blake, an English prisoner held on a French ship. Blake had been entered, passed and raised by Bro. Alexander Louis Aug. Chatteau, a member of La Triple Esperance on Mauritius and the recorder and head of court of appeals on the Isle D'France. Freemasonry had smoothed the transition from Dutch to English rule in 1795, and then back to short lived Dutch authority. When the Cape reverted to British rule the new governor, brother John Craddock, was always invited to lodge events. In his reply to the lodge's invitation to the December 1812 feast of St. John, Craddock replied, "Sir John embraces this opportunity to assure the Lodge of his highest respect, and as a zealous Brother will always be happy to afford them every protection and assistance in his power." Three times in two decades, freemasonry had given the Brethren immediate and preferential access to the colony's incoming rulers. Masonry at the Cape thrived under English rule, and de Goede Hoop continues to be an active lodge today.

The Craft in the African Atlantic Diaspora

The next record of an English lodge in Africa appeared in the 1793 Calendar, which included among the foreign lodge section a heading for AFRICA with one lodge, Bulam on the Coast of Africa, at number 495. Though this lodge officially appeared in 1793, given the precedents in Malta, the West Indies, and North America it may have existed for years or even decades prior. In 1797 lodge number 568 in the Island of St. Helena has joined the list; five years later provincial grand masters were appointed for St Helena and South Africa.[5]

The question of African exposure to freemasonry in these lodges is highly interesting, but unfortunately lack of records leaves the possibility of speculative answers only. As a general rule, English lodges abroad made a practice of initiating local elites from an early period. This was clearly the case in India and among Native Americans. The *Calendar*'s "Remarkable Occurrences" beginning in 1778 lists the initiation the previous year of Omdat-u-Omrah, eldest son of the Nabob of the Carnatic at Trichinopoly, Madras, an event Smith describes in detail. In some English factories such as the one at Bunce Island, the English used mixed race creoles as intermediaries. These and perhaps local merchants and rulers would potentially have made appealing initiates. The Dutch lodge at the Cape of Good Hope did not initiate blacks, but rather kept slaves, a practice that may have been echoed in the English and French establishments on the African coast and the isles of America. Labor at European factories was largely performed by slaves. The large masonic halls on Jamaica, Antigua, Barbados and other islands would have required labor similar to that performed by the slaves at Goede Hoop in Cape Town. Based on the records of Goede Hoop and those of the Dutch lodges in what is now Indonesia, it seems that Dutch masons were more averse than their English counterparts to initiating non-whites.[6]

French masonic practice regarding Blacks was mixed. Blacks entered free-masonry in France with increasing frequency as the ideals of the revolution took hold, but there was also resistance to Black initiations in both the metropolis and the islands. On Saint Domingue mixed race elites were limited to the role of 'frere-servant' and French made colored masons excluded from visiting lodges for some time. This changed during the revolution, with mixed race elites and even at least one African brother from Senegal appearing in lodge *tableaux* from Saint Domingue by 1800. Limited mixed race initiations on Martinique in the form of *frère-servant* also happened. The possibility of initiation of Africans by the French lodge Triple Alliance on Mauritius and any unrecorded French lodges is thus impossible to gauge but would likely have fluctuated over time; such lodges may also have included slaves. Boston's Reverend John Elliot, writing in the mid-1790s, considered it "remarkable [that] white and Black Masons do not sit together in their lodges [in Boston]." Not even the precedent of the "fraternal life of France, [which was] given to no distinction of colour [could] influence Massachusetts Masons to give an embrace less emphatical or tender affection to their black brethren." Elliot was sufficiently aware of the principles and practices of masons around the world to be of the belief that Boston's segregated lodges were an anomaly, and cited France as the integrated counterexample.[7]

In the Caribbean mixed race planters were sometimes initiated. The most famous Black French mason was the swashbuckling composer Chevalier St George. Born on Guadeloupe to a plantation owning father and slave mother, St. George, "Black Mozart", served as a colonel in the French Revolution. Many free Blacks and escaped slaves throughout the Atlantic took to the sea, a profes-sion closely linked to freemasonry. Common sailors frequently entered Ancient masonry. The records of African lodges in Boston and Philadelphia bear this out, and based on demographics the membership of the Black lodge in Providence was probably composed of mariners as well. The Blacks in Philadelphia who sought a charter from Prince Hall's African lodge in particular include Black sailors entered abroad. Julie Winch's research of Philadelphia's African lodge finds that more than one third of the members of that second African Lodge became masons in either Europe or the Caribbean. The letter from Peter Mantore of March 2, 1797 to Prince Hall requesting a charter for the lodge included six men made masons in London and five in "Ancient York Lodge". The location of the latter is not included other than that it was not in Philadelphia, where racism prevented their being initiated by white masons.[8]

Freemasonry held the same obvious appeal to Blacks that it did to whites—inclusion in a universal brotherhood which includes many of the elite, assistance at home and abroad, an entry into the intellectual world of the enlightenment, and the belief that they were part of something ancient and important. The advantages of all of these to Black creoles whose color kept them in the lower ranks of mundane society were equally obvious to them as to the Jews who sought inclusion in freemasonry as early as the 1730s. However, the similarity of freemasonry to analogous West African societies was also a unique pull factor drawing together the Black Atlantic and the republic of Masonry. In *Exchanging Our Country Marks: the Transformation of African Identities in the Colonial and Antebellum South,* Michael Gomez gives a richly detailed description of West African secret societies and their survival in the slave cultures of the Americas. Gomez acknowledges this similarity briefly, stating, "Another possible area in which elements of these societies were retained or merged with non-African influences is freemasonry." He then cites the first-hand accounts of three separate British travelers in Africa, all of whom, "likened the activities of the Poro and Bundu [Sierra Leonean secret societies] to European Freemasonry." The WPA slave interviews of the 1930s provide evidence that remnants of these societies persisted in Gullah speaking regions of the American south through the final generation of slavery in the U.S. Jill Lepore's *New York Burning*, the best narrative of the 1741 New York slave conspiracy, also discusses masonic and Akan-Coromantee rituals overlapping among the conspirators.[9]

Gomez gives an excellent description of the nature and social role of West African secret societies and their transformation and survival among African Americans. He briefly mentions a possible connection to freemasonry, but as Gomez's focus is on African societies and not on masonic studies, he does not highlight the parallels as clearly as he might have. Indeed, his descriptions of the Poro, Bundu, and other African fraternities demonstrate considerable parallels with freemasonry in terms of ritual structure, philosophy, and social utility which would have combined to make masonic membership an understandable and highly desirable part of Western society to an African slave or creole sailor. These were, according to Gomez, ". . .the functional equivalents of social, cultural, and governmental agencies". While freemasonry did not have genuine governmental power, it was structured as if it did, and it did hold genuine social, cultural and political influence. Both types of societies stressed secrecy as an "organizing principle." In Africa, they moderated commercial and diplomatic issues between autonomous areas, offered relief to families and individuals in need, regulated proper behavior, and offered various forms of education as well as status which grew as one progressed through the society. These were all functions which masonry aspired to and frequently provided for its brethren.[10]

The similarities grow deeper when considering ritual practice. Both in West Africa and in the global masonic republic local structures were largely autonomous yet loosely connected, maintaining a considerable uniformity of practice. Speaking of the Sande and Bundu, Gomez chose to call these structures "lodges". They were based on a system of grades or degrees which included the swearing of solemn oaths and ceremonies. Maintaining secrecy was a major part of each new grade. The Poro system of grades or degrees, "walking the path of Poro" was meant to lead one to "responsibility, wisdom, authority and power". Likewise, a mason "traveling to the East" passed the Masonic pillars of "Wisdom, strength, and beauty" in the form of the master, senior and junior wardens as well as the brazen pillars on either side of the entrance to king Solomon's Temple, Jachin and Boaz, which represent strength and "to establish". Both Poro and the lodges, which Jacob called "schools of government" prepared men for, as Gomez puts it "responsible and enlightened leadership". Just as a master mason seeks to shape himself from a rough to a perfect ashlar, so the final grade of Poro, was the "finished man".

The most striking similarity, however, is what the initiate taking his final degree in societies such as the Senku or Poro or the masonic lodge underwent. In both cases, the candidate experienced a ritualized death and spiritual regeneration. Essentially, they both followed the ancient mystery religion formula and put initiates through an analogous path that involved initiation and birth into the society, education and expanded responsibility, and the final ceremonial death and rebirth that led to mastery, perfection, and the link between the temporal and spiritual worlds. Expounding on the implications of the path of Poro among slaves and creoles, Gomez writes, "The celebration of death to life would take on new meaning within the North American context... [the Sierra Leoneans] probably had a more profound understanding of its implications than did their christian enslavers." Similar societies existed down the coast as far as Angola. As proof of the receptivity of Africans to freemasonry on its deepest levels, Gomez cites the rapid spread of masonry from Americo-Liberians to become a major social force in Liberia.[11]

In West Africa these societies were politically potent and if necessary responsible for organizing revolution against unjust authority. Though this was antithetical to the stated rules of the Craft, radical masons used lodges as organizing nodes in revolutions across the Atlantic world. Combine this with the growing accusations against freemasonry not only in the Catholic world but even in the

Netherlands and in Britain and her colonies and the stated openness and universality of freemasonry to all breeds of men and the at first incongruous link, probably more imagined than real but nonetheless frightening to whites, between freemasonry and slave uprising is understandable.

The *St. James Chronicle* of December 21–23, probably reprinting from the *Middlesex Journal* of June 16–19, reported that in 1770 on the island of St. Kitts there was, "a grand plan laid by the Negroes. . .to cut off every white man on the island". This plot was led by a slave named Archy, who stood to be coronated king if it had succeeded. The newspapers proclaimed that, "The conspirators held an assembly, which they called the Free-Masons meeting, and were overheard drinking toasts to the 'success to their war and liberty'". It seems improbable that Archy and his conspirators on St. Kitts could have entered the local lodge, but they may have had some limited masonic exposure through their masters, enough to associate it with the societies of their native lands which would have born responsibility for devising such a plot in Africa. Though less certain, the 10–12 Barbadian slaves called True Blue who in 1773 signed articles of agreement to destroy every white person they met with may have taken their name from the masonic blue lodge.[12]

These incidents in the islands in the 1770s were neither the first nor the last in which freemasonry and slave conspiracy combined in the minds of frightened whites, and perhaps of the conspirators themselves. In New York in 1738, some Blacks arrested for the theft of gin from a tavern claimed to be freemasons. Three years later, the three stood accused of the far more serious crime of plotting to burn down the city, kill all the whites save several co-conspirators, and install a new king. The complete story, and the most astute analysis of this incident, is given in Jill Lepore's *New York Burning*. Lepore found that there were in effect two overlapping secret societies operating among the accused Blacks. A mock freemasons lodge formed as a prank by white petty criminal John Hughson and a group led by Hughson's neighbor, Jack, a slave tied to Comfort's Tea House, based on Akan secret society practices. Blacks with Akan names comprised about 4 % of the slave population of New York City, but they comprised 19 % of those accused in the 1712 revolt and 38 % of the conspirators burned at the stake in 1741. Of these, several, including Jack, had come to Manhattan after having been 'seasoned' in the Islands. Lepore calls this second group, "a brotherhood whose best English translation was 'Freemasonry'".[13]

The relationship between the two societies ran deeper than a simple matter of imprecise translation. It involved several of the biggest names in the colonies including, tangentially, Benjamin Franklin, and more directly printer

Peter Zenger fresh off his acquittal for sedition. In 1737, Evan Jones and other Philadelphia freemasons went on trial for the death of a gullible young man whom they had promised to make a freemason, only to put him through a false initiation that ended with Jones accidentally lighting the youth on fire, burning him to death. The incident garnered the fraternity considerable bad press. Andrew Bradford, printer of the *American Weekly Mercury* in Philadelphia and professional rival of Benjamin Franklin, seized on the opportunity to accuse Franklin and discredit the masons. Bradford's father, William Bradford, was the printer of the *New York Gazette*. The elder Bradford was involved in his own feud with the masons in New York. The fraternity had arrived in the City early in 1737 when James Alexander, dancing master Henry Holt, formerly of Boston instituted Solomon's Lodge in Charleston South Carolina, and other gentlemen of the Country Party started the city's first lodge. The lodge met at the Black Horse Tavern, headquarters of the Country Party, located opposite Peter Zenger's print shop.

Due to a lack of surviving records it isn't clear whether or not Zenger was a mason, but he frequently published masonic news and pro-masonic pieces, generally written by Alexander. It is highly likely, considering the tendency of lodges to recruit printers and Zenger's close personal and political associations with the highly politicized lodge which often served as a vehicle for the Country Party. In any event, the ascendancy of the Country Party had resulted in Zenger's displacing the elder Bradford as the official printer to the colony. In August of 1737, Bradford printed an essay from the *London Magazine* stating that "Englishmen should not tolerate Masonic lodges. . .dark and clandestine Assemblies where Plots against the State may be carried on under the Pretense of Brotherly Love and Good-Fellowship." Zenger's *New York Weekly Journal* responded on November 14 with a mock classified add by Alexander poking fun at the Court Party's watering hole, the Todd Tavern. Bradford responded with an anti-masonic letter of his own on November 28 which attacked the secrecy of the masons and finished with reprinting the oath taken by an entered apprentice which had, by this time, been exposed by Pritchard and others.

While all this strife was brewing between the gentleman of the Black Horse and Todd Taverns, less prominent men were conspiring in more modest establishments. John Hughson owned a tavern where alcohol and other vices were available to Blacks, including slaves. Hughson made ends meet by working as a cobbler and fencing stolen goods. While no gentleman, Hughson was literate as was his Black patron Cuffee. Lepore deduced that Cuffee and Hughson probably found Jones' prank funny, and created a mock gentlemen's club of their own. The newspapers had reprinted both the actual oath of a freemason and the less digni-fied oath given to the unfortunate Mr. Rhees, which had involved kissing Jones' posterior and swearing allegiance to the devil, and thus they had the material necessary to create their own Freemasons Club.

A week before Cuffee, Caesar, and Prince broke into Richard Baker's Tavern to steal quantities of gin, they and Hughson had attended a cockfight at another low class establishment where Hughson, almost certainly drunk, met a slave named Adam and according to testimony latter given by Adam asked him to swear on his book to join in a plot "to set fire to the Houses of the town, and to kill the white people." As Lepore points out, it seems unlikely that Hughson would involve someone he'd just met in a real plot- it was probably a part of his prank masons. After the break in and gin theft the three thieves took to calling themselves the Geneva club (for the Geneva gin they'd stolen). This club was soon arrested and forced to confess. En route to the whipping post one of the three, probably Cuffee, yelled, "Make room for a Free Mason."

William Bradford took full advantage of the incident, mocking Zenger's recent report of a masonic procession. On January 30 he satirically reported on the robbery as a masonic meeting and on the public whipping of the culprits after the fashion of a masonic parade—only months following Boston papers' tales of the first masonic procession in America. Alexander did not find this funny, and the next day attacked the "vicious" and "bawdy" tone of the *Gazette*, resulting in a response which admonished him for defending the three black thieves. The Bradfords, father and son, shared and reprinted each other's anti-masonic mate-rial, which served both of their political, professional, and personal agendas.[14]

Hughson was hanged along with his wife and 17 Blacks, in addition to thir-teen who were burned at the stake in 1741 based on the sensational testimony of his embittered and criminally inclined indentured servant, Mary Burton. The city had experience 13 suspicious fires in short order and had read about recent slave risings in the West Indies. Speculation then and ever since has accused Burton of falsifying the entire story. Indeed, not long after "saving" the city she was frequently spat on and accused of making the whole thing up. Her testimony was reinforced, also unreliably, by Irish born soldier William Kane. Though he had migrated to the colonies at the age of 6, Kane had previously been accused of being a catholic, which he denied. The first white implicated in the plot, Kane gave a confession quite different from those of the blacks who had been inter-rogated in the affair. In addition to implicating two other soldiers, he wove a tale of Catholic intrigue centered at Hughson's and described a bizarre initiation ceremony.

Kane may have been exposed to real freemasonry as a soldier. His ceremony included both pseudo-masonic elements and pieces that bear some similarity to West African ceremonies. It included the removal of one shoe, which has masonic parallels not described in Bradford's short ritual expose. Most interesting were the different oaths sworn by black and white plotters. Blacks swore, according to Kane, an oath which invoked supernatural powers, swearing by thunder and lightning that "God's curse and Hell Fire fall on them that first discovered the Plot." Whites, on the other hand, swore an oath with aspects of the penalties of the first two masonic degrees, with the addition that "his privy parts were to be cut out and thrown in his face." Furthermore, after they had vanquished their foes the rebels, "were to burn what they could of the City, and get what Money and goods they could and carry them to Mr. Alexander's House, which was to be reserved for Hughson."[15]

Regarding "Hughson's Plot", Lepore deduces that it ". . . was, essentially, a prank that grew out of proportion. At meetings at Cuffee's and at Hughson's, Hughson, Cuffee, Caesar, and Prince parodied gentlemen's clubs and conducted mock Masonic initiations. This plot was real— it happened- but it was also fake; it was meant as mockery." The mock masons, inspired largely through the stories printed by Bradford, gave the printer ammunition to use in his political battle with the real masons. Even if it was a prank in Hughson's mind, his gullible recruits may have considered themselves real masons, or believed in the plan to burn down the city. Lepore further postulates that Hughson did not understand the depths of anger and resentment against whites his satirical oaths stirred up in the hearts and minds of oppressed Blacks. Indeed, the testimony of Burton and of many of the blacks arrested stated that there were two types of meetings, the mixed race pseudo-masonic meetings at Hughson's and all Black meetings led by the slave Jack at nearby Comfort's Tea House.

At Comfort's the rebels took oaths more like those of Akan ceremonies. Here, as Lepore puts it "not only the oaths but much of the plotting to which slaves confessed in 1741 bears considerable resemblance to ceremonies known to have taken place among other Akan-influenced communities in the New World." Confessions differed as to whether Hughson or Cuffee was to be king, with the other as governor. It appears that a real conspiracy based on West African secret societies overlapped a pseudo-Masonic conspiracy at a time when the real masons in the city were themselves embroiled in political power struggles. The black conspirators included creoles and Africans, several of whom had first experienced slavery in the Caribbean, where freemasonry was becoming established among whites. The tales of black criminals claiming to be masons made their way into newspapers in several colonies and were circulated and read among both blacks and whites.[16]

Fear among whites of Black freemasonry leading to slave rebellion and appropriation of the title of freemason by blacks who saw the society as the American equivalent of the African societies which would have born responsibility for altering, and if necessary overthrowing, the political order continued throughout the antebellum period. As the eighteenth century closed, these fears were conflated with the fear of French revolutionary conspiracy brought about by the influx of French masons, many of them refugees from Saint Domingue, with their exclusive higher degrees. One of the most insightful findings in Bullock's *Revolutionary Brotherhood* is that it was the higher degree bodies of the Scottish and York rites which were most suspect. Reverend Jedidiah Morse and Yale University president timothy Dwight both published anti-French and anti-Masonic pamphlets in which they differentiate the traditional blue lodge masonry with its associations with the American revolutionary leaders and the new republic from the conspiratorial French masonry now infecting the young nation. The presence of black, mainly mixed race, masons in New Orleans and possibly to a to a lesser extent elsewhere among the French diaspora, which included slaves tainted by their association with those who had driven their masters from the island, added to this fear.

In the United States, slave's appropriation of the title of freemason and white fear of black masonic rebellion began with Gabriel's conspiracy. One of Gabriel's main accomplices Benjamin Woolfolk's testimony, taken on September 19, 1800, clearly demonstrates that slaves used the name of freemasonry to plot rebellion. "That the first time he heard anything of a conspiracy and insurrection among the blacks was from the prisoner [George], that he came to his house at dusk or dark where he was cutting wood, and asked him if he would join a free-mason society; this deponent [Ben Woolfolk] replied no, because all free-masons would go to hell; upon this, the prisoner [George] said it was not a freemason society he wished him to join, but a society to fight the white people for their freedom, [Ben] who replied he would consider it;. . . ." Woolfolk's testimony reveals several things. That he first refused "because all free-masons would go to hell" demonstrates the extent to which anti-masonic ideas had already permeated American society 30 years before the purges of the anti-masonic party. It is revealing that even a slave was aware of the religious objections to the masons. Furthermore, he is then told that rather than real freemasons, they are a conspiracy against the white order. Thus, blacks associated the masons with conspiracy, as well as with the white power structure.[17]

Corey Walker offers speculation that black French masons may have facilitated aspects of the plot including its geographical reach. This seems tenuous at best, since free black masons from Saint Domingue tended to be slave owners themselves, however, it is worth considering that Walker has reproduced the fearful thinking of whites who feared French revolutionary freemasons and black slave rebels, and might have connected the two in various ways. Indeed, contemporary observers offered the following observations, "Now under the clause of the oath, with the negro's superstitious dread of the horrible Masonic penalty for violating it, conspiracies without number may be hatched and matured." A later author echoed this fear, writing, "Let Freemasonry once spread its baneful influence thoroughly amongst the slaves of our Southern and Western States, and the scenes of St. Domingo would be sunk into insignificance, compared with those which would follow."[18]

While Gabriel was unlikely to have been a regularly initiated mason, white southerners did hear threats of violence from a bona fide Black mason: Boston's David Walker, author of the incendiary 1829 *David Walker's Appeal to the Colored Citizens of the World* which justified violence as a means to end slavery. Indeed, the Black masons of Boston were frequently involved in organizing the fight for Black civil rights in their state. More fancifully, whites also spread rumors of Nat Turner's rebellion having a masonic element. The two fears came together in the *Boston Free Press* of March 14, 1832, during the height of the anti-masonic movement, "The fact is well known that Walker, the author of the famous incendiary pamphlet that produced so much disturbance at the South, was a member of the African Lodge. . . . It has also been stated that 'General Nat,' who headed the massacre in Southampton, was a black Mason. Who knows how much of the machinery then used has been left among the blacks, both free and slaves, at the South, to be re-produced after the lapse of a certain number of years, like their own periodical locusts?" The leaders of Boston's Black community who made up a forceful element in the abolitionist movement were nearly all members of Boston's African Lodge.[19]

While the sea lanes of the slave trade may have synergized the spread of freemasonry in the 1730s, by the end of the century Freemason's Hall had become the physical headquarters of the abolition movement in England. Leading abolitionists masons included Granville Sharpe, Thomas Clarkson and others, and the grand lodge would not have made its opulent hall available to a cause which the bulk of the brethren did not support. That the general sentiment among masons was anti-slavery is evidenced in the December 1794 edition of the *Freemason's Magazine: or General and Complete Library*, contained the following under the heading "Acknowledgements to Correspondents": "The Poem *In favor of the Slave-trade* is of a complexion unsuitable to a Work which, on all occasions, shall promote, as far as its influence can extend, the cause of *Universal Benevolence*. We at the same time beg to express our acknowledgements to the Gentleman who did us the favor to transmit it."

Freemasonry therefore appealed to the Black Atlantic on several levels, for reasons stemming from both European and African cultural associations. Freemasonry also mimicked the ritual, spiritual path, and social roles played by analogous societies in West Africa. Blacks had ample opportunity to be exposed to the craft, particularly as the more egalitarian Ancient brand of freemasonry spread throughout the British Empire and as abolitionist sentiment in England and France led to more frequent initiation of Blacks in both of these masonic metropolises. Elite mixed race and Black planters as well as slaves serving white and Black masonic masters had ample opportunity for exposure to masonry in the Caribbean. This was also true at least to an extent in Africa, where there is also the possibility that local elites and traders gained initiation. Masonic initiation was a way to acquire a measure of equality, preference and brotherhood from whites, as well as a source of security, as in the case of the three Blacks kidnapped from Boston. The fight to free the three sailors was led by Prince Hall, founder and master of Boston's African Lodge. African Lodge made Black freemasonry a trans-Atlantic society, a major element of African American culture, and a distinctive subculture of the Republic of Masonry, but white masons also accepted Black men as brothers around the Atlantic basin.

Notes

1 Kent Henderson, Tony Pope, *Freemasonry Universal: A new guide to the Masonic World, Volume I- The Americas* (Victoria, Australia: Global Masonic Publications, 1998), 332.

2 Smith, Uses and Abuses of Freemasonry, xvii–xviii, 237, 243; *Almanach des Francs-Macons 1767*, 30; 1768, 37; *Freemasons' Calendar, 1789*, 44. Thaddeus Mason Harris copied the information from Smith's section on Africa, with acknowledgement, in his Freemasonry Around the World printed in Boston in 1798 but adds no new information or commentary other than the visit of Algerine brethren to Grand lodge in the 1790s; these three appear in the records of St Peter's Lodge in Newburyport as well.

3 Calcott, *Candid Disquisition*, 94; Gould, *Freemasonry around the World*, 230–1.

4 All data on Good Hope Lodge taken from O.H. Bate, *Lodge of Goede Hoop, Cape Town*, Standard Press Limited, 1972. This lodge history contains reproductions of much of the lodges' correspondence with the Grand Lodge in the Netherlands beginning in 1772 as well as excepts from the minutes and analysis thereof.

5 *Freemasons Calendar 1797*, 48; *Freemasons Calendar 1802*, 22–3.

6 Paul W. van der Veur, *Freemasonry in Indonesia from Radermacher to Soekanto, 1762–1961* (Athens, Ohio: Ohio University Center for International Studies Southeast Asia Program, 1976). According to van der Veur the Indonesia elites were not accepted into a lodge in the Dutch East Indies until 1844.

7 *Tableau des Membres La R. L. . . . de Reunion Desiree Port-au-Prince* (Port-au-Prince: La Grange, 1800); *Tableau des Membres Composant La R. . . L. . . de Saint-Jean, Reg. . . const. aux deux rites, A L'O. . . de St. Pierre, Isle-Martinique, 1826* (St. Pierre: printed by the lodge, 1826); Jean K. Gousse, "La Franc Maconnerie aux Antilles et en Guyane Francaise de 1789 a 1848" unpublished MSS. Philadelphia, Grand Lodge of Pennsylvania Library; Taken from Crosby and Nichols, *Sketches of Boston, Past and Present, and of some Places in its Vicinity* (Boston: Phillips, Sampson, and Company, 1851), 74, cited in Chernoh Momodu Sesay, Jr., "Freemasons of Color: Prince Hall, Revolutionary Black Boston, and the Origins of Black Freemasonry, 1770–1807, unpublished dissertation, Northwestern University, 2006. Accessed through Proquest dissertations, UMI Number: 3230175;

8 Peter Mantore to African Lodge, March 2, 1797; African Lodge, Minutes and Records, African Lodge Microfilm; Hinks, *All Men Free and Brethren*, 5–6; Julie Winch, *Philadelphia's Black Elite: Activism, Accomodation, and the Struggle for Autonomy, 1787–1848* (Philadelphia: Temple University Press, 1988), 171, quoted in Corey Walker, *A Noble Fight: African American Freemasonry and the Struggle for Democracy in America* (Champaigne, IL: University of Illinois Press, 2008), 250 ftn 56.

9 Michael A. Gomez, *Exchanging Our Country Marks: The Transformation of African Identities in the Colonial and Antebellum South* (Chapel Hill: University of North Carolina Press, 1998), 90–101; Jill Lepore, New York Burning: *Liberty, Slavery and Conspiracy in Eighteenth Century Manhattan* (New York: Alfred A. Knopf, 2005), 99–102, 138–43.

10 Ibid., 90–95.

11 *Ibid.*, 97–101.

12 Andrew Jackson O'Shaughnessy, *An Empire Divided: The American Revolution and the British Caribbean* (Philadelphia: University of Pennsylvania Press, 2000), 39. O'Shaughnessy's work describes these events, but does not draw the link to West African societies or freemasonry in general.

13 Lepore, *New York Burning*, 145–8.

14 *Ibid.*, 99–102, 139–43.

15 *Ibid., 178–9.*

16 *Ibid., 199–205.*

17 Reprinted in Corey Walker, *A Noble Fight: African American Freemasonry and the Struggle for Democracy in America* (Urbana: University of Illinois Press, 2008), 34–5.

18 Ibid., 57–62. Unfortunately, Walker is not always clear on the sources and dates of his quotes.

19 Ibid., 62–3; James Oliver Horton and Lois E. Horton, *Black Bostonians: Family Life and Community Struggle in the Antebellum North* (New York: Holmes & Meier, 1999), 30–1, 75–6; African Lodge, Minutes.

13

Perfect Scots, Peevish Gauls, and American Republicans: The Far—Flung Masonic Networks of the French Caribbean

French Caribbean freemasonry illustrates the tightly woven interconnection between commerce and the Craft. Jamaican indigo smugglers unofficially brought British masonry to Saint Domingue in the same year Massachusetts merchants established it on Antigua and French merchants carried the light of masonry to Martinique. The networks that formed followed the lines of trade: from Bordeaux to St. Pierre to New Orleans and from Jamaica and Bordeaux to Saint Domingue, and thence back to Jamaica. Guadeloupe, more isolated, also had masonic lodges by 1765 at the latest. All of the correspondence of the French lodges included the latitude of the sending lodge, and in the case of New Orleans of its mother in Martinique and its grandmother lodge in France. Merchants carried the charters, petitions, ritual degrees and letters, and along with planters and administrators—the two groups with whom they conducted business- made up the bulk of the Masonic community. Masonic membership brought cosmopolitan enlightenment and fraternal trust and connection to the backwaters of the colonial world.

Freemasonry in the French West Indies brought together many unlikely characters, notably the irascible creole smuggler and Masonic evangelist Etienne "Stephen" Morin, Moses Michael Hayes, the ubiquitous Jewish Mason of New England and New York, and a host of other French, Dutch and American personalities who clashed and cooperated in spreading new masonic ideas and degrees. On Martinique, personal pique between Frenchmen claiming the title of "Perfect Scots" was so rancorous that lodges in Marseille and Bordeaux wrote to each other trying to sort it out. It brought together the two major splits in the trans-continental republic of Masonry, English vs French degrees and Ancients and Moderns, and more importantly spread the aristocratic French Higher Degrees into the egalitarian Blue Lodge Masonry of the United States. French masonic networks distributed printed *tableaux* with detailed demographic information on lodges, lodge members, and the lodges on both sides of the Atlantic with which they maintained communications. These *tableaux* served as excellent sources of information for the freemason merchant or sea captain, providing an instant network of brotherly business contacts in several empires. They connected French, English, American, Dutch, and Spanish American lodges and brothers. One such *tableaux* was held up by Rev. Jedediah Morse as proof of a French Revolutionary conspiracy afoot in America. The spread of the Higher Degrees, now called the Scottish Rite, became a major factor in the anti-Masonic movement of the 1830s in the United States.

French masons, like French bureaucrats, kept far more detailed accounts than their Anglo- Saxon counterparts. Their meticulous records and correspondence have much to tell about masonic communication within and between empires. Through the *tableaux* exchanged by lodges and the letters exchanged between Saint Domingue and Pennsylvania as well as between all the French Islands and France, entire trans-Atlantic and inter-imperial commercial networks unfold. French Creole masonry also has much to say about race, class, and identity in the early colonial world. As with the British Americas, many but not all of the lodges which existed in the French colonies appear in masonic guides and almanacs published in Europe and later in the United States, illustrating the extent and the limits of information flow across the Atlantic. Finally, their correspondence and writings have much to say on the topic of masons' self-perception and identity, and the extent to which the unlikely combination of mythologized histories and modern republican ideals were a part of the shared masonic worldview of the eighteenth century.

The Scottish Chevalier and French Higher Degrees

While the most widely studied Masonic schism of the eighteenth century is that between the Ancients and Moderns within the British Masonic orbit, the international implications of the additional degrees created in France by the early 1740s under the auspices of the Count of Clermont as grand master were farther reaching. Like the Ancient-Modern split in England, class and social hierarchy played a major role. Also at stake was the legitimation of native French masonic authority, which could claim to have 'revived' older and higher degrees than the three practiced in English freemasonry. The two splits overlapped in ironic fashion, as the newly created, aristocratic and royalist French degrees drew on the masonic legacy of Scotland, referring to many of its new degrees as "*Ecossaise*". Displaying the French flair for drama and pageantry, a great number of degrees emerged, first in France and then elsewhere in Europe.

Freemasonry arrived in France in 1725, with the appointment of Lord Derwentwater as provincial grand master. English diplomat Lord Bolingbroke was likewise a major force in the earliest Paris lodges, which became homes for anglophilic French and ex-patriot British aristocrats and elites, and an active force for promoting English cultural ideas. This contributed to official suspicion regarding the new organization, and from 1737 until 1743 Herault, head of the Parisian police force, investigated the order under a royal decree which barred royal advisors and administrators from lodge membership and empowered the police to search the lodges for traitors. These raids included the lodge held at the home of the British ambassador Lord Waldegrave. Herault found that the group, which included several personal friends and many prominent nobles, was not seditious, and based on his findings and the influence of aristocratic brethren the king ceased receiving reports after 1743.

According to Margaret Jacobs many key English—derived political terms and ideas first appear in French in early masonic documents. Prominent members included Montesquieu, initiated in the Horn Lodge in London. By the latter half of the 1730s many notable east and central European nobles with ties to Paris were freemasons. This was largely due to the personal influence of the Duke of Villeroi, who in 1737 brought in Venetian ambassador Count Farsetti, Prince Caraffa of Lombardy, Swedish diplomat Baron Scheffer, Danish ambassador Count Platte, Prince Wemille of Nassau, Prince Lubormirski of Poland and Prince Nariskin of Russia. From this time on, French masonry joined its English parent as an active force for penetration of the Craft into the interior of Europe.[1]

The transplantation of English political culture was strong enough that a conflict arose in the French grand lodge between an actively Jacobite faction headed by Lord Derwentwater and an anti-Jacobite faction under the Duke D'Antin. D'Antin's faction had won by 1737, and the new grand master, the first native Frenchman to hold that position, actively suppressed Jacobite activity and deflected the attacks of political and religious authorities. By the early 1740s, however, another conflict had arisen within French masonry. New ritual degrees began to appear based on medieval and ancient history which expounded more clearly and openly upon the philosophical, spiritual, and political ideas buried in the highly symbolic English blue lodge degrees. These new ceremonies gave Parisian freemasonry a decidedly French character. By adding a hierarchy which stretched up to the 33rd degree, they allowed for noble rank to re-enter the overly egalitarian lodges.

In England, the Modern lodges headed by noble grand masters and elite grand lodges tended to cater to the upper and upper middle classes while the Ancients arose to bring freemasonry to the middle and aspiring middle class. Likewise, in France, except that the split occurred in reverse order, with the more exclusive degrees developing for the benefit of the aristocratic French from Modern English masonry, which was by French standards radically inclusive. The emergence of these new degrees led to administrative and social rifts in French freemasonry. They also opened the way for Catholic and aristocratic ideas to merge in novel ways with republican and dissenting religious ideals of the Enlightenment. By 1743 the schismatic English Grand Lodge of France had garnered recognition from the Grand Lodge of England and the Parisian Scottish Rite innovators. The Duke of Clermont became its first grand master and issued sweeping new regulations giving himself and his officers extraordinary powers.[2]

The new degrees began with the larger than life masonic character of Andrew Michael Ramsay, better remembered as "Chevalier" Ramsey. His eccentric career brought together the important Masonic concepts of Scottish ancestry, connection to the knights Templar, and the interplay between Whig and Jacobite political ideas and served a key role important in creating an integrated Masonic and Catholic identity. Born in Ayr, Scotland, in 1686, Ramsay first set foot on the continent as a soldier serving in the Netherlands. In Paris he became a student of Francois Fenelon. During this time he converted to Catholicism and embarked on a career as a political and theological author. In 1724, Ramsay briefly served as a tutor to young exile Charles Stuart in Italy, returning to Paris when the position did not work out. In Paris he associated with both Derwentwater and Bolingbroke, and despite his political leanings he was able to enter the prestigious Horn Lodge when in London from 1729 to 30 and among his many professional honors was granted an honorary degree from Oxford University and elected to the Royal Society. Ramsay was also created a member of the unofficial Jacobite Peerage and a knight of Scotland. Of importance to the masonic philosophy he helped to create, he was further knighted into the Order of St. Lazarus of

Jerusalem. Membership in this crusader order as well as his employment with the crusader descended Bouillon family probably inspired him to connect freemasonry to the Knights Templar, a fantasy so enduring that many modern day freemasons cling to their imagined Templar heritage to this day.[3]

Though a Jacobite, the Chevalier was closely linked in England to important Whig masons, including Desaguliers and his colleagues in the Royal Society and the Horn Lodge, where he was active at the same time as his French Masonic brother Montesquieu. Masonic connection assuredly assisted Ramsay in gaining admission to the several learned and professional societies he belonged to in England. In 1736 the Jacobite Chevalier Ramsay denounced the Jacobite faction of Parisian freemasonry under Lord Derwentwater and was appointed grand orator the following year under the ascendant Duke D'Antin. Derwentwater left the Paris Masonic scene, suffering execution on returning to Scotland in 1745. Ramsay's writing and orations were a major force in reconciling English and Scottish masonic ideas with Catholic and royalist French ideals. By 1743, the year of his death in Paris, he had dramatically influenced the ideology and intellectual orientation of the new French degrees.

Bolstering the idea of masonry as a parallel republic, one of Ramsay's more famous orations claimed that one goal of freemasonry was the creation of, "an entire spiritual nation". In 1738, the year of the first papal bull denouncing the masons, Ramsey's *Le Discours* included the statement that the Knights Templar lived by masonic principles and proceeded to draw further parallels between the two brotherhoods through the masonic ideas of benevolence, justice and virtue as well as the prominent presence of French nobility and loyalty to the church among both groups. Ramsay played on the popularity of Templarism among the French, who were quick to embrace the idea of a link between freemasonry and the mediaeval knights. The idea of an order loyal to the church which set out to destroy it based on false accusations held an obvious parallel for French masons faced with the Pope's condemnation. That the French chose to call their new degrees *"Eccossaise"*—Scottish- was likely influenced by Ramsay's nationalism, the Jacobite connections of many early French masons, and the recognized fact that the oldest masonic lodges in the world worked in Scotland. This meant that a claim of Scottish origin could give the innovative degrees an aura of antiquity and legitimacy over even those of the English. Schuchard has demonstrated that freemasonry was likely part of the Stewart court exiled to France, providing further Scottish influence.[4]

By Ramsay's death in 1743 his blending of loyalty to church and crown, a Templar creation myth with a Scottish component, and orthodox British

Masonic ideology had been expanded by the Parisian masonic ritual writers into the basis of the new *Ecossaise* degrees. The "Original Constitution and Statutes of the Order of the *Chevaliers Hospitaliers et Militaires de Saint Jean de Jerusalem dits Frey-Macons*" overtly outlines this admixture. It states that, "Our order is religious and military . . . for rendering Christians perfect. . .''; and that "Nobody will be initiated in the order who has not sworn an inviolable attachment to the Religion, the King and the Custom." Several other passages reinforce the overtly Christian nature of this order. This may be in part a genuine expression of the members' religiosity as well as a defense against the charges leveled by the papacy against the order. It then specifies that, "Any merchant in incredulity who may have spoken or written against the sacred dogmas of the old Belief of the Crusaders, will for ever be excluded from the order; unless he will renounce his blasphemies in a general meeting and will refute his doings." That questioning the beliefs of the crusaders was a common practice among French masons seems unlikely, rather, this appears to have been intended to confirm the Templar connections of "the knights of St. John of Jerusalem, called Free Masons." The reference to Clermont as grand master place the "Constitution and Statues" no later than 1743. This constitution was written in Bordeaux's La Parfaite Harmonie Loge de Saint- Jean de Jerusalem, a lodge whose founders included one of the most influential masonic luminaries of the New World, Etienne "Stephen" Morin.[5]

Etienne Stephen Morin: The Desaguliers of the French Caribbean

Conflicting hypotheses abound regarding Morin's origins and saga. Whether he was a creole of Saint Domingue, a native of Cahors in Quercy as indicated by a certificate issued by the admiralty in Bordeaux March 27, 1762, or less likely, a creole of Martinique as stated in Jacques Blancard's June 15, 1751 letter to the Mother Grand Lodge *Ecossais* of Bordeaux, remains uncertain. Morin went by two first names, Etienne and Stephen, both of which combined with his surname were fairly common at the time. Since there is general agreement that he was born in 1717, a date that coincides with the Bordeaux admiralty certificate, and that he was instrumental in the founding of Bordeaux's earliest *ecossaise* lodge, La Parfait Harmonie Loge Ecossaise de Saint-Jean de Jerusalem, Cahors, France seems like the most likely birthplace. Regardless, his masonic career is well documented. Morin spread the new degrees, with innovations of his own, to Martinique, Saint Domingue- where he mainly resided, and Jamaica, from whence his disciple Henry Andrew Francken brought "Scottish Rite" degrees to colonial New York. The new degrees spread, largely thanks to Jewish merchant Moses Michael Hayes, and were bolstered with a fresh influx of Saint Domingue masons escaping the Haitian Revolution at the close of the century.[6]

Morin's story is illustrative of the importance of freemasonry to West Indian commerce as well as being an important part of the development of the craft throughout the New World. Etienne was the center of controversy and conflict everywhere he went. He navigated masonic politics adroitly and utilized his French masonic standing to his advantage during his several stints as a prisoner of war, returning with authentic or fabricated English and Scottish masonic experiences and qualifications which he then parleyed into greater masonic legitimacy in France. Throughout his masonic career, Morin claimed French, English, and Scottish authority. That at least one of his captures led him from London to Edinburgh to Kingston indicates that he was able to turn his situation to commercial advantage. He ended his life in Jamaica, where he created higher degree rituals, masons, and organizations among the bustling fraternity in Kingston.[7]

Etienne participated in the first *Ecossaise* lodges in Bordeaux, La Parfait Harmonie, and according to some sources served as its master in 1744. He claimed this same year to have received a Scottish grade from Governor and Provincial Grand Master of Antigua William Matthews. This is a difficult claim to interpret; Matthews had been initiated by Massachusetts provincial grand master Robert Tomlinson in 1738 and oversaw the active English Modern lodges on the island. If there were any Scotts lodges on Antigua at this time no records of them remain. During that year he was captured and spent several months in London, then traveled to Edinburgh and Kingston. On returning to France, Morin claimed to have received, on June 25, 1745, the 'Constitution of the Respectable Mother Lodge of London'. Whether this was a fabrication or an exaggerated translation of a more mundane masonic certificate is difficult to say. His signature appears on the July 8, 1745 regulations of La Parfaite Loge d'Ecosse de Bordeaux with the quality, "*par mandement de la Grand Loge d'Ecosse*." Certainly he visited British lodges during his captures. That his trip to Edinburgh resulted in any actual recognition by the Scottish grand lodge seems unlikely, yet he managed to claim authentic Scottish masonic credibility among the newly formed French '*Ecossaise*' masons, bolstering his standing in Bordeaux and Paris.[8]

Morin arrived in Saint Domingue in 1748, where he formed an Ecossaise lodge, St. Jean de Jerusalem Ecossaise, in Le Cap. The first two lodges on the island only received official sanction from France in 1749, probably as a result of communications carried by Morin, whose signature appears on St. Jean's

Constitution in Bordeaux, where he attended lodge in June and July of 1750. Etienne also visited lodges in Bristol, a commercial hub with a strong masonic presence, after another brief capture by the English on this round of voyages. His name appears on a 1750 patent for a lodge in Abbeville, La Parfaite Harmonie, as "*Grand Maitre Ecossais.*" He therefore wielded authority in metropolitan and creole masonic circles at this time. In 1751 he brought *Ecossaise* masonry to Martinique, founding a lodge there, and in 1752 was orator of the lodge at Le Cap, where personal pique led to complaints to Bordeaux from the Brethren, the first in a series of personality conflicts with rival brothers. Meanwhile, Morin installed a new lodge at Port-au-Prince. By 1757 Morin had conferred the higher degrees on members of the lodge La Concorde in Aux Cayes, where he had taken up residence.[9]

The increasingly bitter conflict between Morin, Bordeaux, and Le Cap seems to have been the result of a jurisdictional dispute. Morin had first introduced . the new degrees to Saint Domingue on an earlier voyage, as evidenced by the June 6, 1748 letter requesting Bordeaux's sanction for the *Ecossaise* lodge at Le Cap, which states, "As some children of our Wor. Lodge have established an *Ecossais* Lodge here, and as this growing Lodge desires to be reckoned among your children. . . Bro. Morin, who will visit this country again, will gladly receive your instructions." Morin clearly viewed Saint Domingue as his Masonic territory, at least where the higher degrees were concerned, and cited authority from Bordeaux for that purpose dating from 1747. For whatever reason, on December 24, 1752, Bordeaux issued a patent to Lamorlele de Feuillas, making him their deputy in America. Feuillas soon issued a deputation for the installation of an *Ecossaise* lodge at St. Marc. This very exclusive lodge, limited to seven officers and 12 members, included several very prominent citizens who held or later took important administrative posts. After this initial move, Feuillas, who held a plantation at Cap which he rarely left, became less active in spreading masonry than Morin, a merchant who traversed the entire island. He did created a craft lodge in 1755, but his letters indicate that the dispersal of brethren and the discord created by disputes among them had caused the lodge at Cap to cease working temporarily around that time.[10]

Cap Francais' letter to Bordeaux on February 13, 1753 sheds some light on the brewing conflict, indicating that, "after he gave us the pleasure to pass onto us all the letters and knowledge, he brought with him," Morin, ". . .asked for his resignation from the Lodge and his withdrawal, without us knowing as yet the reason, which the Lodge could only grant him." They further complained that, "Our Lodge, your dear daughter, has equally learned with sorrow, that Bro.

Morin, after having enlightened it from your side, having conducted it unto the Sacred Vault among the ruins and the destruction of the Temple of Jerusalem, has given you the information, that confusion had started among us, and that we would only make a game of Freemasonry. He sent to you, as well as to the Wor. Lodge of Paris, a list of those, whom he had chosen to be vindicated, asking for the interdiction of other Brethren and the Lodge." They went on to express shock at his sudden "change and bitterness."

It would seem that the arrival of the Feuillas deputation led to his leaving the Cap lodge, which recognized it, and to reach out to Paris, which had poor masonic relations with Bordeaux. This letter includes other important insight into the workings of masonic bureaucracy in the French empire. The brethren indicated that they had issued a constitution for a craft lodge which had been operating without official sanction and ordered it, ". . .to write to various Craft Lodges, to enter into correspondence, and to make itself known." They ask that this information be shared with the other lodges at Bordeaux so that its certificates will be recognized there.[11]

Morin paid no heed to Feuillas' new authority, and continued to create new lodges. On June 24, 1757 he wrote to Bordeaux to inform them that he had created three higher degree bodies at Cayes, a Perfect *Ecossais* Lodge, a council of Knights of the Orient, and a chapter of the Knights of the Sun. In this letter, Morin used reverent language to skillfully indicate that while he respected the mother lodge at Bordeaux, he considered their deputation to Feuillas null and void. He reminded them of his superior authority, stating, "in order that they may work to the Perfection of the Art Royal, I have given them the certificate, which your Wo.Lodge has given me, dated July 25, 1747, at the end of which are the Constitutions, which were handed to me by the Wo.Mother Lodge of London, dated June 25, 1745, which you certified, in order that they may rely on it if needed." Thus, he reminds *Les Elus Perfaits* not only of the authority they have given him, but that he also held authority through the English grand lodge. The lodge to which these new bodies were attached, La Concorde, claimed to be the second oldest on the island and held its charter from La Française, a Bordeaux lodge with which Elus Parfaits had friendly relations. Morin had astutely developed close relations with the leading brethren at La Concorde, ceding Le Cap to Feuillas. He asked Elus Parfaits to recognize the new bodies and take on other administrative oversight. This was a brilliant strategem as it left Les Elus Parfaits two choices: they could recognize and receive authority over the new lodge, at the same time recognizing Morin's continued authority over the island; or, they could refuse, knowing that it would change nothing on the ground and that

Morin would simply claim authority based on his English warrant and the standing of La Française in Bordeaux.[12]

Correspondence yields demographic information for 10 of the original members. These include four *habitants* (plantation owners), four merchants, one of who was born in Martinique and conducted business in Port-au-Prince, another of whom returned to France to play a major role in the grand orient in later years; an army general, and Sauveur Balanque, Commander of the King's Frigate—most likely the corsair captain warranted in 1767 as captain of the port of Cap-Français. That the *Ecossais* lodges were exclusive in number and held higher authority over local masons probably embittered the conflict between them. The personal pique between Morin and Feuillas was likely exacerbated by the latter's youth and the general tension between planters and merchants. If Morin was indeed born in Cahors and not in Saint Domingue this may have added a European vs. creole dimension to the conflict. The new lodge opened a correspondence with Bordeaux on its own account. The French opted to maintain their authority over the island by tacitly recognizing Morin's and accepting his new charges as their own.[13]

The brethren at Cap resumed their masonic work in 1759, blaming Morin for their long break. That they were not active when Morin's new lodge formed probably assisted in making up Bordeaux's mind regarding recognition, since to not recognize them at that point would have left Elus Parfaits with little masonic turf on the island. The further correspondence from Cap to Bordeaux sheds some interesting light on race, with Bordeaux in 1770 forcing the resignation and masonic ostracism of brother Pescayne as master of lodge La Vérité because he had married a woman of color. The lodge's renunciation of Pescayne was demanded in a report to the grand orient on the recommendation of merchant Francois Lamark, a.k.a. the American, one of Morin's 1757 initiates.[14]

The conflict was far from resolved. The renewed complaints against Morin in 1759 caused him to play a political trump card. In 1761, back in France, he received authority from La Grande Loge des Maitres de Paris, ditte de France empowering him as grand inspector charged with spreading the higher degrees of perfection. His forced stay in England in 1762, during which time he visited lodges whenever possible, led to Morin's claiming a similar deputation under English Modern grand master the Fifth Earl of Ferrers, though this seems dubious. The grant of authority from Paris led Morin to a spurt of Masonic activity. In 1765 he wrote to Paris to report on various administrative matters and expressing the hope not to be in default, however, by 1766 a Brother Martin had been deputed to replace Morin. The issue this time was at least partly one of residence, as Morin was accused of living in Jamaica, thus necessitating a new deputy for Saint Domingue. Jurisdictional and personal conflicts were probably at issue as well.

Morin not only continued to act under his Parisian deputation but apparently altered it to give himself greater powers as the years proceeded. In 1764 he compiled and added to the 25 degree system which became, through his discipline Henry Francken, the basis of the American Scottish Rite. Francken was one of many deputy grand inspectors authorized by Morin. A Dutch native and naturalized citizen living in Jamaica, Francken brought the degrees to Albany in 1767, creating the first higher degree bodies in British North America. Now living in Jamaica, Morin created the Kingston Grand Chapter of Sublime Princes of the Royal Secret on April 30, 1770. His last known official act was the conferral shortly thereafter of the degrees on a brother from Saint Domingue. Stephen Morin passed away in Kingston on November 17, 1771. During his lifetime he had dramatically altered the ideology and practice of freemasonry in the Old and New Worlds. His influence continued after his death, dramatically influencing the course of freemasonry in the United States, the Caribbean, and the Spanish empire as well as in Europe. As in his life, this influence exerted itself mainly through commercial networks.[15]

Knighthood on Martinique and New Orleans

Before discussing the trading networks that carried Morin's Scottish Rite to the British colonies, it is worth briefly considering the overlapping yet distinct French network which spread from Bordeaux through Martinique to New Orleans. 1738 had been a momentous year in West Indian freemasonry, as it saw the craft spread from Boston to Antigua, from England to Jamaica via the coast of Africa, and thence to Saint Domingue. In this same year the first lodge in Martinique originated under a French warrant. The Gaulish gall which led to Morin's frequent personality clashes became equally evident. The records of the *Ecossaise* lodges of Martinique and New Orleans have much to say on communication and race in the French Caribbean and on the importance of masonic beliefs and ideals to French masons. It also reveals the transmission of masonic ideas from the colonies back to the metropolis, intellectual exchange between English and French masons, and the 'irregular' work of masons outside the sanction of the European grand lodges. The story picks up several years after Morin's departure with three merchants and members of Bordeaux's Elus Parfaits, now on Martinique, who wrote to Bordeaux wishing to form an *Ecossaise* lodge. Among other things, they informed the mother lodge that Morin, who they named "a creole of this island" who had "founded your very respectable lodge" had established an *Ecossaise* lodge at Port Royal but that its work has deteriorated considerably in quality.[16]

Nor was Morin the only evangelist of high degree masonry who had created dysfunctional masonic bodies on the island. The official lodge, La Parfait Harmonie, had been joined by another "bastard" lodge of the same name created by a colorful character called Pierre de Sicard. Sicard claimed to have received the degrees in Palestine, where lodges existed by 1743, from the English Consul Franck and from thence to have traveled the world on a series of adventures, assembling a portfolio of high masonic degrees. He appeared on Martinique in 1747 and founded the second La Parfaite Harmonie. Sicard was excluded from the Ecossais Lodge of St. Pierre in 1752 and moved that year to Guadeloupe, where he founded the lodge Les Vrais Amis, returning to Europe in 1760. Unlike Morin, Sicard never held official powers from Europe yet he took it upon himself to found lodges in the New World, an example of the clandestine masonic activity that occurred throughout the world. Letters report several other lodges that do not appear in French records which the correspondents considered illegitimate. They also state that there was a "Black Lodge" of higher degrees functioning which was the only regular one in the islands and awaited Bordeaux's constitution.[17]

Before the lodge could even be installed, a conflict broke out between a faction under Jean-Francois Pechagut on one side and Jean-Baptiste Veyres and Collison on the other. Collison and Veyres accused Pechagut of mixing with improper masons in order to ensure that he could be master, and even claimed that the three had planned to meet at the estate of Brother Dubolay on Sunday at four o'clock to discuss matters, only to receive a summons to the installation of the lodge at the meeting place of La Parfaite Union- the irregular one, they assumed—at three on the same afternoon. This led to a series of letters between Veyres and Collison on one side and Pechagut and his deputy Pierre Fauchier, a Provencal resident of Granada and captain of militia, on the other to Elus Parfaits in Bordeaux. Bordeaux tended to agree with Veyres and Collison but found the issue so confusing that they exchanged several letters with the higher degree lodge in Marseille, which also had members on the island embroiled in the conflict. This led to a request to inform each other of the lodges each chartered more regularly "in order to be able to correspond with these lodges", but did not resolve the issue. On the problems created by the illegitimate lodges, Marseille's May 25, 1752 letter to Bordeaux stated that, "...the adverse times made such illegitimate establishments common," indicating that they were more a rule than an exception. Elus Parfaits dispatched Bernard Seyssaton on a fact finding mission. His June 8, 1752 report took the side of Veyres and Collison. Despite this, it is Pechagut and Fauchier's lodge which continued in the correspondence and records, indicating either a change of heart or that Pechagut's side simply won out. A February 20, 1753 letter from Elus Parfaits dodged the particulars and deputed Seyssat, Peirre Thouron, and Worshipful Bro. Leysson, member of an influential merchant family in Bordeaux, to reconcile the issue and install the one and only lodge which they would recognize.[18]

Pechagut's lodge returned a list of the 13 original members of the *Ecossaise* lodge, including merchants Collison and Veyres, and one other who "have not yet been present in our lodge." Of Veyres, the document states that, "his illness is the reason why he has not yet labored with us", and describes him as "from Bayonne, merchant in this town, he must soon go back to France." Collison, who along with Pechagut and Captain Pierre Thouron is described as "well known to you" meaning a member of Elus Parfaits, is treated more harshly as unlike the excusably ill Veyres, his "indifference caused his absence from our labors." The list also included Granadan militia captain and planter Fauchier. Other members hailed originally from all over France, including Antoine Bertoux, Picardian, resident (planter) in this town, Norman confectioner Louis Tihpaine, Breton master surgeon Etienne Voison, Francois Doyhamboure, from Bayonne but now a merchant in Martinique, local druggist Jean Pelouze, originally from Languedoc; ship's captain Michel Couture of Provence, Denis Piveteau, creole of Martinique now a merchant at Nantes, and finally brother Duboulay, a French merchant who claimed to be connected with Elus Parfaits in Bordeaux. Thouron and Voisson carried most of these documents, a task merchants almost invariably performed. Thus, this small lodge, which presided over the larger blue lodge, itself likely composed mainly of merchants and planters, connected men from throughout France including merchant houses in Bordeaux and Nantes and planters on both Martinique and Granada.[19]

Thouron, a captain from Bordeaux, carried much of the correspondence between the lodges and even brought the degree of 'Architect', and the appendant body called a 'Workshop of Architecture', to Bordeaux from Martinique. He had received this rare degree in Paris, but due to poor relations between the two metropolitan masonic establishments Bordeaux had been unable to obtain it directly. Therefore, the merchant Thouron carried this masonic knowledge from Paris to the West Indies and back to Bordeaux. Other documents and letters between St. Pierre and Elus Parfaits also speak to the seriousness with which the brethren took their masonic rituals. For example, in their letter of June 15, 1751, they explain their reasoning for keeping the degree of Elect Mason exclusive, "Beside the other conditions prescribed in the Rules which we sent to you, it is certain that there are Elect Masons who were the Guards around the [King Solomon's] Temple & had the keys to it. This confirms us in our resolution to give this degree only to those who want to go further. . ." The letters regarding the conflict between Pechagut, Veyres and Collison are filled with masonic terminology and moralism.[20]

A window into the extent to which they believed at least some masonic history to be true is opened by the February 1754 letter of Fauchier, commander of the militia of Granada and master of the *Ecossaise* lodge, to Brother Dupin of the Elus Parfaits describing discoveries made by Brother Guyot:

> Who is here one of the most worthy Masons, has made some time ago a trip to Palestine. It is in that centre, that our first masters have worked, and hoping to find there traces of their work, he asked to see subterranean caches and waste, of which he had heard speaking. He and an English Brother were taken by some natives to an area around Sidon and near Tyre where he was shown several tombs of an antiquity, which one cannot prove less than two thousand years old, on which were painted all the attributes of the art, with colours, which had been respected by time. He was with an English Bro., whom the same zeal had conducted, and they parted, moved and filled with the most profound respect for an order which they had regarded, until then, as it is regarded by the ordinary Masons. . . Since that period. . .he examined everything with masonic eyes, . . .

Fauchier's sincere belief in the discovery of brother Guyot indicate that he, like many of the authors of eighteenth century masonic literature, took even the more fantastic elements of masonic legend seriously even if some "ordinary masons" did not. The letter goes on to state that recently a very old house, "regarded even as one of the first which had been built in that town [Marseille], which is a daughter of Athens and a sister of Rome. . .In the foundation various stones were found on which were engraved the attributes of Freemasonry." Here we see the internationalism of Freemasonry—a brother on Martinique writing to France with a description of findings in Palestine made by French and English brethren acting together as masons—and the extent to which devout masons took the Craft's boasted antiquity seriously. The letter refers to Fauchier's having early sent a translation of the famous—and probably fake—John Locke letter of May 6, 1696 with the caveat that because the translation is literal it has lost much of its masonic character. Of this letter he explains, "We have received it here by way of the English, who seem to me in general much better Masons, than we are." The reverence for the quality of British Freemasonry echoes Morin's use of British bona fides in his Masonic career.[21]

Ships passing between New Orleans and France generally stopped at St. Pierre, and it was from the *Ecossaise* lodge of St. Pierre that freemasonry first reached French Louisiana. The members overlapped, with Norman master confectioner Tiphaine the motive force behind the lodge and with the influence of Thouron and other Martinique masons playing an important role. Morin's influence continued, though he was not personally involved in the lodge. The overlapping of English and French masonic practices and authorizations was present here as well. The surviving records of New Orleans French masonic lodges include the names of several of the most elite merchants and administrators. The lodge membership and the leadership of the 1768 revolt against Spanish rule and the short lived independent state that followed tightly overlap. In the wake of this revolt and its suppression freemasonry was purged by the holy inquisition and many members either disappear or were executed or imprisoned.

Louis-Francois Tiphaine served as junior warden at the establishment of Martinique's *Ecossais* lodge, but disappears from the records of that island after June 15, 1751 and on December 13 of that year wrote to the Comte de Clermont for constitutions for a lodge he had assembled with some brethren. Brother Pierre Caresse carried the letter which was delivered through a brother Lichigaray. Lichigaray replied on Oct. 25, 1752 that as a matter of secrecy he could not send the higher ritual degrees, but instead sent a book of songs. This was the beginning of a frustrating process of trying to obtain official sanction for the higher degrees in New Orleans, while craft masonry grew under Tiphaine's leadership. Tiphaine had become a mason at Martinique, but his letters indicate that he had learned further masonic "perfection" in lodges in the British colonies, "where I learned many points which are essential, which are ignored at La Martinique, which you will learn through Bro. Rousillon, orator of our lodge, who is charged to inform you, if you have not learned it already." Rousillon, made a mason at New Orleans, was charged with most of the communication between New Orleans, St. Pierre, and France. The constitution for an *ecossaise* lodge, requested in 1756, was granted by Martinique but because Rousillon was detained in France until 1764, this lodge had only a clandestine existence until that year, when its officially installation commenced.[22]

The minutes of La Parfaite Harmonie of New Orleans for August 4, 1754 include as senior warden Jean Milhet, the wealthiest merchant in the city, and Pierre Francois Rousillon, secretary, also a wealthy merchant whose brother,

Guillame received his third degree that night and went on to become master of the *ecossaise* lodge on his return from France. The constitution which St. Pierre eventually gave the higher degree lodge included the stipulation that it supervise the craft lodges in the city, implying that there were multiple lodges operating. Of the "black lodge" working without official authorization, Tiphaine, who by this time is listed as "planter" implying that he had turned from baking with sugar to growing it, wrote to Bordeaux in 1756 explaining that he had received only tacit consent for the lodge from Martinique, and that, "As I have been authorized by the English Grand Lodges, and having been without support for even years, and living more than 800 miles from any lodge of Perfects, I acted accordingly. I made a choice of five good Elect brethren, member of the Lodge of New Orleans". Thus, Tiphaine, like Morin, parlayed his experience in British masonic lodges into real or imagined authority in the French masonic realm. His letter further speaks to the view of British masons having a superior knowledge of the craft.[23]

The constitutions granted by St. Pierre for the New Orleans craft lodge on July 16, 1752 stipulated that, "by the particular laws of this lodge, which do not allow anybody, under what pretext this may be, to be admitted, without being of pure blood, free of his passions, and without having entered into any alliance which would dishonor the purity of the society." This seems to be a reference to race, and to keeping the lodge white. These by-laws ensured an elite membership, as evidenced by the April 13, 1756 request sent to St. Pierre for the *Ecossaise* constitution: Tiphaine, Master Knight of the East, planter, Villere perfect Ecossais and Grand Warden, royal scrivener, Carlier, Grand Second Warden, royal scrivener, Rousillon orator and Secretary, planter, Milhet treasurer, Grand Tyler and acting secretary—though the document does not list Milhet's occupation, he was a very prominent merchant. Villere's July 28, 1765 letter to the lodge from New York, carried by otherwise unknown brother Musculus, is the latest document related to the New Orleans French lodges; that it was written and delivered by lodge brethren in New York, demonstrates the geographical scope of the lodge members' networks.[24]

The correspondence, dated May 23, 1759, between St. Pierre and New Orleans deputy Rousillon while the latter was at Bordeaux include instructions for several ritual degrees and suggest that Thouron, who was at Bordeaux, could teach Rousillon the degree of Architecture which he had brought there from Martinique. A second letter, dated the following day and delivered together, both by Mr. Mouton, secretary to the commissariate, sheds light on Morin's role in both the Caribbean and in Bordeaux. It explains that, "with regard to the *Ecossais*

Lodge, or perfect Elect, we have a copy of the authorization, on the ground of which Bro. Morin has founded it. Our register, in which this authorization was transcribed, is the basis of our foundation, and I regard this Lodge as founded well and legitimately." A marginal note adds, "I found, and will send it to you a copy of the constitutions, given to Bro. Morin." Thus, Morin was perceived as a legitimate source of authority, and had created several of these degrees. This last quality may be the reason he was so important in the founding of Bordeaux's Elus Parfaits, playing a creative role somewhat analogous to Desaguliers in the Grand Lodge of England. The writers credit other degrees to other authorities.[25]

Many of those in the lodge were involved in the uprising which followed the Spanish take-over, after the Seven Years' War. Bro. Jean Milhet had been sent to supplicate Choiseul to try to get the annexation cancelled. Lodge members involved in the Oct. 1768 revolt included Foucault, the organizer and head of the administration of the colony; La Frenière, the attorney general, Villere, an officer of Canadian origin, the senior grand warden in 1756; Marquis, another officer of Swiss origin; Doucet, a lawyer, and Jean Milhet. Spanish Governor Ulloa fled and the rebels declared a republic of sorts. This new nation was to have a short history, however, as Alexander O'Reilly, an Irish officer serving Spain, arrived in July 1769 and quickly put down the rebel republic. On October 24 the principle leaders- La Freniere, Noyan, Villere, Marquis, and Joseph Milhet, the brother of Jean, who may also have been a mason, were arrested and after a sham trial put to death the following day.[26]

Jean Milhet and some others stood condemned to a six year term of imprisonment. Many others were jailed without any trial. Tiphaine, Guillaume Rousillon, Pierre Caress and other lodge members who disappear from the records may have been among these. Hammering the final nail into the coffin of New Orleans first masonic lodges, the Holy Inquisition arrived with O'Reilly and set about persecuting the freemasons. There is no more record of Carlier, Chantalou, Grandchamp or other names which appear in the fragmented masonic records. In 1770 the king of France secured the release of the surviving prisoners, who were expelled from the French Antilles. Some of our 'Perfect Elect' may have been among these survivors.

It is impossible to determine if masonry had a causal role in the uprising. Many of the members had cause to be involved in the rebellion in any case. However, shared lodge membership gave them tighter bonds of brotherhood, particularly for the 'military and religious' masonic knights of the higher degrees. It provided a structure which was amenable to being co-opted into political action when necessary, as occurred during the American War of Independence the Irish

Rebellion of 1798, the European *Carbonari* movement, and other Atlantic revolutions. Even if it was not an organizing tool, the intellectual combination of British republicanism and pseudo-crusader knighthood likely impacted their ideological stance. That unique world view would be adapted in novel ways as West Indian commerce carried French masonic ideas to the new United States, where new personalities became essential in adapting the catholic French crusader myths to the mores of the young Anglo-American republic.

Jewish Merchants & Scottish Knights

The importance of individual actors is very clear. Etienne "Stephen" Morin was a major force in creating the Bordeaux *Ecossaise* lodge whose influence spread across Europe and southwest to the islands of America. Morin personally carried the new degrees to the sugar islands of Saint Domingue, Martinique and British Jamaica. He innovated and altered these degrees to suit the character and culture of the islands, and in so doing impacted French masonic practice as well. Etienne engaged in political and personal conflicts with the metropolis, often successfully, and in so doing created lodges and evangelistic Deputy Inspectors who carried his version of 'Scottish Rite' freemasonry wherever their business took them. Morin's influence and authority came to be recognized and held on Masonic documents from New Orleans to New York and New England.

This came about largely through the actions of his Deputy Grand Inspector Henry Andrew Francken, Dutch native and naturalized British citizen who created in 1768 Albany's Lodge of Perfection. An early initiate, the Jewish merchant Moses Michael Hayes, covered perhaps more ground in the growing republic of masonry than even Morin, serving as master of lodges in New York, Rhode Island, and Massachusetts, where he rose to grand master, and creating his own deputy grand inspectors to spread a new, fully American version of the "Scottish" degrees. These deputies, appointed during wartime business in Philadelphia, were overwhelmingly Jewish masons with business interests in the Southern states and West Indies.

Henry Andrew Francken was born in Holland around 1720. He arrived in Jamaica in 1757 and attained British citizenship the following year. In 1762, probably around the time he became involved with Morin, Francken was appointed Marshall in the admiralty court. Twenty years later he became interpreter of the Dutch and English Languages in the vice-admiralty court and from there went on to hold several other official positions: master of the revels in 1793–5, assistant judge of the common pleas court in Port Royal in 1794, and finally commissioner of the supreme court for Kingston and Port Royal in 1795. This last position could not have lasted long, as he died May 30 of that year. According to the surviving minutes of the Ineffable Lodge of Perfection of Albany he initiated two masons, William Gamble and von Pfister, into the higher degrees a few days after having met them on October 7, 1767. Francken then proposed to create a Lodge of Perfection in Albany with Gamble as master pro tempore pending the approval of New York grand master William Johnson. On January 11 of the following year the lodge came into being, immediately initiating six brothers.[27]

The Lodge of Perfection's Charter described Morin as "Grand Inspector of all Lodges relative to the Superior degrees of Masonry, from Secret Master to the 29th Degree." Francken's authority was "Confirmed by the Grand Council of Princes of Masons, in the Island of Jamaica." The 1762 secret constitution Morin and Francken used described the office of senior grand inspector general as being for life- an answer to those in France who had sought to replace him—and claimed authority from the "three Orients" Modern, Ancient, and Scottish. On December 6, 1768, Francken appointed Samuel Stringer, a prominent local doctor, and Moses Michael Hayes as 'deputy inspectors general'. The minutes are sparse, but the lodge continued to initiate Albany and New York masons into the degrees, performed in English as in Jamaica. One of the more interesting and revealing minutes indicates the wide reaching mercantile and masonic connections of the members. In Sept 1770 "Deputy Inspector General Stringer informed the Lodge of Perfection at Albany that he: 'had received an Order from the Founder to transmit the Minutes of the Lodge & the state thereof to be forwarded to Berlin; in order that Minutes & Accounts might be regularly enter'd and Posted in their proper books purchased for that use'." Various documents related to Morin's authority cited both Paris and Berlin, where Masonry was very active by this time. Whatever the connection, it added a further authority to Morin and charters descended from him. Scottish Rite titles appear among the New York subscribers to William M'Alpine's edition of Calcott's *Candid Disquisition*, indicating that the Jamaica- Albany masonic network was connected to the lodges in Boston. Though Stringer did little to spread the degrees of perfection, Hayes had one of the most influential Masonic careers in the Early Republic.[28]

Moses Michael Hayes was born May 9, 1739 in New York. His grandfather and merchant father had immigrated from the Dutch Republic in 1729. Father Judah was a mason and a merchant who built his reputation as captain of the privateer *Duke of Cumberland* in the French and Indian War. He conducted extensive business in the Caribbean like many Sephardim and frequently advertised masonic items in the New York press. Son Moses Michael Hayes' masonic career probably began in New York. A February 23, 1769 warrant made him the first master of the newly founded King David Lodge. The other listed officers, senior and junior wardens Myer Myers and Isaac Moses, were also Jewish merchants and based on the name of the lodge it seems safe to assume the membership was largely if not entirely Jewish. The warrant describes Hayes as, "a Hebrew of Masonic distinction." With the outbreak of war Hayes took the lodge to Newport, where he was already active in both trade and Freemasonry. Lodge members here included Moses and Isaac Isaacs, masons since 1760, Jacob Isaacs, (1763), David Lopez (1762), Moses Lopez (1763), and Isaac Elizer (1765). Membership in the lodge was mixed, with Christians serving as secretary and treasurer at times. Since many of the known members were masons early on it appears that Jews made up an important part of Newport's masonic community.[29]

It bears noting here that members of the Lopez family appear among the business correspondence of Boston merchant William Palfrey. Palfrey's correspondence with Moses Brown stated that early in his career he met many prominent businessmen in Rhode Island while attending lodge, illustrating the way masonic networks overlapped. Though there are no records of a Lodge of Perfection in Rhode Island before the revolution, a letter to Hayes dated New York, August 24, 1774 is addressed, "To the most illustrious prince Moses M. Hays- of the Ineffable Lodge of Perfection at Newport Rhode Island," implying that Hayes was active in spreading the Scottish degrees by then. He visited Boston's Massachusetts lodge on July 3, 1781 and January 1, 1782. Massachusetts lodge had received its charter in 1770 from Grand Master Joseph Warren and was an offshoot of the Lodge of St. Andrews; the recently deceased Palfrey had served as its first master. Hayes was a member of Massachusetts Lodge by the time extant records begin in 1785. Based on his mutual connection to lodge Master Palfrey's via Lopez and the appearance of Scottish Rite officials in the Wellin's book printed in 1772, it seems Hayes connected to the lodge from an earlier date. This might explain why Bostonian future war hero Henry Knox extended six months credit to Hayes for books and stationary for his story. Though not certain, Knox probably joined Massachusetts lodge around this time. The Independent Ledger, Dec. 24, 1781 announced Hayes' opening a shop in Boston. Hayes and Aaron Lopez were among the Jewish shipowners who funded 6 % of privateering voyages during the war.[30]

Hayes served as master of Rhode Island lodge in 1782–3 and on removing to Boston served as the master of Massachusetts Lodge, of which Palfrey had been the first master, from Dec. 3, 1783 until the middle of 1785. In Boston, Hayes and his son were extensively involved in the West Indies and Gulf coast trade, as well as serving as insurance brokers. Hayes served as Grand Master of the Massachusetts Grand Lodge from June 1788 until the 1792 merger with St. John's. Locally he also issued in 1797 a charter for a Martha's Vineyard Lodge of Perfection in his capacity as Deputy Grand Inspector and gave it the privilege of performing the Royal Arch, the key degree of the Ancients and the recently organized York Rite, and as the most prominent Jew in Boston funded various public projects and was a founder and the initial depositor in the Massachusetts Bank, now part of Bank of America.[31]

More important than his local activity in New England, however, is Hayes' actions in spreading the degrees of perfection during the War of Independence. While on business in Philadelphia on June 25, 1781 and October. 23, 1782, Moses held two meetings at which he appointed seven Deputy Inspectors General, all, with one possible exception, Jewish merchants. He had apparently already granted the title to his associate Moses Seixas. As a result, rituals devised by aristocratic Frenchmen aiming to forge a closer connection between freemasonry and the Catholic church were spread throughout North America and beyond largely by American Republican Jews. Jewish trading networks and masonic networks overlapped considerable in the New World, where Jews were involved in lodges on the Dutch Islands of Curacao and St. Eustatius, and on Barbados and Jamaica as well as in Georgia and the Carolinas.[32]

Hayes' deputies were: Isaac De Costa for South Carolina, Solomon Bush for Pennsylvania, Barend M. Spitzer Deputy Grand Inspector for Georgia, Joseph M. Myers DIG for Maryland, Simon Nathan for North Carolina, Thomas Randall for New Jersey, and Samuel Myers for the Leeward Islands. Isaac Da Costa was born in London in 1721. At the age of 29 he migrated to South Carolina, one of many wealthy Jews to do so, and was involved in the first synagogue there. Da Costa was a member of Solomon lodge No. 1 at Charleston- originally chartered by Boston- by 1753. He served as treasurer of the lodge as well as being an officer of the congregation Beth Elohim. He continued as a merchant in Charleston until the British took the city, confiscating all of his property, at which point he moved to Philadelphia. He attended both of Hayes' meetings. On returning to Charlestown he constituted in February of 1783 a Lodge of Perfection which functioned till it's building burned down in 1796. This was De Costa's last major Masonic act- he died Nov. 23, 1783.[33]

Solomon Bush was a physician who attained the rank of lieutenant colonel in the Continental Army. He was the motive force in founding Pennsylvania's

Lodge of Perfection and was also active in that state's patriotic Lodge No. 2, where he served as master until departing for Europe at the close of the decade. Barend Moses Spitzer also evacuated Charleston when the English arrived. He attended both of Hayes' meetings. A merchant with business interests in the Caribbean, Spitzer was involved in founding Scottish Rite bodies in Charleston and appointed two deputies of his own. Abraham Forst, or Furst, received his patent as a deputy grand inspector on April 4, 1781. It described him as, "...late of the city of London, Merchant, now of the city of Philadelphia." Appointed for Virginia, he is on record as having assisted Myers in organizing a Council in Charleston in 1788, and in 1790 he aided Moses Cohen in re-establishing the degrees in Jamaica, where Francken's group had run its course. A vise on his patent attests to his having visited the lodge La Vérite à l'Orient du Cap in Saint Domingue on April 26, 1791.[34]

Of the other Hayes appointees, Joseph M. Myers deputy for Maryland, moved to Richmond in 1783. That year Hayes appointed him deputy for South Carolina on the death of De Costa, Virginia already having a deputy. In 1788, acting with Spitzer and Forst, Myers established a Grand Council of Princes of Jerusalem at Charleston. The Charleston council was officially the first on the continent, though the rituals had been performed in New York and Philadelphia. Myers emigrated to Europe in 1795. English Born Simon Nathan moved to New York where he engaged in business and was a member of King David Lodge until the British arrived. Nathan was appointed deputy for North Carolina but instead returned to New York after the war, where he was a prominent citizen until he died in 1822. Samuel Myers was born in New York in 1755, the son of Jewish mason and Hayes associate Myer Myers. Myers appointment as deputy inspector for the Leeward Islands indicates that he was a merchant with business there. The younger Myers moved to Petersburgh, Virginia and was prominent in business and civic affairs, marrying Moses Michael Hayes' daughter Judith. Finally, Moses Cohen was a broker and shop keeper. In spring of 1790 he arrived at Kingston Jamaica where Abraham Jacobs lived; shortly thereafter they were reunited with brother Abraham Forst. The three deputy grand inspectors renewed the 'sublime degrees' together.[35]

Though not one of Hayes appointees, one other Jewish merchant whose networks overlapped several of the most important masonic groups in the United States bears mentioning. Abraham Jacobs was among the most active in spreading the degrees of perfection. Born in New York in 1757, he took his second degree on July 22, 1782 as a visitor in Boston's St. Andrew's, where his Fellowcraft certificate was signed by master Paul Revere. Jacobs was raised to the third degree at

Solomon's lodge in Charleston, where in 1787 he took the degrees of perfection thanks to the aforementioned deputy grand inspectors. On November 9, 1790, he took further degrees, advancing to Knight of the Sun, one of the degrees often discussed between Bordeaux, Martinique and St. Domingue, under the direction of Hayes appointees Forst and Cohen. Jacobs reached the highest degree in the new system, that of "Grand Master *Ecosse*" in Savannah two years later from yet another Jew, Israel Delieben. The well-traveled Jacobs actively spread the new "Scottish Rite" in Georgia and New York. The certificate Delieben gave Jacobs on his attainment of the degree is highly interesting, as it cites his authority as deriving from the Irish Duke of Leinster and the Grand Inspector of the Sublime Degrees of Stockholm, Sweden.

It is plausible that Delieben's business may have brought him into contact with the noble masons named on Jacobs' certificate, or that he had received the degrees from someone who had. Conversely, he may have been another masonic pretender citing higher authorities the veracity of which could not easily be checked. In any case, the new degrees written in Bordeaux and Paris and carried abroad by Morin and others like him had by the closing decade of the eighteenth century criss-crossed the Atlantic sufficiently often that a Jewish merchant like Jacobs might, in the course of his masonic sojourning, undergo rituals under the authority of Boston Patriots, Morin's proteges, an Irish Duke and a Swedish aristocrat. Each such master would have interpreted their craft differently, yet at its core freemasonry was something which created a common bond and a realm of shared understanding and community across these vast distances.

The Farthest Reaches of French Freemasonry

Over a dozen ex-patriot French lodges sprang up in the early decades of the United States as well. The annual *tableaux* of one such lodge, L'Amite No. 73 of Philadelphia, illustrate just how widespread and well-organized the French networks were. It included a list of affiliated lodges which named in France two lodges in Marseille, one in Paris, and a lodge in D'Anvers named Les Amis du Commerce—the Friends of Commerce, at which the lodge kept a deputy. In the islands, the lodge was affiliated with two lodges in St. Pierre, Martinique, where it maintained an active deputy, Simon Chaudron, as well as a third lodge on the island. Chaudron also served as deputy to the affiliated L'Union Francaise Lodge in New York. There was another affiliated lodge in New Orleans. Lodges in correspondence included in the United States two in Charleston, and one in

Baltimore; in the Caribbean two lodges on Guadeloupe, the abovementioned Matrinique lodges, and one each on Trinidad, St. Bartholemy on the Iles du Vent, and a lodge on Havana Cuba, where masons fleeing Saint Domingue had re-established the Grand Lodge of St. Domingo. They corresponded with seven lodges in various parts of France, including Les Neuf Soeurs.[36]

The *Etat du Grand Orient de France, Tome Troisième, Première Partie, 1779* includes two lodges on Isle de Bourbon and one on Isle de France, with which the the Dutch lodge at the Cape of Good Hope corresponded and were aware of at least one other "clandestine" lodge. French freemasonry had also reached East Africa, as it had Guyana in the form of a regimental lodge. In the French West Indies, Saint Domingue boasted nine official lodges by 1779, the tiny island of Grenada supported one lodge while Guadeloupe boasted five, officially dating from the 1760s and 1770s, and spread around the island in five separate communities. Martinique boasted two lodges in Saint-Pierre, though the networks described previously demonstrate the activity of multiple grand lodges as well as clandestine lodges there.

On Saint Domingue, La Vérité in Cap, listed as its top two officers a royal notary and the head of treasury for the navy. Correspondence for La Verite in Europe could be posted from Bordeaux through the Lodge L'Amitié or from Toulouse by the Chevalier de Saint-George, officer of the Grand Orient. This may have been either the famous mulatto composer, fencer, and member of Franklin's *Neuf Soeurs,* Chevalier St. George, or possibly the St. George, 'nobleman of Rouen, France' who served as inspector of military hospitals for Saint Domingue and the lesser Antilles. The latter visited lodges in Gloucester, Massachusetts, where he celebrated the feast of St. John on June 24, 1773 with Paul Revere and other luminaries of the Patriot movement, and at Portsmouth New Hampshire in 1774. Postage was to be prepaid in both cities. St. Jean de Jerusalem Ecossaise was still present and being led by a merchant and a merchant— pharmacist.[37]

Several of the other lodges boast contacts in Europe; for each the top two officers are listed as local contacts. These tended to be merchants, military men, or administrators of note. In Cavaillon the Venerable Master and his second-in-command were the commander of the militia and a wine merchant. Les Freres Unis of aux Cayes was led by a retired infantry officer and an eminent attorney. Au Fond de Negres boasted a provincial grand lodge under the auspices of the local commandant and an "officer of the militia", both planters. The former, V. Buttet, *Chevalier de l'Ordre Royal & Militaire de Saint Louis,* was also master of the local lodge. Correspondence from Europe for either body was to be directed either through the captain of the port of La Rochelle or T.V.F Tassin, banker and officer of the grand orient. The King's Lieutenant headed the Leogane lodge, while in Petit—Goave a militia officer and merchant headed a lodge for which correspondence might be sent through parliamentary advocate and grand orient officer Brother Oudet. Finally, the Saint Marc lodge boasted a lawyer and merchant as its top officers. The tightly organized bureaucracy of the grand orient insured that lodges and brethren throughout the French empire maintained highly effective communication.[38]

Notes

1 *Ibid.,* Jacobs, *Origins of Freemasonry,* 20–21.
2 Wesiberger, *Freemasonry on Both Sides,* 299–345; Jacobs, *Living the Enlightenment,* 89–90, 205–7.
3 William Weisberger, "Parisian Masonry, the lodge of the nine sisters, and the French enlightenment" in *Freemasonry on Both Sides of the Atlantic: Essays Concerning the Craft in the British Isles, Europe, the United States and Mexico* (New York: East European Monographs, 2002), 299–345; Jacobs, *Living the Enlightenment,* 3–12; John Robinson, *Born in Blood: the Lost Secrets of Freemasonry* (NewYork: M. Evans & Company, 1989) reignited belief in the Templar myth among modern masons based on dubious historical analysis.
4 *Ibid.,* Jacobs, *Origins,* 22–3; Schuchard, "Jacobite vs. Hanoverian Claims for Masonic 'Antiquity' and 'Authenticity'" *Heredom,* 121–186.
5 "Original Constitution and Statues of the Order of Chevaliers Hospitaliers et Militaires de Saint Jean de Jerusalem dits Frey-Macons," Sharp Documents, Volume 1, Document 1. Lexington: Van –Gordon Williams Library, Museum of Our National Heritage.
6 "Jacques Blancard to the Mother Grand Lodge Ecossais of Bordeaux," June 15, 1751. Sharp Vol. 2, document 30; Charles Porset, Cecile Revauger, *Le Monde Maçonnique des Lumières (Europe-Amériques & Colonies) Dictionnaire prosopographique, Volume III* (Paris: Honoré Champion Editeur, 2013), 2032–5.
7 Porcet, *Le Monde Maçonnique,* 2032–35.
8 *Ibid.*
9 *Ibid.*; Sharp Documents, Vol III "The Story of the Ecossaise Lodge in the Isle of San Domingo", Documents 34, 38, 56.
10 Sharp Documents, Vol. III, Doc. 6, Trutie to Papillion, June 6, 1748; Doc 109 Lamolere de Feuillas to Elus Parfaits, Feb. 27, 1755; Doc. 45 Warrant of Lamorlere de Feuillas, Dec. 24, 1752; Feuillass' delegation of authority to Berthomieux, Sept. 18, 1753, Minutes of the Installation of *Parfaite Lodge d'Ecosse de Saint Marc.*

11 Sharp Documents, Vol. III, Doc 35, Saint Jean de Jerusalem Ecossaise of Cap-Francais to Bordeaux, Feb. 13, 1753.

12 Sharp Documents, Vol. III, Doc. 56, Etienne Morin to Les Elus Parfaits, June 24, 1757.

13 Sharp Documents, vol. III, Doc. 56; Doc 57, "Brethren of Cayes to the Elus Parfaits of Bordeaux", June 30, 1757.

14 *Ibid.*, docs. 59, 62, 63, 112, 114.

15 Porcet, *Le Monde Maçonnique*, 2032–35.

16 Sharp Documents, Vol. II, "The Story of the Lodge La Parfaite Union on the Island of Martinique", ii–iii, Doc. 19.

17 Sharp Documents, Vol. II, Docs. 19, 16, 32, 50.

18 Sharp Documents Vol. II. Docs. 3a, 19, 29, 30, 32, 33, 36, 50.

19 Sharp Documents, vol. II, docs 13–14,

20 Sharp Documents, Vol. II docs. 47, 121.

21 Sharp Documents, vol. II doc. 48.

22 Sharp Documents, Vol. IV "The Story of the Ecossais Lodge of New Orleans", introduction, Documents, 40, 41, 72.

23 *Ibid.*, docs. 49, 50, 54, 102.

24 *Ibid.*, Docs. 49, 50, 64, 66, 72.

25 *Ibid.*, docs. 50, 60, 61, 102.

26 Ibid., introduction / translator's notes.

27 Samuel Bayard Harrison, Jr. *History of the Supreme Council, 33rd Degree Ancient and Accepted Scottish Rite of Freemasonry Northern Masonic Jurisdiction of the United States and Its Antecedants, Volume 1* (Boston: 1938), 46–60. This work contains original minutes of the Albany Lodge of Perfection and other assorted primary documents or excerpts from primary documents, as well as institutional history and biography of figures connected with the Scottish Rite, the US offshoot of the French derived higher degrees. It also discusses on page 21 possible French origins for the degrees which formed the basis of the York Rite.

28 *Ibid.*

29 *Ibid.*, Michael Hoberman, *New Israel / New England: Jews and Puritans in Early America* (Boston: University of Massachusetts Press, 2011), 206–226, 254.

30 Ibid.; MasonicGenealogy.com

31 *Ibid.*

32 *Ibid.*, 61–66.

33 *Ibid.*, 61–72.

34 *Ibid.*, 71–3.

35 Ibid., 72–5.

36 Tableau des Composant La T.R.L Francaise L'Amite, No. 73, Regulierent Constituee a L'O de Philadelphie, Par Le Grand Oreint De Pennsylvanie. (Philadelphia: Bloquerst, 1811), 12–14.

37 *Etat du Grand Orient de France, Tome Troisième, Première Partie,* 1779. Paris: Grand Orient de Francaise, 1779, 117–21, 149–50; Tyrian Lodge, Gloucester, Minutes and Records, Book 1; St. John's Lodge, Portsmouth, Minutes and Records, book 1, Musée Grande Loge Nationale de France, personal communication, December 31, 2009.

38 *Ibid.,* 117–21.

14

Commerce, Connections, and Conspiracy Theorists: Pennsylvania's Grand Lodge of Santo Domingo

French Masonry was most active on Saint Domingue, where John Garrigus in *Before Haiti* estimates that by 1789 there were as many as 20 orients—founding lodges or bodies- and 40 lodges with approximately 1000 members by the end of the 1780s. These included at least one more lodge of English origin dating to the 1740s. The membership was overwhelmingly white, so that these 1000 masons were drawn from a total population of around 30,000. This included about 10,000 unpropertied whites unlikely to qualify for membership. Thus, this 1000 represent a substantial portion of the male elite. Freemasonry was an important part of the new sociability and cosmopolitanism which swept the island following the Seven Years' War. Masonic marks frequently appeared on various documents to make ones' masonic membership known when conducting business with strangers, including transactions with foreign crews.

On February 3rd, 1786, Bro. P. Barbier Dupleissis, future grand secretary of the Grand Lodge of Pennsylvania, laid before the grand lodge two letters that he had from the original French. These proved to be a petition, addressed to "His Excellency, Monseigneur Washington, General of the Armies of America and Serene Grand Master," requesting a charter for a lodge in Cap Francois on the island of Saint Domingue. It was the first of two such unsolicited requests, the second, received several years later and officially considered at the December 18,

1789 meeting of grand lodge, was sent by a group of Brethren in the city of Port-au-Prince. In the first case the Americans acted too slowly, so that by the time they issued the requested charter the French brethren had already obtained one from the English Provincial Grand Lodge of the Southern District of North America, which had recently migrated from St. Augustine to Jamaica. The second request, however, resulted in a fruitful Masonic relationship between Philadelphia and Saint Domingue which led to the formation of a provincial grand lodge on the island and a tightly-knit network of Masonic lodges that maintained itself among the Saint Domingue diaspora and connected lodges from New Orleans to Cuba to New York.[1]

The correspondence of the brethren of Saint Domingue with their brothers in Philadelphia explicitly explain how freemasonry created inter-imperial commercial networks. In their August 11, 1789 petition requesting a warrant for De la Reunion des Coeurs Franco Americains Lodge in Port-au-Prince the French brothers stated, "We have, very much honored Grand Master, shown our zeal for the American Free masonry still further,—the majority of the brethren, forming our Orient, live on the coast where your merchant ships land,—and we have appointed a representative to give us information of all the vessels, as they arrive, and as soon as we are informed that the Captain or some of the crew are free masons, we offer them all the service which circumstances will permit to be useful to them." *Tableaux* of the various Saint Domingue and Martinique lodges are replete with the names of planters and merchants, as well as a smattering of administrators, military officials, and skilled craftsmen. The lodge was thus likely to be able to offer considerable service to their American brethren.[2]

The association with republican values suited those who wished for colonial autonomy and sympathized with the new United States. Their letters show that like the Dutch brethren who sought fraternal relations with Philadelphia after the war, they considered American political values and American masonry to be closely linked and wished to emulate both. Again, the importance of individual masons with wide ranging connections comes into play in the character of Brother P. Barbier Duplessis, whose masonic career began in France. He first entered the masonic minutes of the western hemisphere in Boston in 1779, where the proceedings of the grand lodge stated that on March 5, "A petition from a number of Brethren, subjects of his Most Christian Majesty, now resident in Boston, to erect a Lodge under the title of "Friendship Lodge," was read, whereupon voted, September 3, (after ascertaining the character and merit of the petitioners from the French consul) that a charter be granted, and delivered to a Brother La Barbier Dupleissis at his request." Huguenot descended Paul Revere took an active role in Dupleissis' Friendship Lodge. Such lodges of French ex-patriots appear in England on the *Engraved Lists* and elsewhere in the Anglophone world, including one such lodge in Philadelphia of which Dupleissis later served as master. It was in Pennsylvania where he reached the height of his masonic career.[3]

Pierre Le Barbier Dupleissis first appeared in Pennsylvania freemasonry in January, 1787 at Montgomery Lodge. No. 19, where he served as master three years later. He was the founding master, in 1792, of a new lodge of French Emigres, St. Louis No. 53. In grand lodge Barbier served as grand secretary from 1790 to 94 and as deputy grand master from 1808 to 13. He also held high rank in the local Scottish Rite bodies. Dupleissis not only translated the petitions and letters received from Saint Domingue but, as those letters show, he had known at least one of the petitioners from masonic lodges in France.[4]

The first petition opened by explaining that as the master had argued to the brethren "most parts of the Lodges of France having neglected the Discipline Established by the English & which have been the principle of Masonry, it is proper to apply to the head spring and to a Scotch Lodge. . .Therefore he thought the application should rather be made to General Washington, Grand Master of the Lodges in North America, in the grand lodge at Philadelphia." The misconception that George Washington reigned as grand master of the whole United States aside (such a plan had been raised but quashed, largely by Massachusetts), this impeccable masonic logic carried the day and the vote to seek sanction from Philadelphia carried unanimously. The *Tableaux* sent by the lodge shows that 60 % of the membership were merchants, 20 % administrators, with planters and one watchmaker making up the final quintile.[5]

The Pennsylvanians voted to grant a warrant and directed the secretary to make out the pertinent documents. Before they could be delivered to Saint Domingue, however, suspicions developed regarding the masonic legitimacy of the bearer of the petition, the aptly named Brother French. Masonic Jurisprudence was an essential matter in all such dealings, and so before the new warrant could be transmitted to the West Indies French wrote to one Anthony Ernest, then at New York, who vouched for his having received the commission from the lodge at Cap. He further stated that they were impatient to receive the charter and had implored him, should he see French in America, "to urge him to get the business done as quick as possible." He then gently admonished the Pennsylvanians that, "From the particular attention & respect paid to several Brethren from the difft. States while I was there, It gives me a deal of concern to learn that in return for their Civilities, their Business has been so long delayed. . ." This letter of March

1, 1786 was directed to the grand master of Pennsylvania, William Adcock, at French's request.

Grand lodge officially read their final letter in December. In it, the lodge at Cap explained that they had indeed empowered Brother French, who claimed to belong to a lodge in Philadelphia, and had intimated that the process would be easier than had been the case. It politely explained that since they had had nothing from the Americans after so long, they applied to the Provincial Grand Lodge of St. Andrew at Morant Bay, Jamaica, and had received a constitution. The letter informs that they would be "exceedingly happy to see any of their American brethren that may pass that way." However, the minutes of the grand lodge also state that they returned the warrant sent from Pennsylvania, opting to continue under Jamaican authorization. The republican ideology associated with America appears to have been more important to the second, successful solicitation of an American warrant for a Dominguan lodge.

On December 18, 1789 the Grand Lodge of Pennsylvania voted to issue a warrant for lodge No. 47, De la Reunion des Coeurs Franco Americains. This time they acted more decisively, voting to issue the charter on the same day the petition was read, so that on Christmas day they created a warrant for The Union of Franco-American Hearts Lodge located in Port-au-Prince under Master Pierre Augustin Riquet du Belloy. Considering how many lodges were active in Saint Domingue by this time, why would two groups of Dominguan masons bother to seek a warrant in far off, English speaking Pennsylvania? How did they know who to contact, and how to delivery their petition to the grand lodge? These are questions which they addressed in rich detail in their petition. The document is replete with flowery masonic stylings including their motivation to seek a Pennsylvania warrant:

> The seven arts which we know and which have been transmitted to us by the wise Hermes, the conquering Nimrod, and which your nation practice with so much distinction and honor, have at all times contributed to the formation of temples, erected to the virtue and to good order; – it is principally in your country that these famous monuments of Masonic zeal exist- as your plans and edifices are astonishing the whole universe, it is therefore not surprising that Free Masons from another Kingdom seek to claim light at your hearth and to place themselves under your colors.

The idea that it was 'principally' in the United States that glorious temples and edifices existed in 1789 could not have been meant literally. Rather, they refer to 'edifices of Masonic zeal', meaning institutions that represent the values of freemasonry—secular, republican government, social equality unmatched in the world, and the growth of commerce and education. At a time when Saint Domingue merchants and planters sought greater autonomy and free trade and intentionally expressed their desires in language similar to that of the American revolutionaries, the ties between the real world political significance of American ideals and their masonic counterparts was by no means superficial or superfluous to the Creole petitioners.

The petition described its membership as composed of. "Several Free masons of different Nationalities, living at present under the torrid zone." They explain that, "we have opened, and will welcome with emotions of sensitiveness and of pleasure all of our American brethren to our Lodge (erected under the distinct title of the 'Reunion of the hearts- Franco American'), who come invested with authentic certificates from the different lodges of which they are members." That their hospitality will extent to those with 'authentic certificates' speaks to the importance of masonic diplomatic protocol, legality and legitimacy. It also serves to reassure the Pennsylvanian grand lodge officers that the applicants will follow the fraternity's jurisprudence and maintain the quality and standing of the grand lodge in the greater masonic world.

The personal connections which led to the petition's arrival and delineate a further framework for the relationship. The creoles had decided to, "confer upon T...M... Bro. Pierre Le Barbier Dupleissis- whom we chose for our representative, all the necessary powers to solicit our constitution, together with a sufficient number of certificates to prove and attest to the whole universe that we are invested with the ineffaceable character of Free Masons." Dupleissis' personal connections to the petitioners and his ability as a translator were vital to the relationship. That they saw fit to include certificates of their members reinforces the importance of legitimacy and of documenting their international bona fides. After specifying their intent to pay the associated fees, they request, "if you find it *a propos*, to give to the first Masonic American captain, who casts anchor in this Port, a special order that, together with the illustrious brother Lefebre, he examine our Orient, and to judge our work."

The first point, that of ritual correctness, was important enough for the petition to elaborate on, bringing together the orthodoxy of British ritual and the clout of French higher degrees. "Although made masons in France. . . we practice the modern English Masonry which is in use in the most part of your lodges." the Grand Lodge of Pennsylvania was by now militantly Ancient, however, this reference to 'Modern' British masonry did not dissuade the Pennsylvanians. To support this, they further refer to brethren described in the enclosed certificates,

"...our very dear brother Osson de Verrieres is-himself- an English Mason...". Calling on personal connections, they state another member has worked, "during his last voyage in several of your Lodges, assisted by T...M... Bro. Le Barbier Dupleissis Sovereign Prince of the Royal Secret, with whom he had before worked in France in the lodges of symbolic masonry." Brotherhood formed in France altered both the masonic alliances existing across national boundaries in the Americas and formed the basis for solid and expansive trading relations among brother freemasons from Pennsylvania and Saint Domingue, by extension facilitating further connections to other lodges throughout the French empire.

The closing paragraphs of the petition reinforce the important relationship between the two nations, and emphasize the close connection between the political, social, and Masonic relationship. "Already harmony, friendship and mutual services have united our two nations, which the Royal Art and the practicing of the Sublime mysteries unite in still stronger ties, principally between the Free Masons of the two nations, who undoubtedly are the elite and the best support of the countries, by the virtuous principles which direct them." The unifying nature of freemasonry and its enlightenment role as a virtuous, principled, moral elite of politically active citizens is clearly evident, as is the reference to the recent Franco-American alliance and the belief that America as a nation is in a very real sense an expression of masonic values. So began a relationship which in less than two decades led to the formation of at least eight more lodges and a provincial grand lodge on Saint Domingue. This Franco-American brotherly connection did not die with the whites in the Haitian Revolution, but evolved into a functional network within the refugee diaspora that continued to grow in new homes across the United States and the islands. It also served to introduce freemasonry to Cuba, one of the first successful masonic inroads into the Spanish empire.

The Grand Lodge of Pennsylvania dispatched the warrant and next heard from Lodge No. 47 on June 6, 1791, when they received a package dated May 15 containing a letter directing their representative, Bro. Dupleissis, to lay before the lodge "several paper written in the French language, such as extracts from their Minutes and Resolves, Blanks of their Certificates as well for actual as Honorary Members, a list of their Officers and Members printed on white Satin &c." The September 5 minutes report that correspondence of the "greatest importance" had been received from the lodge. These included information on the death of the founder and first master of the lodge, P. Augustine Riquet du Belloy, which must have been personally upsetting for his friend Dupleissis. On a happier note, the political instability on the island had not interfered with the operations of the lodge. Getting down to business, they also informed the grand lodge that they would forward the outstanding payment for their warrant "as soon as a safe opportunity presents."

The minutes of lodge No. 47 sent to Philadelphia cover only a short period of the lodge's first year of operation, but nonetheless include ample evidence of an active, cosmopolitan lodge. One of the officers was name Churchill, clearly neither a Frenchman nor a native of Saint Domingue. The lodge received visitors from overseas including an American whose private petition for assistance the lodge granted. There were Portuguese visitors in the lodge's first month of operation, February 1789, in which the lodge held five meetings. Multiple meetings in a single month were common. There is also a note of receipt of a letter from the Grand Lodge of Madeira. Following a long gap in communication, the lodge's letters to grand lodge of November 17, 1799, December 6 1799 and January 11, 1800 reached Philadelphia. After explaining that the turbulence on the island had led to the lodge's suspending operations for a time, the brethren noted that since resuming their masonic work there had been a succession of foreign visitors.

The first, Savard, appears to have come from Bogota; he was followed successively by Robert Maxiwell (sic), lodge No. 58 Halifax North Carolina; William Whetten, lodge No. 37 Curacao; William Baxter of lodge No. 8 in Maryland, and Nicholas Fitz Simon from lodge No. 8, South Carolina. Thus, in a short and unstable period the lodge had entertained visitors from lodges in the Dutch and Spanish colonies and three American states. The first letter also recommended a member, Bro. Gettin, "whom we find to have been taken and carried to Jamaica," the lodge perhaps hoping that American masons may have had contacts there. Most of the latest letter offered condolences on the death of Bro. George Washington along with an extract of their proceedings for January 11, 1800, on which day they held an elaborate masonic funeral for Washington by the lodge members and other masons, "performed agreeably to usage among Ancient Masons". They also included a list of 51 members.

The correspondence, though voluminous on masonic matters, offers little in the way of specifics regarding the hardships the brethren faced due to the ongoing Haitian Revolution. The handwritten *tableau* for 1798 included only 25 names- 6 fewer than the previous year- but the printed *tableau* submitted the following year had the lodge back at 52 active members with two listed as away on business and three honorary members in Saint Domingue. Dupleissis was also an honorary member. The demographics of the 1799–1800 roster included 23 merchants, seven planters (most immigrants), a goldsmith, two retailers, a pair of bakers, two notaries, one journalist, a printer, one lawyer, two building contractors and their supervisor, a chief clerk, and several administrators: the municipal secretary, inspector general of the health service, and a bailiff, military officer and administrative officer. Only a handful—as few as four—were listed as born in Saint Domingue with one from Prague.

The opening year of the nineteenth century gave white planters on or returning to Saint Domingue a false sense of optimism for the future of their colony. Whether through direct connection with Reunion of Franco-American Hearts or of their own volition, three more lodges appeared under warrant from Pennsylvania. Lodge No. 87, Les Freres Reunis at Le Cap, received its warrant on December 15, 1800. Pennsylvania granted a warrant for lodge No. 88, La Concorde at St. Marc on May 4, 1801 and Lodge No. 89, Les Frères Sincèrement Re-Unis at Aux Cages, du Fond de L'Isle Vachas on the same date, indicating that their petitions were most likely received simultaneously from the same bearer. The explosion of Pennsylvania authorized Ancient freemasonry on the island led to the brethren soliciting, through their representative Dupleissis, a provincial grand lodge to superintend their work locally.

Grand Master Jonathan B. Smith informed the grand lodge of his approval of their request on December 7, 1801. In his letter he explained that "six lodges are now regularly constituted on that island," implying that more lodges arose from this association which are no longer recorded, and that "applications are made for two more." On ritual, Smith stated that, "I am well informed they are much pleased with the antient mode of working, and as far as they can procure instruction wish to conform to it exactly, and that they profess an inviolable attachment to the Grand Lodge of Pennsylvania." This last matter was an important one in Pennsylvania, where the dominant Ancient grand lodge had refused a masonic funeral service for eminent Modern mason and former grand master Benjamin Franklin. Ironically, the egalitarian British— Irish Ancient masonry and the elitist French "Scottish" masonry had formed an unlikely hybrid among Saint Domingue's Pennsylvania-oriented creole masons. The provincial grand lodge of Santo Domingo was founded on January 9, 1802. It chartered four known lodges in its short existence on that island: Lodge No. 95, La Humilité, at Anse-à-Veau, December 6, 1802; Lodge No. 97, and Parfaite Harmonie (no location given) on September 5, 1803. On December 5, 1803 the grand lodge received a return from provincial grand master Hacquet, reporting a total of eight lodges including two new ones, which were given the numbers 98 and 99 on the Pennsylvania role that day: La Preserverance at Abricots, and La Temple du Bonheur at Arcahaye.

The constitution of lodge No. 89, Sincere Reunion of Cayes de Fond de L'Isle-A-Vache, a printed copy of which the lodge sent to grand lodge bound with their *Tableau* for the year 1801, is particularly interesting. It was dated in both the masonic and Revolutionary calendar, with the masonic date of the 15th day of the 6th masonic month corresponding to 27 Thermidor year 9. Speaking to masonic jurisprudence, the constitution included a summary of the foundation of the Grand Lodge of Pennsylvania as warranted by the Ancient Grand Lodge of England in 1764, as transmitted from Edwin of York. The constitution shows ample evidence of the brethren's ideals of masonry as a unified nation, opening "The masons widespread upon the face of the Earth, make up a family whose members, scattered and separated, are still united by the rectitude of their intentions and fraternal charity; they are mutually shown these sentiments when ills occur in any part of the world; differences of religion, of government, and the Masonic Rite under which they work, must not disturb the harmony between them. . ." The lodge thus declared itself open to masons Modern, Ancient, or working under a French or European higher degree system.

Their constitution speaks to interplay between the two sides of the masonic world. The members included holders of French higher degrees, such as Saint Domingue native, brigadier general, and *"Commandant le department du Sud"* Jean-Joseph Laplume, who held the rank of *"Elu des 9"*. At the same time, the constitution states that, ". . . jealous to work under the Ancient Rite, in which SEVERAL of our member were initiated, . . . we solicited the Constitutions of our friends and neighbors the Americans. . .". Brethren like those of Sincere Reunion sought both the aristocratically oriented French-Scottish degrees and the working class Irish Ancient degrees in the belief that they represented a deeper level of Masonic understanding. Ironically, the Ancients' Royal Arch degree had most likely been derived from a French higher degree in the first place. The lodge's membership was, with only a few exceptions, European rather than creole, and included a number of administrators, military men, and professionals with a smaller proportion of merchants than other lodges under the provincial grand lodge.[6]

Exodus

Whatever the aspirations of the brethren in these newly warranted lodges may have been, their former slaves had a different agenda. On May 6, 1806 the Grand Lodge sent a letter, addressed only to "Wor. Sir & Bror", apparently meant for whomever remained of the provincial grand lodge. That a reply was forthcoming only a few months later implies that someone at grand lodge in Philadelphia knew where to deliver the message. It informed the surviving brethren that as of

April 7 the warrant of their provincial grand lodge had been vacated, "by reason of its having ceased on account of the unhappy disturbances in St. Domingo." Even in view of these "unhappy disturbances" -an interesting euphemism for genocidal race war- Philadelphia hoped that the legal niceties of the republic of masonry might be followed. They requested that, "If you are in possession of the Warrant, Papers, &c. or if not in your possession but in your power to procure them you will have the goodness to transmit them to me agreeably to the said Resolution & the regulations of the G. Lodge, but if they cannot be procured I would request the favor of you giving me what information you can respecting them." The writer goes on to state that he has enclosed, "for the like purpose, Circulars to the late officers of the late Lodges No. 47, 87, 88, 89, 95, 97, 98 &99…"

The Grand Lodge then requested that it be "fully informed" if possible, on several subjects. Namely, the warrants of lodges 87, 88, and 89. The letter explains that three warrants for these lodges were delivered to Brother Duplessis to be forwarded to Saint Domingue. Duplessis was to receive the remittances and pay them to the grand lodge. No payment for the warrants or subsequent dues were ever received. Further, "The Grand Lodge has never rec'd any Thing on accot of the Lodges No. 95, 97, 98 &99 all which were established by the said late Provincial Grand Lodge." This culminates in the statement that said provincial grand lodge has never sent any payments on its behalf either.

Pennsylvania seems to have maintained some hope of being paid for masonic services rendered. They ask if any of the aforementioned funds had been remitted and if so which lodges had paid which outstanding accounts, "by whom sent, at what time? and by whom received here?" These were, as far as the grand lodge was concerned, important documents and meaningful financial obligations, equivalent to taxes and corporate charters in a conventional republic. The response they received and read before the grand lodge on September 1 answered the American queries with skillfully diplomatic language in both French and English from "The Past Master's Council of the R…L…N… No. 88, York's Constitution [i.e. Ancient] under the distinctive name of Concordia, Constituted by the most Ill…G..L… of Pennsylvania in the case of St. Marc in the Island of St. Domingo on the 4th of May 1801 Now re-established & Sitting at St Yago in the Island of Cuba."

The letter opens by congratulating James Milnor on his ascension to the position of Grand Master. The Provincial Grand Lodge explained that, "The most R…B.. Barbier Dupleissis, sent towards you in the capacity of its deputy, will give you an account of the facts and motives he is to present you in its name…"

Apparently Duplessis had either met in person or received personal correspondence from one or more members of the lodge. They asked the new grand master to decide whether their provincial grand master, Mathieu Dupostel, acted legally in authorizing their lodge to continue its operations in Cuba and further requested that if this exceeded his authority, that the grand lodge itself authorize the continuation of the lodge or allow them to constitute a new one with the same number. They listed six documents as included in their package: an authorization of the provincial grand master dated "the sixth day of the sixth month, 5805"; an invoice to their master, Moret de Guiramand of the same date, probably for provincial grand lodge expenses; records of the installation of the lodge "on the seventh day of the month" implying that they resumed their operations in June, 1805 based on the PGM's authorization; their *tableau* for the year, and a payment of $50. Guiramand signed the letter on behalf of the past masters council of lodge number 88.

The grand lodge appointed a three man committee of correspondence chaired by Duplessis to handle communications with the St. Domingo diaspora. A report of the committee appears in the proceedings of the Grand Lodge of Pennsylvania for September 15, 1806. It lists communications received from the refugees as the communication from Lodge La Concorde, No. 88, described above as well as a letter from R.W. Mathieu Dupotet, the former Provincial Grand Master, and an address and petition from Lodge No. 98 formerly meeting at Abricots; this last document was received and presented to the committee by Duplessis. The report explained that "a considerable number of brethren" under the Grand Lodge's jurisdiction "as well as several other masons" had escaped to Cuba, particularly St. Yago and Baracoa. This, "gave room to frequent private committees and clandestine makings, to scandal and abuses of all kinds." Mathieu Duportel, late provincial grand master of St. Domingo and several members of the provincial grand lodge now resided at Baracoa. "The good masons" had been "informing him of what was doing every day and requested he would by virtue of his authority and powers grant warrants for new lodges on dispensation to open the lodges, late from St. Domingo, whose officers were then at St. Yago, pleading the necessity to put an end to the said scandals and irregularities, by giving to true masons a central point to unite themselves in and establishing a tribunal that might judge and punish the guilty, or at least give them an opportunity to return and follow the paths of Wisdom and virtue."

It is difficult to know what 'scandals and abuses' had grown serious enough to warrant a tribunal. Perhaps it was more of the sort of personal pique that had characterized French colonial freemasonry as exemplified by Morin's constant clashes. The report later mentions a complaint of lodge number 88 against number 98, as well as correspondence from the latter lodge, which it referred to Duportel and the Provincial Grand Lodge of St. Domingo and Cuba rather than attempting to adjudicate it themselves. In any case, the suggestion of a tribunal, a pseudo-legal body, shows how seriously these masons viewed masonic legalities. The report continues the story, stating that Duportel believed his and the provincial grand lodge's authority to have expired when they left Haiti, but, "yielding to the imperiousness of circumstances and convinced that the establishment of a lodge at St. Yago was the only means to put a stop to those evils and to render to Masonry those advantages it would otherwise have lost..." called a grand committee at Baracoa on "August 6th, 5805" and resolved to authorized Morel de Guiramand to open, as master, lodge number 88 *La Concorde* until instructions arrived from Pennsylvania. The committee agreed with the actions taken at Baracoa, "to save masonry from disgrace in a country where the people are already so much prepossessed against it." They called Duportel's actions "laudable" and deserving of "approbation and thanks."

This led the committee to advance four resolutions, all passed unanimously, that the resolution rescinding the authority of the provincial grand lodge of St. Domingo and the warrant of lodge number 88 be vacated, and that instead its authority be extended to Cuba. Furthermore, they confirmed the proceedings of La Concorde since August 6th, 5805 (1805) and referred the petition of lodge no 98 La Perseverance and La Concorde's complaint against them to the newly re-authorized provincial grand lodge and grand master. Duplessis paid La Concorde's $50 to the grand treasurer and the grand lodge resolved to transmit through the committee of correspondence copies of their report and proceedings to the provincial grand lodge and lodge La Concorde.

The *tableaux* of lodge No. 98, the last of which dates from 1809 after the lodge had relocated to Cuba, included 19 members. None were merchants. These either fell on the opposing side of the post—exodus controversy between No. 98 and the rest of the provincial grand lodge or had relocated elsewhere. Eight were listed as proprietors of Saint Domingue, of whom only one was born there. He was one of two Saint Domingue natives; one member was from Guadeloupe and the rest were French. The other members were professionals, including four goldsmiths, two physicians, a distiller, artist, and maritime officer.[7]

It is interesting to note that the rosters of French lodges in the United States following the Haitian Revolution tended to include far more natives of Saint Domingue, generally listed as planters. It appears that the masonic circle acquainted with Dupleissis were largely French ex-patriots like him. Since Saint

Domingue had a very large masonic community with overlapping jurisdictions and territorial disputes, it seems reasonable that one of the unspoken motivations for seeking authority from Pennsylvania may have been the contentious relationship between the merchants and new immigrants found in No. 47 and her sister lodges and the established social and masonic elite of Saint Domingue. Tension between merchants and planters and between old and new whites as well as the fractious and jealous nature of Saint Domingue freemasonry imply that such motivation was plausibly at play. The French masonic tradition of writing to the metropolis to resolve colonial disputes and the seriousness with which the brethren took their masonic identity led to a remarkably voluminous correspondence on the 'scandalous' and even 'perverse' actions of lodge number 98 which is interesting more for the importance placed on it by men undergoing such extreme trauma and dislocation and what it says about the gravity with which they viewed their membership in the masonic fraternity than for the minutiae of the feud.

So began the ironic history of Cuban freemasonry. The lodges survived persecution and suspicion, sometimes overtly and sometimes covertly. The institution introduced by white slave owners gradually opened to Cubans of various shades. More interesting, it was involved in political intrigues against Spanish rule throughout the eighteenth century. Freemasons were involved in the filibuster expeditions and in locally originated movements. The leaders of the independence struggle, Jose Marti, Antonio Maceo and Carlos Manuel de Cespedes, were all freemasons. By the closing decades of the century, masons involved with the movement left Cuba and Puerto Rico for New York in the wake of their movement's failure. There, they came under the jurisdiction of the African American Prince Hall Grand Lodge of New York. Notably among these masons, was Aurturo Schomberg, also a member of "Los Dos Antilles", a revolutionary group with heavy masonic overlap. Schomburg became a noted black scholar, activist, and high ranking member of the Prince Hall grand lodge in New York in the close of the nineteenth century and the early decades of the twentieth.[8]

Lodges La Concorde and La Perseverance were not the only survivors of the provincial grand lodge of St. Domingo to relocate and resume contact with the grand lodge of Pennsylvania. The original Saint Domingue lodge, no. 47, reconnected with Duplessis, now deputy grand master, in 1808. Their petition, which he presented to the grand lodge on September 15, 1808, informed Pennsylvania that the lodge had retained its original warrant and was now operating in New Orleans. The nine signers of the petition include both refugees and masons who they met in their new home. They asked to be able to continue working under their old name and number, or if that was not possible, to establish a new lodge

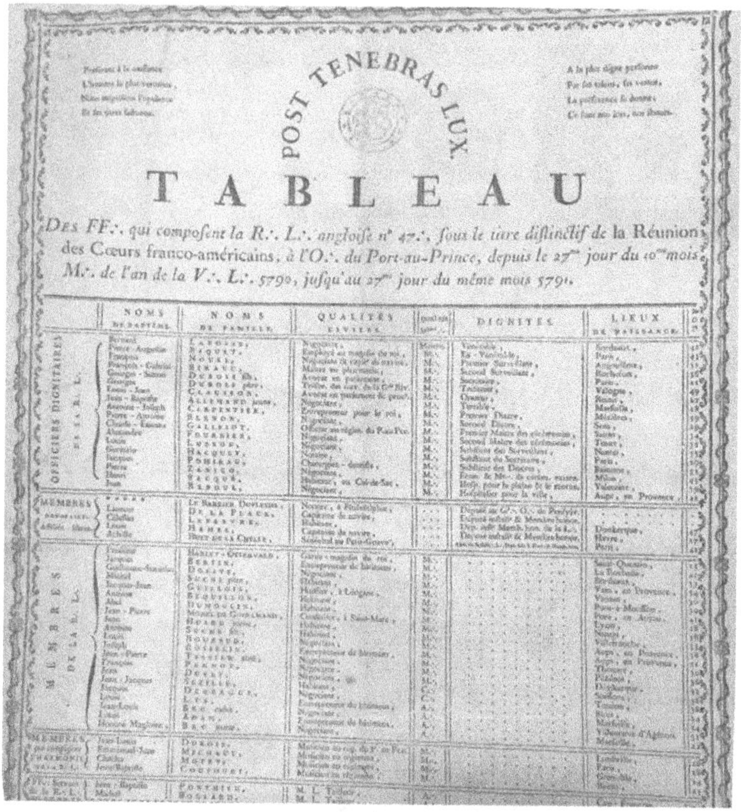
POST TENEBRAS LUX.

TABLEAU

DES FF∴ qui composent la R∴ L∴ angloise nº 47∴, sous le titre distinctif de la Réunion des Cœurs franco-américains, à l'O∴ du Port-au-Prince, depuis le 27me jour du 10me mois M∴ de l'an de la V∴ L∴ 5790, jusqu'au 27me jour du même mois 5791.

NOMS DE BAPTÊME | NOMS DE FAMILLE | QUALITÉS CIVILES | DIGNITÉS | LIEUX DE NAISSANCE

Figure 14.1. 1790–91 Tableau of lodge No. 47. Of the members, only the two "frere Sevans", both tailors, were natives of Saint Domingue. Of the 45 members and five honorary members (including Dupleissis, listed as Notary in Philadelphia), there were: 16 merchants, 8 planters—all immigrants from France; two ships captains, one of whom was also listed as "merchant"; 2 lawyers, an employee and a guard of the royal magazine, a pharmacist, a royal contractor, 4 building contractors, a surgeon—dentist, a regimental officer, military official, bailiff, a notary, a seneschal and 4 regimental musicians. (Courtesy Masonic Library and Museum of Pennsylvania).

"under the name of the desired re-union." As the warrant of lodge number 47 had been vacated as of April 7, 1806, the grand lodge voted to charter a new lodge, No. 112, as requested, and directed the installing brother to receive the old warrant and return it to the grand lodge.

The fate of the other lodges of the Provincial Grand Lodge of St. Domingo is not clear. Some may have been among the French lodges which appeared up and down the coast of the United States at this time, choosing to affiliate with the grand lodges of the states in which they landed. The rest either disappeared or removed to the Spanish dominions or elsewhere without resuming contact with Pennsylvania. The French Lodges of the United States, both those originated through Pennsylvania and a number of others, at least 14 or 15 in all, created a network which included their relocated Cuban brethren, lodges on the remaining islands in the French Caribbean and France, as well as elsewhere in both Europe and the United States. Their *tableaux* show a membership swelled by the influx of refugees from Saint Domingue in the immediate wake of the Haitian revolution. Over the following decades they continued bringing in new members from France and locally born young men of French descent, functioning in many cases at least until the anti-masonic frenzy of the 1830s shut down so many lodges across the United States.

Nor was freemasonry erased from the Haitian soil when the last white man left; indeed, it was to re-emerge as a vibrant force in Haitian politics and society, with both English and later French authorized bodies as well as syncretic local variations emerging in the aftermath of revolution. That the lodges of the Grand Lodge of Santo Domingo's last *Tableaux* from Saint Domingue included revolutionary leader and Governor General Toussaint Louverture's secretary and a new initiate born in Senegal, not to mention the US consul, demonstrates that well placed Blacks had received the secrets of freemasonry before the last white masons evacuated. One can only speculate to what extent these highly placed Black initiates may have aided their white brothers in first fitting into the new social order and finally in escaping the bloody climax of the Haitian Revolution. The 1810 edition of the *Freemasons Calendar* includes two Haitian lodges, number "603 La Loge de L'Amité des Frères Réunis, Port au Prince, 604 La Loge de L'Heureuse Reunion, Aux Cayes Island of Hayti", "Hayti" is also added to the regional listings for the West Indies. Two years later, the *Calendar* also included a provincial grand master, John Goff, for the island. Boston's Prince Saunders used his masonic connections in both England and Haiti as an envoy from Christophe to England. In Haiti, freemasonry flourished on the highest levels of society and also had a marked influence on vodoun and other syncretic traditions from the early nineteenth century on.[9]

Exiles from Saint Domingue continued to spread freemasonry and create masonic degrees. Among the members of Lodge No. 47, Joseph Cerneau remains notorious among U.S. Scottish Rite masons to the present day. French born Cerneau was, by 1800, a member of Loge La Reunion Desiree in Port-au-Prince under the auspices of the Grand Orient of France. By June of 1801 Lodge No. 47

listed him as a member and goldsmith in its *tableaux*. Cerneau served as junior grand warden of the provincial grand lodge and after exile led in the 1804 petition for a warrant for Le Temple des Vertus Theologales from brethren in Havana to the Grand Lodge of Pennsylvania and served as the first master of the lodge. By 1809 Cerneau had migrated to New York, where he became an active member of Washington Lodge No. 21. From this time until his return to France in 1827, Cerneau created several active and cosmopolitan higher degree bodies. Eventually the Scottish Rite organization linked to Charleston, South Carolina, now aiming for nationwide influence, attacked Cerneau's followers as "clandestine" and forcibly replaced them with what become the Scottish Rite's Northern Jurisdiction.[10]

Perhaps the strangest masonic innovation to issue Saint Domingue's refugees arose in their French motherland. The *Sublime Ordre Militaire des Pacificateurs Americains, Chevaliers Princes des Tropique,* was a pseudo military order of 100 brethren formed to retake their lost island. Formed on January 12, 1813, their first article stated that, "The order has no other goal but that of the restoration of the colony of Santo Domingo; the return of the legitimate authority; and the installation of every owner colonist in his dwelling." Rather than a standard lodge room, their council chambers resembled a warship and they wore military-masonic regalia. Their charter did not explain how 100 masonic "knights" aimed to succeed where 100,000 French soldiers had failed, and in the end the reconquest of Haiti by masonic chevaliers did not come to fruition.[11]

French Freemasons and American Conspiracy Theorists

While masonry flourished among Blacks in Haiti, many of the white masons of Saint Domingue who survived carried their networks to the United States, where the fears wrought by the Haitian and French Revolutions combined to cause many Americans to view these new French masons with a suspicious eye. Back in Boston, Reverend Jedediah Morse obtained a copy of a letter and from the lodge La Sagasse in Portsmouth, Virginia, to the Lodge l'Union of New York dated "the 17th of the fifth month of the year of True Light 5798" along with the membership *tableaux* La Sagasse had included with their letter. Morse's *A Sermon, Exhibiting the Present Dangers, and Consequent Duties of the Citizens of the United States of America. Delivered at Charlestown, April 25, 1799. The day of the National Fast, By Jedediah Morse, D.D. Pastor of the Church in Charlestown,* presents these two documents in both their original and an English translation as evidence of a French Revolutionary plot to invade the United States from Haiti with an army of Blacks which was foiled only by Touissant's victory. Of the intercepted documents, Morse informed his listeners that:

> I have, my brethren, an official, authenticated list of the names, ages, places of nativity, professions, &c. of the officers and members of a Society of *Iluminati*, (or as they are now more generally and properly styled *Illuminees*) consisting of *one hundred* members, instituted in Virginia, by the *Grand Orient* of FRANCE. This society has a deputy, whose name is on the list, who resides at the Mother Society in France, to communicate from thence all needful information and instruction. The date of their institution is 1786, before which period, it appears from the private papers of the European Societies already published, (according to PROFESSOR ROBISON) that several societies had been established in America* The seal and motto of this society corresponds with their detestable principles and designs. The members are chiefly Emigrants from France and S. Domingo, with the addition of a few Americans, and some from almost all the nations of Europe. A letter which enclosed this list, an authentic copy of which I also possess, contains evidence of the existence of a society of the like nature, and probably of more ancient date, at *New –York*, out of which have sprung *fourteen* others, scattered we know not where over the United States. Two societies of the same kind, but of an inferior order, have been instituted by the society first mentioned, one in Virginia, and the other at St. Domingo. How many of equal rank they have established among us I am not informed.[12]

The membership, as Morse points out, included lists of both resident and non-resident masons, many former planters or merchants of Saint Domingue as well as men from all over Europe, the United Kingdom and several states in the US. The letter to New York's L'Union, which Morse warned was one of 14 such cells—an accurate figure of the number of French lodges on American soil—informed them of the establishment of higher degree bodies, one in Virginia and the other in Saint Domingue. Morse cautioned readers that these groups were sending member lists, correspondence, and deputies between the US, Saint Domingue and France. The reverend cited a letter he had received from Yale president Timothy Dwight, who had published a similar screed the previous year, in which Dwight had informed Morse that "Illuminatism exists in this country" and that furthermore, "the impious mockery of the Sacramental Supper, described by Mr. ROBISON has been acted here." Robison's *Proofs of a Conspiracy* brought combined Russian and English anti-masonic fears to New England. Dwight had informed Morse that, "his informant, a respectable Free Masons, declares, that among the Higher Orders of Masons in this country, this piece of illuminism is, at time, I known not how often, practiced."[13]

The reverend did not, however, conflate the local masonic establishment in Boston with this conspiracy, but explained that, "The titles of some of their dignitaries, their seal and motto, they [Boston masons] declare are not Masonic. These societies have presumptuously assumed the forms of Masonry; but are not of the order of true and good Masons. They are imposters." Dwight and Morse's exposes reprinting the *tableaux* of French masons as proof of a revolutionary conspiracy infecting the otherwise innocuous and innocent freemasonry of the United States was not the only piece connecting French freemasonry and its invented connection to the Knights Templar to French Revolutionary conspiracies at home and abroad. Several other rare but highly interesting pieces of anti-French and anti-masonic conspiracy literature were also inspired by the influx of French masonic degrees.[14]

Masons reacted strongly to such works, including those in Boston who wrote to President John Adams assuring him of their patriotism. Salem's Reverend William Bentley responded defensively to their charges, saying, "If there were any error, it must be in commencing the Revolution in the Lodges; and that was never proved upon the Lodges in France, more than upon them in America, and never will be proved. They will never take the praise or the blame." This cryptic defense certainly implies a revolutionary role for the lodges in America. After all, Bentley was speaking to a lodge founded during the Revolution by several veterans. Apparently not convinced of the innocence of his French brethren, Bentley found it necessary to distinguish the American lodges from their French counterparts, ". . .there is a very important distinction in our favor, between the state of France after the revolution and before that event. We express the greatest affection to our own government unequivocally, now that we are its lawful subjects."[15]

Morse's was not the first such anti-French- masonic—illuminati piece to appear in Boston. *The Tomb of James Molai; or, the Secrets of the Conspirators,* anonymous and purportedly "Translated by a gentleman of Boston" and "Addressed to those who wish to know every thing" played off the Templar legend. This 22 page booklet describes how "James Molai", (meaning Jacque de Molay, executed final grand master of the Knights Templar) had created from his prison four "mother lodges" in Naples, Ediburgh, Stockholm and Paris. These took an oath, "To exterminate all Kings and the race of the Bourbons, to destroy the power of the Pope, to preach the liberty of nations, and to found one universal Republic." To achieve these goals, they then created the lodges of freemasons, who unwittingly serve their ends. The author connects these conspirators to various rebellions including, somewhat contradictorily, Oliver Cromwell, who "re-established free-masonry in England" and killed its king as well as the superiors of the Jesuits. Not just any jesuits, but, "those Jesuits who caused Henry IVth and Louis XVth to be assisinated[sic], who stabbed Stadtholder Maurice, of Nassau, who poisoned the Emperor Henry VII in a sacramental wafer. . .and who have been convicted of thirty-nine conspiracies and twenty-one regicides." This impressive legacy of jesuit regicide was not the end. He mentions the actual Jacobite Grand Master Lord Derwent, Waters[sic], Portugal's 1640 split from Spain, a conspiracy against Catherine II of Russia and of course the French Revolution.[16]

The next year, 1798, Yale president Timothy Dwight, D.D., who had informed Morse of the conspiracy as described in Morse's 1799 sermon, preached and published a fourth of July sermon claiming that Voltaire and various *philosophes*, including "the principal compilers of the *Encyclopedie*" concocted an atheistic conspiracy to take over the French Academy, publish attacks on christianity, and "undermine morality and government." There are grains of truth in the masonic connections of those he lists and the prominence of masons in the French Academy and most European learned societies, though he twists these associations in the darkest possible way. Similarly, Dwight, who like Morse shared the common clerical distrust of freemasonry, described the activities of European lodges to support his claims:

> In the mean time the Masonic Societies, which had been originally instituted for convivial and friendly purposes only, were, especially in France and Germany, made the professed scenes of debate concerning religion, morality, and government, by these philosophizes, who had in great numbers become masons. For such debate the legalized existence of masonry, its profound secrecy, its solemn and mystic rites and symbols, its mutual correspondence, and its extension through most civilized countries, furnished the greatest of advantages. All here was free, safe, and calculated to encourage the boldest excursions of restless opinion and impatient ardour, and to make and fix the deepest impressions. Here, and in no other place, under such arbitrary governments, could every innovator in these important subjects utter every sentiment, however daring, and attack every doctrine and institution, however guarded by law or sanctity. In the secure and unrestrained debates of the lodge, every novel, licentious, and alarming opinion was resolutely advanced. . . .[17]

This description, stripped of its negative and accusatory tone, is not so different from Margaret Jacob and other scholars' interpretation of the influence of freemasonry during the French Revolution. Dwight similarly includes a largely accurate description of the relationship between freemasonry and Illuminism:

> While these measures were advancing the great design with a regular and rapid progress, Doctor Adam Weishaupt, professor of the Canon law in the University of Ingolstadt, a city of Bavaria (in Germany) formed, about the year 1777, the order of Illuminati. This order is professedly a higher order of Masons, originated by himself, and grafted on ancient Masonic Institutions. The secrecy, solemnity, mysticism, and correspondence of Masonry, were in this new order preserved and enhanced; while the ardor of innovation, the impatience of civil and moral restraints, and the aims against government, morals, and religion, were elevated, expanded, and rendered more systematical, malignant, and daring.[18]

At the same time, Barruel and Robison's more fanciful accusations were being published, the former centering on the French Revolution and the latter on secrets Robison had "discovered" in Russia, where masonry was undergoing suppression. That Dwight had a reasonably accurate, albeit twisted view of the role of freemasonry's connection to both the French Revolution and the illuminati imply that such knowledge was more common that one might expect. If so, it would help to explain the anti-masonic eruption that occurred in the decades to come.

Though this initial burst of anti-masonry was minor and short lived, a major movement including an anti-masonic political party and massive public organizing forced the fraternity to go underground and seriously reduced its numbers, preventing it from ever achieving the prominence it had once held in American life. The trigger for this was the 1826 disappearance and assumed murder of William Morgan, who had threatened to publish an expose of the craft. No body was ever found and Morgan was rumored to have fled to Canada, however, the presence of multiple masons on the jury which acquitted the accused meant that the not guilty verdict raised more suspicions that it allayed. This widespread animosity was due to both perceived and actual nepotism practiced by masons in important offices across the country. Kathleen Smith Kutolowski's study of New York State, in which there were around 20,000 masons in 450 lodges by 1825, found that masonic connections were a tremendous advantage in gaining entry into local, county and state government during the period. Bullock also highlights the interplay of social tensions more generally, the secretive and hierarchical nature of the lodges, and religious objections in the evangelical climate of the early nineteenth century.[19]

One of the most astute insights in Bullock's comprehensive chapters on the anti-masonic movement of 1826–1840 is that anti-masonry was aimed primarily at white freemasons—those able to wield actual social and political power—and at the higher degrees. These existed in two major bodies in the United States by this time. The Scottish Rite was the direct inheritance of the French *"Ecossaise"* degrees imported by Etienne Morin's disciple Frankel and by the refugees from Saint Domingue and spread in part by Moses Michael Hayes. The York Rite is a collection of three smaller bodies. The first, Chapter, confirms degrees culminating in the Royal Arch. Of these, the Royal Arch and the preceding Most Excellent Master appear to have been early variants of French degrees imported to the British isles. While the French system did not survive there, several of the degrees apparently did. The Chapter also includes the Mark degree, purportedly an extremely old Scottish version of the second degree. This may be so, as it includes a reading of the Old Charges and the rest of the content is a combination of Biblical lore and matters specific to operative stonemasonry. The second body, Council, includes rituals supposedly made up in America; the Consistory, is fully dedicated to chivalric degrees culminating in the Knights Templar. As with the Royal Arch, these degrees made it to Ireland and from thence to the English ancients but are most likely derived from the corresponding French degrees.

Unlike the blue lodge, these bodies were highly hierarchical, extending up to a 33rd degree. Bullock documents cases of anti-masons, echoing Morse, essentially ignoring or overlooking the masonic membership of men solely involved in blue lodge masonry. Though the initial anti-French and anti-illuminist conspiracies petered out, the seeds they planted fed into the later feelings against the higher degree lodges. It is also ironically fitting that the degrees conceived to separate French aristocrats from common masons and to make the craft more amenable to the Catholic social order—and perhaps with Jacobite influence as well—were viewed by the democratic, protestant Americans as so highly dangerous, elitist, and anti-democratic. The writings of Morse and the anonymous author of the *Tomb of Jacque Molai*, while rife with paranoid conspiracy theories, did contain some elements of truth in regards to the elitist nature of the degrees and a knowledge of their claimed—albeit invented—connection to the Knights Templar. At the same time, the ideas of secularism, opposition to the Catholic church, and radical republicanism the two authors interpreted as a conspiracy against all monarchies were transmissions from the blue lodge ideals of 1717's 'grand architects'. Beginning in New York, the ideals and aspirations of London's FRS and well-heeled grand architects, and Clermont and Ramsey's circle of aristocratic French Templar enthusiasts combined to inspire the young nations' first third party movement as part of a massive anti-masonic with hunt.

Notes

1 Villain, Senior to George Washington / Grand Lodge of Pennsylvania, 1785. MSS Grand Lodge of Pennsylvania Archives, Vol. L, Paquet 72, folio 4; reprinted in Julius Sasche, *Old Masonic Lodges of Pennsylvania Vol. II 1779 –1791* (Philadelphia: 1913), 242–4; *Ibid., 242–282.* Where translations are available in Sasche I have generally stuck to his English version, as they appear to have been translated accurately and correctly when compared to the original in every case.

2 Ibid., 252–5.

3 Thaddeus Mason Harris, *Constitutions of the Ancient and Honorable Fraternity of Free and Accepted Masons; Collected and digested from their old records, faithful traditions, and Lodge Books; For the Use of Lodges. Together with the History and General Regulations of the Grand Lodge of Massachusetts. Compiled by the Rev. Thaddeus Mason Harris, A.M. Member of the Massachusetts Historical Society, and Chaplain to the Grand Lodge of Massachusetts Second Edition, revised and corrected, with large additions* (Worcester: Isaiah Thomas, 1798), 197.

4 Sasche, *Old Masonic Lodges of Pennsylvania, 254–7.*

5 *Ibid.,* 244–6; St. John's Lodge of Scotland to Grand Lodge of Pennsylvania, MSS Grand Lodge of Pennsylvania Library, and Sasche, *Old Masonic Lodges; the translation used here is Sasche's.*

6 *Constitutions De La R.L. No. 89, sous Le Titre Distinctif Des FF. Sincerement Reunis de L'Ancienne Maconnerie D'Yorck, A L'O. Des Cayes Du Fond De L'Isle-A-Vache, Isle Saint Domingue.* (Port Republicain: Gauchet, LaGrange et Co., Imprimeurs du Gouvernement, 1801) Grand Lodge of Pennsylvania Library, MS-81-1286- 1300.

7 Tableau Des FF. composant la R.L. No. 47 Sous le titre distinctif de la Reunion Des Coeurs Franco-Americains, a L'Orient du Port-Republicain, depuis le 27me, jour du 10me. mois M. de l'an de la V.L. 5799, jusqu'au 27e. jour du meme mois 5780. (MSS. Philadelphia: Grand Lodge of Pennsylvania, MS-81-1264); Tableau Lodge No. 47, 1798 (MSS. Philadelphia: Grand Lodge of Pennsylvania, MS-81-1248); Tableau of Lodge No. 47, 1797 (MSS. Philadelphia: Grand Lodge of Pennsylvania, MS-81-1247); Tableau of the Members Composing Lodge No. 98, 1809 (MSS. Philadelphia: Grand Lodge of Pennsylvania, MS-81-1317).

8 "Los Dos Antilles", New York: Schomberg Center, microfilm.

9 *Freemason's Calendar 1810*, 45, 48; 1812, 22–3; Eoghan Craig Ballard. "Caliban and the Widow's Sons: Some Aspects of the Intersections and Interactions between Freemasonry and Afro-Caribbean Religious Praxis". Prepared for the 2016 American Historical Association's annual meeting.

10 Alain Bernheim, "Joseph Cerneau, His Masonic Bodies, and His Grand Consistory's Minute Book –Part 1". *Heredom, 18,* 2010, 25 –84.

11 Neil Morse, " 'The American Peacemakers': An INtroduction to a French Colonial Masonic Order" in *Freemasons in the Transatlantic World,* ed. John Wade (London: Lewis Masonic, 2019), 17–44.

12 Jedediah Morse, D.D., *A Sermon, Exhibiting the Present Dangers, and Consequent Duties of the Citizens of the United States of America. Delivered at Charlestown, April 25, 1799. The day of the National Fast, By Jedediah Morse, D.D. Pastor of the Church in Charlestown.* Published at the request of the hearers (Charlestown: Samuel Etheridge, 1799), 15–6.

13 *Ibid.,* 16–17, 32–35, 46.

14 *Ibid.,* 46; Bullock, *Revolutionary Brotherhood,* 174–7.

15 Rev. William Bentley, Mr. William Bentley's Address to Essex Lodge Upon the Festival of St John the Evangelist at the Induction of Officers (Salem: Mary Crouch and Company 1799), 8–9.

16 A Gentleman of Boston, *The Tomb of James Molai; or, the Secrets of the Conspirators.* (Boston: Benjamin Edes, 1797).

17 Timothy Dwight, D.D. *The Duty of Americans, at the Present Crisis, Illustrated in a Discourse, Preached on the Fourth of July, 1798; by the Reverend timothy Dwight, D.D. President of Yale-College; at the Request of the Citizens of New-Haven* (New Haven: Thomas and Samuel Green, 1798), 11.

18 *Ibid.,* 12.

19 Kathleen Smith Kutolowski, "Freemasonry and Community in the Early Republic: The Case for Antimasonic Ancieties," *American Quarterly* 34, no. 5 (Winter, 1982): 543–561.

Epilogue: "To Vie with the Best Established Republic"

The Light of Masonry: Education and Progress in the Early Republic

Former Grand Master, senator, and New York Governor DeWitt Clinton addressed the Grand Lodge of New York on September 29, 1825, only months before the disappearance of masonic apostate William Morgan in his state unleashed the anti-masonic crusade that nearly destroyed the fraternity in the United States. Coming to the topic of the history of freemasonry, Clinton derided the "gratuitous assumptions and fanciful speculations" of masonic histories. He dismissed "the absurd accounts of its origin and history, in most of the books that treat of it" which in his view had "proceeded from enthusiasm operating on credulity and the love of the marvelous." In lieu of this credulous enthusiasm, Clinton pressed his listeners to avoid "giving the rein to erratic imagination" but rather "to sober down our minds to well-established fact." Clinton did not, however, expect this fact-based, sober investigation to lead to the conclusion that the Craft's history had largely been invented between 1717 and 1723. Rational investigation, in the view of the highly educated and erudite former governor, would show that freemasonry was "the most ancient society in the World."[1]

In the early United States, masonic lodges met in nearly every community. As Stephen Bullock points out, "more lodges met in the United States in 1825 than in the entire world fifty years before." Cornerstone laying ceremonies such as the one conducted by Grand Master Paul Revere were common sites as on September 18, 1793 when President Washington in full masonic regalia led the brethren in the dedication of the U.S. capital. Freemasonry was a ubiquitous part of the social order, particularly at the higher levels of society. Masons dominated business and politics in much of the nation. Brethren saw their fraternity as a bulwark of the republican order, but those excluded from their ranks or threatened by the Craft's reach had reason for suspicion and jealousy.[2]

Ancient masonry predominated, and the republican and rational values of the fraternity had come to be held identical with those of the new nation itself. Masonic membership offered instant connection to the brother traveling west to settle along the frontier. It also became increasingly ensconced in places of power, so that nepotism real and imagined as well as masonry's position as a spiritual force outside of the church eventually led to accusations of conspiracy, corruption and ultimately murder and cover up in the 1826 disappearance of William Morgan,would-be betrayer of the fraternity. This in turn generated the nation's first third party movement, the Anti-Masonic Party. Yet the influence of freemasonry on the early Republic on analysis appears far less sinister than hysterical anti-masons believed.[3]

In the intellectual climate of the early United States with its emphasis on learning, the consequence was, as David Hackett puts it, that "postwar Masonic spokespersons revived interest in scientific learning and education." American

Figure E.1. Left—Allyn Cox's 1793 depiction of George Washington laying the cornerstone of the U.S. Capitol in a masonic ceremony. Note the masonic apron and gloves of Washington and his assistant. Right- a second contemporary mural. (Public domain)

masons knew of the importance of science to masonry's roots, as demonstrated by a 1793 address by Clinton given before Holland Lodge on his installation as Master. A naturalist as well as a politician, Clinton told the assembled brethren: "It is well known that our Order was at first composed of scientific and ingenious men who assembled to improve the arts and sciences and cultivate a pure and sublime system of morality." Clinton even emphasized the importance of masonic print culture, explaining that ". . .when the invention of printing had opened the means of instruction to all ranks of people, then the generous cultivators of Masonry communicated with cheerfulness to the world those secrets of the arts and sciences which had been transmitted and improved from the foundation of the institution. . ." DeWitt Clinton's final public service was to oversee the construction of the vastly important Eerie Canal.

Other masonic orations from the day echo Clinton's emphasis on science, as for example the one given at the consecration of the new Grand Lodge of Maine in 1820. This speech included the ideas that "[t]he liberal arts and sciences were formerly taught in Lodge." This may have been a reference to masonic mythology or to the lectures of the previous century, or both. The speaker expounded further on the importance of education to masons, saying "To no order in society is the encouragement of schools and the advancement of knowledge more valuable than to the fraternity."[4]

In the new intellectual climate of the United States, many voluntary societies and educational institutions formed, and masons were admonished by speakers such as DeWitt Clinton or the anonymous orator from Maine to be involved in these endeavors out of masonic duty. Isaiah Thomas, who succeeded Paul Revere as grand master of Massachusetts in 1803–5 and again in 1809, was the primary founder of the American Antiquarian Society and one of the nation's most successful publishers. The extensive masonic collection in the Society's library is largely built around Grand Master Thomas' personal collection, including his copy of William M'Alpine's 1772 Boston printing of Calcott's *Candid Disquisition*. That he possessed such a collection of masonic print and served as grand master for several terms demonstrates that the ideas of the fraternity were important to Thomas.

George Washington's lodge in Alexandria, Virginia founded a museum using its members' collections. Washington was personally involved in founding a free school in the city and the bequest he left for a national university eventually ended up funding what is now Washington and Lee University. In Georgia Abraham Baldwin and other masons were heavily involved in the free school system and the University of Georgia, the majority of the early trustees being masons. Masons were also involved in forming the universities of Virginia and North Carolina, as well as frontier and southern schools such as the one which met in the lodge hall in Danville, Virginia or the Marietta, Ohio school largely funded by the local lodge. Boston's Prince Hall masons were the driving force behind the first Black schools in that city after Prince Hall's activism failed to achieve educational equality; they were also leaders in the fight which eventually led to school integration in the 1840s.

Following on William Allen and Benjamin Franklin's founding of the Philadelphia Academy, now the University of Pennsylvania, Middlebury College received the entire estate of mason Gamaliel Painter; freemason Michael Myers founded Oneida Academy; John Dickinson served as president and benefactor of Dickinson College; Samuel Kirkland was the founder of Hamilton College, as was brother mason Stephan Girard in the case of Girard College. These were not masonic project per se, but project of high ranking masons influenced by the ideals of their craft. DeWitt Clinton was likewise operative in the founding of New York's public schools system. Boston masons Henry Burbeck and Henry Knox, both veteran officers of the Continental Army, were prime movers in the foundation of West Point Military Academy. In Wareham, Massachusetts, freemason John Kendrick began the town's free school. In Lexington, Massachusetts a portion of the masonic Temple provided space for the nation's first normal school. Though masonry was not the only impetus that compelled these men to form educational institutions, its teachings reinforced that impulse, and the fraternity provided a network of like-minded, influential men on which these educators could depend when needed.[5]

Though the craft's many members around the world may have seen their institution very differently, Governor DeWitt Clinton's addresses in the final years before America's anti-masonic purge demonstrate just how effective the history and ideology created a century before in the taverns of London truly was. The craft had been created by "men of science", and was indeed, "the most ancient society in the world." That these were the sentiments of one of the most influential politicians in the Republic, and that masonry and the belief in its ideas were a hallmark of that Republic's leadership speaks to the incredible achievement of the grand architects who sat in the Premier Grand Lodge of All England at the Apple Tree Tavern in 1717.

All of the different evolutionary paths taken by freemasonry stemmed from the reinvention of the fraternity from its roots in late renaissance mysticism by the founders of the first grand lodge in 1717. Some of the twists it took would certainly have bewildered Jean Theophilus Desaguliers and company, who were concerned primarily with creating a society which would support the Whig order in Hanoverian England and promote the ideals of the British enlightenment at home and abroad. While the association with radicals in England and her colonies might have disturbed the Whig leaders and Fellows of the Royal Society of the Premier Grand Lodge, they would have been gratified to see the manner in which their fraternity spread both science and republicanism throughout Europe from its first introduction to the continent in 1725 through to middle of the nineteenth century. Lodges such as the Neuf Souers and its sisters in Prague, London, and Moscow which served as learned societies with trans-Atlantic membership roles comprising a who's who of the Enlightenment certainly must have been equally gratifying.

Likewise, they would have been pleased with the manner in which the craft became a bulwark of the British empire and a major force in the new American republic, where it acted as a support of education, religion, and the political establishment until its reach spurred a massive backlash against the society in 1826. In Haiti and Liberia, two nations of liberated slaves created long after the grand lodge first met, freemasonry became a supporting establishment of the elite. In continental Europe and Latin America, the penetration of freemasonry had both conspiratorial and elitist, establishment—supporting implications. Masonic penetration of these regions and its impact there was very much in keeping with Masonry's early role as a vehicle for British republicanism.

The Masonic networks which migrants and creoles who shared a sense of masonic identity and brotherhood, made official in the certificates of their transnational society with its systems of citizenship, diplomacy, political and legal structures which paralleled and overlapped those of the "profane" world played an important role in the trans-Atlantic lives of thousands of masons from every corner of the Atlantic. This is clear in the many connections these networks had, and the ways in which they influenced each other. Boston's Modern masonic empire of 40 or more lodges from Canada to Surinam connected to the brethren of Saint Domingue as early as 1742, and helped spread the craft into Canada, 10 of the original 13 colonies, and the Caribbean ahead of their metropolitan brethren. French masons in the West Indies maintained vast networks of fraternity and commerce, include Pennsylvania's Provincial Grand Lodge of St. Domingo. French and Dutch merchants brought the French "Scottish" degree system as far north as New York, where the Jewish merchant Moses Michael Hayes, student of Etienne Morin's Dutch disciple Francken, spread it through the aid of a network of Jewish merchant -patriots.

The connections between Boston, Charleston and Philadelphia also appeared in London's West India and American Lodge and to the Grand Lodge of England. Boston's African Lodge entered the trans-Atlantic world of Masonic print as had its white predecessors, as well as forming connections both in England, Philadelphia, and on Haiti after the brethren of Pennsylvania's provincial grand lodge there had evacuated the island, some bringing masonry with them to a new home in the Spanish Caribbean. The world of masonic print continued to connect all of these brethren in the years to come, not only with lists of lodges around the globe which any regular brother might visit, but through continuing to expound on the masonic history, ideology, and moral philosophy created by Desaguliers and the grand architects from the medieval traditions of actual stonemasons preserved in the Old Charges and the traditions of the four lodges which formed the Premier Grand Lodge of All England in 1717.

Though American Freemasonry became largely focused on the growing United States, David Harrison in *The Transformation of Freemasonry* demonstrates that for English masons with business in the United States, its role in trans-Atlantic trade continued unabated long after independence and England's Unlawful Societies Act of 1799. Jessica Harland-Jacobs points out that it was a major facet of networking in the North Atlantic realm that remained to Britain, and was ubiquitous with British presence throughout the globe and served as a support of the empire and its far flung subjects. In Europe and Latin America, the craft followed a number of paths which correspond to the various strains introduced by the grand architects and the French *Ecossaise*. The mysticism of Schaw's Scottish Renaissance found a revival in lodges in central and Eastern Europe. Masonry penetrated the Spanish and Portuguese Americas as radicalized republicans initiated in Europe such as Miranda, San Martin, O'Higgins and Bolívar brought English and American masonic experience to their homelands as did officers fleeing the French onslaught in Europe. Though the historiography is far less developed, there is evidence of masonry in various nations of Latin America playing roles as sources of political intrigue, elite status, and mysticism.

During this period, freemasons led by brothers Bolivar, O'Higgins, San Martin, Hidalgo and many others fought for independence and established new societies from Mexico to Cape Horn, aided at times by brethren like those in London who raised funds for Bolivar, or Boston's Captain Zebina Sears. Argentina had a particularly strong pro-Independence masonic faction due to the high number of Spanish and Italian masons who had migrated there following the turbulence of the Revolutionary period in Europe. Masonic conspiracies cropped up in Argentina and Mexico as well as among the Spanish officers who

created and ran the constitutional government in Spain in 1820. There is tantalizing evidence that Hidalgo and fellow revolutionaries Primo Verdad, Allende,
and Dominquez joined the first lodge in Mexico City. Mexico's first president
Augustin de Iturbide was a freemason, and freemasonry in Mexico has a bewil-
dering history of political intrigue. Nor was Portuguese Brazil exempt from
masonically organized nationalist plots; Jamie E. Rodriguez describes several
such separatist groups in Recife and other parts of Northern Brazil in 1817.[6]

Recently, Roderick Barman has contributed greatly to scholarship on freemasonry's role in Brazilian independence, from its emergence around 1800 and the
role of cosmopolitan Brazilian masons such as Hipolito de Costa, exiled advocate
of independence, to newly initiated Emperor Dom Pedro's coronation as Brazil's
first independent monarch. Barman presents groundbreaking evidence for widespread masonic organization in support of Brazilian independence analogous to
masons' roles in the Sons of Liberty and the Irish Brotherhood. He describes
how in Pernambuco tensions between creoles and Europeans and economic woes
led Creole masons to foment the rebellion that led to the very brief existence of
an independent republic in 1817. Though this led to proscription of the craft for
several years, it reemerged in 1821 in the wake of the new Portuguese liberal government's attempts to regain control of their colony. Lodges in Rio De Janeiro
were essential to convincing Dom Pedro to stay and then in promoting and supporting his declaration of independence. The Prince's most important advisor,
José Bonifácio de Andrada e Silva, became the first grand master of the Grand
Orient of Brazil and performed Dom Pedro's initiation on August 2, 1822, a few
short months later in October, the newly made brother became the first emperor
of an independent Brazil.[7]

In Haiti's new governments freemasonry took on an important role, and
by 1810 the *Freemason's Calendar* included merchant John Goff as Provincial
Grand Master for Haiti, indicating that Haitian masonry continued to play role
in Atlantic commerce. In Europe most masons took part in polite society and
harmless fraternalism while others organized the *Carbonari,* and similar movements. Of the various subversive movements fomenting across the continent from
1800 to 1848, the Italian Carbonari, a militant republican and nationalist faction, show the clearest evidence for masonic involvement. Indeed, the Carbonari's
ritualistic initiations, organization, ideology, and membership evidence clear
derivation from freemasonry. Though more tenuous, there are also indications
of ideological and organizational masonic linkages in other radical movements
leading into the Revolutions of 1848. In Catholic nations, masonry remained, as
John Dickie phrases it, part of a "culture war" between the church and a more

modern, secular worldview. European masonry, justifiably or not, carried enough conspiratorial and political associations in the popular mind that it faced repression under the fascist regimes of Franco, Hitler, and Mussolini and as in Britain and the United States continues to fuel conspiracy theories to the present day.[8]

Even while radicalism peaked among Europeans and some European masons in the period leading up to 1848, the bulk of the brotherhood were not radicals or revolutionaries. On the continent, freemasonry had become very much a bourgeoisie movement. British masonry served as a pillar of the empire and the establishment. It was a major facet of networking in the North Atlantic realm that remained to Britain, and that it was ubiquitous with British presence throughout the globe and served as a support of both the empire and its far flung subjects. American anti-masonry gained impetus from the brethren's status among the political, social and economic elite.

Captain Zebina Sears' great escape from a Spanish prison on the Moorish coast and his odyssey through masonic ports of call in France and England to freedom in masonry's New World birthplace, Boston, was one of many masonic triumphs in the first quarter of the nineteenth century. A few years later a decade long purge began that dramatically reduced the size, prominence and reputation of the American craft. Though freemasonry survived and even recovered much of its former presence, it did so in a dramatically altered fashion as a patriotic, charitable fraternal group of the establishment and middle class. African American masonry continued to organize Black communities and activism well into the twentieth century, while mainstream masonry became ever more indistinguishable from the many fraternal organizations popular among American men in the 19th and 20th centuries.

As the 1800s proceeded, both Massachusetts and freemasonry lost much of their role in the nation's international commerce. Yet they did not fade entirely. The Grand Lodge of Massachusetts chartered a French lodge in Puerto Rico in 1821. In 1853 American businessmen in Chile obtained a Massachusetts charter for Bethesda Lodge, forming four other Chilean lodges in 1858, 1869, 1877, and 1884. Chile remained a district of the Grand Lodge until 2010, when Grand Lodged moved authority for them to the District Grand Lodge of Panama. This district grand lodge dates to the days before Panamanian independence, when Massachusetts formed a lodge in Panama city in 1866. Though this lodge eventually shifted its orientation to its national grand lodge, Massachusetts has had an ongoing Masonic presence in the Canal Zone up to the present day, with six thriving lodges. They had also created a lodge in Peru in 1866, though that lodge disappeared after a severe earthquake in 1868.

The Grand Lodge of Massachusetts also contributed to the growth of freemasonry in Asia in the 19th and 20th centuries. In 1863 American businessmen in Shanghai received dispensation for Ancient Landmark Lodge. An official charter followed two years later. Three more petitions for American lodges in China succeeded in 1903. One, Pei-He Lodge was short lived but Orient Lodge and Sinim Lodge lasted for decades. From 1916 to 1929 seven more Massachusetts lodges sprang up in China. Communist victory in 1949 ended five of the six lodges which remained active, but Sinim Lodge relocated to Tokyo and continues to be an active lodge to this day. These lodges in South America, Panama and Asia are a direct continuation of the international expansion begun by Worshipful Henry Price and Robert Tomlinson carried on by traveling merchants and businessmen of a later epoch.[9]

Though not the preeminent social network that it used to be, freemasonry remains an international brotherhood. Charity continues to be a major feature of the masonic Craft. The Shriners, a masonic body, run 22 free hospitals for children across the United States and Canada. The Lodge of St. Andrew, once operated by Patriot leaders, runs the Angel Fund in conjunction with local Massachusetts lodges, buying necessary items anonymously for disadvantaged schoolchildren in local communities. Lodges and grand lodges offer a plethora of scholarships and discretionary charitable contributions, and lend out needed medical supplies. There is a Knight's Templar Eye Center run by the York Rite, among other major masonic charitable institutions in the United States. The Scottish Rite, descended from Ramsey, Morin, Francken and Hayes, operates 43 Children's Dyslexia Learning Centers across the United States. Masons in other countries run extensive philanthropic undertakings as well. Speaking to the dual interest in charity and science, Utica, New York hosts the Masonic Medical Research Institute while the signature charity of the Grand Lodge of Massachusetts is the Masonic Medical Research Laboratory.

All of these organizations are the legacy of the charter granted by Viscount Montague to Henry Price in 1733. Freemasonry in the eighteenth century Atlantic had a profound effect on the direction of the American colonies and the early Republic, indeed on all of the new Republics founded in the Revolutionary ferment of the long eighteenth century. A modern day freemason will not experience the epic adventures of Zebina Sears. Even so, the Craft's influence, though greatly diminished in the modern day, has yet to completely fade. It's endurance is the culmination of the vision of the Grand Architects of the Premier Grand Lodge of London, and of the "citizens of the Masonic democracy", a democracy, "which in its institutions may vie with the best established republic".

Notes

1 "The Address of De Witt Clinton" [to the Grand Lodge of New York, 29 Sept. 1825] quoted in Steven C. Bullock, "Initiating the Enlightenment?: Recent Scholarship on European Freemasonry," *Eighteenth Century Life* 20, no. 1 (1996): 80–92.
2 Bullock, *Revolutionary Brotherhood,* 137–238.
3 Bullock, *Revolutionary Brotherhood,* 138–9, 220–38, 277–319.
4 DeWitt Clinton Quoted in Berman, *Loyalists and Malcontents,* MSS; David Hackett, *That Religion in which All Men Agree* (Oakland: University of California Press, 2014), 70–1; *Proceedings of the Grand Lodge. of the State of Maine,* I, 25–26 quoted in Bullock, *Revolutionary Brotherhood,* 148.
5 Bullock, *Revolutionary Brotherhood,* 143–9; James Davis Carter and Walter Prescott Webb, *Background, History, and Influence to 1846* (Waco: Committee on Masonic Education and Service for the Grand Lodge of Texas A.F. and A.M., 1955), 119 –154. Accessed online, July 29, 2016 at http://web.mit.edu/dryfoo/Masonry/Essays/jdcarter.html.
6 Jamie E. Rodriguez, *The Independence of Spanish America* (New York: Cambridge University Press, 1998), 165, 192–4, 202; Jeremy Adelman, *Sovereignty and Revolution in the Iberian Atlantic* (Princeton: Oxford University Press, 2006), 314–5; Adrien Royo Caldiz, "Freemasonry in Argentina" *The Argentina Independent,* Oct. 14, 2009; Maria Eugenia Vazquez Semadeni, "La imagen publica de la masoneria en Neuva Espana, 1761–1821" *Relaciones* 125, Invierno 2011, Vol. XXXII, 167–207; Hugh Hamill, *The Hidalgo Revolt: Prelude to Mexican Independence* (Westport: Greewood Press, 1966), 101–2.
7 Roderick Barman, publication pending.
8 John Dickie, *The Craft: How the Freemasons Made the Modern World* (New York: Public Affairs, 2020), 121–150, 222–245, 303–343; John R. Rath, "The Carbonari: Their Origins, Initiation Rites, and Aims," *The American Historical Review* 69, no. 2 (Jan. 1964): 353–370; Eric Hobsbawn. *The Age of Revolutions, 1789–1848* (New York: Vintage Books, 1962), 58–59, 218, 256.
9 Walter Hunt, "The Neo-Colonial Expansionism of Massachusetts Masonry" in *Freemasonry on the Frontier,* ed. John Wade (London: Lewis Masonic, 2020), 215–242.

Works Cited

A Deceased Brother, for the Benefit of his Widow. *The Beginning and First Foundation of the Most Worthy Craft of Masonry, with the Charges thereto Belonging.* London: Printed for Mrs. Dodd, at the Peacock without Temple-Bar, 1739.

A DEFENCE OF FREE-MASONRY, as Practiced in the REGULAR LODGES, both FOREIGN and DOMESTIC, Under the Constitution of the ENGLISH GRAND-MASTER. In which is contained, A REFUTATION of MR. Dermott's absurd and ridiculous Account of FREE-MASONRY, in his Book, entitled AHIMAN REZON; and the several queries therein, reflecting on the regular MASONS, briefly considered, and answered. London: W. Flexney, 1765.

A Discourse upon Masonry. As Spoken by the Author when Master of a Lodge in England, in the year 1772, from the Words of the Prophet Amos, Ch. i. v. 9. In Which Discourse is sent Forth Masonry as it stood in the Days of Noah, and from his Generation down to this Present Time. Second Edition. Dublin: T. Wilkinson, 1772.

A FREE-MASON'S ANSWER TO THE Suspected AUTHOR of a Pamphlet, ENTITLED JACHIN and BOAZ; or, an authentic Key to Free-Masonry; LONDON: Printed for J. COOKE, at Shakespeare's – Head, in Pater-noster-Row, 1762.

A Gentleman of Boston. *The Tomb of James Molai; or, the Secrets of the Conspirators.* Boston: Benjamin Edes, 1797.

A Gentleman of London / R.S.. *JACHIN AND BOAZ OR, AN AUTHENTIC KEY TO THE DOOR OF FREE-MASONRY, Both ANCIENT and MODERN. Calculated not only for the Instruction of every new-made MASON; but also for the Information of all who intend to become BRETHREN.* London: W. Nicolls, 1762; Fifth Edition, London: Nicholls, 1764; Sixth

Edition 1765; updated edition, Nicholls, 1776, 1785; London: 1995; London: E. Newberry, 1797; London editions – 1828; Boston: J. Bumstead, 1787, 1798; West Springfield, Massachusetts: Edward Gray, 1798.

A List of Regular Lodges A.D. 1737. London: John Pine, 1725 (facsimile), 1736, 1737, 1738; London: Benjamin Cole, 1761, 1764, 1766, 1766, 1768, 1770, 1778; reproduced in Hughan, *A List of Regular Lodges*, 1729, 1734, 1735, 1739, 1740, 1744, 1745, 1754.

A Member of Royal Arch. *Hiram: or the Grand Master-key to the Door of both Ancient and Modern Free-masonry: Being an Accurate Description of Every Degree of the Brotherhood, as Authorized and Delivered in all Good Lodges.* London: W. Griffin, 1764; Chelmsford, T. Toft, 1764.

"A Partial List of the Exposes of Freemasonry" found on web.mit.edu. http://web.mit.edu/dryfoo/Masons/Misc/exposures-list.html accessed April 1–3, 2016.

A Pass'd Master. *Shibboleth: or, Every Man a Free-Mason. Containing An History of the Rise, Progress, and Present Stat of That Ancient and Noble Order.* London: J. Cooke, 1765.

A Pocket Companion for Freemasons. Belfast: James Magee, 1751.

"A True and Exact Account of the Celebration of the Festival of Saint John the Baptist by the Ancient and Honourable Society of Free and Accepted Masons, at Boston in New England, on June the 26, 1739. Taken from the Boston Gazette and Rendered into metre, that Children may more easily commit it to and retain it in their Memory," *MSS.* Lexington: Museum of our National Heritage.

"Acknowledgements to Correspondents." *Freemason's Magazine: or General and Complete Library, July 1794.* Vol. III. London: J.W. Bunny, 1794.

Adelman, Jeremy. *Sovereignty and Revolution in the Iberian Atlantic.* Princeton: Oxford University Press, 2006.

African Lodge. "An ORATION Delivered Before the Grand Master, Wardens, and Brethren of the Most Ancient and Venerable Lodge of AFRICAN MASONS." *The Columbian Magazine* 1 (August 1788): 467–9.

African Lodge, Minutes and Records, African Lodge. *Microfilm.* Boston: Grand Lodge of Massachusetts.

Almanach Des Francs- Macons. Amsterdam, 1757, 1758, 1759, 1760, 1762, 1764, 1767, 1768, 1769, 1772.

Almanach oder Taschen-buch für die Brüder Freymaurer der ereingten Deutschen Logen. 1776, 1777, 1778.

Amory, Hugh, and David D. Hall, eds. *A History of the Book in America Volume One the Colonial Book in the Atlantic World.* New York: Cambridge University Press, 2000.

Anderson, James. *The Constitutions of the Freemasons.* London: 1723; London: J. Scott, 1756.

Ballard, Eoghan Craig. "Caliban and the Widow's Sons: Some Aspects of the Intersections and Interactions between Freemasonry and Afro-Caribbean Religious Praxis". Prepared for the 2016 American Historical Association's annual meeting.

Barman, Roderick. *History of Brazil.* MSS, publication pending.

Bate, O.H. *Lodge of Goede Hoop, Cape Town.* Cape Town: Standard Press Limited, 1972.

Beitheile, Francis. *Autobiography. MSS* The Beitheile Manuscripts. Boston: Grand Lodge of Massachusetts.

Beithelie, Francis. *The Beitheile Manuscripts*, Muriel Davis Taylor, ed. Boston: Grand Lodge of Massachusetts, n.d.

Bentley, Reverend William. *Mr. William Bentley's Address to Essex Lodge Upon the Festival of St John the Evangelist at the Induction of Officers*. Salem: Mary Crouch and Company, 1799.

Berman, Ric. *The Foundations of Modern Freemasonry: The Grand Architects, Political Change and the Scientific Enlightenment, 1717–1740*. Portland: Sussex Academic Press, 2012.

Berman, Ric. *Schism: the Battle that Forged Freemasonry*. Sussex: Sussex University Press, 2013.

Berman, Ric. *The Grand Lodge of England & Colonial America: America's Grand Masters*. Oxfordshire: The Old Stables Press, 2020.

Blackwell, Thomas. *Forma Sacra, or, A Sacred Platform of Natural and Revealed Religion;: Exhibiting, a Scriptural and Rational Account of Those Three Important Heads. /By the Pious and Learned Thomas Blackwell; to Which is Now Added, an Introduction. by Simon Williams, A.M. Minister of the Gospel in Windham, N.H.* Boston: William M'Alpine, 1774.

Blancard, Jachques. "Jacques Blancard to the Mother Grand Lodge Ecossais of Bordeaux," June 15, 1751. Sharp Vol. 2, document 30.

Boehme, Adam Friedrich. *Alphabetisches Verzeichnis aller bekannten Freimaurer Logen aus Oeffentlichen Urkunden Dieser Ehrwurdigen Gesellschaft Zusammen Getragen*. Boehme: Leipzig, 1778.

Boston Evening Post, "From the Political State, January, 1736," April 26, 1736; June 28, 1736; July 11, 1737; October 23, 1737; August 28, 1738; September 11, 1738; September 18, 1738; "A True and Exact Account of the Celebration of the Festival of Saint John the Baptist by the Ancient and Honourable Society of Free and Accepted Masons, at Boston in New England, on June the 26, 1739. Taken from the Boston Gazette and Rendered into metre, that Children may more easily commit it to and retain it in their Memory." July 2, 1739; October 8, 1739; June 8, 1741; June 6, 1743; June 20; 1743; January 1, 1750; January 15, 1750; February 5, 1750; May 10, 1756; August 19, 1765; August 26, 1765; September 2, 1765; "At a Lodge of Free and Accepted Masons Held at Hartford," January 24, 1766; April 7, 1766.

Boston Gazette, July 31, 1721, "London" June 15, 1730; April 1, 1734; July 8–15, 1734; June 26, 1739; April 25, 1737; June 28, 1737; Janaury 1, 1770.

Boston Gazette or Weekly Journal, April 25, 1737, February 16–23, 1738, November 3, 1741, *New York Weekly Journal*, November 23, 1741.

Boston Gazette and Country Journal, December 7, 1763; February 6, 1769.

Boston Maritime Society Records, 1752–1762. Masschusetts Historical Society, Boston. Microfilm P-377.

Boston, Massachusetts Town Records, 1770–1777. Boston Public Library Database: www.arch ive.org.

Boston News-Letter, "Philadelphia, Feb. 7, 1737." March 9, 1738; July 14, 1737; October 6, 1768, October 10, 1768, April 2, 1769.

Boston Post Boy, July 14, 1735; January 1, 1750; "Newport, RI." January 15, 1750; June 29, 1752; November 11, 1762; February 3, 1766; April 4, 1766; September 14, 1767; November 23, 1772; December 2, 1772; December 12, 1772; January 14, 1773.

Boston Weekly News Letter, January 5, 1719; September 21, 1721; "London.March." May 25, 1727; "London, January 17." March 30 – April 5, 1733; June 21–28, 1739; June 23, 1743.

Boston Weekly Rehearsal, "[London.] April 26." July 24, 1732; "Dublin" September 27, 1731; "Dublin" October 20, 1731.

Brigham, Clarence S. *Paul Revere's Engravings.* New York: Atheneum, 1969.

Briscoe, Sam, J. Jackson, J. Weeks. *The Secret History of the Free-Masons Being an accidental discovery, of the ceremonie made use of inn the several Lodges, upon the admittance of a Brother as a Free and Accepted MASON. With the Charge, Oath, and private Articles, given to him at the Time of his admittance.* London: 1724.

Brogden, Reverend William. *Freedom and Love. A Sermon Preached before the Ancient and Honourable Society of Free and Accepted Masons, in the Parish Church of St Ann in the city of Annapolis on Wednesday, the 27th of December, 1749.* Annapolis: J. Green, 1750.

Bulkily, John, John Cummins, *John Bulkily, A Voyage to the South Seas, in the Years 1740–1. Containing a Faithful Narrative of the Loss of His Majesty's Ship the the [sic] Wager on a Desolate Island in the Latitude 47 South, Longitude 81:40 West . . . Interspersed with Many Entertaining and Curious Observations, not Taken Notice of by Sir John Narbourough, or Any Other Journalist, with Many Things not Published in the First Edition. By John Bulkely and John Cummins, Late Gunner and Carpenter of the Wager.* London, Printed. Philadelphia: Reprinted by James Chattin, 1757.

Bullock, Stephen. *Revolutionary Brotherhood: Freemasonry and the Transformation of the American Social Order, 1730–1840.* Chapel Hill: UNC Press, 1996.

Bullock, Steven C. "Initiating the Enlightenment?: Recent Scholarship on European Freemasonry." *Eighteenth Century Life* 20, no. 1 (1996): 80–92.

Calcott, Wellins, P.M. *A Candid Disquisition of the Principles and Practices of the Most Ancient and Honorable Society of Free and Accepted Masons; Together with Some Strictures on the Origin, Nature, and Lesson of that Institution.* London: Brother James Dixwell, 1769; Marlborough: Brother William MacAlpine, 1772.

Caldiz, Adrien Royo. "Freemasonry in Argentina" *The Argentina Independent,* Oct. 14, 2009.

Care, Henry. *English Liberties, or the Free-born Subjects Inheritance.: Containing Magna Charta, Charta de Foresta, the Statute de Tallagio non Concedendo, the Habeas Corpus Act, and Several Other Statutes; with Comments on Each of Them. . . with Many Law-cases Throughout the Whole. Compiled first by Henry Care, and continued, with large additions, by William Nelson, of the Middle-Temple, Esq;- The Sixth edition, Corrected and Improved.* Providence: John Carter, 1774.

Carter, James Davis, and Walter Prescott Webb. *Background, History, and Influence to 1846.* (Waco: Committee on Masonic Education and Service for the Grand Lodge of Texas A.F. and A.M., 1955) 119–154. Accessed online 7/29/2016 at http://web.mit.edu/dryfoo/Masonry/Essays/jdcarter.html

Case, James R. *Connecticut Masons in the American Revolution.* Hartford: Grand Lodge of Connecticut A.F. & A.M, 1976.

Case, James Royal, and Merle P. Tapley. *A Bicentennial History of the Grand Lodge of Connecticut.* Hartford: Grand Lodge of Connecticut, 1989.

Churchill, Charles. *Poems by Charles Churchill.* New York: [publisher unlisted, Rivington import edition], 1768.

Clark, Anna. "The Chevalier d'Eon and Wilkes: Masculinity and Politics in the Eighteenth Century." *Eighteenth-Century Studies* 32, no. 1 (1998): 19–48.

Colville, Alexander, 7th Baron Colvill. http://www.biographi.ca/en/bio/colvill_alexander_3E.html, accessed April, 18, 2016.

Connecticut Courant. "At a Lodge of FREE-MASONS, held at the Fountain Tavern, in New-Haven, Tuesday, 19th March, 1765." April 1, 1765; July 27, 1767; September 28, 1767; November 9, 1767; July 28, 1772, August 3, 1772.

Connecticut Gazette, January 5, 1770.

Connecticut Journal, June 1, 1770; December 3, 1772; June 18, 1773.

Constitutions De La R.L. No. 89, sous Le Titre Distinctif Des FF. Sincerement Reunis de L'Ancienne Maconnerie D'Yorck, A L'O. Des Cayes Du Fond De L'Isle-A-Vache, Isle Saint Domingue. Port Republicain: Gauchet, LaGrange et Co., Imprimeurs du Gouvernement, 1801. Grand Lodge of Pennsylvania Library, MS-81-1286- 1300.

Coustos, John. *Unparalleled sufferings of John Coustos, Who Nine Times Underwent the Most Cruel Tortures Ever Invented by Man, and Sentenced to the Galley Four Years, by Command of the Inquisitors at Lisbon, in Order to Extort from him the Secrets of Free-Masonry; from whence he was Released by the Gracious Interposition of his Late Majesty, King George II.* London: Strahan, 1746; Birmingham: Swinney, 1790; New York: Jacob Mott, 1797. *-Ausserordentliches Verfahren der Potugiesischen Inquisition Wider die Freymaurer / von einem aus Der Inquisitions Freygkommenen Mitbruder [i.e. Johann coustos] Bescrieben. Aus dem Franzosischen Ubersetzt.* Hamburg: 1756.

Crosby, Nichols. *Sketches of Boston, Past and Present, and of some Places in its Vicinity.* Boston: Phillips, Sampson, and Company, 1851.

Currier, John. *History of Newburyport, Mass. 1764–1909. 2 Vols.* Newburyport: John Currier, 1906–1909.

Dermot, Lawrence. *Ahiman Rezon, or A Help to a Brother.* London: Brother James Bedford, 1756.

Dermot, Lawrence. *Ahiman Rezon, or a Help to All that are (or would be) Free and Accepted Masons, Containing the Quintessence of All that Has Been Publish'd on the Subject of Free Masonry: With Many Additions, which Renders this Work More Usefull than Any Other Book of Constitutions.* London: Robert Black, 1764.

Dickie, John. *The Craft: How the Freemasons Made the Modern World.* New York: Public Affairs, 2020.

Drake, Francis S. *Tea Leaves: Being a Collection of Letters and Documents Relating to the Shipment of Tea to the American Colonies in the year 1773 by the East India Company.* Boston: A.O. Crane, 1884.

Dwight, Timothy D.D. *The Duty of Americans, at the Present Crisis, Illustrated in a Discourse, Preached on the Fourth of July, 1798; by the Reverend timothy Dwight, D.D. President of Yale-College; at the Request of the Citizens of New-Haven.* New Haven: Thomas and Samuel Green, 1798.

Egnal, Marc, and Joseph A. Ernst. "An Economic Interpretation of the American Revolution." *The William and Mary Quarterly*, 3rd series, 29, no. 1 (January 1972): 3–32.

Elliot, Paul, and Stephen Daniels. "'The School of True, Useful and Universal Science'? Freemasonry, Natural Philosophy and Scientific Culture in Eighteenth-Century England." *The British Journal for the History of Science* 39, no. 2 (Jun., 2006): 207–229.

Ernest, John. *A Nation within a Nation: Organizing African American Communities Before the Civil War.* Lanham: Rowman & Littlefield, 2011.

Essex Gazette, January 16–23, 1769.

Fay, Bernard. "Learned Societies in Europe and America in the Eighteenth Century." *The American Historical Review* 37, no. 2 (Jan., 1932): 255–66.

Ferling, John. "The New England Soldier: A Study in Changing Perceptions." *American Quarterly* 33, no. 1 (Spring 1981): 26–45.

First Lodge. Minutes and By-Laws, 1738–1754. Boston: Grand Lodge of Massachusetts. Microfilm.

Fischer, David Hackett. *Paul Revere's Ride.* New York: Oxford University Press, 1994.

Fleet, Thomas Jr. *Fleet's Pocket Almanac / Fleet's Massachusetts Register.* Boston: Thomas Fleet. Series from 1779–1793.

Forbes, Esther. *Paul Revere and the World He Lived In.* Boston: Houghton Mifflin, 1942.

Foss, Gerald. *Three Centuries of Freemasonry in New Hampshire.* Somersworth, NH: The New Hampshire Publishing Company, 1972.

Free-Mason's Vocal Assistant, and Register of the Lodges of Masons in South Carolina and Georgia. Charleston: Brother J.J. Negrin, 1807.

Freemasons Victoria Library and Museum, https://www.freemasonsvic.net.au/history-and-heritage/

Garrigus, John D. *Before Haiti: Race and Citizenship in French Saint-Domingue.* New York: Palgrave-MacMillian, 2006.

Georgia Gazette, April 7, 1763.

Gloucester, Massachusetts Archives. Vital Records, Selectman's Records, Town Records, Revolutionary War Muster Rolls. Gloucester Archives committee, Gloucester MA.

Gomez, Michael A. *Exchanging Our Country Marks: The Transformation of African Identities in the Colonial and Antebellum South.* Chapel Hill: University of North Carolina Press, 1998.

Gore, Christopher, Esq. *An Oration: Delivered at the Chapel, in Boston: Before the Ancient and Honourable Society of Free and Accepted Masons, June 24, 1783.* Boston: Brother William Green, 1783.

Gould, Robert Freke. *History of Freemasonry around the World, Vol. IV.* New York: Charles Scribner's Sons, 1936.

Gousse, JEan K. "La Franc Maconnerie aux Antilles et en Guyane Francaise de 1789 a 1848" unpublished MSS. Philadelphia: Grand Lodge of Pennsylvania Library.

Graham, John Hamilton. *Outline of the History of Freemasonry in the Province of Quebec.* Montreal: J. Lovell & Sons, 1892.

Grand Lodge Of Massachusetts A.F. & A. M. *The constitutions of the Ancient and Honorable Fraternity of Free and Accepted Masons: Containing their history, charges, addresses, &c. Collected and digested their old records, faithful traditions, and lodge books. For the use of Masons. To which are added The History of Masonry in the commonwealth of Massachusetts, and the Constitution, laws, and regulations of their Grand Lodge. Together with a large collection of songs, epilogues, &c.* Worcester: Isaiah Thomas, 1792.

Grand Lodge of Massachusetts A.F. & A.M. *Proceedings in Masonry: St John's Grand Lodge 1733–1792; Massachusetts Grand Lodge 1769–1792; with an Appendix Containing Copies of Many Ancient Documents, and a Table of Lodges.* Boston: published by the Grand Lodge of Massachusetts, 1895.

Grand Lodge of North Carolina and Tennessee. *Proceedings of the Grand Lodge of North Carolina and Tennessee, for A.L. 5807.* Raleigh: Wm. Boyan, 1808.

Grand Orient de France, *Etat du G. O. de France, Tome Troisieme*, Premiere Partie, 1779.

"Green Dragon Tavern," *The Hotel: Its Interest and Management* I, no. 8 (November, 1893): 1–4.

Green, Joseph. *Entertainment for a Winter's Evening: Being a Full and True Account of a very Strange and Wonderful Sight seen in Boston on the Twenty-Seventh of December 1749 at Noon-Day, the Truth of which can be attested by a Great Number of People, who actually saw the same with their Own Eyes, by Me, the Honble B.B. Esq; by Joseph Green of Boston.* Boston: G. Rogers, 1750.

Green, Joseph. *The Grand Arcanum Detected: or, A Wonderful Phaenomenon Explained, Which has baffled the scrutiny of many Ages. By ME, Phil. Arcanos, Gent. Student in Astrology.* Boston: G. Rogers, 1755.

Hackett, David G. "The Prince Hall Masons and the African American Church: The Labors of Grand Master and Bishop James Walker Hood, 1831–1918." *Church History* 69, no. 4 (Dec. 2000): 770–802.

Hackett, David G. *That Religion in which All Men Agree.* Oakland: University of California Press, 2014.

Hall, Prince. *A Charge Delivered to the African Lodge on the 25th of June, 1792.* Boston: T. Fleet, 1792.

Hall, Prince. *A Charge Delivered to the African Lodge, June 24, 1797, at Menotomy.* Boston: Benjamin Edes, 1797.

Hall, Prince. "The Lives of Some of the Fathers and Learned and Famous divines in the Christian Church from our Lord and Saviour Jesus Christ." n.d. Microfilm, Boston: Grand Lodge of Massachusetts.

Hall, Prince to William White, n.d. / 1793, Microfilm. Boston: Grand Lodge of Massachusetts.

Hall, Prince / African Lodge to William Moody, May 18, 1787. Microfilm, Boston: Grand Lodge of Massachusetts.

Hamilton, Dr. Alexander. *The Itinerarium of Doctor Alexander Hamilton.* (original: Annapolis, 1744) ebook: https://books.google.com/books?id=c1OIz-UCgmsC&pg=PT211&lpg=PT211&dq=dr+alexander+hamilton+1744+penguin+books&source=bl&ots=AEsuPbHsG-&sig=iVRcH-8lC8BXraZHoRqEJHCUNf0&hl=en&sa=X&ved=0ahUKEwiQ6Nysg vHNAhUMPD4KHWRKAXwQ6AEIHDAA#v=onepage&q=dr%20alexander%20hamilton%201744%20penguin%20books&f=false

Hans, Nicholas. "UNESCO of the Eighteenth Century: *La Loge Des Neuf Soeurs* and its Venerable Master Benjamin Franklin." In *Freemasonry on Both Sides of the Atlantic: Essays Concerning the Craft in the British Isles, Europe, the United States and Mexico*, ed. William Weisberger, Wallace McLeod, and Brent S. Morris, 279–298. Boulder: East European Monographs, 2002.

Harland-Jacobs, Jessica. *Builders of Empire: Freemasons and British Imperialism, 1717–1927.* Chapel Hill: UNC Press, 2001.

Harland-Jacobs, Jessica. "Hands Across the Sea: The Masonic Network, British Imperialism, and the North Atlantic World." *Geographical Review* 89, no. 2 (Apr. 1999).

Harris, Reginald, P.G.M. Nova Scotia, A.J.B. Milborne, Grand Historian, G.L. of Quebec, Col James R. Case, Grand Historian, G.L. of Connecticut. "Freemasonry at the Two Sieges of Louisbourg 1745 and 1758". The Papers of the Canadian Masonic Research Association, 1949–1976, Vol. 2, paper 46. May 13, 1958. Accessed online: http://pictoumasons.org/libr ary/CDN%20Masonic%20Research%20-%20Freemasonry%20at%20Louisbourg%20 [pdf].pdf.

Harris, Thaddeus Mason. *Constitutions of the Ancient and Honorable Fraternity of Free and Accepted Masons; Collected and digested from their old records, faithful traditions, and Lodge Books; For the Use of Lodges. Together with the History and General Regulations of the Grand Lodge of Massachusetts. Compiled by the Rev. Thaddeus Mason Harris, A.M. Member of the Massachusetts Historical Society, and Chaplain to the Grand Lodge of Massachusetts Second Edition, revised and corrected, with large additions.* Worcester: Isaiah Thomas, 1798.

Harrison, David. *The Transformation of Freemasonry.* Suffolk: Arima Publishing, 2010.

Harrison, David. "Freemasonry and the French Revolution," https://dr-david-harrison.com/pap ers-articles-and-essays/freemasonry-and-the-french-revolution/, September 1, 2015.

Harrison, David. "The York Grand Lodge", https://dr-david-harrison.com/papers-articles-and-ess ays/the-york-grand-lodge/ Sept. 5, 2015.

Harrison, Samuel Bayard Jr. *History of the Supreme Council, 33rd Degree Ancient and Accepted Scottish Rite of Freemasonry Northern Masonic Jurisdiction of the United States and ITs Antecedants, Volume 1.* Boston: 1938.

Heaton, Ronald E. *Masonic Memberships of the Founding Fathers.* Silver Spring: The Masonic Service Association, 1974.

Henderson, Kent, and Tony Pope. *Freemasonry Universal: A New Guide to the Masonic World, Volume I- The Americas.* Victoria, Australia: Global Masonic Publications, 1998.

Hinks, Peter P., and Stephen Kantrowitz, eds. *All Men Free and Brethren: Essays on the History of African American Freemasonry.* Ithaca: Cornell University Press, 2013.

Hiram Lodge No 1, Ancient Free and Accepted masons 1750–1916. New Haven: John J Corbett Press, 1916. http://www.historyofparliamentonline.org/volume/1660-1690/member/clay ton-sir-robert-1629-1707

Hoberman, Michael. *New Israel / New England: Jews and Puritans in Early America.* Boston: University of Massachusetts Press, 2011.

Hughan, William, ed. *A List of Regular Lodges A.D. 1734.* London: Grand Lodge of England, 1907.

Hutchinson, William. *The Spirit of Masonry in Moral and Elucidatory Lectures, the Second Edition,* Carlisle: F. Jollie, 1795.

J***G******. *Mahabone: Or, the Grand Lodge Door Open'd. Wherein is Discovered the Whole Secrets of Free-Masonry, Both Ancient and Modern.* London: Johnson and Davenport, 1765; Liverpool, J. Gore, 1765.

Jacob, Margaret C. *The Radical Enlightenment: Pantheists, Freemasons and Republicans.* London: George Allen & Unwin, 1981.

Jacob, Margaret C. *Living the Enlightenment: Freemasonry and Politics in Eighteenth Century Europe.* New York: Oxford University Press, 1991.

Jacob, Margaret C. *Strangers Nowhere in the World: The Rise of Cosmopolitanism in Early Modern Europe.* Philadelphia: University of Pennsylvania Press, 2006.

Jacob, Margaret C. *Origins of Freemasonry: Facts and Fictions.* Philadelphia: University of Pennsylvania Press, 2007.

Jacob, Margaret C., and Wijnand Mijnhart. *The Book That Changed Europe: Picart and Bernard's Religious Ceremonies of the World.* Cambridge, MA: Belknap Press of HArvard University, 2010.

JFM, II (1785) Part 3, 114–7 (408).

Johnson, Melvin M. *The Beginnings of Freemasonry in America: Containing a Reference to All that is Known of Freemasonry in the Western Hemisphere Prior to 1750, and Short Sketches of the Lives of some of the Provincial Grand Masters.* Kingsport, TN.: Southern Publishers, Masonic Publications Division, 1924.

Jones, Stephen. *Masonic Miscellanies, in poetry and prose. Containing 1. The Muse of Masonry, comprising one hundred and seventy masonic songs, 11. The Masonic Essayist. III. The Freemason's Vade-Mecum.* London: Vernor and Hood, 1797.

Kutolowski, Kathleen Smith. "Freemasonry and Community in the Early Republic: The Case for Antimasonic Ancieties." *American Quarterly* 34, no. 5 (Winter 1982): 543–561.

Lang, Ossian. *History of Freemasonry in New York.* New York: The Hamilton Printing C. 1922.

Laws of the Marine Society at Boston in New-England, Incorporated by the Government, as by CHARTER, February 2, 1754. Massachusetts Historical Society, Boston.

Laws of the Marine Society, At Salem, in New England March 25, 1766. Massachusetts Historical Society, Boston.

Laws of the Marine Society at Newburyport, New England, commencing the 13th day of November, 1772. Massachusetts Historical Society, Boston.

Lepore, Jill. *New York Burning: Liberty, Slavery and Conspiracy in Eighteenth Century Manhattan.* New York: Alfred A. Knopf, 2005.

Lodge No. 47 Minutes, February 1789– June 1790. MSS. Philadelphia: Grand Lodge of Pennsylvania Library, MS-81-1174 – MS-81-1185.

Lodge of St. Andrew. Minutes Of Meetings, 1756–1778. Lodge of St Andrew. Minutes of Master's Lodge Meetings 1762 – 1802. Lodge of St Andrew. Charters and By-laws, 1762–1802. Master's Lodge, Minutes of Meetings, 1755–1768. Boston: Grand Lodge of Massachusetts, microfilm.

Lodge of St. Andrew. *Centennial Memorial.* Boston: Press of Arthur W. Locke and Co. 1870.

Lodge of St. Andrew. *Commemoration of the One Hundred and Fiftieth Anniversary of the Lodge of Saint Andrew.* Boston: St. Andrew's Lodge, 1906.

Lodge of St. Andrew. *Lodge of St. Andrew Bi-Centennial Memorial.* Boston: St. Andrew's Lodge, 1956.

London Daily Post, March 20, 1741.

"Los Dos Antilles", New York: Schomberg Center, microfilm.

Lyon, E. *An Antique History of the Orders of Freemasonry from the Assyrian Monarchy Down to the Present Times, with an Appendix by Way of Admonition.* London: W. Owen, 1752.

Mackey, Albert Gallatin. *The History of Freemasonry in South Carolina, from its Origin in the Year 1736 to the Present Time, Written at the Request of the Grand Lodge of Ancient Freemasons of South Carolina by Albert G. Mackey, M.D., Grand Secretary of the Grand Lodge.* Columbia: South Carolinian Steam Power Press, 1861.

Mantore, Peter. *To African Lodge,* March 2, 1797. Microfilm, Boston: Grand Lodge of Massachusetts.

Marrant, John. "A Sermon Preached on the 24th Day of June 1789, Being the Festival of St. John the Baptist, at the Request of the Right Worshipful the Grand Master Prince Hall and the Rest of the Brethren of the African Lodge of the Honorable Society of Free and Accepted Masons in Boston, by the Reverend Brother Marrant, Chaplain." Boston: Bible and Heart, 1789.

Maryland Gazette. "London." February 9, 1732, "London. December 16." April 6, 1733.

MasonicGenealogy.com

Massachusetts Gazette and the Boston Post Boy and Advertiser, September 7, 1772.

Massachusetts Lodge, *Celebration of the 125th Anniversary of the Massachusetts Lodge 1770–1895.* Boston: Massachusetts Lodge, 1896.

MASONRY farther DISSECTED; OR, MORE SECRETS Of that Mysterious SOCIETY REVEAL'D. Faithfully Englished from the French Original just published at Paris, by the Permission and Privilege of M. DE HARRAUT, Lieutenant-General of Police. With Explanatory NOTES (both serious and comical) by the TRANSLATOR. London: J. Wilkes, 1738.

Masonry the Turn-Pike Road to Happiness in this Life, and Eternal Happiness Hereafter. Dublin: James Hoey, 1768.

MASONRY THE WAY TO HELL, A SERMON: Wherein is clearly proved, Both from REASON and SCRIPTURE, That all who profess these MYSTERIES are in a state of DAMNATION. London: Robinson and Roberts, 1768.

Masonry Vindicated: A Sermon. Wherein is Clearly and Demonstratively Proved, that a Sermon, Lately Published, "Intitled Masonry the Way to Hell," is an intire piece of the Utmost Weakness, and Absurdity; at the Same Time Plainly Shewing to all Mankind, that MASONRY, if Properly applied, is of the Greatest Utility, not only to Individuals, but to Society and the Public in General: and is Impartially Recommended to the Perusal, as well as to clear up, and obviate all the Doubts Entertain'd, of those who are not Masons; and to the Fair Sex in Particular. London: J. Hinton, 1768.

Massey, D.A. *History of Freemasonry in Danvers, Mass. From September, 1778 to July, 1896.* Peabody: Press of C.H. Shepard, 1896.

Money, John. "The Masonic Moment; Or, Ritual, Replica, and Credit: John Wilkes, the Macaroni Parson, and the Making of the Middle Class Mind." *The Journal of British Studies 32,* no. 4, *Making the English Middle Class, ca. 1700–1850,* Oct., 1993.

Moore, William. *The Elements of Freemasonry Delineated.* Kingoston, Jamaica: William Moore, 1782.

Morse, Jedediah D.D. *A Sermon, Exhibiting the Present Dangers, and Consequent Duties of the Citizens of the United States of America. Delivered at Charlestown, April 25, 1799. The day of the National Fast, By Jedediah Morse, D.D. Pastor of the Church in Charlestown.* Published at the request of the hearers. Charlestown: Samuel Etheridge, 1799.

Morton, Perez. *An Oration; Delivered at the King's Chapel in Boston, April 8, 1776, on the re-interment of the Remains of the Late Most Worshipful Grand-Master Joseph Warren, Esquire; President of the late Congress of this Colony, and Major – General of the Massachusetts Forces; Who was Slain in the Battle of Bunker's-Hill, June 17, 1775.* Boston: J. Gill, 1776.

Musée Grande Loge Nationale de France, personal communication, December 31, 2009.

Museum of African American History, www.afroammuseum.org/site14.htm, accessed July 28, 2015.

New England Weekly Journal, "London, May 14." July 27, 1730.

New Hampshire Gazette, April 12, 1765; January 5, 1770.

New Hampshire Gazette and Historical Chronicle, "Books to be Sold at Public Auction", April 12, 1765.

New York Gazette, June 6, 1751; June 17, 1751; July 8, 1751; July 15, 1751; October 26, 1761; November 2, 1761; November 30, 1761; December 28, 1761; "Nassau, New Providence, Dec. 30." March 3, 1762; March 7 1763, March 21, 1763, March 28, 1763, April 18, 1763, August 8, 1763; November 8, 1764; November 22, 1764; November 29, 1764; May 13, 1765; May 20, 1765; June 3, 1765; June 15–26, 1767; June 29– July 6, 1767; July 6– July 13, 1767; September 7– September 14, 1767; March 7, 1768; March 21, 1768; April 4, 1768; April 18; 1768, April 25, 1768; May 2, 1768; June 26, 1775.

New York Journal, December 10, 1767; December 17, 1767; "Advertisements." September 1, 22, November 10, 1768; August 8, 1771.

New York Magazine, December 28, 1761; March 21, 1763; March 28, 1763.

New York Mercury, "Bristol. October 27" February 4, 1754; November 20, 1752; November 27, 1752; April 19, 1756; April 26, 1756; May 3, 1756; May 10, 1756; August 3, 1761; November 8, 1764; November 14, 1761; June 11, 1764; "advertisements", "Moses Judah," September 28; May 4, 1767, June 3, 1775.

New York Weekly Journal, "Wednesday January 17. 1738/9." January 22, 1738; July 25, 1743.

Newburyport Herald, September 1, 1818.

Newell, Aimee. *Curiosities of the Craft: Treasures from the Grand Lodge of Massachusetts Collection.* Lexington: Museum of Our National Heritage, 2013.

Newport Mercury, September 12, 1763; December 31, 1764; "At a Lodge of Free and Accepted Masons Held at Hartford," March 3–10, 1766; September 21, 1767.

Norwich Packet and the Connecticut, Massachusetts, New Hampshire and Rhode Island Advertiser, April 21–28, 1774.

Onnerfors, Andreas. "Swedish Freemasonry in the Caribbean: How St. Barthelemy turned into an Island of the IXth Province." *REHMLAC Revista Estudios Históricos de la Masonería, Latinamericano y Caribeña* 1, no. 1: 18–41.

"Original Constitution and Statues of the Order of Chevaliers Hospitaliers et Militaires de Saint Jean de Jerusalem dits Frey-Macons," *Sharp Documents, Volume 1, Document 1.* Lexington: Van– Gordon Williams Library, Museum of Our National Heritage.

O'Shaughnessy Andrew Jackson., *An Empire Divided: The American Revolution and the British Caribbean.* Philadelphia: University of Pennsylvania Press, 2000.

Paine, Thomas. *Thomas Paine: On the Origin of Free-Masonry.* New York: Elliot and Crissy, 1810.

Palfrey Papers, Letters of William Palfrey, Letters to William Palfrey, 1762–1780. Cambridge: Harvard University, Houghton Library.

Palfrey, William. "An Alphabetical List of the Sons of Liberty who Dined at Liberty Tree, Dorchester, Aug. 14, 1769." *Proceedings of the Massachusetts Historical Society 1869–70.* Boston: Mass. Historical Society, 1871.

Palfrey, William, and Moses Brown. *The Course of True Love in Colonial times Being the Confessions of William Palfrey of Boston and the Friendly Advice of Moses Brown of Providence Concerning Polly Olney.* Boston: The Merrymount Press, 1905.

Pennsylvania American Weekly Journal, June 30–July 7, 1743.

Pennsylvania Chronicle, June 26 1769; July 3, 1769; July 1 – 8, 1771; July 8–15, 1771; July 15–22 1771; July 22–29, 1771.

Pennsylvania Gazette, July 9, 1730; "London, May 14." August 13, 1730; December 8, 1730; May 13, 1731; "London." July 22, 1731; "Dublin." May 11, 1732; August 22, 1745; September 5, 1745; October 3, 1754; October 17, 1754; November 21, 1754.

Picart, Bernard. Louis Fabricius Dubourg, Claude du Bosc, "Les Free Massons" (engraving), circa 1735. Boston: Grand Lodge of Masons.

Porset, Charles, and Cecile Revauger. *Le Monde Maçonnique des Lumières (Europe-Amériques & Colonies) Dictionnaire prosopographique, Volume III.* Paris: Honoré Champion Editeur, 2013.

Portsmouth, New Hampshire. *Town Records, Vol. II, No. 1 & 2.* Portsmouth Public Library, Special Collections, Portsmouth, New Hampshire.

Portsmouth Sons of Liberty, *Correspondence. Belknap Collection, Microfilm Box 61.* Boston: Massachusetts Historical Society.

Preston, William. *Illustrations of Masonry First Edition,* 1772. Accessed online at http://picto umasons.org/library/Preston,%20William%20-%20Illustrations%20of%20Masonry%20 %5Bpdf%5D.pdf.

Preston, William. *Illustrations of Masonry, Second Edition.* London: J. Wilkie, 1781. 221–4, 226–33, 288–97. Digital version: https://play.google.com/books/reader?id=cGljAAAAc AAJ&printsec=frontcover&output=reader&hl=en&pg=GBS.PR5-IA3. Wilkie printed runs labelled "the Second Edition" in 1775 and 1781.

Pritchard, Samuel. *TUBAL-KAIN: Being the Second Part of SOLOMON IN ALL HIS GLORY, OR MASTER MASON: Containing an Universal and Genuine DESCRIPTION OF All its BRANCHES, from the ORIGINAL to the PRESENT TIME. . . WITH A new and exact LIST of REGULAR LODGES accourding to their Seniority and Constitution. . .* Dublin: Thomas Wilkinson, n.d.; reprinted from London: Nicholls, n.d.

Pritchard, Samuel. *Masonry Disected (sic); being a universal and genuine description of all its branches, from the original to this present time. As it is delivered in the Constituted regular lodges both in city and country according to the several degrees of admission. Giving an impartial account of their regular proceedings in initiating their new members in the whole three degrees of masonry. VIZ. I. enter'd'prentic, II. Fellow craft III. Master To which is added, the author's vindicaton of himself.* London: Printed by Thomas Nichols, 1730.

——— *The Fifth Edition.* Edinburgh: William Gray, 1752.

——— Kilmarnock: John Stevenson, 1780.

——— Newport R.I, 1749. The publisher of the 1749 Newport edition is not listed, a pencil annotation on the copy at the Grand Lodge of Massachusetts library attributes it to Franklin.

——— *Het Vrye Metselaarschap ontleed; in alle deszelfs Deelen, van zynen Oorspronk af tot dezen tyd toe.* Translated by Ingelstelde Kamer, Printed by Erven van J, Ratelband en Compagnie, op de hoek va de Kalverstraat, aan den Dam.

Providence Sons of Liberty, *Correspondence. Peck Manuscripts* III 63–70. Providence: Rhode Island Historical Society.

Racine, Karen. *Francisco de Miranda, a Transatlantic Life in the Age of Revolution.* Washington: Rowman & Littlefield, 2003.

Rath, Jon R. "The Carbonari: Their Origins, Initiation Rites, and Aims." *The American Historical Review* 69, no. 2 (Jan. 1964): 353–370.

Revere, Paul. *Receipt for Masonic Jewels issued to Tyrian Lodge,* Feb. 13, 1770. Tyrian Lodge, Gloucester, MA.

Revere, Paul. Summons to Tyrian Lodge, September 2, 1811 (originally engraved 1773). In collection of Philips Library, Salem, Massachusetts.

Revere, Paul. Summons to St. Peter's Lodge, February 2, 1797 (originally engraved 1773). In collection of Philips Library, Salem, Massachusetts..

Revere, Paul. Statement on his Ride and Capture. 1775. From americanrevolution.org/revere.html.

Revere, Paul. "A letter from Col. Paul Revere to the Corresponding Secretary". In *Collections of the Maschusetts Historical Society for the year MDCCXCVIII,* 106–111. Boston: Samuel Hall, No 53, 1798.

Rivington's New York Gazette, or the Connecticut, New Jersey, Hudson's River and Quebec Weekly Advertiser, December 2, 1773.

Roberts, Rev. Oliver A. *St. Peter's Lodge: The History of a Masonic Body Organized 1772.* Manuscript, Grand Lodge of Massachusetts Library, Boston, MA.

Robinson, F.J.G., and Wallis, P.J. *Book Subscription Lists: A Revised Guide.* Newcastle upon Tyne: Harold Hill & Son LTD, 1975.

Rodriguez, Jamie E. *The Independence of Spanish America.* New York: Cambridge University Press, 1998.

Rowe, John. *Letters and Diary of John Rowe.* United States: New York Times and Arno Press, 1969.

Rylands, W. Harry F.S.A. Last Master. *Records of the Lodge of Antiquity No. 2 Vol. I.* London: Harrison and sons LTD., Printers in ordinary to his majesty, 1928.

Safier, Neil. "A Courier Between Empires: Hipolito de Costa." In *Soundings in Atlantic History, Latent Structures and Intellectual Currents 1500–1830,* eds. Bernard Baylin and Patricia L. Denault, 265–294. Boston: Harvard University Press, 2011.

Sasche, Julius. *Old Masonic Lodges of Pennsylvania Vol. II 1779–1791.* Philadelphia: 1913.

Sasche, Julius Friedrich. *Old Masonic Lodges of Pennsylvania Vol. II 1779–1791.* Philadelphia: 1913.

Schomburg Exhibition Curatorial Committee. *The Legacy of Arthur A. Schomburg: A Celebration of the Past, a Vision for the Future.* New York: New York Public Library, Astor, Lenox and Tilden foundations, 1986.

Schuchard, Martha Keith. *Restoring the Temple of Vision: Cabalistic Freemasonry and Stuart Culture (Brill's Studies in Intellectual History).* Leiden: Brill, 2002.

Sears, Barbara McRae. "Zebina the Privateer, Pirate or Patriot?" *New England Ancestors Magazine* 9, no. 1 (Winter 2008): 35–37, 42.

Second Lodge. *Minutes 1760–1778.* Boston: Grand Lodge of Massachusetts, microfilm; transcription of same, Lexington: Museum of Our National Heritage.

Seraile, William. *Bruce Grit: the Black Nationalist Writings of John Edward Bruce.* Knoxville: University of Tennessee Press, 2003.

Sesay, Jr. Chernoh Momodu. "Freemasons of Color: Prince Hall, Revolutionary Black Boston, and the Origins of Black Freemasonry, 1770–1807." Unpublished dissertation, Northwestern University, 2006. Accessed through Proquest dissertations, UMI Number: 3230175.

Sharp Documents, Vol. II. "The Story of the Lodge La Parfaite Union on the Island of Martinique", ii–iii, Docs. 3a, 13, 14, 16, 19, 29, 32, 33, 36, 47, 48, 50, 121.

Sharp Documents, Vol. III, Doc. 6. Trutie to Papillion, June 6, 1748; Doc 109 Lamolere de Feuillas to Elus Parfaits, Feb. 27, 1755; Doc. 45 Warrant of Lamorlere de Feuillas, Dec. 24, 1752; Feuillass' delegation of authority to Berthomieux, Sept. 18, 1753, Minutes of the Installation of *Parfaite Lodge d'Ecosse de Saint Marc.*

Sharp Documents, Vol. III, Doc 35. Saint Jean de Jerusalem Ecossaise of Cap-Francais to Bordeaux, Feb. 13, 1753.

Sharp Documents, Vol. III. "The Story of the Ecossaise Lodge in the Isle of San Domingo", Documents 34, 38, 56, 57.

Sharp Documents, Vol. IV. "The Story of the Ecossais Lodge of New Orleans", Introduction, Documents, 40, 41, 49, 50, 60, 61, 64, 66, 72, 102.

Sheppard, Harvey Newton. *Freemasonry in North America St. John's Lodge AF&AM 1733–1916.* Boston: Seaver-Howland Press, 1917.

Sherman, John M. "The Green Dragon Tavern: Ancient Colonial Tavern on Union Street, "Headquarters of the Revolution."" Unpublished: Boston, January 30, 1975; Grand Lodge of Massachusetts Library.

Slade, Alexander. *The Free Mason Examin'd: or, the World Brought out of Darkness into Light. Being, an authentick account of all the secrets of the ancient society of free masons, which have been handed down by oral tradition only, from the institution, to the present time. In which Is particularly described, the whole ceremony used at making masons, as it has been hitherto practised(sic) in all the lodges round the globe; by which any person, who was never made, may introduce himself into a Lodge. With Notes, explanatory, historical, and critical. To which are added, the Author's reasons for the publication hereof, and some remarks on the conduct of the author of a pamphlet, call'd Masonry dissected. With A new and correct lost of all Regular Lodges, under the English constitution, according to their late removals and additions.* London: R. Griffiths, 1754.

Smith, Captain George. *On the Uses and Abuses of Freemasonry: A Work of the Greatest Utility to the Brethren of the Society, to Mankind in General, and to the Ladies in Particular.* London: G. Kearsley, 1783.

Smith, Douglass. "Freemasonry and the Public in Eighteenth Century Russia." *Eighteenth-Century Studies* 29, no. 1 (1996): 25–44.

Smith, Douglas. *Working the Rough Stone: Freemasonry and Society in Eighteenth -Century Russia.* Dekalb, Ill.: Northern Illinois University Press, 1999.

Smith, Mary Ann Yodelis. "William M'Alpine." In *Boston Printers, Publishers and Booksellers, 1640–1800,* 358–60. Benjamin V. Franklin, ed. Boston: G.K. Hall & Co., 1980.

Smith, Thomas Webb. *The Freemason's Monitor, or Illustrations of Masonry: In Two Parts.* Albany: 1797.

Smith, William. *A Pocket Companion for Freemasons.* Dublin: E. Rider, 1735. http://www.dublin citypubliclibraries.com/image/wea40-freemasons.

Smith, William. *Freemason's Pocket Companion.* London: John Torbuck, First Edition, 1735, Second Edition, 1738.

St. Andrew's Royal Arch Chapter. *Exercises Commemorating the150th Anniversary of St. Andrew's Royal Arch Chapter 1769–1919.* Boston: St. Andrew's Royal Arch Chapter, 1920.

St. James Evening Post, "Boston, June 27th." August 20, 1737.

St. John's Lodge. *Synoptic History of St. John's Lodge No. 1 F. & A.M. Portsmouth, New Hampshire 1736–1976.* Portsmouth, St. John's Lodge, 1976.

St. John's Lodge No. 1, Portsmouth. *Minute Books.* St. John's Lodge, Portsmouth, New Hampshire.

St. John's Lodge No. 1, Portsmouth, *Archival Database.*

St. John's Lodge Newburyport. *Two Hundredth Anniversary.* Newburyport: St. John's Lodge, 1966.

St. John's Lodge of Scotland to Grand Lodge of Pennsylvania, MSS Grand Lodge of Pennsylvania Library, Vol. L, paquet 72, folio 6.

St. Peter's Lodge, *Minute Books, Book 1.* Grand Lodge of Massachusetts, Grand Secretary's Vault, Boston, MA.

Stearns, Samuel, LLD. *THE FREEMASON'S CALENDAR, AND ALMANAC; for the YEAR of our LORD 1793: CONTAINING, Astronomical calculations,---An account of the Ancient and Honorable Society of Free Masons, with other things necessary for an Almanac.* New York: Samuel Stearns, LLD. 1793.

Steblecki, Edith. *Paul Revere and Freemasonry.* Boston: Paul Revere Memorial Association, 1985.

Stevenson, David. *The Origins of Freemasonry: Scotland's Century, 1590–1710.* Cambridge: Cambridge University Press, 1998.

Stevenson, David. *The First Freemasons: Scotland's Early Lodges and Their Members.* Aberdeen: Aberdeen University Press, 1988.

Stewart, Larry. "Newtonians, Revolutionaries, and Republicans." *Canadian Journal of History* 17, no. 2 (1982): 314–21.

Stokes, Durward T. "The Baptist and Methodist Clergy in South Carolina and the American Revolution." *The South Carolina Historical Magazine* 73, no. 2 (Apr., 1972): 87–96.

Supreme Council of the Northern Jurisdiction of Scottish rite Freemasonry, "History," http://www.supremecouncil.org/index.tpl?&ng_view=16 (accessed June 26, 2009).

Tableau Des FF. composant la R.L. No. 47 Sous le titre distinctif de la Reunion Des Coeurs Franco-Americains, a L'Orient du Port-Republicain, depuis le 27me, jour du 10me. mois M. de l'an de la V.L. 5799, jusqu'au 27e. jour du meme mois 5780. MSS. Philadelphia: Grand Lodge of Pennsylvania, MS-81-1264.

Tableaux des Freres de la R. L. . . des Neuf Soeurs, a L'O. . . de Paris, 5782. Paris: Loge Des Neuf Soeurs, 1782.

Tableaux des Freres de la R. L... des Neuf Soeurs, a L'O... de Paris, 1783. Paris: Loge Des Neuf Soeurs, 1783.

Tableau des Membres La R. L... de Reunion Desiree Port-au-Prince. Port-au-Prince: La Grange, 1800.

Tableau des Membres Composant La R... L... de Saint-Jean, Reg. const. aux deux rites, A L'O... de St. Pierre, Isle-Martinique, 1826. St. Pierre: Printed by the Lodge, 1826.

Tableau of Lodge No. 47, 1797. MSS. Philadelphia: Grand Lodge of Pennsylvania, MS-81-1247.

Tableau of Lodge No. 47, 1798. MSS. Philadelphia: Grand Lodge of Pennsylvania, MS-81-1248.

Tableau of the Members Composing Lodge No. 98, 1809. MSS. Philadelphia: Grand Lodge of Pennsylvania, MS-81-1317.

Taschenbuch fur Freymaurer, Almanach oder Taschen-Buch für die Bruder Freymaurer der Vereinigten Deutschen Logen, and *Taschenbuch für Brüder Freimaurer Enthaltend Sämmtliche mit der g.u.v. St. Joh. Loge Pforte zur Ewigkeit i. O. v. Hildesheim theils correspondirende, theils derselben Seit 5794. bekannt gewordene Logen, als Manuscript für Brüder Freimaurer.* Hildesheim: Joh. Christ: 1796, 1801.

Tatsch, J. Hugo. *Freemasonry in the Thirteen Colonies.* United States: Kessinger Rare Reprints, 1933.

The Complete Freemason, or Multa Paucis for Lovers of Secrets. No publisher or date.

THE FREE-MASONS' CALENDAR: OR, AN ALMANAC, For the Year of CHRIST 1776, and Anno Lucis MMMMMDCCLXXV, being the Third after Bissestile, or Leap-Year: CONTAINING, Besdies an accurate and useful Calendar of all Remrkable Occurences for the Year, Many useful and curious Particulars relating to Masonry. Inscribed, with Great Respect, To the Right Honourable Lord Petre, Grand Master, By a Society of the Brethren, London: Printed for the Company of Stationers, 1775. —1776, 1778, 1780, 1782–1789, 1791–1813.

The Free Mason's Pocket Companion; Containing, the Origin, Progress, and Present State of that Ancient Fraternity; the Institution of the Grand Lodge of Scotland; Lists of the Grand Masters and Other Officers of the Grand Lodge of Scotland; Their Customs, Charges, Constitutions, Orders and Regulations: For the Instruction and Conduct of the Brethren. Also, a Complete Collection of Masonic Toasts, Songs, Prologues, Epilogues, &c. Lists of all the Regular Lodges in Scotland and England; and Many Other Particulars, for the Use of the Society. Glasgow: Joseph Galbraith, 1765.

The Free Mason's Pocket Companion; Containing, the Origin, Progress, and Present State of that Ancient Fraternity; the Institution of the Grand Lodge of Scotland; Lists of the Grand Masters and Other Officers of the Grand Lodge of Scotland; Their Customs, Charges, Constitutions, Orders and Regulations: For the Instruction and Conduct of the Brethren. Also, a Complete Collection of Masonic Toasts, Songs, Prologues, Epilogues, &c. Lists of all the Regular Lodges in Scotland and England; and Many Other Particulars, for the Use of the Society. To which is Now Added, a Collection of the Most Approved English, Scotch and Irish Songs. Air (sic): John and Peter Wilson; Edinburgh: W. Anderson; Stirling: J. Duncan & Son; Glasgow: J&M Robertson, J&W Shaw, and A. MacCauley, 1792.

The Freemason's Pocket Companion; Containing the Origin, Progress and Present State of that Ancient Fraternity; the Institution of the Grand Lodge of Scotland; Lists of the Grand Masters and other Officers of the Grand Lodges of Scotland and England; Their Customs, Charges, Constitutions, Orders and Regulations; for the Instruction and Conduct of the Brethren. To which is Added an

Appendix, Act of the Associate Synod Against the Free Masons, with an Impartial Examination of that Act; Charges and Addresses to the Free Masons on Different Occasions; A Complete Collection of Free-Mason Songs, Prologues, Epilogues, &c. with Lists of all the Regular Lodges both in Scotland and England with Many other Particulars, for the use of the Society. Edinburgh: Ruddiman, Auld, and Company, 1761; Edinburgh: Auld and Smellie, 1765.

The Grand Mystery of Free-Masons Discover'd. Wherein are the several questions put to them at their meetings and installations: as also their oaths, health, signs, and points, to know each other by. As they were found in the custody of a free –mason who dyed suddenly. And now publish'd for the information of the publick. London: Printed for T. Payne near Stationer's Hall, 1724.

"The Green Dragon Tavern." *The New England Freemason* I, no. 4 (April 1874): 151–163.

The History of Masonry or the Freemasons Pocket Companion: Containing the History of Masonry from the Creation to the Present Time; the Institution of the Grand Lodge of Scotland; Lists of the officers of the Grand Lodges of Scotland and England; Their Customs, Charges, Constitutions, Orders and Regulations. To which is added, a large collection of Songs, prologues, epilogues, &c. [the third edition]. Edinburgh: William Auld. 1772; London: John Donaldson, 1775.

The Lodge at Fredericksburg a Digest of the Early Records Abstracted from the Record Book of Minutes, 1752–1771; Lodge Accounts to 1785; with an account of the Members of the Lodge in the American Revolution; and a nominal roll of all names in the Records, Complied by Ronald Heaton & James Case. Silver Spring: Masonic Service Association of the United States, 1981.

The Old Constitutions Belonging to the Free and Accepted Masons. Taken from a Manuscript Wrote Five Hundred Years Since. London: J. Roberts, 1722, 2–3. Reprinted in *The Old Constitutions of Freemasonry Being a Reprint.With a Foreword by Joseph Fort Newton.* Anamosa, IA: The National Masonic Research Society, 1917. This rare work includes a photostat of the original.

The Pocket Companion and History of Free-masons, containing their Origine (sic)*, Progress, and Present State: an Abstract of Their Laws, Constitutions, Customs, Charges, Orders and Regulations, for the Instruction and Conduct of the Brethren: a Confutation of Dr. Plot's False Insinuations: an Apology, Occasioned by Their Persecution in the Canton of Berne, and in the Pope's Dominions: and a Select Number of Songs and Other Particulars, for the Use of the Society.* London: J. Scott, 1754; Second Edition, 1759.

The Secrets of the Free-Masons Revealed by a Disgusted Brother. Containing an Ingenious Account of their Origin, their Practices in the Lodges, Signs and Watch-Words; Proceedings at the Making, and the Method Used to Find a Mason, when in a Foreign Country, &c. &c. as it ever was, and ever will be. The Second Edition. London: J. Scott, 1759, 1–8; *Sixth Edition.* London: J. Scott, 1762.

The Vocal Companion, and Masonic Register. In two parts. Part I. consisting of original and selected masonic songs, anthems, dirges, prologues, epilogues, toasts, and sentiments, charges prayers, funeral procession, Part II. A concise account of the original of masonry in America; with a list of the lodges in the six Northern states, viz, Massachusetts, New Hampshire, Rhode-Island, Connecticut, New-York & Vermont. With the names of the officers and the number of members of which each lodge consists. Boston: Brother John Dunham, 1802.

Triber, Jayne E. *A True Republican: The Life of Paul Revere.* Amherst: University of Massachusetts, 1998.

Two Letters to a Friend. The First, Concerning the Society of Free-Masons. The Second, Giving an Account of the most Ancient Order of Gormogons, In its original institution, excellency, and design: its rules and orders, and the manner of its introduction into great Britain. With an intire collection of all that has been made publick on that occasion. Together with the supposed reason of their excluding the free-masons, now first set forth for the satisfaction and emolument of the publick. London: Printed by A. Moore, near St. Paul's, 1725.

Tyrian Lodge A.F. & A.M. *Bicentennial Celebration 1770–1970.* Gloucester: Tyrian Lodge, 1770.

Tyrian Lodge, *Minute Books, Book 1.* Tyrian Lodge, Gloucester, MA.

United Grand Lodge of England. *THE MINUTES OF THE GRAND LODGE OF FREEMASONS OF ENGLAND, 1723–1739. Illustrated with plates and facsimiles. With introduction and notes by William John Songhurst.* London: Quartuor Coronati Lodge, 1913.

van Brankle, Samuel. *Masonic Oration Delivered 27ᵗʰ of December, A.L. 5852, A.D. 1852. At Bethel Church, At Philadelphia, For the Benefit of the Poor of Said Church, By Samuel Van Brankle, Most Worshipful National District Deputy Grand Master, for the Middle District of the United States of America, Comprising the States of Pennsylvania, New Jersey, and Delaware.* Philadelphia: Committee of Arrangements, 1852.

van der Veur, and Paul W. *Freemasonry in Indonesia from Radermacher to Soekanto, 1762–1961.* Athens, Ohio: Ohio University Center for International Studies Southeast Asia Program, 1976.

Vazquez Semadeni, and Maria Eugenia. "La imagen publica de la masoneria en Neuva Espana, 1761–1821." *Relaciones* 125, Invierno 2011, Vol. XXXII, 167–207.

Villain, Senior to George Washington / Grand Lodge of Pennsylvania, 1785. MSS Grand Lodge of Pennsylvania Archives, Vol. L, Paquet 72, folio 4.

Wade, Dr. John, ed. *Freemasons in the Transatlantic World: Papers Delivered to the Quatuor Coronati Lodge Conference at the George Washington Masonic National Memorial 14–16 Septmenber 2018.* London: Lewis Masonic, 2019.

Wade, Dr. John, ed. *Freemasonry on the Frontier: Papers Submitted for the 2020 Conference for Quatuor Coronati Lodge in the United States of America, the Grand Lodge of Massachusetts, Boston, Massachusetts 18–20 September 2020.* London: Lewis Masonic, 2020.

Walker, Corey. *A Noble Fight: African American Freemasonry and the Struggle for Democracy in America.* Urbana, IL: University of Illinois Press, 2008.

Wallace, Maurice. "Are We Men? Prince Hall, Martin Delany, and the Masculine Ideal in Black Freemasonry, 1775–1865." *American Literary History* 9, no. 3 (Autumn 1997): 396–424.

Warren, Charles. *The FREE-MASON Stripped Naked; or, the Whole Art and Mystery of FREE-MASONRY, Made Plain and Easy to All Capacities; – by a Faithful Account of Every Secret, from the First Making of a Mason, till he is Completely Master of Every Branch of his Profession.* Dublin, printed. London Reprinted: Isaac Fell, n.d.; Sixth Edition, London: Scott, 1762.

Warren, John, Esq. S.G.W. *A Charge Delivered to the Antient and Honourable Fraternity of Free and Accepted Masons, at Boston, on the Festival of St. John the Baptist. A.D. 1782 .* Boston: 1782.

Warren, John Esq. S.G.W. *A Charge Delivered to the Antient and Honourable Fraternity of Free and Accepted Masons, at Boston, on the Festival of St. John the Baptist. A.D. 1782.* Boston: 1782; Christopher Gore, Esq. *An Oration: Delivered at the Chapel, in Boston: Before the Ancient and Honourable Society of Free and Accepted Masons, June 24, 1783.* Boston: Brother William Green, 1783.

Weisburger, William. "Parisian Masonry, the Lodge of the Nine Sisters, and the French Enlightenment." In *Freemasonry on Both Sides of the Atlantic: Essays Concerning the Craft in the British Isles, Europe, the United States and Mexico,* William Weisberger, Wallace McLeod, and Brent S. Morris, ed., 299–345. Boulder: Columbia University Press, 2002.

Wetherbee, Winthrop. "Prominent Mason Addresses Banquet." *Prince Hall Masonic Digest* 9, no. 2 (August, September, October 1960): 4–9, 23.

Williams, William, M.A. *Masonry Founded upon Scripture; in a Sermon Preached Before the Lodges of Gravesend. On New Year's Day, 1752: and Published at their Request. The Second Edition.* London: C. Burnett, 1764. *Third Edition.* Aberdeen: James Leslie, 1771.

Willingly Wou'd – Be, Esq. *Wou'd Be's Reason: or, an Impartial Review of the Principal Arguments for and Against the Antient Society of Free and Accepted Masons. Advanced in Two Late Pamphlets on that Subject.* Dublin: Henry Pepyat, 1760; Richard Lewis. Corrector of the Press. *The Freemasons Advocate. Or, Falsehood Detected. Being A full refutation of a scandalous libel, entitled, A Master-Key to Free-Masonry. With A Defence of the Brotherhood and the Craft, Against all the calumnies and Aspersions, that ever have been, or can be thrown on them, by the weakness of some, and the Wickedness of others.* Dublin: J. Hunter, 1760.

Wilson, Thomas. *SOLOMON in all his GLORY: OR, THE MASTER-MASON. BEING A TRUE GUIDE To the inmost Recesses of FREE-MASONRY, Both ANCIENT and MODERN.* London: Robinson and Roberts, 1766; Dublin: T. Wilkinson, 1777.

Winch, Julie. *Philadelphia's Black Elite: Activism, Accomodation, and the Struggle for Autonomy, 1787–1848.* Philadelphia: Temple University Press, 1988.

W—O—V—n. Member of a Lodge in England at this time. *The Three Distinct Knocks; or the door of the most Ancient Free Masonry: opening to all men, neither naked nor clothed, bare-footed nor shod, &c. Being an universal description of all its branches, from its first rise to this present time, as it is delivered in all lodges.* London: H. Serjeant, 1760.—*Fifth Edition.* London: H. Serjeant, and Dublin Reprinted, 1762.—n.d. Dublin, T. Wilkinson.—London: J. Limbird, n.d.

Index

abolition movement
  African Lodge Boston's leadership in 120,
    237, 239, 252, 254, 275–6
  among French Revolutionaries leaders who
    were freemasons 59
  John Montagu support of abolitionish
    Ignacio Sanchez 18
accepted mason
  see also acception 22, 47
acception
  see also accepted mason 22, 47
Adams, Samuel
  correspondence from William
    Palfrey 227, 236
  and Paul Revere Massachusetts State
    House cornerstone ceremony 193
  and Joseph Warren 218
  reported to by revolutionary
    "mechanics" 218
  visits to Masonic lodges 214
African Lodge, Boston vi, 10–11,
    127, 237–58
  demographics of 267
  fight to free black sailors 276

in *Freemason's Calendar* lodge lists 112
and military lodges 36
southern reaction to membership of David
    Walker 275
in subscription list of M'Alpine's edition of
    Calcott 100
trans-Atlantic print culture 336, 342,
    347, 350
African Lodge, Philadelphia 267
African Lodge, Providence 267
Ahiman Rezon 68–79
  and lists of lodges 96, 97, 105
American Philosophical Society 55–7
Ancient and Honorable Artillery
    Company 212, 226
Anderson, Reverend James 45–6
Anderson's Constitutions
  see also *Constitutions of the Freemasons* 68,
    70, 72, 78, 90, 111
Annapolis Lodge No. 1,
    Maryland 145, 162
anti-masonic party 32, 34, 326,
    328, 332
Antigua, freemasonry on

in *Engraved List of Lodges*, 92
established by St. John's, Boston 11, 12,
   29, 37, 128, 135–9
in other lodge listings 107, 109, 113
Provincial Grand Masters 30, 31
Ashmole, Elias 25, 39, 47, 51

Barbadoes (sic) lodge 100, 122–4, 128,
   139, 183
Barret, Samuel 194, 213, 219
Batt, Sergeant John 226, 236, 237
Belcher, Governor Jonathan 130, 131,
   134, 136, 181, 184
Belknap, Jeremy 216, 244, 249
Betheile, Francis 131
Bolivar, Simon 336
Boston Marine Society ix, 151, 154
Boston Tea Party 194, 203
   St. Andrew's Lodge members
      involvement 211–13, 217–18
   St. Andrew's Lodge and planning of 225–
   7, 234
Bowen, Dr. Jabez 201–2, 220
Brissot, Jacques 59
Brockwell, Reverend Charles 70, 133,
   135, 146, 150, 156, 175, 185–6.
Brown, John (British chemist) 53
Brown, John (Rhode Island political
   leader) 220
Brown, Moses 200, 209, 352
   correspondence with William
      Palfrey 220, 235, 298
Bulam Lodge No. 495

Coast of Africa 266
Burbeck, William 36, 195–6, 211, 226;
   artillery service with Richard
      Gridley 144, 148, 206;
   relationship with Paul Revere 234
   Sons of Liberty 216–17
Calcott, Wellins, *A Candid Disquisition
   of the of the Principles and Practices*

*of the Most Ancient and Honorable
   Society of Freemasons* 16, 41, 80, 88,
   100, 186, 234, 344.
Carbonari 33, 296, 337, 340, 353
Chase, Thomas 215, 217
*Chevaliers Hospitaliers et Militaires de
   Saint Jean de Jerusalem dits Frey-
   Macons* 284, 303, 351
Chiron, Abraham 261–2, 264
Church, Benjamin Jr. 186, 203, 218–19
Clayton, Sir Robert 23–5, 39
Clinton, Governor DeWitt 331, 333–
   4, 340
Constitutions of the Freemasons
   see also *Anderson's Constitutions* 5, 19, 25–
      6, 44–8, 68–73, 76, 80, 85, 87, 90
   advertised in colonial press 175, 186
   influence on Masonic Africanist
      literature 238–9
   and lists of lodges 90, 96, 111–12
Colson, Adam 195
*Columbian Parnassid / Columbian
   Magazine* 238–9, 243–7, 249, 342
Colville, Lord Alexander 136, 146–7,
   154, 156, 181, 345
Comins / Comyns, Captain Robert 141
Coustos, John 69–70, 112, 178, 345
Cox, Daniel 28, 31, 162, 332

Dalton, Thomas 252
Danton, Georges 49, 59
Delafaye, Charles 18, 53
Dermot, Lawrence 35, 69–80, 87,
   341, 345
   correspondence from William
      Palfrey 200, 202, 209
   and lists of lodges 96
Desagulier, Dr. John Theophilus 26,
   45–68, 72
   in colonial press 180, 190
   and Etienne Moran 283–4, 295
   legacy 334, 336

Deshon, Moses x, 194, 211, 217, 220

Desmoulins, Camille 49, 59

"Dissertation Upon Masonry 1734, A", Boston, 133, 152

Douglas, Captain William 29, 31, 138, 259, 354

Druids / Druidism, and freemasonry 47–8, 67, 68–70, 84–5

Duc D'Orleans, Philippe
see also Egalite, Philippe 59

Duminy, Francois 263, 264, 265

Dupleissis, Pierre Barbier x, 307–9, 311–14, 316, 318, 320

Dwight, Reverend Timothy 274, 323–6, 329, 345

Ecossaise
see also French higher degrees 35, 281, 303–4, 354
Etienne Morin and Bordeaux *Ecossaise* Lodge 296
European and Latin American legacy 336
influence on anti-masonry 327
on Martinique 289–93
in New Orleans 293–4
on Saint Domingue 284–8, 302

Encyclopedie 54–5, 85, 325

Engraved List of Lodges 32, 90, 152, 353
evolution in *Freemasons Calendar* 112
in figures vii, ix, 91
Henry Price included in 165
inclusion of French ex-patriot lodges 309
inclusion of Indian lodges 263
inclusion of New World lodges 101, 122, 131, 138–40, 162, 183, 190
reprinted in other sources 101
West India & American lodge listed first in 124

Egalite, Philippe
see also Duc D'Orleans, Philippe 59

Ellery, William 201, 220

Elliot, John, A.M. 208, 210, 267

Eureka Lodge 257

Falmouth Lodge 205, 212

Farwinter, Captain Ralph 30

First Lodge, Boston
see also St. John's Lodge, Boston 28, 129, 151, 152, 153, 260, 346
Captain Scott's cross membership in West India & American lodge 122, 241
Caribbean connections 138
colonial press, use of 179
correspondence of 155–72
in correspondence of African Lodge 242
figures vii, ix, 91, 99
Francis Beteihle's autobiography 132
introduction of freemasonry to Canada 141
King George's War and Siege of Louisburg 142–4
lists of lodges 109
Lord Colvill's membership 146
relationship with lodge of St. Andrew 194, 196, 201
revolutionary activities and organizations 215, 219, 220, 225, 234

Fleet, Thomas Jr. 100, 203, 346, 347
Boston Evening Post 175, 179, 182, 216

Francken, Henry Andrew 285, 289, 296–7, 300, 335, 339

Franklin, Benjamin 7–9, 37, 51, 84, 209, 218, 224, 314
in Atlantic print culture 43, 45, 47–9, 71, 86, 102, 178–82, 185, 355
and Boston freemasonry 98, 126, 129, 146, 162, 353
and learned societies 55, 56–8, 63, 334
master of *Neuf Soeurs* 5, 67, 302, 347
Rhees scandal 178, 270–1
and West India & American lodge 122

Fredericksburg Lodge 223, 235, 357

Freemasons' Calendar, or an Almanac 23, 25–7, 35, 39–40, 45, 48, 151, 152, 153, 355, 356
African and Indian lodges in 266, 276, 277
and African Lodge 238, 241–4, 250

Caribbean lodges mentioned in 138, 139
cited in other sources 94, 98–9, 106–7, 112, 113
in figures viii, ix, 93
on German lodges 60, 65
Goede Hoop in 260, 261–2
Grand Lodge takeover of 91
Haitian lodges in 321, 328, 337
Henry Price in 130, 166
Knights Templar mentioned in 68, 251
French Higher Degrees
see also Scottish Rite Freemasonry
Ecossaise 26, 48, 60, 68
in French colonies 280, 311, 315
French and Indian War 36–7, 142, 147, 161, 205, 220, 297

Gabriel's Rebellion 274–5
Gerry, Elbridge 212
Girondin 59
Goose and Gridiron Lodge
see also Lodge of Antiquity
West India and American Lodge 24, 31, 122–4, 253
Gore, Christopher, *An Oration: Delivered at the Chapel, in Boston: Before the Ancient and Honourable Society of Free and Accepted Masons* 149, 151, 207–8, 210, 346, 258
Grand Lodge of All England (York) 23
Grand Lodge of England (Ancients) 38, 104, 315
Grand Lodge of England (Moderns)
see also Premier Grand Lodge of England 6, 16, 27, 49, 90
in colonial press 178, 181, 282, 295, 336, 348, 358
connection to Royal Society 51
correspondence with African Lodge, Boston 238, 251
correspondence with other American freemasons 113, 343

correspondence with white Boston freemasons 129–30, 137, 160
and *Freemasons Calendar* 152
merger with Grand Lodge of England (Ancients) 35
Grand Lodge of New York 28, 205, 221, 253, 319, 331, 340
Green Dragon Tavern
see also Masons' Arms 127, 194, 218, 225–7, 347, 354, 357
in figures x, 229
Gridley, Jeremiah 30–2, 148, 157–60, 162–3
and Boston Marine Society 150
charter to Pitt County Lodge 146
death of 136, 173–4
Gridley, Richard 142, 144, 147–8, 169–70, 203, 206, 216, 240

Hall, Captain 140
Hamilton, Dr. Alexander 6, 15, 145, 154, 347
Hancock, John 37, 122, 126, 202, 205, 240, 241
Boston Tea Party involvement 226, 227, 229
Lodge of St. Andrew membership 173, 195–6, 200, 213
in Merchant's Lodge 147, 184, 194
Hartford Lodge No. 1 185, 191, 205, 343, 351
Hartnett, Cornelius 224
Hayes, Moses Michael 128, 187, 202
and Scottish Rite Freemasonry 279, 285, 296–301, 327, 335, 339
Hughson, John 270–3
Hutchinson, Governor Thomas 169, 212, 215, 234
Hutchinson, William, *Spirit of Masonry* 69, 80–3, 88, 348
lists of lodges in 112, 117
Russian translation 62

Illuminati 33, 323, 324, 326

Jefferson, Thomas 49, 56, 58, 59
Jeffries, Dr. John 49, 216, 218, 232
Johnson, John, watercolor of Green
    Dragon with Masonic and Tea Party
    references 229
Jones, John Paul 9, 58, 137

King George's War 142–4
King's Chapel, Boston 129, 140,
    177, 189
    orations delivered at 210, 231, 351, 358
Knights Templar 9, 35–6, 47–8, 68–9,
    85, 284
    American / York Rite degree bodies 327
    and anti-masonry 324, 328
    Eye Center 339
    in *Freemasons Calendar* 68, 251
    Ramsey's connection to 282–3

L'amite No. 73 115, 301, 304, 321
Lodge No. 1, Philadelphia (Ancients)
    see also Lodge No. 2;
        Lodge No. 4, Philadelphia
        (Moderns) 37–8, 223–3
Lodge No. 1, Philadelphia
    (Moderns) 28, 98, 129, 135,
    146, 165
Lodge No. 2
    see also Lodge No. 4, Philadelphia
        (Moderns); Lodge No. 1, Philadelphia
        (Ancients); Lodge 222–3
Lodge No. 4, Philadelphia (Moderns)
    see also Lodge No. 1, Philadelphia
        (Ancients); Lodge No. 2 37–8
Lodge No. 47, *De la Reunion des Coeurs
    Franco Americains* 310, 312–13,
    316, 319–22
    primary documents 349, 354, 355, 356
Lodge No. 169, Boston 28
lodge of antiquity

see also West India and American Lodge;
    Goose and Gridiron Lodge 41, 125–6,
    264, 353
Lodge of Good Hope see *Loge de
    Goede Hoop*
Lodge of St. Andrew
    see also St. Andrew's Lodge 10, 77, 87,
    111, 193–209, 231, 300, 339
    African lodge and 239–40
    and Boston Tea Party 229–5
    in colonial press 179, 183–4, 187
    in figures ix, x
    formation of Massachusetts Grand
        Lodge 10, 127, 156, 194, 298
    notes and citations 234, 235, 236,
        254, 349
    relationship with Boston Moderns 127,
        139, 150, 154, 169, 170, 174
    and Sons of Liberty 211–19, 220, 224
Lodge of the Nine Muses, London 59
Lodge of the Nine Muses,
    Moscow 59, 62
Lodge of the Nine Muses, Paris see *Loge
    Neuf Seours*
Loge Neuf Seours
    see also Lodge of the Nine Muses, Paris 7,
        49, 56–64, 332
    correspondence with Caribbean
        lodges 302
    Dr. John Jeffries' membership in 218
    in references 347, 355, 356
    Thomas Paine's membership in 67
    Voltaire initiated in by Benjamin
        Franklin 181
Loge de Goede Hoop 13, 258–66,
    277, 342
Loge D'Union de L'Orient 263
Long Room Club 217–18, 226, 236
Lopez, Aaron 202
Louisburg, Siege of 143–5, 153, 348
Lowell, John 195, 200, 203, 213
    relationship with Prince Hall 240, 247
Loyal Nine 194, 215–16, 217, 226

M'Alpine, William 100, 161, 186, 202–6, 213, 297, 333
  in citations 16, 209, 234, 343, 344, 355
Mantore, Peter 267, 277, 350
Marblehead Lodge
  see also philanthropic lodge 150, 162, 212, 219
  African lodge correspondence to Grand Lodge of England regarding 242–3
  membership of John Pulling 195, 197, 230
Marquis de Lafayette 59
Marrant, John 239, 241, 245, 247, 249–55, 350
Masons' Arms *see* Green Dragon Tavern
Massachusetts Grand Lodge 120, 198–9, 205, 299
  African lodge's relationship with 240
  founded by Lodge of St. Andrew 10, 127, 156, 298, 194
  intellectual activity in 206, 208
  members involved in Sons of Liberty 213, 215–16, 218, 220
  merger with St. John's Grand Lodge (Moderns) 170, 233
  in notes and citations 151, 347
Massachusetts Lodge 200, 204, 225, 298, 350
Matthews, William, Governor of Antigua 30, 138, 161, 183, 259, 285
Merchants' Lodge, Quebec 112, 194
Milhet, Jean 293–5
military lodges
  see also traveling lodges 38, 127, 141–2, 148, 221, 237
Mirabeau, Honore 49, 56–7, 59
Molyneux, William 147, 169, 214, 218, 219
Montagu, John 2nd Duke of Montague 17–19, 46, 50, 52, 72, 160, 180, 339
Moray, Robert 47, 51

Morin, Etienne Stephen 279, 284–6, 291, 296, 304, 327, 335
Morse, Reverend Jedediah 115–16, 274, 280, 322–7, 350–1
Morton, Perez 231, 232, 243, 351

Nantucket Lodge 150, 154, 204, 212
Newburyport Marine Society 150–1, 349
North End Caucus x, 195, 212, 217–18, 226–8

Old Charges 19, 21–3, 44–6, 63, 72–3, 85, 336
  in notes and citations 39
  in Price's oration give at John Rowe's installation 149
  in York Rite degree ritual 327
Oxnard, Thomas 31, 143, 145–6, 157, 160, 167, 174
Otis, James 159, 173, 217
  Lodge of St. Andrew activities of 194–5, 213
  Modern masonic activities of 147, 149, 194, 219

Paine, Robert Treat 214
Paine, Thomas 49, 56, 58, 67, 84, 352
Payne, George 25, 52
Palfrey, William 158
  masonic activities and connections 194–6, 199–203, 205, 298
  in notes and citations 126, 209, 234, 235, 236, 255, 352
  political and Revolutionary activity 211, 213–14, 216, 218–20, 226–7, 233, 241
La Parfaite Harmonie Loge de Saint- Jean de Jerusalem 284–5
Peck, Samuel 211, 226
Petion, Jerome 49, 59
Perkins, Thomas Marriot 31, 41, 121–5
philanthropic lodge, Marblehead Massachusetts *see* Marblehead Lodge

Pitt County Lodge, North Carolina 146, 161, 163–4
plan of incorporation 169
Plott, Dr. Robert, *Natural History of Staffordshire* 23, 72, 77
Premier Grand Lodge of England *see* Grand Lodge of England (Moderns)
Preston, William *Illustrations of Masonry* 69, 80–4, 88, 352
Price, Henry 31–2, 130–3, 136, 140–2, 145–6, 242, 339
  and Benjamin Franklin 126, 129
  charge delivered at John Rowe's installation as grand master 149–50, 206–7, 208
  correspondence 99, 136–7, 158–61, 163–9
  in figures vii, viii, 92, 93, 95
  resumption of grand mastership in 1767 174–5
Primus Hall 226, 237–8, 239, 241
Prince Hall 120, 127, 226, 240–1, 245, 247–67, 276
Prince Hall freemasonry 10, 120, 127, 247–67, 319, 334
  in citations 342, 347, 350, 354, 358, 359
Prince Saunders 252, 321
Pritchard, Samuel, *Masonry Dissected* ix, 54, 73, 75, 86, 271, 352
  and other masonic exposes 102–6, 110
Pulling, John 195, 197, 230
Purkett, Colonel Henry 227

Quincy, Edmond 137
Qunicy, Samuel 169, 170, 218

Ramsay, Chevalier Michael 35, 55, 57, 74, 282–3, 327, 329
Regius Manuscript
  see also Old Charges 44
Revere, Paul 37, 139, 189, 302, 332, 333

in citations 192, 209, 210, 233, 234, 235, 236
in figures ix
and French ex-patriot Friendship Lodge 308
Masonic career and business connected thereto 193–207
overlapping masonic and political network 211–13, 217–19, 226, 227–8, 230–1
urn containing lock of George Washington's hair 9
Rising Sun Lodge 185, 194, 204, 219, 242
Roberts, J., *The Old Constitutions Belonging to the Ancient and Honourable Society of Free and Accepted Masons* 46, 48, 70
Robison, John, *Proofs of a Conspiracy* 323, 326
Rowe, John 31, 160, 206
  charter issued to Rising Sun Lodge by 185
  in citation 126, 171, 353
  masonic and mercantile networks 147–9, 180, 238, 240
  petition to Grand Lodge of England for grand master appointment of 161, 164, 166–7
  political involvement 169–70, 212, 214, 215, 218, 227
Royal Society of England 7, 19, 25, 50–5
  accepted masons among founders 22, 47–8
  Benjamin Franklin's membership in 57
  Chevalier Michael Ramsay's membership in 282–3
  John Montagu's membership in 17

St. Andrew's Lodge *see* Lodge of St. Andrew
St. Eustatius 13, 28, 109, 299
St. George, Chevalier 267

St. John's Grand Lodge
  see also First Lodge 127–74, 175
St. John's Lodge, Boston *see* First Lodge
St. John's Lodge, Newburyport 34, 149,
  150–1, 219, 355
St. John's Lodge, Portsmouth 149, 204
  in citations 153, 154, 235, 305, 355
  in Henry Price's correspondence 135, 137
  members at Siege of Louisburg 143–4
  revolutionary political involvement of
    members of 212, 219, 302
St. Peter's Lodge, Newburyport ix, 89,
  116, 197–8, 206, 212, 276
Schaw, William 21–2, 336
Scott, Captain Joseph 122, 126, 200
Scottish Rite freemasonry
  see also French higher degrees 35–6, 282,
    285, 289, 321–2
  Albany Sons of Liberty cross-
    membership of 221
  and anti-masonry 280
  Barbier Dupleissis involvement in 309
  Etienne Morin's role in spreading 296–7,
    327, 339
  Moses Michael Hayes role in
    spreading 298, 300–1
Sears, Captain Zebina 3–8, 182, 336,
  338, 339
Sears, Isaac 221
Second Lodge, Boston 204, 206, 216,
  219, 225, 230, 242
  Abraham Savage, past master of 148
  Andrew Oliver ceased to visit after Stamp
    Act 214
  in citations and references 209, 234, 254
  in *Engraved List of Lodges* 109
  Lord Alexander Colvill, master
    of 146, 156
  payment for charter carried to
    England 161
  relationship with St. Andrew's Lodge 194,
    200, 201, 220
  visited by William Molyneux 215, 218

Scald Miserable Masons 71, 74–5, 135–
  6, 177
Sheftalls, Mordecai 225
Sicard, Pierre de 290
Sieyes, Abbe 49, 56, 59
slave trade 28, 245, 259, 260, 263, 275
Smith, Captain George *Use and Abuse of
  Freemasonry* 7, 69, 80–1, 83, 258–
  9, 266
  in citations and references 15, 276, 354
Smith, Reverend William 37, 55
Snelling, Jonathan 150, 194, 213
Sons of Liberty 194–5, 199, 201, 203,
  211–28, 241, 337
  in citations and references 233, 234, 241,
    352, 353
  in figures x
Spencer, Samuel 78
Stamp Act 34, 169, 195, 211–16, 220–5,
  232, 234–5
strict observance 60–2
Stuart, King James VI 22, 45

Temple Lodge in Elizabeth Town New
  Jersey 146, 162, 189
Third Lodge, Boston 145
Three Crowned Stars Lodge, Prague 60
Tomlinson, Robert 12, 30–1, 130, 137–
  9, 143, 160, 166
  chartered lodge on Antigua 160, 259,
    285, 339
  obituary 174
traveling lodges *see* military lodges
True Harmony Lodge 61–2
Tyrian Lodge, Gloucester 77, 87, 154,
  197–9, 204, 212
  in figures ix, x, 198, 199, 217
  in references 353, 358

Unlawful Societies Act of 1799 32, 336
Urann, Thomas x, 203, 211, 213,
  218, 228–9

vann Brankle, Samuel 252, 256, 358

Warren, Dr. Joseph 37, 51, 121, 239–40
  in British masonic periodicals 84
  in figures x, 217
  funeral 170, 231, 232, 351
  lodge of St. Andrew membership
    of 211–13
  provincial grand master 38, 185, 199,
    200, 208, 216, 298
  revolutionary political importance of 194,
    196, 218–19, 226, 227
  subscription to purchase M'Alpine's
    edition of Calcott 203, 206
Warren, Dr. John 51, 207, 210
Washington George 150, 170, 223, 309,
    313, 333

capital building cornerstone laying
    ceremony performed by x, 332
  in citations and references 15, 328, 358
  lock of hair preserved by Grand Lodge of
    Massachusetts 9, 197
Webb, Joseph x, 170, 194, 211, 213, 217
Weishaupt, Adam 33, 326
West India and American Lodge
  see also Goose and Gridiron Lodge;
    Lodge of Antiquity, Thomas Marriot
    Perkins 121–6
White, William 241–2, 255, 347
Wooster, David 142, 144, 145, 220
Wren, Christopher 24–5, 78, 126
Wyllys, Samuel 220

Zenger, Peter 178, 179, 190, 271, 272